P

Homicide by t

"Dr. Scott provides an organized, accessible collection of some of the most intriguing crime stories of elite American culture. Without resorting to sensational reporting, she nevertheless has penned a page-turner."

—Katherine Ramsland, professor of forensic psychology and author of *The Science of Cold Case Files*

"An unsparing examination of the power of wealth and fame over justice that roasts American values over a brilliant flame of indignation."

—Marvin J. Wolf, author of *Perfect Crimes*

"Ms. Scott's book demonstrates that homicides are not just confined to the inner city or gang violence. No one is immune from this deadly violence or its consequences. It is often good 'old-fashioned police work' that brings these cases to justice."

—Peter Dunbar, deputy chief, Oakland Police Department

"*Homicide by the Rich and Famous* is an exciting read. Gini Scott is an excellent researcher . . . a real page-turner. Reading this book will change people's reactions to crime news forever."

—Alma H. Bond, Ph.D., psychoanalyst, faculty of the Institute for Psychoanalytic Training and Research (IPTAR) and Writers School, and author of *The Deadly Jigsaw Puzzle* and *Murder on the Streetcar*

Homicide *by the* Rich and Famous

A Century of Prominent Killers

Gini Graham Scott

BERKLEY BOOKS, NEW YORK

THE BERKLEY PUBLISHING GROUP
Published by the Penguin Group
Penguin Group (USA) Inc.
375 Hudson Street, New York, New York 10014, USA
Penguin Group (Canada), 90 Eglinton Avenue East, Suite 700, Toronto, Ontario M4P 2Y3, Canada
(a division of Pearson Penguin Canada Inc.)
Penguin Books Ltd., 80 Strand, London WC2R 0RL, England
Penguin Group Ireland, 25 St. Stephen's Green, Dublin 2, Ireland (a division of Penguin Books Ltd.)
Penguin Group (Australia), 250 Camberwell Road, Camberwell, Victoria 3124, Australia
(a division of Pearson Australia Group Pty. Ltd.)
Penguin Books India Pvt. Ltd., 11 Community Centre, Panchsheel Park, New Delhi—110 017, India
Penguin Group (NZ), Cnr. Airborne and Rosedale Roads, Albany, Auckland 1310, New Zealand
(a division of Pearson New Zealand Ltd.)
Penguin Books (South Africa) (Pty.) Ltd., 24 Sturdee Avenue, Rosebank, Johannesburg 2196,
South Africa

Penguin Books Ltd., Registered Offices: 80 Strand, London WC2R 0RL, England

HOMICIDE BY THE RICH AND FAMOUS

A Berkley Book / published by arrangement with Greenwood Publishing Group, Inc.

PRINTING HISTORY
Praeger Publishers hardcover / 2005
Berkley mass-market edition / September 2006

Book design by Stacy Irwin

For information, address: The Berkley Publishing Group,
a division of Penguin Group (USA) Inc.,
375 Hudson Street, New York, New York 10014.

ISBN: 0-425-21131-2

BERKLEY®
Berkley Books are published by The Berkley Publishing Group,
a division of Penguin Group (USA) Inc.,
375 Hudson Street, New York, New York 10014.
BERKLEY is a registered trademark of Penguin Group (USA) Inc.
The "B" design is a trademark belonging to Penguin Group (USA) Inc.

PRINTED IN THE UNITED STATES OF AMERICA

10 9 8 7 6 5 4 3 2 1

CONTENTS

Introduction

Today the world of the rich and famous is more fascinating than ever. Not only do hordes of photographers report on their doings, but also recent films such as *Rich Kids* and TV shows such as Robin Leach's *Life of Luxury*; MTV's *Rich Girls*; Fox's *The Simple Life*, featuring Paris Hilton and in which Beverly Hills meets rural America; and NBC's *The Apprentice* with Donald Trump celebrate this world. However they acquire their fortunes, the rich and famous have become part of a modern-day royalty based on celebrity.

Now, more than ever, this fascination has been extended to the homicides committed by the rich and famous. This interest is deep rooted because the public has long been intrigued by the crimes and trials of the high and mighty, particularly since the advent of the penny press in the United States and Western Europe in the 1830s. Then, with the arrival of mass-produced photography and yellow journalism in the 1880s and 1890s, the news of such crimes made even more lurid and titillating reading; and today, the Internet, cable TV, investigative TV programming, along with the print media, have turned the homicides of the rich and famous into a form of popular entertainment. The O. J. Simpson case in 1994, dubbed by some "The Trial of the Century," was only the beginning of this modern explosion of interest.

Part of this fascination arises simply because of the wealth and fame of the victims and the accused. Another reason is that murder by the wealthy is much rarer than murder by members of other social classes, so it gets more coverage and attention because the news emphasizes what's new and different. Coverage of these homicides also opens up the lives of the wealthy and famous in an even more intimate way, and it reveals the personal vulnerabilities and problems in relationships that are normally kept concealed. Then, too, people are fascinated by these murders for a reason especially emphasized in this book: because they are often very different from the murders committed by others. As one chronicler of the wealthy, F. Scott Fitzgerald, once said, "The rich are different from you and me"; and Ernest Hemingway responded, "Yes, they have more money."

Likewise, the rich are different from the rest of us when it comes to homicide. They kill for some of the same reasons but in different ways. The crimes they commit often remain officially unsolved because the increased public attention is more likely to interfere with the usual police procedures and make the cases more difficult to solve or prove. Then, too, the rich often lawyer up, protecting themselves from being more intensively investigated or charged, even if the police have their suspicions. Although many street and gang killings also remain unsolved or uncharged, the reason is different: Commonly, people fear to say anything about what they know, so they don't come forward, thus leading the case to a dead end; it is not because public curiosity and media coverage have trampled through and disturbed the crime scene or because the prime suspect brings in his or her lawyers. Furthermore, should a case end up in court, rich suspects are more likely to be acquitted or serve less time, though the public might be convinced they are guilty.

Cases involving the rich and famous are also more likely to become the subject of media attention, whether the charges are murder or other serious crimes—witness the media frenzy drawn to the Phil Spector case after a former B-list actress and lounge hostess Lana Clark was found shot in the head in his house. Also consider the excitement surrounding the Michael Jackson child molestation accusations or the Kobe Bryant rape charges. One reason for the added attention is because the suspects are already in the public eye. But even if relatively unknown before, their involvement quickly draws the press, like flies to savory meat, such as when the eccentric Robert Durst, living as a woman in a seamy neighborhood, though a member of a very wealthy family, was accused of killing and chopping up a neighbor. The case was weird enough that it might have gained media attention anyway. But add in a super wealthy heir to a fortune, and the story becomes even juicier.

Then, too, these cases compel attention because many of them are like intriguing mystery stories that are more complex and more difficult to solve. The mystery is intensified because the rich and famous often use more complicated, hard-to-detect methods or have other people commit the crime or provide alibis or protection for them. Adding to the complexity is the help they often get from their families and high-powered lawyers; in addition, they have more resources to hire investigators. Consequently, they are better able to deflect suspicion to other suspects or make it more difficult to obtain evidence against them. The trial often becomes a drama, too.

What also fascinates about these cases is the way these homicides differ in style, methods, motives, and other characteristics, reflecting the different lifestyle, and culture, of the rich and famous. For example, these murders often involve more quiet, genteel methods, along with planning to execute and cover up the killing. The killers frequently use covert methods, such as poisoning or creating the appearance of an accident or burglary that results in death. Plus, these killers are more apt to have help, from having the funds to hire a hit man to calling on a friend or associate to take the victim away or provide an alibi.

Another difference is that the rich and famous are unlikely to be serial killers or mass murderers. Although these are both rare occurrences, a growing number of murders in America, especially since the 1970s, do involve serial killers or multiple rage killings. But these types of crimes are usually committed by someone who kills to show power and control over a victim or are due to an act of anger or revenge by someone who has felt mistreated or exploited. But the rich and famous generally already feel powerful, so they don't have the motive to kill a large number of victims to gain that power or take revenge. Certainly, they may kill to show their power at times, but then their act is usually up close and personal. It is directed against a particular person who has threatened their power—say by leaving a relationship or threatening to do so—not against a generalized victim to help them feel good.

Most commonly, killings by the upper classes and celebrities tend to arise out of the classic motives for homicide, which are very personal—money, jealousy, failed relationships, the difficulty of getting a rejected partner to leave, and feelings of being trapped in a loveless marriage, with no other desirable way out. Yet these classic motives are shaped by wealth, since it takes a much greater amount of money to motivate a person to kill than is the case for people who have less money, where a much smaller amount—a few thousand, a hundred, or even less—may lead to murder. Thus, these homicides are generally not killings by strangers; instead, they are very personal, emotional killings, such as those involving spouses, lovers, parents, children, siblings, other relatives, friends, and business rivals. Yet, even with these personal connections, the killings may be difficult to solve, especially when the rich hire others to commit the crime, bring in their lawyers to protect them, or the evidence gets trampled or mishandled in the ensuing media circus.

Then, after the crime is committed, the investigation to solve the crime and try the suspect is often especially difficult. One reason is the investigators often have to get testimony from witnesses and unravel complicated paper trails; in addition, high-tech and scientific methods, like analyzing DNA and trace evidence, may be required because rich and famous killers often know their victims. Another difficulty is the seal of protection that often surrounds wealthy and celebrity killers, which includes a bevy of lawyers who tell their clients not to talk and friends and family who clam up, making it harder to both investigate and prosecute. Also, many high-profile killings attract a ravenous press eager for details—and more recently, parties and witnesses eager for book deals, which interfere with the investigation and court process.

Homicide by the Rich and Famous highlights such notable cases in the United States from the nineteenth century to the present, focusing on what makes these cases different. In selecting these cases, I have chosen only those where the perpetrator can be described as rich and powerful, whether he or she became rich by being born into wealth, earning it, or marrying into it. I have also limited the cases to those where the perpetrator has been charged and prosecuted for committing at least one murder (or attempted murder in the case of one victim as good as dead in a permanent coma). However, the perpetrator may not necessarily be convicted or might win an appeal after a first conviction, since in many cases, the rich and powerful do get off through good lawyering and the problems with the police investigation and crime scene that result from media coverage, as well as from the special consideration sometimes given to the wealthy charged with crimes. I have not included such cases where the suspected killer isn't actually charged. I have additionally left out any discussion of victims of murder who are rich and powerful where the perpetrator was neither; these cases typically involve robbery, burglary, kidnapping, or other schemes to acquire money and do not follow the same pattern as murders committed by the rich and powerful. Finally, I have excluded the killings involving organized crime, which might be the topic for a book by itself.

I have focused each chapter on one of the major themes that characterize these homicides. After a brief discussion of that theme, each chapter points out how these cases reflect that theme using one or usually two cases to illustrate. For each profiled case, I describe what happened; the motive; how the police, FBI, or other detectives investigated the case; and what occurred in court. In addition, many of the most recent cases feature highlights from the examinations of psychologists and psychiatrists into the minds of the killers. I have drawn the stories from book, newspaper, and magazine accounts about individual cases.

Although many of these cases illustrate multiple themes—for example, a wealthy man accused of hiring others to commit a murder may gain strong family support and have the financial resources to hire top legal power to win an acquittal—I have organized the cases based on what seems to be their strongest theme. A mix of cases from different historical periods illustrating these themes is presented chronologically to show how these same patterns can be found throughout history. The date or dates in the chapter subheads for each case indicate when the murder occurred or came to police attention and when a verdict was rendered in the case, or in a few cases when the case was settled without a trial or a verdict occurred in a second trial.

So what are the key patterns that make these homicides by the rich and famous so different? I've already mentioned many of them in this introduction. In brief, they are the following, with one chapter devoted to each theme:

- Motive—highlights how personal motives typically include factors, such as jealousy, power, success, money, prestige, and not losing one's fortune or prestige, that often drive the rich and famous to murder.
- Method—highlights the emphasis on preplanning, waiting for the right moment, creating an organized crime scene, and the types of weapons used, including unusual methods, such as using special poisons to conceal the crime.
- Finding hired help—highlights how the wealthy often hire or persuade others to do the actual killing.
- Cover-ups—highlights how the wealthy are more skilled at covering up the crime; for example, they may be better able to dispose of the body or stage the crime scene.
- Family and friends in high places—highlights how the wealthy often gain strong backing from family and people in power, which enables them to successfully fight back against the charges.
- Police power, politics, and the media—highlights how the wealthy often get special police consideration, which can lead to manipulation of the investigation and the police compromising the crime scene. At the same time, personal connections and the power of the press can delay or influence the outcome of the investigation and trial.
- Legal power—highlights how the suspect's ability to get a strong legal/investigative team behind them can help them beat the case or get a lesser punishment if convicted. This chapter also highlights the ability of the wealthy to influence the trial process, including jurors and judges.
- Kids who kill—highlights how some rich kids are drawn to killing, either as a challenge or as a way of striking back at their parents.
- Losing it—highlights how some of the rich become killers in the course of falling away from a life of luxury by becoming weirdly eccentric; having problems with alcohol, drugs, or mental illness; or living a life that spins out of control.

CHAPTER 1

A Matter of Motive

The rich and famous are typically driven to murder by the kinds of personal motives that contribute to any murder, such as love, jealousy, power, success, money, and prestige. What is different are the circumstances that distinguish how these motives play out.

Consider money. The rich and famous, used to dealing with large sums, are generally motivated by large amounts of money, killing perhaps for an inheritance or a business gain of hundreds of thousands or millions of dollars. By contrast, middle- and low-income killers might kill for much smaller amounts—say a few thousand or more at the middle-income level or a few hundred or even less for those with low incomes. Then, too, for someone with a lot of money, the thought of losing one's fortune and the social connections or prestige that go along with that money can be a reason to kill.

Similarly, ideas of power, success, and prestige are defined differently. For example, a slight or an exclusion from an exclusive club, which a person without wealth or prominence could not even consider joining, could trigger a response. An example is the Molineux case, described in this chapter, where a member of an elite New York society club developed an enduring hatred for another member, which led to murder. Another reason a very successful wealthy person might be led to murder is if he (and commonly it is a male when achievement or job success is the motivator) feels someone is standing in his way of job advancement or threatens to topple him from an already achieved high position. For a rich and powerful women whose source of wealth and high status is through marriage or being the mistress of a wealthy and powerful man, the trigger may be a rivalry for her husband's or lover's affection, leading her to kill her husband, rival, or both, before a divorce can take away that money and status.

Still another difference is that feelings of love and jealousy are often intertwined with motivations for success, money, and power, such as when a woman's love for her husband is, in part, due to his money and lifestyle. In such a case, when a rival threatens or he is losing interest in her or wants his freedom, she may be motivated by losing both his love and the good life to which she has become accustomed. Alternatively, for the wealthy man, feelings of love are often tied to feelings of power that often arise because money commonly provides status, authority, and the ability to pay for whatever one wants. Thus, a wealthy man losing a mistress or a wife might not only feel threatened by the loss of love, but of his power over her, as illustrated dramatically by the Capano case, described in Chapter 4, where a high-powered prominent lawyer, unwilling to let a former mistress go after she was eager to move on and marry someone else, turned into a stalker and ultimately a killer.

Certainly, those such as the controlling husband or the wife who fears losing her comfortable suburban life as well as her husband, who are not rich and famous may be influenced by a mix of love, jealousy, and financial or power motives. But the rich and powerful have more money and power, and often those motives become far stronger motivators than love. For example, a wealthy man may decide that it is time to get rid of his mistress, though he has loved her, because she threatens his social position and status.

Then, too, the rich and famous are typically motivated to commit murders directed toward a particular victim, so usually these are one-on-one murders or, at most, murders involving two victims (such as a spouse and a lover). And usually the victim has a close personal relationship with the perpetrator.

Finally, as explored more fully in Chapter 9, there are the murders that spring out of cases where the rich are losing it mentally or financially and kill due to delusions, paranoia, or a desperate effort to hold onto the wealth and status they have once known. Still other reasons for losing it might be living a double life or engaging in kinky sexual activity that leads to the threat of exposure or blackmail, although such cases often involve outwardly ordinary middle-class people, too.

The following cases illustrate the way these more personal motives of love, power, honor, and money play out for the rich and famous. While there are many dozens of cases to choose from, I have chosen two cases from different time periods—the first, from early in the twentieth century, shows how a slight to honor and respect, mixed with love and jealousy, can lead to murder (the Molineux case); the second, from mid-century, shows how the threat of losing a life of luxury and one's high social position, along with love for someone else, can result in murder, too (the Mossler case).

A Matter of Love and Honor: The Case of Roland Burnham Molineux (New York, New York, 1898–1902)

Roland B. Molineux, an aristocrat of old New York, not only killed once, but twice, and each time with a different motive. The first time was out of love and jealousy, when one man threatened to take away the woman he wanted to marry; the second time was when a fellow member of an elite New York club demeaned him with petty insults and humiliations. Unfortunately, Molineux's search to restore his honor in the second instance backfired and led to an investigation into his first murder as well. His problem was that the second time around he poisoned the wrong person; her death launched an investigation that led the police to him and resulted in two trials that were the talk of turn-of-the century New York.

The case began a few days after Henry Cornish, the athletic director of the posh Knickerbocker Athletic Club in New York, received a bottle of Bromo Selzer in the mail shortly before Christmas. It came in a pale-blue box that looked like a gift from Tiffany's, one of the most fashionable stores in the city. Inside he found a silver toothpick-holder in the shape of a two-inch-square candlestick, and beside it he saw a one-ounce blue bottle of Bromo Seltzer, which could fit into the holder. Though a small envelope lay in the box, it contained no card, so he couldn't tell who sent the package.[1]

Cornish thought the package a Christmas joke and presumed that a friend had playfully sent it to caution him not to drink too much over the holidays. His fellow Knickerbocker Club members similarly thought it a joke when he showed it around. But who sent the gift? At his assistant's suggestion, he pulled the manila wrapper from the wastebasket and cut off the address, hoping he might eventually recognize the handwriting and identify the prankster. Though he didn't notice it at the time, the envelope held an important clue: the address number at 45th and Madison was misspelled as "fourty." Later, this error would provide a crucial clue for investigators.[2]

A few days later, on December 27, Cornish brought the present home to his boardinghouse and showed it to his landlady Mrs. Katherine Adams, also his widowed aunt, and her daughter Mrs. Florence Rodgers. Then, he put the bottle in his room, along with the wrapper. When Mrs. Adams awoke the next morning with a splitting headache, her daughter remembered the Bromo Selzer and asked Cornish to give some to her mother. Graciously, he poured her a glass with about a half-teaspoonful of medicine. As Mrs. Adams drank some, commenting that it tasted bitter, Cornish drank a bit of what remained, commenting that it tasted all right. But unfortunately, it wasn't.[3]

A few minutes later, after Cornish had returned to his room, Adams went into convulsions. She vomited, writhing and screaming in pain, and fell unconscious on the floor. Mrs. Rogers knocked urgently on Cornish's door, begging him to come quickly. Minutes later, they sent a boy out to get Dr. Edwin Hitchcock, who soon arrived with a stomach pump and emergency bag. But by then, Mrs. Adams was near death, lying almost motionless on her back. Meanwhile, Cornish began retching, with the same symptoms as Mrs. Adams, though not as severely.[4]

Dr. Hitchcock quickly suspected the medicine. To check, he tasted a bit of the remaining powder by putting a drop on his finger against the tip of his tongue. Soon he felt a slight nausea, though this quickly passed. But Cornish, who had sipped a little more, was ill for days.[5]

Meanwhile, as Cornish recovered over the next few days, the police, led by Detective Carey, began to investigate. At first, they considered a simple manufacturing flaw in the Bromo Seltzer and sent it out for testing. But after the results came back, they discovered the bottle contained cyanide of mercury, one of most deadly drugs known. The press had already started following the story, and now it began to speculate about who could have been the poisoner, surmising that Cornish was the intended victim because the package was sent to him. So who might have hated him enough to have sent it?

Detective Carey and the other police officers wondered, too, and they went to the Knickerbocker club to ask club members who might want to harm Cornish. Several club members recalled that a former club member, Roland Molineux, had had several run-ins with Cornish. Perhaps, he might have continued to hold some ill-feelings toward Cornish after resigning his membership in the club.[6]

Yet, the conflicts seemed strangely trivial. Could they have really inspired murder? In one case, Molineux, a champion gymnast and member of the club's athletic committee, had asked Cornish to order a certain type of horizontal bar, but Cornish didn't order it. Molineux had also complained to other members that Cornish let athletic members and their guests use obscene language around the club swimming pool, which offended Molineux's aristocratic sensibilities. Then, perhaps most humiliating of all, Cornish had shown he could lift heavier weights in a dumbbell-lifting contest.[7] Eventually, Molineux told the board members to fire Cornish or he would resign, and when the board members refused to fire Cornish, that's what he did—he resigned from the club in 1897.[8] Could such minor incidents possibly be a motive? police wondered.

To find out, the police began to look into whether Molineux could have sent the package. They soon found a suggestive lead in the address on the manila package Cornish had received. Two club members, secretary John D. Adams and club steward Andre Bustanoby, thought the handwriting on it looked a little like Molineux's. So, a few days later, the police called Molineux in for questioning, and the morning newspaper reported their interest with the headline: "The Police Want Roland B. Molineux."[9]

At first, Molineux showed his eagerness to cooperate. The next day, he and his father, the prominent Civil War general, Edward Leslie Molineux, showed up at the home of the Chief of Detectives, Captain McClusky. At once, Molineux insisted he had nothing to do with sending any package to harm Mr. Cornish, and because there was no evidence that he had sent it, Captain McClusky let him go.

Then came some tantalizing new evidence. When the police interviewed the club doctor Wendell C. Phillips, he remembered that about a year prior another club member, Henry C. Barnet, had died from symptoms similar to Cornish's. As Phillips explained, Barnet had taken a dose of another patent medicine called Kutnow powder, and it had been mailed to Barnet anonymously.[10]

Soon, the police located Barnet's doctor, Henry Douglass, and questioned him about Barnet's death, which had never aroused earlier police suspicions because it had been considered a natural death at the time. As Douglass explained, he had given the medicine bottle the powder came in to a chemist for analysis and learned it contained cyanide of mercury. But because he had believed that Barnet died of diphtheria, he didn't make the connection between the cyanide poison and Barnet's death. Thus the report was never sent to the police.[11]

Returning to the club, the police learned even more suspicious details. Now club members told them that before Barnet died, he had taken an interest in a beautiful young woman named Blanche Cheeseborough and was courting her. But Molineux was attracted to her, too, and a few weeks after Barnet's death in October 1898, Molineux married her.[12] Was his death just a fortunate coincidence? Or was it Molineux's way of eliminating the competition? the police wondered.

After more questioning, the police discovered that Molineux's father, the general, was not only a chemist but also the superintendent of Morris Herrmann and Company, a factory across the river from Manhattan in Newark, New Jersey.

It manufactured dry colors, using all kinds of chemicals. One was cyanide of mercury.[13]

The police learned that before Barnet died and Cornish fell ill, someone had established a fictitious letter-box account in the names of both men at a post office on 42nd Street—the Barnet box in May 1898 and the Cornish box on December 21, 1898. Significantly, the Cornish box was opened just two days before Cornish received the Bromo Seltzer bottle. Whoever opened these boxes used the two men's names to place a number of orders, as the mailboxes' proprietor Nicholas Heckmann reported.[14] What orders? One order, as the police discovered, was for Kutnow powder for Barnet; several other orders were for a cure for impotence and other patent medicines.

Then, in looking more closely at the correspondence, Detective Carey noticed several misspellings, and one in particular caught his attention. The writer had misspelled the word "forty" as "fourty"—just as it was misspelled on the package sent to Cornish. Another piece of the puzzle came when Heckmann identified Molineux as the renter of the box and reported that Molineux had stopped in about two dozen times to pick up mail and packages. The police additionally found that Molineux's handwriting on the box rental slip also seemed to match the handwriting on the Cornish package.[15]

But even if Molineux had sent the package, worked in a paint factory, and had a motive due to jealousy or anger, did he actually poison the medicine? There was still no clear proof of a crime, a problem that often arises in rich and famous cases involving deceptive and surreptitious methods.

Detective Carey was determined and continued his investigation. Then, he found even more convincing proof. He located saleswoman Emma Miller at the Hartdegen jewelry store in Newark, who told him that she remembered selling the silver toothpick holder to a man in a Vandyke beard—a man who was looking for something to hold a Bromo Seltzer bottle.[16] Because Molineux had such a beard, that was another persuasive bit of evidence.

Meanwhile, the Newark police, who were assisting with the investigation, found still more evidence when they spoke with an employee who worked with Molineux, Mary Melando. She said she recognized the light-blue stationery used to order the medicine for impotence. She had previously seen it in Molineux's office, she explained to a detective.[17] At a police inquest, Molineux had denied ever seeing such a letter, but Melando's comment contradicted him. Could Molineux explain it away?

Angrily, Molineux insisted he was innocent, claiming that Heckmann, the rental box owner, had set up a plot to extort him. Because Molineux and his family had the resources to put up an extended fight, a long, expensive battle to keep Molineux from going to trial ensued. His father put up far more than the $200,000 the prosecution spent trying to convict him—equivalent to spending millions today. Also, Molineux had a good high-power attorney, Barlow S. Weeks, to represent him.[18]

Soon the legal wrangling turned to fighting about the evidence, although ultimately Molineux's motivation would come into play, as each side sought to show why Molineux, a highly respected member of New York society, would or would not have had a reason for committing the crime. Though motive might not be one of the elements in proving the crime, it would play an important part in convincing the jury to accept either the prosecution or the defense theory of the case.

Initially, all of this legal maneuvering helped to delay the prosecution, always a helpful strategy for the defense. Then, as now, the effort to delay the trial was a usual defense strategy, because with delays, evidence can be lost or degraded, witnesses' memories can fade, and the defense can find more supportive witnesses to create reasonable doubt. To this end, Molineux's lawyer first convinced the judge to dismiss a February 1899 grand jury indictment by arguing there wasn't sufficient evidence for an indictment. Why? Because, he argued, the handwriting wasn't admissible, since one of the samples was sent through the mail, and there was a question of who sent the letters signed by Cornish and Barnet.[19] Additionally, he raised suspicions about Heckmann, suggesting he might be an escaped prisoner from Nashville named Percy Raymond who was trying to set up Molineux. In response, a Tennessee lawyer claimed there was a plot to take Heckmann from New York State to prevent him from testifying.

While the complications were being sorted out, the first

judge decided to dismiss the first grand jury indictment and turned the matter over to the next grand jury.[20] So now Molineux's fate rested in the hands of the new jury members.

Finally, in July, after New York Supreme Court Judge Pardon C. Williams ruled that the handwriting could be admitted if determined genuine, the grand jury decided to indict Molineux. So at last, on December 4, 1899, Molineux went to trial before Judge John W. Goff at the Court of General Sessions of the Peace.[21]

As an eager press followed the story, it was an epic battle for the next eight weeks. Using the evidence Carey and other detectives had collected, District Attorney James W. Osborne tried to show how Molineux had created a grand scheme to get rid of his two hated enemies: Cornish, as well as Barnet. Poor Katherine J. Adams, Cornish's landlady, had simply been an inadvertent victim because Cornish happened to give her the Bromo Selzer for her headache.[22]

But could Osborne prove that Molineux planned to get rid of his enemies? One battle was over whether Heckmann was correct in claiming that Molineux rented the letter boxes or whether another man rented them. An even bigger battle was over the handwriting, which had only recently become admissable evidence in any court. Osborne brought in fourteen expert witnesses who said the handwriting definitely was Molineux's, but Weeks attacked their credibility.[23] Then, it was time for the defense's presentation, but instead of presenting any defense, Weeks immediately began his closing arguments, claiming the prosecution had not established its case. He argued that the prosecution was trying to build a case based on the dubious claims of so-called experts, and he concluded by dramatically throwing down the gauntlet: "Find Molineux guilty of murder in the first degree or nothing."[24] It was an audacious ploy to show that Molineux was so sure of his innocence that the jurors couldn't help but agree.

Would the ploy for innocence work? Unfortunately, no, because seven hours later, the jurors unanimously found Molineux guilty, and the judge sentenced him to the Tombs prison in New York and the death house at Sing Sing. Molineux looked shocked as he heard the verdict, and just before the sentence was announced, he stood up, protesting his innocence. "The yellow journalists put a price on my head," he charged, claiming that Heckmann had been co-opted by this money to testify falsely against him. As he put it, this price was "an invitation to every blackmailer, every perjurer, every rogue, every man without principle but with a price, and to that invitation Mr. Heckmann responded."[25]

But Molineux had the resources to keep fighting and was able to hire a good lawyer and pursue an appeal. As a result, while Detective Carey had no doubts of Molineux's guilt, in 1901, Molineux's appeal was heard by the New York Court of Appeals and the court unanimously reversed his conviction and ordered a new trial. Why? Because Molineux's lawyer successfully convinced the judges that the trial court erroneously let in hearsay testimony from Barnet's physician, who described how Barnet had gotten the Kutnow powder in the mail and became ill after taking it. The court ruled that Barnet wasn't sufficiently ill at the time for his statement to be considered a dying declaration and therefore admissible hearsay. In addition, the court said that the prosecution couldn't bring in any evidence about Barnet's death because the crime wasn't charged in the indictment. Also, the judges raised questions about the letter-box correspondence and the fictitious names, suggesting that it was a stretch to use them to link the two victims.[26] In short, the judges ripped the heart out of the prosecution's case.

As a result, when Molineux was retried in October 1902, after spending eighteen months in the Tombs, much of the evidence against him was excluded. The prosecution couldn't introduce any evidence related to the Barnet poisoning and could only introduce six of the Barnet letters that did not refer to the poisoning to compare these with the letters to Cornish. Also, Mary Melando, key witness against Molineux when she described seeing the blue stationery to order a cure for impotence in his office, refused to appear. And because she lived in New Jersey, the prosecution couldn't compel her appearance in New York.[27]

Molineux's other trump card was that this time he appeared on the stand, and he impressed everyone with his confident aristocratic bearing when he described how he was visiting a Columbia University professor on the day the poison package was mailed. Additionally, he confidently denied writing any of the letters to Barnet or Cornish, and he even claimed he had never heard of cyanide of mercury. He put on a magnificent performance, and after twelve minutes of deliberation, the jury found him not guilty.[28]

After that, Molineux never went back to the paint business. Instead, he became a writer of poetry, plays, and stories, and he based one of his books *The Room with the Little Door* on his experiences in the Tombs, using his writing to help restore his tarnished reputation and regain his standing in New York society. In *The Room*, he described how he had been falsely identified by a "blackmailer" or "crank" by "the yellow newspapers, hungry for sensation,"[29] and he decried the false testimony of the so-called handwriting experts. As he put it:

> The handwriting expert passes no examination, and possesses no diploma. He need not even procure a license. . . . The expert in handwriting may have your life, liberty, and fortune in his hands; but he comes from—where? Who taught him? Who has tested or examined him as to his knowledge or accuracy? . . . All scientific things are recognized by these great colleges and universities. The study of questions arising from disputed handwritings is recognized in none of them; hence this study is not, at least as yet, a science. . . . it is based on the theory of probabilities; it is mere speculation . . .
>
> In courts of justice no experts should be allowed to plead for the side they espouse. . . . Their opinions are tinctured by retainers. . . . The expert will declare it a tracing should his retainer dictate; otherwise not; but whichever way he testifies can never be proved wrong.[30]

He concluded his argument for innocence by imagining a duel between himself and his former prosecutor, Osborne, who had won the first round. Molineux described it as a battle between the bludgeon against the rapier. But in this second round, though Molineux came from his cell, where he had been shut up for nearly four years, looking "pallid and wasted," in the end he made an "excellent witness" and "gave an impression of utter sincerity." In fact, Molineux used this text to deny he had any motive for these crimes. As he explained, he had only given the woman Barnet pursued, Blanche Cheeseborough, a friendship ring shortly after Barnet had died. Thus, there had been no impropriety in his attentions to her, no motive to kill Barnet—she had just been a friend. But instead, Osborne had used the story of the ring as part of a devious plot to destroy him. But finally, in the battle of the bludgeon and the rapier, he had won.[31]

Thus, with any guilt or motive for killing explained away, Molineux resumed his aristocratic place in society, at least for awhile. Though his first wife Blanche divorced him, he remarried. He even became a reporter for several newspapers, covering murder stories, and one of his plays about prison life, *The Man Inside*, was produced by the theatrical impresario David Belasco in 1913. Unfortunately, though, that same year, he had a nervous breakdown and was committed to an insane asylum in Babylon, Long Island; and the following year he was found running away without trousers, wearing only a running shirt and a bathrobe. He was committed to another asylum, the Kings Park State Hospital, where he died in 1917.[32]

So did Molineux commit these murders? Did he have the motive to do so? Almost assuredly he did. But with the power of upper-crust money and the confident bearing of an aristocrat, he escaped conviction, though he kept on trying to convince the world of his innocence through his writing. And ironically, despite all his protests about the power of handwriting to destroy, his handwriting is what gave him away in the first trial.

For Love and Money: The Case of Candace (Candy) Mossler (Miami, Florida, 1964–1966)

The Candy Mossler case is a perfect example of the woman, married to a very wealthy older man, whose motives are money, freedom from the relationship, and a desire to be with someone else. The case had all the elements that would turn it into a front-page story as the 1964 version of the trial of the century—"incest, adultery, money, greed, passion, hatred."[33] The charge? Mossler, a platinum blonde and bouncy 39-year-old woman, was accused of killing her husband, Jacques Mossler, with the help of her nephew and lover, Melvin Powers. To defend herself, she hired a team of five lawyers, led by the formidable legal powerhouse, Percy Foreman, who mounted a strong and spirited defense.

The case began in the early morning of June 30, 1964, when Candy, claiming a severe migraine headache, left her apartment at the exclusive Governor's Lodge in Key Biscayne, Florida, at 1 a.m. to take her four adopted children, who ranged in age from eleven to twenty, for a car ride to a hospital emergency room. But was this really her reason or was it an excuse to be out of the house when the murder occurred? After a long, meandering drive, she returned to her apartment at 4:30 a.m. There, she found her husband, Jacques, lying dead on the floor, in a pool of blood resulting from thirty-nine stab wounds and a massive blow that fractured his skull.[34] Possibly, the blow was from a large shattered ceramic swan that was on the floor near the body, though later prosecutors would claim the weapon was a large Coke bottle obtained from a nearby bar. Also, the police found a bloody palm print on the kitchen counter.[35]

At once, after finding the body, Candy called to report the homicide, and soon after, the police arrived and began questioning Candy and the neighbors. They soon learned that at about 1:30 to 2:00 a.m., the neighbors had heard thumps and screams from Candy's apartment, as well as the loud barking of the Mossler's boxer, Rocky, who the police found chained to the kitchen doorknob. One neighbor down the hall, Mrs. Peggy Fletcher, reported hearing the plaintiff cry: "Don't—don't do that to me!," after which the dog began to bark. Then, as she went to the door to find out what was going on, before opening it, she heard the door close across the hall, followed by the sound of footsteps walking down the hall. Afterward, she heard the intruder running down the concrete outer stairway. According to the neighbors who heard the footsteps, they sounded heavy, like those of a man.[36]

Meanwhile, to help deflect any suspicion from herself, Candy was quick to suggest to the detectives what might have happened. She told police that Jacques might have been killed by a homosexual lover or someone he had met at the beach, since he had this secret sex life and often brought his lovers home.[37] And early on, the police did arrest a suspect who was gay, though they quickly released him after questioning. Additionally, they picked up a few other suspects, including a man found near Key Biscayne dressed in bloody clothing, who claimed he had been beaten up by a gang of teenagers.[38]

However, very soon, the police had other evidence that pointed to Candy and her 24-year-old nephew Melvin Powers, who ran a trailer sales lot in Houston that Mossler financed. Among other things, they learned that Candy appeared to be having an intimate relationship with Powers. They also discovered a note from Mossler that stated: "If Mel and Candace don't kill me first, I'll kill them"; in addition, they found a match between Power's palm print and that left on the kitchen counter. Thus, on the theory that Powers had flown from Houston to Florida, killed Mossler, and returned to Houston within forty-eight hours, the police arrested Powers.[39]

Immediately, Candy flew back to Houston, where she and Mossler had another of their luxurious homes. There she hired a top lawyer, Percy Foreman, to defend Powers. At the time, Foreman was the most famous criminal lawyer in Texas, known for his great success in keeping defendants in murder cases out of prison or from getting the death penalty.[40]

A few weeks later, Candy was herself arrested, accused of "being the brains behind the murder" whereas "Mel was the brawn."[41] Now she brought in her own team of four lawyers, consisting of two lawyers from Houston, Clyde Woody and Marian Rosen, and two well-known Miami lawyers, Harvey St. Jean and Henry Carr. The four then combined forces with Foreman, who headed up the defense. For about a year, Powers fought against being extradited from Texas to Florida for the trial, but finally, on January 16, 1966, the trial began with jury selection.[42]

Meanwhile, as Candy and Melvin remained free on $50,000 bail each, the newspapers and news magazines began the build-up that would turn the trial into a media circus. It had all the elements. One was the very brutal murder of Jacques Mossler, a millionaire with three luxurious homes in Miami, Houston, and Chicago who had made his fortune in oil and had investments in banks and finance companies. Another was the beautiful and flamboyant Candy, who looked like an aging Hollywood star. Before marrying Jacques in 1948, she had run away from her poor Georgia home, been a model, and owned her own modeling agency in New Orleans.[43] Additionally, there were salacious allegations that Candy had been having an incestuous relationship with her nephew and that she and Jacques had an unusual family arrangement with ten children. Jacques had four grown daughters from his first marriage; Candy had two very attractive children from her last marriage; and together, Candy and Jacques had adopted four teenagers, who had become homeless orphans after their father, a mentally disturbed war veteran, had killed their mother and was committed to a mental institution.[44]

And that intriguing background was just for starters. As the trial unfolded, there would be reports that Jacques had been leading a secret and perverse life that included hookers, transvestites, and gay lovers. At the same time, Candy proved to be a glamorous, easy-to-talk-to interviewee for reporters, beginning with her arrival for the trial at the Miami airport. There she met the hordes of reporters waiting for her and turned on her southern charm, as she "declared her innocence and her faith in the good people of Dade County."[45]

Though Candy firmly denied the allegations that her nephew Melvin Powers was also her lover, her claims were questioned when reporters asked about some letters to Powers in which she called him "darling" and expressed her love. But she had a ready answer for that, claiming that she used these words of affection for everyone, or as she put it: "I write to everyone, 'Darling,' I love you. I want you in my arms.' I say the same thing to my lawyer. It doesn't mean I really love him."[46] She even told reporter Theo Wilson in an interview that her alleged love letters, with phrases like "I love you" and "I miss you," were simply the comments of a "loving aunt."[47] Yet the suspicion lingered, especially when reports surfaced that Powers had described how he had gotten his aunt to give him all sorts of favors—such as giving him good clothes and a good car—by performing oral sex on her, or as he put it: "scarfing" her.[48]

Needless to say, such lurid tidbits made great copy, and the public ate it up. Theo Wilson and other reporters even wrote a song to the tune of "Frankie and Johnnie Were Lovers," called "Candy and Melvin Were Lovers" which featured the popular sentiments about the couple and spread around the world.

So as the trial proceeded, even the press and public believed that Candy and Melvin, as lovers, had a good reason for getting rid of Jacques, especially because Candy would inherit his millions.

But what would the jury decide?

Foreman immediately sought to get a more receptive jury pool by making sure that the jurors would not be likely to convict if they believed the defendants had engaged in adultery, fornication, or incest and would be open to separately considering whether there was reasonable doubt of a homicide. Thus, to eliminate jurors who might be swayed to convict if morally offended, Foreman repeatedly asked each prospective juror: "If you were satisfied there had been adultery, fornication, an incestuous relationship beyond a reasonable doubt, but were not satisfied that the prosecution proved homicide, would you convict them of murder?"[49] Eventually, the jurors who were selected did agree that they could tell the difference between such allegations and homicide.

The prosecution case was relatively straightforward and compelling, showing a strong motive of love and money, backed up by strong evidence of guilt. The prosecution team, which included Arthur Huttoe[50] and Richard Gerstein,[51] argued that Powers had killed Mossler at Candy's request, so that she would inherit over $7 million after his death and then be free to marry.[52] By some accounts, the prosecution showed that Mossler's estate was worth much more—over $200 million in gross value, $22 million net.[53] Whatever the amount, this was a huge amount of money, as the prosecutor argued, and therefore the prospect of losing it was a strong incentive to kill.

Presumably, Mossler had discovered their affair and was planning to seek a divorce and drop Candace from his will. So that's what prompted Powers to fly from Houston to Miami, where he drove the white car he obtained from Candy, which some witnesses had seen in the area. Then, the prosecution argued, several hours before the murder, Powers had gone to the

Stuffed Shirt Lounge, located on the way to Key Biscayne, where he had ordered a drink and asked the bartender for a large empty Coke bottle. After this, he had gone to the Mossler house to kill Jacques, while Candy was driving to the hospital and back with her children from 1:00 a.m. to 4:30 a.m. to provide an alibi. Finally, after the murder, he had driven the car back to the airport and returned to Houston.[54]

Based on these facts, as the lead prosecutor Huttoe emphasized to the jurors, the motive was clear: "The motive for this murder was a personal hatred of the deceased by Melvin Lane Powers and a sordid, illicit love affair between the deceased's wife and her sister's son."[55] Plus there were the millions of dollars to be reaped from Jacques's demise, half of which would go to Candy.

To back up this theory, the prosecution provided plenty of supporting evidence. For one thing, Power's fingerprints were not only in the car, but in the bloody print on the kitchen counter. Some witnesses saw a man with dark hair running away from the apartment and/or driving a white car, much like the one Candy had driven in the afternoon.[56] The prosecution also introduced several witnesses who spoke about Candy's earlier efforts to find someone to kill her husband, including one witness, William Frank Mulvey, who claimed that Candy had given him $7,500 to murder her husband, though he never carried out the killing, nor intended to do so. Further, Mulvey claimed that after he was sent back to prison for another crime, he had met Powers there and Powers had boasted about killing Mossler.[57]

Additionally, the prosecution brought in witnesses to testify that Candy and Powers did have a hot and steamy relationship. One ex-convict, Edward Bart Diehl, described how he and his wife worked as caretakers on Jacques's ranch near Galveston, Texas, and how his wife cleaned up a trailer that Candy and Mel used, which was "always a mess," with beds that were left rumpled and unmade into the middle of the day. He claimed that Powers had once described the affair to him, explaining that he could get good clothes and a good car from Candy and "all he had to do was scarf her," which Diehl translated as to "eat her box"—in other words to satisfy her through oral intercourse. Then, "he could get anything he wanted," Diehl explained.[58] And one handyman, Earl Martin, testified that not only did Powers offer him some fast money to kill Candy's husband, but that he had seen Candy at Power's office kissing and hugging him in her car.[59]

Thus, the prosecution built what seemed to be a very strong case to show not only motive, but the acts in which the defendants engaged, which demonstrated both their affair and their acts to carry out the murder plot.

But then, led by Foreman, the defense struck back, presenting its own theory of the crime and attacking every bit of evidence the defense presented. The bloody palm print? Why shouldn't it be in the house, since Powers was a business associate of Jacques and perhaps he could have innocently cut himself, say on the kitchen knife? Besides the print could have been there for days. The witnesses claiming offers for a hit job? They were not to be believed because they were shady criminals, and Mulvey was not only a known drug addict with many convictions, but also he would easily lie to get out of prison. And he couldn't have heard anything anyway, because his cell was four cells away from Power's cell and they never spoke.[60] Moreover, on the dates when one witness, Arthur Grimsley, a mail-order minister serving time in the Arkansas State Penn, testified that Powers told him he was living with a relative and they wanted her old man killed, Powers was in the hospital for several operations.[61]

On and on Foreman's attack on the prosecution theory and witnesses went. The high point of the defense came in an attack on Jacques's character, coupled with intimations that any number of people who hated Jacques could have killed him. As Foreman described him, Jacques was an "insatiable sex pervert" and a "ruthless pirate" hated by thousands of people,[62] thereby setting himself for either blackmail or murder. Among his vices were engaging in transvestism, homosexuality, voyeurism, masochism, and sadism.[63] When Candace testified, she added to this seedy profile by describing how her husband would bring many of the men he picked up back to the house, which is why she thought he was murdered. As she explained, in her soft, gentle southern drawl that made her sound so sweet and innocent:

> My husband, unfortunately, very unfortunately, just picked up strangers. The children and I would walk into the apartment and the house would be full of strangers. They were young men, mostly, and they'd just clear out as soon as we walked in. . . . He'd just pick them up, sailors and young men, on the beach and in bars, in restaurants, on the highways.[64]

Alternatively, if the killer wasn't one of Jacques's low-life sex partners, Foreman suggested that he had plenty of people from his business dealings who might hate him and want to kill him. Among them were dozens of auto dealers that he had ruined, thousands of people whose cars were repossessed, and many unhappy former employees.[65]

In short, Foreman used the tried-and-true strategy of many defense lawyers: he attacked the victim and planted ideas about other killers to get the jurors to forget about the likely motivation of his own clients. Moreover, since he was working with four other lawyers, Foreman was able to give the last closing argument, normally reserved to the prosecution, because he had not called any defense witnesses himself. He had left that role to the four other lawyers representing Candy, and in his closing argument, he spoke for almost five hours, powerfully advocating the defense theory, which attributed the motive to kill Jacques to potentially thousands of sex partners, disgruntled employees, and business associates.

So who would prevail? It was a long, tormenting wait of over sixteen hours because the jury initially deadlocked. But after a number of ballots, the jury returned with a "not guilty" verdict, finding insufficient circumstantial evidence to convict.[66] Candy was joyous, and as she left the courtroom, she kissed members of the jury, as well as Powers and Foreman. Later, she had a big victory acquittal party celebration, and her children went around the room with one of the big murder trial posters to collect signatures.[67] It was a total win, for now that the trial was over with an acquittal, Candy was free to inherit her husband's $33 million real estate and banking business. She turned it into Candace Mossler Enterprises, which became an empire worth over $100 million by the late 1960s.[68]

Her relationship with Powers was soon over, however, though she did not want to talk about what happened. She had put that "regrettable circumstance in Florida," as she referred to the trial, behind her[69] and was ready to move on. When she married again a few years after the trial, it was to an electrician, Barnett Wade Garrison, who was eighteen years younger than she was. Oddly, though, he suffered a strange fall from the house in 1972. When he returned home one night and found the door locked, he tried to climb up to an unlocked window on the third floor. But as he climbed using only one hand, because he had a small automatic pistol in the other, he slipped and fell, sustaining a two-week coma and permanent mental damage. His reason for climbing with a pistol wasn't clear. Could he perhaps have had a motive for attacking Candy? Whatever the case, the marriage ended in divorce in 1975, and a year later Candy died, after an overdose of sedatives. Despite her glamorous appearance at her trial a decade before and great business success, she had become a drug addict over the years.[70] But at least for a time, her motive for murder had brought her the fortune and freedom from Mossler she craved, even if she didn't gain the love of Powers, which seemed to be one of her motives, too.

CHAPTER 2

What's the Method?

Certainly, the rich and famous employ some of the usual methods and weapons of murder. They shoot to kill in a lover's quarrel; they use a kitchen knife in a fight with a family member; they use everyday poisons to dispatch a no-longer-wanted mate or lover.

However, they are more likely to use other methods that involve premeditation and planning, such as creating an elaborate setup for the crime, including buying the weapons and plotting an alibi (as in the Capano case featured in Chapter 4). Also, they are more likely to take their time, waiting for an auspicious moment to strike; for example, they may plan a trip or attend a meeting where they will be seen while someone carries out the murder for them, or they may change insurance documents and wills so that they, or someone they trust as a proxy, will gain the funds expected after their victim's death. Then, too, the rich and famous are more likely to come up with creative ways to engineer the demise of their victim, whatever their motive, because of their greater access to resources or the specialized knowledge they have obtained from their business lives or typically higher levels of education. For example, Albert Luetgert, profiled in Chapter 4 for his creative cover-up, used an unusual method for killing his wife made possible by his ownership of a factory for butchering meat. Because he pushed her into a vat of sulfurous chemicals, it was difficult to find her body or to prosecute him. Not everyone has access to such an efficient way to kill and dispose of a body.

Such knowledge and resources, in turn, can contribute to developing and implementing a creative cover-up, though the use of an unsuspicious murder method can often make an elaborate cover-up unnecessary. Some methods may make the murder appear to be a natural death or an accident, so initially no one even suspects there has been a crime. But when investigators start probing, they may uncover a nefarious plot. In other cases, such as when a slow-acting poison leads to a lingering illness and death followed by a quick cremation that eliminates any traces of poison or any chance of discovery, those close to the victim and perhaps the police may have lingering suspicions, though the evidence is insufficient to charge a crime. Other methods that are difficult to trace and that include premeditation, planning, and elaborate cover-ups include jiggering a vehicle's brakes so that they fail, causing the vehicle to crash in a fiery blast and obliterating any evidence or setting off a delayed time bomb in the house when the perpetrator is nowhere in sight, giving him or her the perfect alibi.

Often, such methods are so covert that the case ends with a suspected murder that can't be proved—for instance, controversy still lingers six years later over the cause of the car crash in a tunnel in Paris that took the life of Princess Diana. Was it murder due to car-tampering, as some conspiracy theorists believe? Or was it an accident caused by a driver who drank too much and was pursued by rabid paparazzi, causing him to veer out of control? As of this writing, this controversy continues, as investigations and inquisitions proceed.

But sometimes, with good police work, or the occasional blunder by the perpetrator, these devious methods are exposed and the alleged perpetrators are at least charged and sometimes convicted.

The following cases illustrate some of the more unusual and devious methods of committing murder; the first case is from early in the twentieth century and the second is a more recent case from the 1960s. I have chosen them from different time periods to show how this use of creative methods spans the decades, though the lifestyles of those profiled and the particular methods chosen are shaped by the available technologies. As is common in these cases, the media turned them into public spectacles, while high-powered lawyers fought to get their clients acquitted.

The first case, from the 1910s, features a wealthy and noted doctor, Dr. Linda Burfield Hazzard, who set up a clinic offering a fasting cure to appeal to wealthy female clients with stomach problems and the delicately termed "female troubles." In the cases of two wealthy British heiresses, she took the starvation cure even further, so that one died and one nearly did, allegedly because she wanted their money and property. But could the prosecutor prove this outlandish scheme of death by starvation?

In the second case, from the 1960s, Dr. Carl Anthony Coppolino, a former anesthesiologist who had become a successful author of several books on medical subjects and hypnosis, was accused of murdering his wife. At first, her sudden death looked like a simple heart attack, but after the death certificate was signed and she was buried, his former mistress accused him of not one but two murders. If he did kill his wife, his method employed the obscure drug succinylcholine chloride, which is used by anesthesiologists and is hard, if not impossible, to detect in autopsies, and his motive was to collect his wife's insurance and marry a longtime lover. So did he do it and could the prosecutor prove it? That question became the subject of a lurid trial that helped make the career of F. Lee Bailey, then a rising young defense attorney.

Starving the Victims: The Case of Linda Burfield Hazzard (Odalla, Washington, 1911–1912)

As described by Gregg Olsen, a Seattle resident, who carefully researched the Hazzard case in *Starvation Heights* and spoke to me in an interview after reviewing this write-up, the story of Dr. Hazzard's scheme to starve patients for their money shocked the nation. The scheme unraveled after Dorothea and Claire Williamson, two wealthy British heiresses, arrived in Seattle on February 27, 1911, and headed for Dr. Linda Burfield Hazzard's office, drawn by her unusual but internationally known fasting cure. They thought the cure would help them both overcome some long-standing stomach problems and female troubles while they enjoyed a few weeks at a world-renowned spa resort that catered to the upper classes.[1] They had no idea that six months later Claire would starve to death and Dora would be a near-death skeleton struggling for her life to escape Dr. Hazzard's sanitarium. Was this outcome due to a fasting cure that turned deadly by accident, or due to starvation as a method for murder, as the prosecutor tried to prove?

On the surface, the tragedy would appear to be the result of a simple medical complication, at a time when modern medicine was still in its infancy, and Dr. Linda Hazzard was one of the few female doctors. It was a time when independent women were distrusted and the male-dominated medical establishment wanted to maintain control and continue to use traditional remedies. By contrast, Linda Hazzard was seeking to promote a new medical breakthrough—a fasting cure to purify the body and soul—and she made her pitch to the elite and moneyed classes in the United States, Britain, and Europe. When the case became an international sensation, bringing in a flood of unwanted publicity questioning her methods, she claimed she was really a victim, not a murderous villainess starving her patients for their money.

At first, though, nothing seemed amiss when Dora and her sister Claire arrived in America to take Dr. Hazzard's cure. They were both very wealthy English heiresses, who had been left more than a million in American dollars by their Scottish-born grandfather when they were living in Australia. Then, they had moved to the sea near Brighton in Sussex County south of London. Despite their wealth, they were vaguely unhappy and began going to several health institutes, seeking to cure a number of not very serious complaints, such as the bloodshot eyes, swollen glands, and knee and head pains.

Then, one day while traveling, Claire saw an ad for Dr. Hazzard's book *Fasting for the Cure of Disease*.[2] It proclaimed the virtues of her revolutionary new treatment, and much like modern New Age seekers, they were excited to read about the remarkable recoveries of patients who suffered from diseases and bodily disturbances because they ate meat or had nutritional imbalances. So, eager to learn more, Claire wrote to Dr. Hazzard describing the complaints she and her sister had, and in response, along with her book, Dr. Hazzard sent a brochure describing her clinic.[3]

Dr. Hazzard's claims were inspirational and appealing, as she described how her approach could cure many common ills, such as cancer, toothaches, psoriasis, heart trouble, tuberculosis, epilepsy, and insanity. Also, she spoke frequently to civic groups, newspaper reporters, and prospective patients and their families about the virtues of her approach. Still, there were some early warning signs; Hazzard wasn't trained as a doctor, even though she had acquired a medical certificate for her cure, and many medical practitioners criticized her for promoting a quack regimen. But at a time when medicine was just leaving behind patent medicines and becoming more of a true science, it was often hard to distinguish between what was valid and what was quackery. On the positive side, Dr. Hazzard's medical certificate gave her the imprimatur of legitimacy as she spread her fasting gospel far and wide. Then, too, she did have a medical background; she was a nurse in Minneapolis and became an osteopath in 1898, before she began promoting her fasting cure in 1903. She quickly worked her way into Minneapolis society, acquired a husband, Samuel Hazzard, and in 1907, with visions of setting up a great sanitarium, she headed for Seattle with a legion of devotees.[4]

Yet, even at this early date, there were intimations of danger associated with her cure. After some patients died, rumors about their strange deaths spread due to local gossip, comments among doctors, and hints of problems reported in the press. But like modern holistic practitioners criticized for untraditional, unproven methods, Hazzard counterattacked with her own literature and talks, decrying the "organized persecution" she experienced from medical sources and the newspapers, which she accused of being "controlled by the profession," out to defeat her revolutionary new cure. She argued that her clients were commonly desperate patients seeking her cure as a last resort after other treatments had failed. Her arguments worked, so despite any early warning signs, her business thrived. Patients continued to pour into her Seattle offices to take the cure, though some mysteriously died.[5]

The two Williamson sisters were intrigued by Dr. Hazzard's book and brochure, and within a few days, Dr. Hazzard's argument that "overeating is the vice of the whole human race" persuaded them to go to Seattle for some therapy. After some correspondence back and forth, they arrived in Seattle on February 27, 1911, ready to begin their treatment. When the Olalla sanitarium, still under construction, was finished, they would continue their treatment there.

They arrived at Dr. Hazzard's office in a recently built brick bank building dressed primly in long skirts and high necked dresses, as horse-drawn wagons and a few new automobiles passed by on the road. Almost immediately they were struck by Dr. Hazzard's strong force of personality and confident manner—she had the look of a self-sufficient farmwife or warfront nurse. Like a minister, she passionately described how her cure had helped so many of her patients achieve remarkable recoveries, convincing Dora and Claire to start the treatment, which would involve a mix of fasting, light broth, enemas, and baths. She began by having each of the sisters take off their clothes and lie on a massage table while she pummeled them with her fists. Afterward, she suggested three or four weeks of the treatment, plus vigorous exercise, to eliminate the poisons in their bodies causing their current malaise. They would have stronger uteruses, their stomachs would be soothed, and they would feel stronger overall.[6]

And so the treatment began, with visits to Dr. Hazzard's office five times a week, while Dora and Claire stayed in a small nearby flat. Oddly, while they gradually came to feel weaker, they came to increasingly believe in the treatment, feeling it was making them cleaner, as well as giving them a pleasant light-headed euphoria.[7] It was a dangerous mix of belief and feelings that made them increasingly dependent on Dr. Hazzard, even as they began to look cadaverous and skeletal and their bodies became wracked with pains, especially as their daily enemas increased from half an hour to two and three hours. Dora even fainted during one of the procedures.

But Dr. Hazzard convinced them that this pain and suffering was for their own good. "We must eliminate the poisons," she assured them.[8] So they continued the treatment.

But was it really a treatment or part of Dr. Hazzard's devious method to kill them to gain access to their fortunes, even though Dora and Claire didn't think anything was amiss? They simply thought they were on their way to even greater purity, once the treatment was over.

The prognosis was ominous, however. By mid-March, the girls could barely walk, even with the assistance of a nurse, Nellie Sherman, now assigned to help them move about. Their arms, hands, and legs had become very bony, and their eyes and mouths were shrunken and emaciated. Still, Dr. Hazzard was persuasive, convincing them that they still needed to clean their tongue, sweeten their breath, and fully cleanse their system. "You are not fit to take food yet," she assured them,[9] and so they went on, their will now subservient to hers.

Now that they were bedridden and fully in her power, Dr. Hazzard advised them that they needed to secure their expensive belongings against anyone coming into their apartments. At first, the sisters demurred, but after several requests, they agreed, turning over their rings and even land deeds to her.[10]

By the end of March, Dora experienced times when her mind wandered and she became delirious. But still the fasting continued. The sisters could not even get out of bed anymore and had to be carried. Yet even though Nellie, their nurse, tried to get them to eat more than the slight broth of tomatoes or asparagus tips that was now their daily diet, they refused to take anymore, thinking they needed to strictly follow the treatment.[11]

Fearing for their safely, Nellie went to local osteopath Augusta Brewer for advice, telling her: "They are absolutely under Dr. Hazzard's dominion."[12] But beyond urging Nellie to try to feed them immediately, Dr. Brewer could do nothing.[13]

Then, in mid-April, Dr. Hazzard gained even more control over the sisters when she moved them to her recently completed sanitarium at Olalla. She used a special ambulance and launch to move them, since after almost two months of treatment, they were like immobile skeletons, each weighing between seventy and eighty pounds and drifting in and out of consciousness as they sped to their new island home.

Once there, they were placed in one of the smaller cabins for patients that were scattered around the grounds, beyond the large wooden main house with two stories. Ironically, the sanitarium seemed outwardly like a beautiful restful resort or spa, with a commanding view of a beautiful bay in a town of 350 people. But in the cabins, most of the patients were starving to death, including Dora and Claire. It was as if Dr. Hazzard had created a death factory for the wealthy that was concealed by a beautiful healing façade. And to facilitate the process, she had help from her husband, Sam Hazzard, who was like a marionette under her control. He offered to assist the patients with any correspondence, but that help gave him the ability to help the dying patients change their wills to leave their property to Dr. Hazzard. But at the time, Dora and Claire seemed thankful for his "kind" help.[14]

There seemed little way out. At the end of April, perhaps sensing her impending death, Claire managed to find the strength to crawl along a path with a message asking for help. On the way, she encountered a small boy, offered him some money, and asked him to send this message in a cable to Dora's family nurse Margaret Convey, who was then in Australia. The cable said simply: "Come SS Marama May 8th, first class. Claire."[15] Beyond that, there was no explanation, but Margaret took the message as a cry for help, and she quickly sailed to Vancouver, Washington, arriving about a month later, on June 1.[16]

When Margaret docked at Vancouver, she learned the worst from Sam Hazzard, who met her boat to accompany her to Olalla. "Miss Claire has died, and Miss Dora is helplessly insane."[17] Margaret was shocked and felt even more concerned when she met Dr. Hazzard in Olalla and saw her wearing one of Claire's dresses.[18] Then, she saw Dora standing weakly at the door of her small wooden cabin by a ravine filled with ferns and brambles. Dora's face looked like a bluish death mask, her body just bones. As she grabbed Dora to her, Dora whispered her plea for help, asking Margaret to take her away. But could she do so, Margaret wondered? Would Dora even survive that long?[19]

At once Margaret began what would become a fight for

Dora's life. But was she in time? And would Dr. Hazzard let Dora go?

At first, Dr. Hazzard resisted Margaret's request to take Dora with her, claiming that Claire had assigned her assets and power of attorney to her, that money was still due for the sisters' bill, and that Dora had become hopelessly insane. Dr. Hazzard also claimed that drugs that Claire had taken as a child were responsible for her death, not her last resort treatment. So Dora couldn't leave.

For help, Margaret turned to Dora and Claire's uncle, John Herbert, who lived in Portland, Oregon, and urged him to come quickly. After he arrived on May 22, Dr. Hazzard took him to view Claire's body in Seattle funeral parlor, but he didn't recognize his niece and wondered if this was really her body. Of course, it was, Dr. Hazzard assured him. Yet he had his doubts, and if it wasn't his niece, where was the real body? Then, when Dr. Hazzard showed him a tiny stomach, liver, and intestines, which she claimed were Claire's organs, he was shocked. They were so small and shrunken.[20]

Despite Herbert's doubts, Dr. Hazzard was still determined to convince him that there was nothing wrong with the treatment. So later that night at dinner in the sanitarium dining room, she pulled out a letter dated April 23, which she said was written by Claire, in which Claire described her faith in Dr. Hazzard's treatment, though she knew it might not work and expressed acceptance of her death. But was this typed, unsigned letter really written by Claire? Or was this part of Dr. Hazzard's scheme to escape any blame and acquire Claire's property?[21]

While Herbert returned to Seattle the next day to determine what to do, Margaret stayed on at Olalla, where she saw Dora become weaker and weaker, lying in bed most of the day. Meanwhile, Dora's new nurse, Sarah Robinson, continued to give her daily enemas and a small bit of tomato or vegetable broth.

Finally, in mid-June, Margaret saw her chance to save Dora and perhaps obtain justice. When Robinson left for the day, Margaret insisted on taking over her care, gained Dr. Hazzard's reluctant assent, and convinced Dora that she had to eat more and began sneaking her extra food. Margaret first fed her some bits of rice and flour, since that was all Dora could eat, and gradually added other food over the next few days. Meanwhile, as she stayed on, Margaret learned that a few other patients were similarly imprisoned with declining health. But they were like captives doomed to death, unable to help themselves because Dr. Hazzard and her husband watched over everything at the sanitarium so closely, and there was no phone within five miles. Dora couldn't see this at first, though, because she had been so trusting and so captivated by Dr. Hazzard's powerful will.[22]

Finally, the turning point came when Margaret found a document that Dora had signed. Though Dr. Hazzard had told her the document was to transfer $500 to an uncle in Toronto, the document actually showed the transfer was to Samuel Hazzard. After Margaret explained this to Dora, Dora realized what had occurred, and Margaret was determined to help her regain enough strength to go with her to Seattle. Then, she planned to contact the authorities to see if anything could be done.[23]

At first, the plan proved daunting, since Margaret was only a nurse and Dr. Hazzard stopped Dora from sending or receiving any mail. But in secret, Margaret drafted a cable letter and sneaked it out to a local store asking Claire's uncle, John Herbert, to return and get them both out. Finally, he did arrive, but then followed several long days of negotiation to secure Dora's release. Eventually, Herbert had to pay Dr. Hazzard an additional $500 she claimed was due on the bill, and at last, she let Dora go. It was July 22, 1911—four months since Dora had started the fasting cure, but at last she was free.[24]

Then, the investigation of Dr. Hazzard and her practices began. But would the authorities be convinced that her cure covered up a scheme to kill patients and take their money? Margaret and Dora went to see Lucien Agassiz, the British vice-consul, in Tacoma, Washington, and he began the investigation of Dr. Hazzard's practices. Furious at hearing Dora's description of her months of brutal treatment and imprisonment and of her sister's death, he was determined to seek justice. He believed Dr. Hazzard was a charlatan doctor who had imprisoned the sisters, stolen their money, forged and cashed their personal checks, and swindled them out of jewels that were family heirlooms.[25]

As a first step, Agassiz enlisted the aid of a private attorney, Frank Kelley, to remove Dr. Hazzard's name from Dora's guardianship papers. Then, he sought to gather enough evidence, so the Kitsap County authorities, where Olalla was located, would act.[26] But would they? This was a small underfunded department, whereas Dr. Hazzard had strong allies in the county, as well as the money and national following to put up a big fight. Could Kelley compel them to act?

Step by step, Kelley began accumulating incriminating evidence to put pressure on the Kitsap authorities to charge Dr. Hazzard with a crime. One odd discovery was that Claire Williamson's body had been taken by a chartered launch from the island without a removal permit. The undertaker said there had been no time, but Agassiz suspected a conspiracy between the undertaker and Dr. Hazzard. He was even more suspicious on learning that Herbert thought the body he saw in the funeral parlor wasn't Claire's. Agassiz also discovered about $6,000 in missing jewelry, which wasn't returned with the sisters' clothing that Margaret had collected when they left.[27]

Determined to see justice done, Kelley went to see the Kitsap County prosecutor, Thomas Stevenson, at his offices in the small town of Bremerton and presented his evidence. He spoke passionately as he made his presentation to convince Stevenson to act, knowing that this lone prosecutor was the only hope. At first Stevenson demurred, explaining that the county had little money and describing how expensive and difficult trying Dr. Hazzard on murder charges would be. In response, Agassiz argued how important it was to act quickly, since Dr. Hazzard could easily move away or continue her dangerous cure on others. Then, he used his trump card, telling Stevenson that if he didn't do anything, there could be an international incident, since this was a British citizen who was murdered. Finally, Stevenson offered a bargain. He would prosecute if Dora would contribute to the costs of pursuing the suit. There would be interviews, travel, hotel expenses for witnesses. Would she do it?[28]

His request for private funding was extraordinary. But finally Dora agreed and Kelley told the district attorney, "If she has to pay to stop her sister's murderer, so be it."[29]

And so the arrest warrant was filed on August 4, 1911, charging Dr. Hazzard with the murder of Claire Williamson by intentionally starving her to death. Then, over the next few weeks, Agassiz, Kelley, and Stevenson, working together, began to locate evidence of other mysterious deaths of patients. Press headlines about the case began to spread from Seattle to the rest of the country—like the *Seattle Tribune* headline: "Starvation Specialist Who Faces Murder Charges" and the *Tacoma Daily News* headline: "Officials Expect to Expose Starvation Atrocities. Dr. Hazzard Pictured as Fiend."[30] Some journalists even compared her to Belle Gunness, the notorious farm owner who had advertised for suitors, then killed and buried them on her property to collect their money. Agassiz was more than willing to help them make this connection, pointing out that just as investigators had found bodies all over Gunness's farm, so he, Kelly, and Stevenson had discovered records and the friends of many patients who died while under Dr. Hazzard's care.[31] Agassiz also noted that the investigators had located numerous bank records, letters, wire transfers, and other documents showing how Dr. Hazzard had repeatedly obtained the property and money belonging to the patients that died. Not only did this mounting collection of evidence help support their claim in court, it contributed to a growing public horror about what Dr. Hazzard had been doing. The American Medical Association even pulled her license to practice medicine.

When the trial finally began, still other negative information began to surface from Dr. Hazzard's days in Minneapolis. Her husband, Sam Hazzard, had committed bigamy to marry her. Plus, some questions about the success of her cure had led her to leave Minneapolis. Especially questionable was the 1902 death of Gertrude Young, who died of a stroke on the thirty-ninth day of her fast. A coroner, holding a postmortem exam, had ruled that Young had died of starvation and weighed only 105 pounds at her death. Then questions arose after the inquest, because Young's jewelry was missing, including the expensive rings that had been on her finger. But Dr. Hazzard denied stealing from a patient, and no charges were ever filed against her.[32]

Although Dr. Hazzard might previously have escaped any

criminal proceedings, these old stories now contributed to Stevenson's case and to the growing negative press against her. Stevenson also brought to court several medical experts who testified that Dr. Hazzard's fasting cure caused Claire Williamson's death from starvation, rather than any other medical conditions such as peronitis, cirrhosis of the stomach, or a generally poor physical condition, as the defense claimed.[33] The roll call of patients who died while under Dr. Hazzard's care was persuasive, too, and Stevenson was heartened when the judge prevented any patients who claimed they benefited from the fasting cure from testifying. Still, the defense argued back that the trial was really about Dr. Hazzard's method of treatment, rather than anything that she had done.[34] As the defense alleged, the trial was really more about politics, using these criminal accusations to attack Dr. Hazzard's unorthodox medical approach of getting rid of toxic bodily poisons through starvation.

So would the prosecution prevail? Would the jury see through Dr. Hazzard's defense?

Finally, on February 4, 1912, the jury did find Dr. Hazzard guilty of manslaughter. Yet, as Sheriff Howe came to take her away, Dr. Hazzard screamed out, still protesting her innocence and claiming that a vendetta against her method by the mainstream medical practitioners was behind her conviction. "The high and mighty with the diplomas and letters after their names have done this!"[35] she yelled. But at last, justice had been done, as Frank Kelley told the press the next day: "This case will, I believe, be a death blow to quack medical and healing individuals and institutions throughout the country."[36] And he credited Lucien Agassiz, along with Dora Williamson, for instigating the prosecution that led to this result.

Using Anesthesia to Kill: The Case of Dr. Carl Coppolino (Freehold, New Jersey, and Naples, Florida, 1965–1967)

In August 1965, Dr. Carl Anthony Coppolino seemed to be living the good life in Longboat Key, near Sarasota, Florida. He had been an anesthesiologist in New Jersey before moving to Florida with his 32-year-old wife Carmela in April four months earlier and had become a very successful author of several books, most on medical subjects and one book on hypnosis. He also had recently begun seeing an attractive divorcee named Mary Gibson.

Then, the morning of August 28, he found his wife dead, apparently of a heart attack, as he told Dr. Juliette Karow, a nearby doctor he knew casually. Given his authority as a doctor and author, Dr. Karow duly signed the death certificate without any further investigation, and soon after Carmela was buried.

And that seemed to be that—until Coppolino's former lover, Marjorie Farber, came forward and told Dr. Karow of her suspicions. And later Mrs. Farber revealed her own romance with Coppolino and claimed that he had killed her husband, who had been buried in New Jersey two years before. She also later claimed she had been hypnotized by Coppolino and fell completely under his power. Once Mrs. Farber came forward, the build-up began to one of the most lurid trials of the decade. These revelations and the trial were accompanied by a media frenzy, and Coppolino's energetic defense helped build the career of a then rising young defense attorney named F. Lee Bailey, who was attracted to high-profile publicity cases and had built his national reputation defending the infamous Boston Strangler in 1964 and 1965 and negotiating a not-guilty-by-reason-of-insanity plea.[37]

The Coppolino case took on new life the morning of November 7, 1965, when Mrs. Farber, a 52-year-old young-looking widow, called Dr. Juliette Karow, a general practitioner who worked out of her home in Sarasota. Mrs. Farber introduced herself as a woman who lived nearby in Longboat Key—an exclusive area of high priced luxury homes, valued at about $50,000 then and equivalent to about $1 million now. Then, she said she had a matter of vital importance to discuss, and soon afterward arrived at Dr. Karow's office. Mrs. Farber called because she was aware that Dr. Karow had signed the death certificate of Coppolino's wife Carmela, after her sudden death, indicating it was an acute coronary. But Mrs. Farber now told Dr. Karow: "I think she was murdered,"[38] and she gave her reasons, which she would later expand upon to investigators and to the courts. As Mrs. Farber explained, she had witnessed Coppolino committing an earlier murder, leading her to think Coppolino murdered Carmela, too.

The accusation came as a surprise, since Dr. Karow had met Coppolino and Carmela through a mutual friend and had dinner with them about four months earlier when they first arrived in Florida from New Jersey. They had appeared to be a happily married professional couple, but as she listened, Dr. Karow began to question her impression and to feel that Farber was more than just a middle-aged crank needing psychiatric care. Maybe her suspicions were worth considering.[39]

As Farber explained, she had been a friend of both Coppolino and Carmela for several years, first when they were neighbors in New Jersey. Several months after the Coppolinos had moved to Florida, she had followed them there and built a home right next to the Coppolino's.[40] She didn't, however, at this initial meeting, tell Dr. Karow that a reason for her move was because she had once been Coppolino's lover and hoped to continue the relationship, even though Coppolino seemed to have lost interest in her. But she described Dr. Coppolino as an active womanizer and said that she had seen him with a good-looking divorcee, Mary Gibson, the day before Carmela's death. Farber emphasized that Carmela had no history of heart trouble, whereas Coppolino did—which is why he had left his medical practice as an anesthesiologist and gotten a disability pension. So why should a woman with no history of heart trouble suddenly die of a coronary—a rare type of death for someone who was only 32? Farber wondered. Plus, wasn't it suspicious that only six weeks after Carmela had died, Coppolino had married Mrs. Gibson, who she had seen with Coppolino the day before Carmela's death?

Dr. Karow began wondering herself, as she reflected back on that August 28 morning when Coppolino had called her at 1:15 a.m. to tell her his wife had died. When she had arrived, she found Carmela in night clothes on her side in bed, and without doing an extensive examination, based on Coppolino's description, she had diagnosed a coronary occlusion. As Coppolino had told her, Carmela had complained of chest pains the day before, but afterward, he had been with her and everything had seemed perfectly normal, until he discovered her lying in bed dead. At the time, Coppolino's description seemed quite reasonable, and Dr. Karow didn't think to question him further because she knew he was a physician, though not licensed to practice in Florida. Thus, she signed the death certificate for him, without thinking an autopsy was necessary. She felt it was a professional courtesy to do so at a time of personal tragedy.[41]

But now, Dr. Karow felt sufficiently suspicious to urge Mrs. Farber to tell her story to a clergyman, who subsequently referred her to the FBI. But the FBI agent Mrs. Farber spoke to told her this was a local matter and referred her to Sheriff Boyer, a tall, portly man with southern charm. A few days later, she arrived in Boyer's office with her lawyer, who tried to keep Boyer from probing too deeply into her background and knowledge of the Coppolino's in New Jersey. After all, Mrs. Farber opened herself up to being complicit in a crime. But Boyer was insistent. If he was going to look into her suspicions of foul play in Florida, he needed to have the full story. Just what did Mrs. Farber know about Coppolino that would lead her to suspect the worst and why? Though Mrs. Farber was initially unwilling to talk, she returned two days later, on November 11, without her lawyer, who she had fired, ready to tell everything, even if this opened her up to a murder charge.[42] It was a bizarre story that soon came to fascinate America.

As she explained, she and her husband, Lt. Colonel William E. Farber, once a dashing military officer before he retired, had moved to Middletown Township, New Jersey, where they lived diagonally across the street from the Coppolinos. At the time, Dr. Coppolino had retired from his work as an anesthesiologist and had turned to writing about health and medical topics, among them *Practice of Hypnosis in Anesthesiology* and *Freedom From Fat*,[43] while his wife went to work at a pharmaceutical firm. Mrs. Farber, whose husband worked during the day at an insurance company, soon began to get to know Coppolino, who worked at home.[44] She began spending more and more time with him, and gradually, their friendship turned into an affair, though Carmela Coppolino didn't seem to know this.

The affair began, Mrs. Farber explained, when she had

trouble stopping smoking and Carmela suggested that her husband might be able to help because he was an expert hypnotist as well as an anesthesiologist. Mrs. Farber agreed to try, and after being hypnotized, she found herself powerfully drawn to the doctor, who was eighteen years younger than herself, and soon their intimate relationship began. They began seeing each other at Coppolino's house while his wife was off working, and they even went on a tryst to Miami together.[45]

That's when, as she later testified in court, Coppolino had told her that her husband had to go, and she felt powerless to resist when he asked her to assist him.[46] As a result, when Coppolino gave her a hypodermic syringe with a deadly drug in it, she agreed to inject it into her husband. Yet, when it came time to administer the deadly dose, she felt ambivalent and only injected a small amount in her husband's leg while he was sleeping. After that he didn't die but became very ill, and she urged Coppolino to help him live. At first it seemed Coppolino would. But the next day, after Coppolino gave Colonel Farber a sedative, the two men quarreled, and Coppolino angrily injected him with more of the drug and placed a pillow over his head to suffocate him.[47] Thus, Mrs. Farber said she had actually seen Coppolino kill her husband, and now she suspected that he had killed his own wife.

Though her story seemed bizarre, Sheriff Boyer sought to check it out and started investigating. As he did, he sent a report of Mrs. Farber's story to Sheriff Joseph Shafto of Monmouth County, New Jersey, where the Farbers and Coppolinos had lived. Sheriff Shafto soon discovered that Carmela Coppolino had signed Colonel Farber's death certificate, stating that he had died of heart failure. But there was no mention of any injection or strangulation, which Mrs. Farber now claimed. So Shafto, nearing the end of his term as sheriff, put the report aside. But when Boyer sent a copy of the report to the new sheriff, Paul Kiernan, Kiernan referred it to the Monmouth County prosecutor, Vincent Keuper, who decided to further investigate the possibility that Farber could have been murdered.[48]

At the time, both investigations—one in Florida, the other in New Jersey—seemed like long shots. After all, Coppolino was a prominent successful author who had been a doctor, with no record of impropriety in the past. But soon, the results of these investigations led to exhumations and charges of murder, and the story of how Coppolino had turned Mrs. Farber into his hypnotized "love slave" became front-page news.

At first, the investigations seemed quiet routine, when Sheriff Boyer and prosecutor Keuper asked the medical examiners in their respective jurisdictions to report on what they had discovered about the buried bodies. Then, Keuper turned up some curious facts about Dr. Coppolino's background in New Jersey. Born in Brooklyn in 1932, Coppolino showed an early ambition to study medicine and was especially interested in learning about chemistry. He finally pursued his medical studies at Fordham University, where he soon met and married a fellow medical student, Carmela Musetto. Though finances were tight for the aspiring doctors, they married in 1958 and Carmela's father helped them finance their studies.[49] Soon after they were both licensed to practice medicine in New York State, Coppolino got a residency at the Methodist Hospital in Brooklyn, where he specialized in anesthesiology, and later he joined the staff of a hospital in Red Bank, New Jersey. Meanwhile, his wife took a public health job but then left that for a well-paying job at a New Jersey pharmaceutical firm.[50] Coppolino additionally took on some private patients at home, and he occasionally hypnotized a few of them to reduce their pain or help them break bad habits.[51]

Though the arrangement might have seemed ideal for a new doctor, especially with the extra earnings from his private practice and his wife's good job, Coppolino, who had long been ambitious and eager to live well, felt he wasn't making enough. He even complained to other doctors that the nurse who helped them administer the anesthesia at the hospital was making too much money and was getting some of the fees that should go to them. Apparently, he did more than complain: soon the nurse began receiving anonymous threatening letters and phone calls telling her to give up her post or face physical injury. At first, the nurse considered these letters and calls the ravings of a psychopath. But after she continued receiving them, she called the police who referred the matter to the FBI. When an agent came to investigate, he checked several typewriters at the hospital and found one that appeared to be the source of the letters. It was located in a room frequently used by Dr. Coppolino and the other doctors, and after the agent learned about Dr. Coppolino's complaints about the nurse's fees, suspicion fell on Coppolino as the mysterious writer and caller.[52]

But there was no prosecution. Instead, the matter was eventually resolved when Dr. Coppolino resigned, and shortly afterward, he claimed he had a heart condition that prevented him from further practicing any medicine, even privately. But at least he wouldn't have to worry about money, since a health insurance policy would pay him $1,800 a month while he was disabled, and Carmela still had her well-paying job.[53] Then, Coppolino found a way to wealth through his writing and hypnosis of patients.

Now the Coppolinos began to move up in the world and bought their expensive new home with a swimming pool in Middletown. Soon after that, the Farbers moved in. Then, that Christmas in 1962, Coppolino met Mrs. Farber at a neighbor's Christmas party. Soon afterward, in January 1963, Carmela had her second daughter and Marge Farber stopped by with a baby gift. As they spoke, Carmela noticed Marge's heavy cough, and when Marge confessed it was due to smoking, Carmela recommended that Carl might help her by hypnotizing her.[54] Their affair started soon after that.

Continuing her story to authorities, Mrs. Farber explained that after Colonel Farber died suddenly on July 30, 1963, Coppolino, who was no longer a licensed doctor, told Carmela that Farber had died of a heart attack. Consequently, Carmela had signed the death certificate stating this was the cause of death without doing an autopsy. Later, after Colonel Farber's body was shipped to Arlington Cemetery as befits a military hero, Coppolino and his wife remained friendly with Mrs. Farber, and Coppolino continued writing about medicine and health.[55]

While Farber's death by itself might be unremarkable, what was especially suspicious to Keuper was Carmela's signature on the death certificate. His suspicion was aroused because he had also learned that Carmela had been at work at the pharmaceutical company at the same time that she said she had attended Farber.[56]

Still other puzzling details were turning up from Sheriff Boyer's investigation of the Coppolinos in Florida. As Boyer discovered, Dr. Coppolino had been very upset when his wife failed the Florida medical licensing exam and therefore was unable to get her license to practice there. He had looked forward to her higher earnings as a doctor, rather than her lower income selling pharmaceuticals. Then, too, her death from a heart attack seemed surprising, since friends who had seen her earlier that day said she had been in excellent health. Plus, shortly before she died, Coppolino had increased her life insurance to $65,000. Upon her death he had collected $40,000 from one company. After another company, the Professional Life and Casualty Company, refused to pay a $25,000 claim on the grounds that he had made false representations about Carmela's good health, Coppolino had sued the company.[57]

In December 1965, both Boyer and Keuper concluded there were enough suspicious circumstances about both deaths to exhume the bodies and perform the examinations that had not been made at the time of death. Accordingly, Farber's body was exhumed from Arlington and Carmela's from her family's burial plot in Boontown, New Jersey. In Carmela's case, the investigators asked her father, Dr. Carmelo A. Musetto, for permission for these procedures and had asked him not to mention anything to Coppolino, to which he agreed.[58]

First, Carmela's body was exhumed and autopsied by Dr. Milton Helpern, the chief medical examiner in New York, who found no pathological reason for her death, since her heart and organs were completely normal. However, he discovered what looked like a needle puncture in her left buttock, and he sent that off for a further examination. In addition, Helpern sent tissues to Dr. C. Joseph Umberger, head of the toxicology lab in the medical examiner's office, asking him to test for unknown poisons, and should that test prove negative, to conduct a further test for succinylcholine.[59] These tests continued over the next six months until a final determination of the cause of death was made in June 1966.[60]

Colonel Farber's body was dug up July 14, and after examining it, Helpern discovered that Farber had not died from a heart attack, but from a strangulation, as Mrs. Farber had suggested. His finding that a cartilage of the larynx had two fractures was consistent with what Mrs. Farber had claimed in describing Coppolino's use of a pillow to suffocate her husband.[61]

As a result of Helpern's findings, the Monmouth County grand jury issued an indictment on July 21 charging Dr. Coppolino with Farber's murder. Meanwhile, prosecutor Frank Schaub in Sarasota County began presenting evidence to the grand jury that Dr. Coppolino had killed his wife. At this point, the media ran with the case, and on July 22, Coppolino's name made national headlines.[62]

A big issue in the case was whether Dr. Coppolino had, in fact, injected such a drug, or whether both had died of natural causes, a theory that Dr. Coppolino's lawyer, F. Lee Bailey, was to argue, claiming a lack of scientific proof for the state's case. His theory was based on that fact that many toxicologists and pharmacologists believed the succinylcholine drug was untraceable in the human body because it would rapidly disintegrate into its components—succinic acid and choline—which were both normally present in the human body.[63] On the other hand, if Dr. Coppolino was a knowledgeable anesthiologist and knew this, maybe he could have injected this lethal drug into Carmela's body, knowing this means of murder was unlikely to be discovered or proved. Given his specialized knowledge, this could very well be the case.

But any proof of murder hinged on the findings of the medical examiners. Their reason for looking for succinylcholine chloride was that it was well-known to anesthesiologists as a muscle relaxant used to keep a surgery patient from breathing for short periods of time, so a surgeon could do delicate work. But in surgery, whenever the drug was used, an anesthesiologist would always be on hand with oxygen in order to force it into the patient's lungs as necessary. But if the drug was used as a poison and was injected into the body as a liquid solution, it would quickly induce a complete paralysis, though not unconsciousness. So a victim might be fully aware of his inability to breathe and impending death—but be unable to do anything. And afterward, the drug would be untraceable. As one scientist, Dr. C. Manuel Gilman, told a pathologist who worked with Dr. Helpern on the investigation:

"If you want to kill a person and get away with it, this is a good drug to use."[64]

Thus, Dr. Gilman sought to develop this proof, working with Dr. Charles J. Umberger, director of Dr. Helpern's toxicological lab to find a way to detect the drug. If they could identify one of the chemical products resulting from the drug's breakdown and show that these chemicals were present in a greater than normal quantity in the body, that might be an indicator that the drug had been used.[65]

To this end, Gilman began injecting rabbits, and later frogs, with an overdose of the drug and burying them for as long as Carmela had been buried. His plan was to determine the components into which the drug broke down and compare these to the chemicals found in Carmela's body. He spent months experimenting with varying doses and with burying the rabbits and frogs for differing time periods.[66]

Finally, after six months he found a way to identify one of the broken-down chemicals—succinymonocholine, also known as succinic acid. Then, employing spectroscopy, a technique using the light spectrum to identify particular chemicals, he examined Carmela's body and found traces of this substance in Carmela's brain—proof that she had received an intravenous injection of the anesthesia.[67]

Meanwhile, the detectives in Florida had made a significant discovery. Shortly before Carmela's death, Coppolino had obtained a large quantity of succinylcholine chloride from a friend who was a pharmaceutical expert, explaining that he wanted the drug to experiment with cats. Yet, as the detectives learned, Coppolino was known to be extremely allergic to cat fur. That information, along with Dr. Gilman's discovery about succinic acid, was the last piece of the puzzle.[68]

Accordingly, while Keuper was proceeding in New Jersey, State Attorney Frank Schaub on July 21 asked the grand jury in Sarasota to consider the case in a special session. Several days later, on July 25, the Sarasota grand jury issued a second murder indictment against Coppolino, which created a further media sensation. The newspapers played up the story of a physician accused of double murder in a case involving "sex, secret drugs and beautiful women."[69]

With two jurisdictions vying for justice, the question was

where would Dr. Coppolino be tried first, and could he, a soft-spoken, thin, preppy-looking doctor, who resembled Gregory Peck, really be guilty of such horrible murders? For several weeks, the legal wrangling went on between prosecutors in New Jersey and Florida. Finally, Florida Governor Haydon Burns agreed to extradite Dr. Coppolino to New Jersey to be tried there first. Perhaps a reason he did is that Florida's case hinged primarily on the circumstantial evidence of finding breakdown products to show the presence of succinylcholine chloride. By contrast, New Jersey seemed to have a far stronger case with a witness who had actually witnessed the crime, backed up by medical evidence supporting her testimony about a strangling. So Florida shipped Dr. Coppolino off to New Jersey, where he was taken to Freehold, the Monmouth County seat.[70]

But what Florida and the New Jersey prosecution didn't count on was Dr. Coppolino's brash young defense lawyer, F. Lee Bailey, who was now defending him in both cases. Much of the evidence pointed to Dr. Coppolino. But could the prosecution prove he did it? Dr. Coppolino's two trials became a national cliff-hanger, as the public followed each lurid detail and revelation in the tabloid press.

At first, Bailey, who had just gained fame in winning a new trial for Sam Sheppard on the grounds of too much publicity, tried to quash the indictment against Dr. Coppolino and change the venue on the same grounds. But after the judge shot down the publicity argument, the first trial began on December 5, 1966.[71] Initially, it looked like a slam-dunk case, as Keuper opened the trial by arguing that Coppolino had killed Colonel Farber out of jealousy because of his affair with Marjorie Farber, and sought to conceal the murder by having Carmela sign the death certificate claiming a heart attack. Moreover, Keuper pointed out that he had the direct evidence—eyewitness testimony from Marjorie Farber—to prove it.[72]

However, Bailey quickly ridiculed the charges, arguing that Farber had not been murdered at all and the murder claim was a "hoax." Rather, he suggested, Farber had instigated the charges because she was angry and jealous after Coppolino dropped her for another woman. "This woman drips with venom," he said, going on to state that "this woman wants Carl Coppolino so badly, she would sit in his lap in the electric chair while somebody pulled the switch, to make certain no one else gets him."[73]

Then, he proceeded to turn Marge's claim that she had been hypnotized by Coppolino to be cured of smoking and felt drawn to him and his power into a joke. When Marge testified that she couldn't take any action to interfere with her husband's death because of the hypnosis, saying, "I had no free will,"[74] Bailey shot back with a barrage of questions suggesting that any "trance" and any control by Coppolino, if it ever existed, ended when Coppolino dropped her. She brought these trumped-up charges as a jealous woman scorned. As Bailey emphasized again and again, Dr. Coppolino had no motive to kill Colonel Farber, since he could continue the affair with Marjorie without Farber's death. By contrast, Marge had a strong motive to "wreak vengeance" on her former lover.[75]

Additionally, Bailey craftily dismissed the evidence of strangulation from the post-mortem exhumation, suggesting that the larynx fractures were caused by the exhumation itself. Perhaps the grave digger might have struck his spade into the dead man's neck, he suggested. Later Bailey brought in two of his own medical experts who insisted that Colonel Farber had died of a coronary, not strangulation.

When Dr. Coppolino took the stand, he made a powerful defense witness, too, as he spoke calmly and professionally about how he had been called to Colonel Farber's bedside and found him gasping for breath. Then, he detected a heart attack and urged Farber to go at once to a hospital. But when both of the Farbers refused to do that, he simply provided some drugs to ease Farber's suffering and withdrew from the case. Coppolino also calmly rejected the idea that he pressed a pillow to Farber's face, as Marge contended. As for Carmela's name on the death certificate? That was easy to explain, too, he said with assurance. Since he had withdrawn from the case as the attending physician, Carmela signed the certificate.[76]

It was a compelling defense, and five hours later, the jury returned with its not-guilty verdict. Bailey left in triumph, assuring Dr. Coppolino that the case in Florida would be even easier to win because it was based solely on circumstantial evidence. If the jurors in New Jersey hadn't been impressed by direct evidence and eyewitness testimony, surely the Florida jurors wouldn't be convinced by the obscure medical testimony to be offered them about Coppolino's method of murder.

The Florida prosecutor, State Attorney Frank Schaub, was well aware of these difficulties. Thus, before trying to explain how chemistry could show that a rarely used drug had led to murder, he decided to focus first on establishing motive. Only after that would he explain the medical evidence by painting a dramatic graphic picture of how Carmela died.

To demonstrate motive, Schaub began by showing that Coppolino was a philanderer, malingerer, and a man captivated by money. As he pointed out, Coppolino had become used to living well on the money he received from his disability insurance—about $20,000 a year—in addition to his wife's earnings and his income from his writing and private clients. But after they moved to Florida, he suddenly saw his income decrease because Carmela had given up her highly paying pharmaceuticals job, and after she failed to pass the state examination, she could no longer earn what she had. Additionally, Schaub suggested, the insurance companies were starting to question Coppolino's disabilities, putting his own income in doubt.[77]

But Coppolino saw a way out, Schaub argued, when he met Mary Gibson, an attractive, wealthy divorcée, and decided to do away with his wife, leaving him free to marry a woman of means and continue living the good life. And to do so, Schaub explained, Coppolino decided to use succinylcholine chloride, a drug he was already familiar with as an anesthesiologist, feeling sure it would leave no trace in the body. Then he used his charismatic power of persuasion to falsely tell others, including the doctor who signed the certificate, that Carmela had suffered a heart attack, which resulted in her quick burial without an autopsy. After that, he thought he was home free. That's why he soon sought to collect his wife's life insurance and, within a few weeks, married Mary Gibson, assuring him the life of luxury that he had felt slipping away.[78]

This time, Schaub's approach was compelling. He brought

in Dr. Karow, who shared her doubts about Carmela's heart attack, though she had signed the certificate based on what Coppolino had told her because he was a once-practicing fellow doctor. Schaub brought in Dr. Helpern to testify that he had not detected any symptoms of heart trouble and had seen a suspicious needle prick, leading him to wonder if Carmela had received a drug injection that proved deadly. He brought in Dr. Umberger to testify that his step-by-step research led him to discover succinic acid in Carmela's brain, showing that she had died of an overdose of succinylcholine chloride. He brought in Marge Farber, who admitted her affair with Coppolino. Finally, he called in a representative of the New Jersey pharmaceutical company who gave Coppolino the drug, thinking he was going to use it for experimental work.[79] Later, in his summation, he emphasized the significance of Carl getting the drug succinylcholine shipped to him about a month before Carmela died. He also pointed out that Mary Gibson was "a woman of means," therefore Carl had all the more incentive to commit the murder because it would free him to marry her and thus compensate for the financial reverses he suffered just prior to Carmela's death.[80]

This time, Bailey couldn't shake the medical witnesses or turn Farber into a subject of ridicule. Plus, Coppolino didn't testify, so he wasn't able to use his charm to sway the jury. Thus, the outcome in this second trial was quite different. After three and a half hours, the jury returned with its verdict: "Guilty of murder in the second degree." The following day, the judge sentenced Coppolino to life imprisonment, the maximum term possible.[81] Coppolino would spend the rest of his life in the Florida State Prison at Raiford. Though Bailey appealed the verdict and sought to set aside the verdict or have a new trial, the sentence stood.[82] Thus, despite an unusual and sophisticated method that was supposed to leave no trace, in the end, it did, and Coppolino was convicted based on circumstantial evidence, which included the results of a novel chemical analysis.

He remained in prison until October 16, 1979, when he was paroled for being a model prisoner who had an "excellent record." During this time, he enrolled in the prison school and was appointed to teach after a few weeks.[83] His second wife,

Mary Coppolino, who visited him regularly, was instrumental in securing his release. She engaged in a campaign to raise doubts about the evidence used to convict him based on a lethal injection of succinylcholine chloride. Among other things, she sought to claim that Helpern and Umberger, who by then had died of natural causes, had fabricated their testimony, resulting in his conviction. The result of her campaign paid off in political support from the then Chairman of the Florida House of Representatives Committee on Corrections, Probation, and Parole, Florida Representative Arnett E. Girardeau, though Dr. Helpern's widow heatedly disputed her claim, pointing out in June 1979 that "Coppolino wasn't convicted on that test alone and to say the evidence was 'fabricated' is to smear two men who are not alive to answer that outrageous charge."[84]

Yet, apparently the campaign worked, and Coppolino was released on a lifetime parole. Subsequently, he wrote his own book titled *The Crime That Never Was* and published by the Justice Press in 1980, in which he disputed the crime. Then, he toured the country to promote sales of the book.[85] In a way, his response is reminiscent of the way Roland Molineux, who was also found guilty of using a poison—cyanide of mercury—claimed he had been wrongly convicted in his book *The Room with the Little Door*. In it, he wrote about his experiences in the Tombs and sought to restore his tarnished reputation and regain his standing in New York society. So just as Molineux used his book to rail against the false testimony of the handwriting experts that linked him to the package that was mailed with the poison, Coppolino argued in his book that he had been subjected to fabricated evidence by the toxicological experts.

So were they guilty? The jurors and the press at the time certainly thought so, though both men subsequently sought to contradict the verdict against them—a ploy that the rich and famous may be better able to use for two reasons: First, they are already in the public eye because of the news attention given their case. Second, they have the resources and connections to help them regain their reputation, even if they can't reverse the verdict and much of the public and press continues to believe they did it—or probably did.

Chapter 3
Hiring Help

The rich and famous differ in another way because of their money and power. They are in a better position than the average person to hire help. They not only can pay more and therefore hire more-qualified help, but also they can often make the hire through their connections. For instance, they can make arrangements through a close and trusted friend, employee, or business associate. Their connections and resources can help them better cover their trail, so they are less likely to get caught. Typically, the wealthy and powerful masterminds behind the scheme set up an alibi, so when the hit happens, they are generally far away or engaged in other activities in a place where they have witnesses. Moreover, the activities they engage in might help their deniability, such as being at a high-level business conference, where many other people may see the person at the time of the murder. Then, too, being at a high-status event can make a claim of arranging a murder even harder to support because it tends to underline the person's good reputation, making his or her involvement in a murder seem even less likely.

But even if they are suspected, such as when a person arranges to get rid of a difficult spouse during a divorce or custody fight, their cases are generally harder to prove. One hurdle is that unless there is corroborating evidence, just the testimony of the person accused of doing the killing isn't enough, because any confession must be supported by corroboration.

By contrast, witness the problems of the average person contemplating getting help in committing a murder. First, there is the financial barrier, since it typically costs several thousand dollars, and sometimes more, to hire a hit man. Another difficulty is that with fewer connections, barring a willing relative or friend, the person seeking a hit man will commonly put out feelers in places such as local bars and night clubs, where people who might kill for money or people who know them might hang out. But the risk of queries to mere acquaintances or strangers, rather than a trusted connection, is that the request is more likely to be passed on to the local police. Thus, there is a greater risk of getting caught by just making an attempt at murder. Or even if the person isn't exposed initially on hiring someone, once a hit is suspected and the police begin investigating, there's a greater chance that the people who heard the request to hire the killer will come forward. By contrast, the wealthy have more discrete ways of making arrangements, including recruiting subordinates dependent on their employment to help in the search.

Also, with more skilled help, a planned homicide is more likely to be carried out successfully. One reason is that rather than just one person, the wealthy may be able to hire a team of killers, or the killer or killers they hire may be more knowledgeable about how to plan the homicide or use less-detectable methods. For example, they may make the hit look like a random shooting on the street or a home invasion robbery gone bad. By contrast, when one offers less money, there's more chance of hiring someone who is less skilled or a novice, thus increasing the likelihood that something might go wrong.

Yet, while the odds of being found not guilty or not getting charged at all are much greater in these rich and powerful cases, sometimes the wealthy eventually do get charged and convicted. However, it often takes a more difficult investigation and prosecution to prove the suspect's guilt, as in the Allen Blackthorne case described in this chapter. After almost ten years of battles over child support and custody, Blackthorne turned to a friend as a go-between to find a killer to get rid of his ex-wife. Then, it took several years to investigate and bring him to trial.

A Deadly Mix of Power, Control, Hatred, Revenge, and Some Hired Help: The Case of Allen Blackthorne (Houston, Texas, and Sarasota, Florida, 1997–2000)

The Allen Blackthorne case typifies that of the man motivated by a mix of power, control, hatred, and revenge to wreak vengeance on a woman who would dare to stand up to him or break away from him. He had the financial resources to keep up his search for revenge for years, and he could readily pay for the help of others. His resources enabled him to both make cash payments of about $20,000 and to offer a substantial ownership interest in one of his properties to an associate he used to recruit a killer. Additionally, Blackthorne had the resources to hire a bevy of lawyers to defend himself.

Why didn't Blackthorne simply walk away from his relationship after his divorce, since he already had a custody arrangement that let him see his kids? It was because Blackthorne had developed such a strong hatred of his ex-wife of twelve years that his emotions led him to engage in a vendetta against her that could only be resolved by her death. Rather than pay a much smaller amount to let her go in a divorce, he used his money to buy her murder. Long a heavy gambler in all sorts of business deals and schemes, he was willing to take the risk to set in motion plans to have her murdered, rather than release her from his desire for vengeance and control.

Blackthorne had always been something of a con artist, and was abusive and controlling with the women in his life. When he struck it rich and became a multimillionaire, he became even more so, until his obsessiveness led to murder. He grew up Allen Van Houte in Salem, Oregon, and after his father abandoned him, he was largely left on his own by his mother. He was mainly raised by his grandparents and an aunt and uncle until his teens, when his father came back into his life.[1]

Early on, Blackthorne showed a cruel, sadistic streak, which was evident in his first marriage to a girl he went steady with in high school. He married soon after high school, and the marriage quickly turned into a nightmare, until she filed for divorce and left him after five years. She couldn't take the physical abuse and his hair-trigger temper. For example, after their dog soiled the carpet, he beat it with a board until it died. He also frequently choked and hit his wife; he also kicked her in the stomach when she was pregnant, and fearing that the baby was damaged, she had an abortion.[2]

His marriage to his second wife, Mary, showed a similar pattern. They moved to Gig Harbor, Washington, and at first he seemed charming. But soon after they married, his violent temper erupted whenever Mary did anything to offend him. Then, he reacted with rage, pushing her and slapping her so that she soon became terrified of him, especially after he threatened to kill her two children from a previous marriage should she ever leave him. Eventually, after three years of escalating abuse, she packed up, fled with her children, filed for divorce, and left Oregon for California to put some distance between them.[3] There, she effectively went into hiding, until she was later located by investigators and subpoenaed to tell the Bexar county grand jury in Texas about her experiences.[4]

In conjunction with his early pattern of abusing and controlling the women in his life, Allen showed an early skill in wheeling and dealing, which would eventually pay off big-time. At first, though, he was involved in one shaky scheme or con game after another, each time hoping this would be his passport to the good life. During the height of the disco era in the 1970s, he worked with his father selling lighted dance floors that his father designed. When the disco craze faded, in 1981, he opened up a hi-fi stereo store in Salem, Oregon, thinking that this would be the next big franchise.[5] But it wasn't. It was just another everyday business.

In 1982, while he was still waiting for his divorce from Mary to become final, he met Sheila Walsh, who was so charmed by him that she agreed to marry him by their third date, oblivious to the warning signs of problems ahead. For one thing, though Allen was thinking big, he was still struggling financially and moved in with her family in 1983. Then, one day, shortly before they married, he tried to force her sister Kerry to have intercourse with him. She pushed him away but didn't tell Sheila at the time. An even more dire warning sign came when he was racing in his sports car with Sheila, after they were married for six months. Irritated by a cyclist who passed him, Allen deliberately sped up and hit the cyclist and his girlfriend, killing them both. He had not the slightest remorse. Instead, he covered up what really happened, telling the police that the cyclist had tried to race him and cut in and out of his path, causing the accident when he came too close. Though Sheila knew the truth, she said nothing because she was already pregnant with their first child and didn't want to create tensions in their marriage.[6]

Then came the first of Allen's many business schemes that would make him a multimillionaire, while leaving many victims in his wake. The scheme began with a loan from Sheila's parents, Don and Gene Smith, so he could open a hi-fi store and buy a sporty Porsche. Soon Don and Gene discovered he was cooking the books and didn't have the collateral to back up their loans. Allen then converted the remaining assets of the business into his name and fled to Hawaii with Sheila, blaming her parents for mismanaging the business. He even quoted the Bible to convince Sheila that it was her duty to stick by her husband rather than her parents, explaining that the bankruptcy was just "bad luck" and he had never promised her parents a "sure thing."[7]

Once in Hawaii, Allen discovered the device that was to make him a fortune, though he left more victims along the way. On a trip to Asia, he discovered a new health product that emitted an electronic pulse that could stimulate muscles and make them contract involuntarily. He thought this stimulator had great potential to help people build muscles without exercising. He called it the Health-Tronic, and soon convinced relatives he had not seen for years to invest in the business, including his father Guy Van Houte. He also persuaded the Bank of Hawaii to give him a sizable loan to fund his start-up.

Unfortunately, Allen began advertising the Health-Tronic

as a cure-all for illnesses and overcoming paralysis in limbs—both an exaggeration and illegal claim—and soon the FDA was seeking to shut down his company. When the business was on the verge of collapse, Allen simply walked away from it and headed to Texas with Sheila and their two baby daughters.[8]

Ironically, after Allen left, Guy and his brother Randy made some electronic modifications to meet the FDA requirements for using the stimulators for health purposes, got approval, and began making money. Allen responded by breaking completely with his father and brother, angry that they were making money from the product he discovered, even though he had run out on what he thought was a financial ruin. To underline this break, he changed his name to Blackthorne, picking the name of the hero of the book and film *Shogun*. Then, he stole their idea to set up a new company in San Antonio, Texas.[9]

With his marketing and sales skills and new partners, his new company, RS Medical, soon left Guy and Randy in the dust. At first, he simply arranged, under the name EMS, to distribute the products Guy and Randy were manufacturing, but then he found investors to create a new company. Though again many business associates lost money and EMS went bankrupt in 1988 due to his poor management and high lifestyle,[10] in 1990, Allen found two new wealthy investors, Rick and Patrick Terrell. This time, he was back in business as RS Medical, using the same EMS-250 electronic stimulator that had been sold by EMS, which he planned to sell or rent to doctors.[11] This device and new business structure would become the means to wealth Allen had been seeking all his life, and it would make him a multimillionaire in a few years.

Meanwhile, around the time of the EMS bankruptcy, his marriage to Sheila was unraveling and becoming a source of ongoing bitterness, because increasingly, Sheila found Allen's abuse and bizarre behavior intolerable. For example, while he accused Sheila of cheating on him, Allen was frequently unfaithful to her. He even hired prostitutes to act out his fantasies of sadism and masochism. Yet, Sheila hesitated to leave for several years, afraid of what he might do. Although she felt sure Allen no longer loved her or wanted her, she was afraid he would kill her if she left.[12]

Finally, though, in 1987, when they were living in the Castle Hill section of San Antonio, Sheila had enough. Once again, Allen accused her of cheating on him, as well as spending too much of his money, and this time, he beat her especially severely with his belt and fists, promising her "she would never walk again" and that he would "mess up" her face. Eventually, though, she was able to call the Castle Hill police, who arrested Allen for battery misdemeanor. She was so afraid of his retaliation that she hid in a church basement for several nights. Then, she fled to Santa Rosa, California, with her two children. When Allen tracked her down there, they had another bitter fight, and this time, after Allen was arrested for assault and battery, she fled to Oregon and spent several weeks there to heal.[13]

After recovering, she returned to San Antonio, where she had good friends and a good job that was still open for her at a law firm. Soon, she found her own apartment and began fighting Allen for a divorce, which was granted in 1988. Then, she fought some more to gain financial support for her children after she won custody rights, while Allen had visitation rights.[14] These were like the first salvos in a growing domestic war that would go on between Sheila and Allen for the next nine years. A reason the combat lasted so long and made Allen increasingly angry is that Sheila repeatedly won court judgments against him. Though he found ways to avoid paying or hid his assets, even as he was becoming a multimillionaire, Sheila would return with another legal attack, which he parried with still another courtroom defense. It was a formula for an escalation of both legal bills and hatred, and Allen now had the money to pay.

Meanwhile, outside the courtroom, by the early 1990s, it seemed that both Sheila and Allen would be moving on. Sheila met and married Jamie Bellush, a pharmaceuticals salesman she met on a plane flight in 1993. Around the same time, Allen met Maureen Weingest through a dating service when the woman he was supposed to meet brought along her friend. He was now wealthy, as well as good looking and charming, and Maureen fell hard for him, eagerly accepting his proposal to marry on November 7, 1993.[15]

Yet, despite his new romance and marriage, Allen continued his court battles and obsession with Sheila, because he hated her so much, especially when she kept winning in court. Thus, though he could well afford the court judgments to pay her share of the assets from their earlier EMS business, as well as pay support for their children, he didn't want her to have anything. And though it cost him more, he continued to fight. Besides, he now had so much money, he could afford the luxury of the extra cost to express his hatred of his ex-wife.

He used every opportunity to control or demean her. For example, when Sheila's girls, Daryl and Stevie, for whom he shared custody, came to visit him, he often had little time for them. Instead, he was usually pursuing his major passion of golf or going on business calls to make more deals. At the same time, he let them do whatever they wanted, undermining the rules Sheila and her new husband Jamie set for them.[16]

Allen also took advantage of a minor argument that Daryl had with Sheila in March 1997. After Sheila warned Daryl that her stepfather Jamie would punish her when he got home, Daryl ran to a neighbor, sobbing about the feared discipline. When the neighbor called Allen to complain, he used the incident to get back at Sheila by calling the sheriff to report child abuse and by reporting Sheila to Child Protective Services. Also, he recruited the neighbor to keep him posted in the future on what Sheila was doing.[17]

Though by now Allen and his new wife Maureen had moved into a huge mansion in an elegant neighborhood, he was still obsessed with his battle with Sheila, and he stepped up his attack in June. This time, he asked the court to hold Sheila in contempt for not allowing her daughter Stevie to see him. He conveniently ignored Stevie's view that she did not want to see her father at all, in part because eight years before he had sexually molested her. Then, when it looked like Sheila might bring up his earlier abuse of Stevie in a court hearing on custody, he suddenly announced on July 22 that he would give up his parental rights entirely, stating that he "could no longer subject his new family to the constant battles with Sheila."[18]

Ostensibly, he was making this grand gesture of doing the noble thing by saying he would no longer be their father. But was he really giving up? Soon after he gave up his rights, he spoke to a golfing buddy and bookie, Danny Rocha, about how he was tired of his ex-wife and wanted to do something about it. He asked Danny if he knew anyone who could get rid of her. In return, he said he planned to invest $20 million in a new golf-course project and would give Danny 25 percent of it. He also offered to help fund a sports bar that Danny hoped to operate with a neighbor.[19] As a multimillionaire, Allen could afford to offer such valuable incentives—which had the potential to be even more financially rewarding than just a few thousand in cash, perhaps reaching millions—to get rid of his wife.

In response, Danny said he would see what he could do, and soon afterward, Sheila and Jamie began to notice strange occurrences in their neighborhood, causing them to feel really scared. For instance, one night a car appeared to be following them, and from then on, Sheila felt frightened when Jamie had to travel for his job as a drug rep.[20]

At the same time, Allen was meddling in Sheila's life, causing additional tension. Sheila, for example, discovered that Daryl was sneaking out to meet Allen, even though Allen had proclaimed in court that he was giving up his parental rights. Then, tensions escalated even more after Sheila argued with Daryl about her sneaky behavior. When Sheila spanked her, Daryl ran over to the neighbors, who were already spying on Sheila and passing information on to Allen, and they called the police. After they briefly arrested Sheila, who had recently had four quadruplet babies with Jamie, the local papers reported the news with headlines like: "Quad Mom Arrested for Child Abuse!"[21]

So life in San Antonio seemed to be turning into a nightmare. Yet Sheila saw a way out when Jamie was promoted and transferred to handle his company's territory in Florida. Finally, she could leave San Antonio and Allen's influence. Thus, she and Jamie eagerly made plans to move to Sarasota in early September, though she still had to return for a criminal hearing about the child abuse charges. They also planned to put Daryl in a YMCA shelter in Florida while they were working out their problems.[22]

The move seemed like the perfect solution—a fresh start in a new city. And because Sheila didn't want Allen to know where they were moving, she and Jamie told only a few close relatives and friends about their plans. She had felt oppressed by Allen for so long; the move was finally a chance to escape from him and his influence over her or her children.

However, within two months, on November 7, when her daughter Stevie was away and Sheila was alone with her four babies, Sheila suddenly confronted a stranger in her garage. He brutally shot her in the head and slashed her with a knife, causing two gaping neck wounds and slashes to her hands as she sought to fight him off. But she was no match for him, and mortally wounded, she collapsed on the floor, the phone dangling because she no longer had the strength to call 911.

So was her killing arranged by Allen Blackthorne and his golf course associate? And if so, could the police and prosecutors find sufficient evidence to prove him the mastermind behind the killing?

The link was uncertain, although almost at once, there was little mystery about Sheila's killer. He was soon identified because some nearby neighbors had noticed a suspicious-looking car on the street; the car and the heavy-set driver in his twenties wearing a camouflage uniform had looked out of place. One neighbor noticed the car was a white late-model Mitsubishi with Texas plates, another noticed the license number YBR-62G,[23] and they both reported their observations to the police. With this information, the police did a computer search for the car. Though a Florida computer search turned up nothing on the car, within a few days a Texas computer search made a match, which led to the car's registered owner, Maria Del Toro, in La Pryor, Texas, a small town near San Antonio and the Mexican border. After detectives interviewed her, they discovered she had bought the car for her grandson, Joey.[24] Then, a few days later, detectives learned that the fingerprints found in Sheila's utility room were his, and they found his car on November 9 parked outside the apartment of one of his girlfriends, Carol Arreola. He had stayed there for a few days and had left behind all sorts of evidence of the crime, including the murder gun, a piece of paper with directions to Sheila's house, a camouflage ski mask, camouflage gear, and assorted receipts from places where Joey had stayed or bought items used in the crime.[25]

The find was like a signpost advertising Sheila's killer, so there was no question about who had committed the crime. But Joey had disappeared, frightened by knowing the police dragnet was zeroing in on him. Later, he turned up in Mexico, where he fought extradition for the following year.

The police very quickly learned that many people suspected that Allen was behind the murder, among them Sheila's husband and her daughters, who described her long court battle with Allen. They cited Allen's deep hatred for her, his obsessive stalking, and her deep fear of him. The day Sheila was killed, they told the police that they suspected Allen was involved, though they had no specific evidence to show this. Stevie, who found her mother dead, told the prosecutors how the family had fled San Antonio and sought to keep their location secret from Allen because they were afraid of him. "I guess my dad . . . just doesn't like my mom," she told the police investigating the case.[26]

The police quickly eliminated Jamie as a suspect, too, since he had been traveling on his drug detailing route and was seen by plenty of people along the way. Also, he was an emotional wreck because of the murder, as were Sheila's two daughters. But Allen also had a solid alibi, based on his high-status connections. As he calmly told the police, he had been at a business meeting in Texas the day of the murder, and many people saw him there. Although being at the meeting helped bolster his image as a prominent successful business man with little reason to plot a murder, the police and Sheila's family believed that Allen could have used surrogates to act for him.

But the problem for the police and prosecutors was making that link between the stranger who did the killing in Sarasota, Florida, and Allen in Texas. Making that connection was even more difficult if Allen didn't hire the killer himself, but used his personal connections to find someone to hire the killer for him.

The key to the case eventually revolved around showing a motive; and Joey Del Toro had no good motive for killing Sheila. After all, why should he drive all the way from Texas to Florida to brutally kill a woman in her own home, when he didn't know her and had never met her before? And why should he have her address written down in his car? Clearly, the address and long drive indicated that the killing was planned rather than random and that Del Toro had been directed to kill Sheila. But could the police show that Allen not only had the motive, but also the means and opportunity to set up her murder?

Gradually, the investigation began to close in, as the police in Florida and then Texas began to connect the links. Soon they connected Joey to his cousin Sammy Gonzalez and then to his friend Danny Rocha, who had played golf with Allen the day Sheila was killed.[27] They got Sammy's name from Joey's girlfriend Carol Arreola, and they learned from Joey's grandmother that Sammy and Joey were cousins. After they found Sammy at the Precision Driving Range where he worked, they had him follow them to the Texas Ranger's office where he began to talk. His initial story wasn't completely accurate, but he told the ranger that his friend Daniel Rocha had asked him if he would beat up a woman. After he declined to do it himself, he had contacted his cousin Joey. Then, he explained, after the woman moved to Florida, it took a few months for Danny to obtain her address. Once he got it, though, he gave it to Joey, who followed her there. Sammy even told the ranger that he thought that Allen Blackthorne had ordered the hit.[28]

Now the Texas police had enough information to arrest Sammy and Danny on November 17 as part of a conspiracy to commit murder based on the Florida charges. But they still needed to connect Allen to this conspiracy. Just Sammy's belief that Allen did it wasn't enough, and Allen now drew on his considerable wealth to thwart the investigation and any charges. The day after Sammy and Danny were arrested, he hired a prominent Texas lawyer, Roy Barrera Jr. and claimed he was innocent. Though the Mexican police captured Joey two days later on November 20, Joey quickly began his fight against extradition—a fight that would last almost two years, apparently fueled by money that Allen secretly channeled to him.[29]

Still, despite such attempts to impede their efforts, the police and prosecution gathered a growing body of evidence to show that Allen both had the motive and the opportunity. For example, many people described Allen's continuing hatred of Sheila, as well as his desire to find someone to beat up his ex-wife. One witness was Sammy Gonzales, who pled guilty to a conspiracy to commit murder. He claimed that Danny Rocha told him that Blackthorne "had ordered his ex-wife beaten so he could get custody of their teenage daughters." Jack Speights, a friend of both Blackthorne's and Rocha's, described Blackthorne's intense anger toward his ex-wife and said that when Rocha and another man went on a business and golf trip with Blackthorne in August, three months before the killing, Allen said he wanted a woman killed "because she was beating the kids." And later, when Speights was at Blackthorne's house, Blackthorne played a videotape showing Sheila's arrest for abusing one of her daughters and commented: "You see what kind of bitch I used to be married to."[30]

In short, plenty of people could testify to Allen's strong hatred of Sheila and desire to see her hurt. Yet there still wasn't enough to connect the killing in Sarasota to Blackthorne in San Antonio; the only link between Blackthorne and Joey, the killer, and Joey's cousin Sammy, who asked him do it, was Danny Rocha, who allegedly recruited Sammy and gave him Sheila's address. But Danny invoked his right to remain silent until he could speak to an attorney because he hoped to negotiate a better deal for himself before he said anything. He continued to hold out, but meanwhile the prosecution gathered enough other evidence that they were no longer willing to deal. As a result, instead of getting a plea deal for providing helpful information, Sammy was tried, convicted, and sentenced to nineteen years, but without implicating Allen for giving him the orders, payment, and address to set the plan in motion.[31]

Meanwhile, through his attorney, Roy Barrera Jr., Allen continued to staunchly maintain his innocence. Barrera argued that Allen was simply being pursued because of his conflict-filled relationship with his ex-wife and because he had frequently golfed with one of the men arrested and charged with her murder.[32]

Thus, though they were convinced that Blackthorne was behind the plot, the police and prosecution didn't have enough evidence to arrest him or file charges. So over the next two years, Allen continued to run his business, play golf, and socialize with the wealthy in San Antonio.

Meanwhile, the police and prosecution kept plodding along, gathering circumstantial evidence to link Blackthorne to the plot. They found records showing that Allen played golf with Danny Rocha on the day of the murder, and they discovered phone bills showing that he made many calls to Danny, to a private detective, and to his daughter Daryl around this time. These records and bills, in turn, supported the prosecution theory that Blackthorne had pieced together information about where Sheila was from the detective and his daughter. Then, he had given that information to Danny, and had made payments or promises of payments to Danny, Sammy, and Joey. These payments or promised payments were quite substantial—$4,000 to Joey, $5,000 up front plus $10,000 more to Sammy after a successful killing, and a promise to give Rocha a stake in a golf course development and money to open a sports bar if he found someone to kill Sheila. At times, the amount Allen offered to advance ranged from $50,000 to $250,000.[33] Obviously, the person who offered these kind of financial incentives had to be rich.

The evidence provided by the phone calls was especially compelling, too. As described by Ann Rule, in her in-depth book about the murder and subsequent trial, *Every Breath You Take*, Texas Ranger Gary De Los Santos found a string of suspicious calls. One was to the A-1 Bail Bonds company, which had issued the bond after Sheila's child abuse arrest, to get information on her present location. Additionally, Allen called a series of hotels and motels following an eastward path, as if he was trying to track the family. Though Allen didn't identify himself, the calls were traced to his residential and business phones. Still other damning information came from his daughter Daryl, who described how Allen had used a pretext that he would try to visit her for Christmas in order to worm some identifying information from her. She was then staying in a YMCA youth center and had promised her mother that she wouldn't give out the family's location. But Allen convinced her to tell him that the street name began with "Mark" and a grocery was on the corner, and her clues were enough to give the location away.[34]

Then, too, the police gradually gathered other evidence showing that Blackthorne continued to track, threaten, and harass Sheila over the years. For instance, during her wedding rehearsal dinner before she married her second husband Jamie, Blackthorne served her with a lawsuit demanding additional visits with their two daughters. Also, investigators found business partners of Allen's and attorneys who once represented Sheila who described his many threats, including one in which Allen told her he would have her "taken care of" if she ever left him or hurt his business.[35] One associate of Allen's company RS Medical even said he heard Allen say he "had the contacts to have Sheila taken to Mexico and she wouldn't return."[36]

But would this evidence be enough to convince a jury in spite of Allen's continued protests of his innocence? He even claimed that Jamie, motivated by problems in the marriage and insurance money, was the real perpetrator behind the killing and had time to arrange it during his drug rep rounds.[37] However, Jamie's timeline and contacts for that day were airtight, and he was so obviously devastated by the murder, the police never considered him a suspect.

Allen continued to deny his involvement when a grand jury began investigating Sheila's death eighteen months after her murder. He confidently began talking to the media, too, including giving a *48 Hours* interview that showed him playing a relaxed game of golf. No, he assured interviewer, Peter Van Sant, he had never wanted Sheila murdered or hurt. And no, he had never given Danny Rocha Sheila's address, and he had no idea how Danny got it. Furthermore, to show his innocence, he described himself as a father and golfer with a strong family, great kids, and an "awesome" ex-wife. So, certainly, he would be able to prove his innocence in court.[38]

But meanwhile, as Allen showed his charm to CBS and other media, portraying himself as the perfect family man, the police gained help from the U.S. Attorney's Office in San Antonio and from the FBI. And soon they uncovered even more evidence of Blackthorne's hidden past before he became a multimillionaire, including stories of domestic abuse and battery of previous wives.[39]

Finally, on January 4, 2000, the grand jury felt it had

enough to act and handed down a sealed indictment charging Allen with using interstate facilities and arranging a murder for hire. Soon after that, police and FBI agents arrested him as he was leaving a golf course, and the subsequent search of his house led to further incriminating evidence. Though the police had already gotten phone, bank, and other records, they now found the negatives of the photos given to Danny Rocha—one picturing Sheila with the kids at a birthday party—so the hit man could identify her. And what was even more telling was that two prints were missing from the set.[40]

Yet, despite all this evidence revealed at his trial, including testimony from an already convicted Danny, who testified that Allen had ordered the hit, Allen maintained he was just being set up. He claimed through his lead attorney, Richard Lubin, that Danny was really the mastermind behind the attack, who did it to extort money from him to open a sports bar.[41] Then Lubin, and later Blackthorne when he took the stand, offered an innocent explanation for the evidence. He claimed he had only reluctantly given up his rights to his daughters in order to protect them from further harm from being beaten by Sheila when they returned from his house. And although he acknowledged that he had tried to find Sheila after she had left San Antonio in secret, he claimed he only did so to help his daughter Daryl who had called him asking for his assistance. As he poured on the charm on the witness stand, he told lie after lie, made excuse after excuse. He even suggested that Danny Rocha must have found Sheila's address next to some tapes that his assistant had left out, which he was planning to send out to alert the neighbors about Sheila's arrest for abusing her children.[42]

But would the jury find his usual sales charm and lies persuasive? Would they believe that Danny had engineered the plot on his own? Or would they believe that Allen had the motive and money to arrange the killing, as shown by the trail of evidence connecting him to the murder?

The decision was a long and hard one, which could have gone either way. But eventually, after looking closely at Allen's state of mind and relationship with Sheila during nine years of custody battles, they found him guilty.[43] Especially convincing were the telephone records linking Allen's phone to places in Florida and his hiring of a private detective to find his ex-wife's address in Florida. Then, too, the jurors thought it odd that despite Allen's protestations that he was making all these calls and doing all this investigating to protect his kids, he never called the children after Sheila died to see if they were okay. Another critical factor was the address that Danny had written down, since there was no evidence that he had tried to find out Sheila's address on his own.[44] But most of all, the jurors were convinced by the graphic testimony of several witnesses about Allen's motivation and state of mind, such as one who heard Allen say that "he wanted his ex-wife's tongue ripped out or her body dumped in the ocean or woods." As one juror told reporter Leonora Minai: "In order for him to intend for her to be murdered, he had to have the state of mind that he wanted her killed. . . . There was state of mind." Another juror who took a lot of convincing agreed, saying: "You have to infer from circumstances surrounding the case that this is what he intended. . . . I think he intended her death."[45]

So in the end, it was Allen's motivation to kill, along with his money to finance the scheme, that helped the jurors decide he was guilty. At his sentencing, the judge sentenced him to two concurrent life terms, without the possibility of parole, a mandatory life term under federal law.[46] Though Allen had achieved what seemed like a perfect luxurious life of a multimillionaire who didn't have to work anymore and could devote himself to his passion for golf, he was so motivated by hatred, revenge, and the desire to exert power and control over his ex-wife, and keep her from being happy, that he couldn't leave her alone. All his money and his luxurious lifestyle, successful business, and new wife, weren't enough to satisfy him. He had to have his ex-wife destroyed, and in the end, that destroyed him, too. Though Lubin appealed his conviction, the appeal was denied in 2002.

CHAPTER 4

The Big Cover-Up

The advantage of having money and influence enables the rich and powerful to better cover up their homicides after the fact—whether they do it themselves or get help.

Some common ways of covering up include driving a distance to dispose of the body, dropping it in a dumpster, leaving it on a quiet country road, burying it in a hole, or covering it up with dirt or leaves. Another type of cover-up is changing the crime scene to make it look like an accident or a burglary gone bad.

When it comes to these cover-ups, the wealthy are often better at implementing unique, even exotic methods because they have access to more resources. They may be more skilled at staging a more convincing crime scene because they may have a higher level of information and education that often accompanies a high social and income status. Also, they are more likely to have skilled help come to their aid—and they may be better able to gain their silence, sometimes by paying them a goodly amount.

Effective cover-ups are one reason that many of these cases remain unsolved. They also make it more difficult to prove the suspect's guilt. For example, if the house is carefully scoured, any incriminating fingerprints may disappear. If the body is dismembered or carefully incinerated, the investigators may not be able to prove a crime because they have no body and they may not have enough circumstantial evidence to suggest the person is not just missing, but dead. Again and again such tactics are used and often work, but not always. In the end, though, because the wealthy have the resources to create more elaborate cover-ups, they are more likely to get off.

The following cases illustrate some of these more unusual approaches to disposing of the body and covering up the crime. Although the particular approaches vary, reflecting the different technologies of the day, they show similar out-of-the-ordinary efforts to cover up. These cases also show some of the other themes discussed in other chapters, such as the personal motives, the power of the media, and the use of high-powered lawyers to better the chances of beating the charges. But these cases are especially unique because of the methods used to cover up the crimes, reflecting the way the rich and powerful are able to hide their deeds.

The first case, from the 1890s, features a wealthy factory owner, Albert Louis Luetgert, whose company became the main sausage manufacturer in Chicago—the Luetgert Sausage and Packing Company.[1] He used his meatpacking facilities and his knowledge of chemical processes to get rid of the evidence—though ultimately a little glitch in the process gave his scheme away, and even the best lawyering couldn't help.

Then, skipping ahead to the 1990s, there's the notorious Thomas Capano case, in which a wealthy, high-profile prosecutor was accused of killing a woman who wanted to leave him. And what did he do with the body? According to the prosecution theory, he stuffed her dead body into a cooler, packed the cooler onto his boat, and dumped the cooler at sea. And in the end, even without a body, the jury was convinced he was guilty, no matter what his high-priced lawyers tried to show.

Concealing the Evidence in the Cooking Vats: The Case of Albert Louis Luetgert (Chicago, Illinois, 1897–1898)

This case began when Albert Louis Luetgert wanted to get rid of a bothersome wife. Like many rich men, he was able to support and conceal affairs with a number of mistresses. He became concerned when his wife learned of his affairs and threatened divorce. His fear was that any hint of divorce might result in a scandal in a conservative age when monogamy and faithfulness were prized. To prevent this, he wanted his wife out of the way, and he used his resources to hide the crime and make the case difficult to investigate.

Luetgert, a successful entrepreneur, had plenty of resources, along with the determination to get his way. At the time of his wife's homicide, he was a big and burly man who weighed about 250 pounds, and he had the look of a swarthy, bearded, middle-aged, lusty pirate, with a hearty sexual appetite.[2] After emigrating from Germany, Luetgert had settled in Chicago. In those days, Chicago was a bustling meatpacking town, where cattle were packed together and slaughtered in steaming, stinky meat vats, leading Walt Whitman to call it the "hog butcher of the world."

Soon after Luetgert arrived, he threw his energy into building up a sausage factory and becoming the sausage king of America. Despite the mounting costs he incurred as he tried to expand his factory, Luetgert became part of the city's wealthy and prominent elite. One reason for his great success is that he had a knowledge of several secret processes that enabled him to manufacturer his products for much less money than his competitors. At his height, his worth was about $300,000[3]—many millions in today's terms. He also was quite the womanizer, though outwardly he presented himself as a proper Victorian husband; his many lusty mistresses included his wife's maid, Mary Simering; a wealthy German dowager, Mrs. Christine Feldt; and a saloon keeper, Mrs. Agatha Tosch.[4]

For a time, his quiet long-suffering wife, the model of proper middle-class Victorian decorum, tried to look the other way. But at times, her anger boiled over, and she and Luetgert fought bitterly. She even threatened to leave, which Luetgert dreaded, because of the terrible stain it would leave on his reputation. He wanted to keep his infidelity well undercover, and a divorce threatened to expose it. Plus, Luetgert was under increasing financial pressure[5] because he was seeking to expand his factory too quickly. Therefore, the idea of getting rid of his wife and collecting her life insurance looked increasingly tempting.[6]

Luetgert soon found the solution in his factory, in the very vats he used to turn his hogs into sausage, and it took investigators some time to find out exactly what happened.

The investigation began on a hot, muggy day on May 10, 1897, when Diedrich Bicknese, Louisa Luetgert's brother, came to the Chicago Detective Bureau to report that his sister was missing. As he explained, he was worried about her because when he called at home two days earlier, the maid, Mary Simering, had told him Louisa wasn't there, and when he returned later that evening, Louisa was still not back. So what had happened to her? This wasn't a time when wives simply went off on their own. No, something was wrong, he was sure, especially since Luetgert said she had been gone since May 1. But if so, why wasn't Luetgert concerned and why hadn't he called the police? Bicknese was further puzzled when Luetgert explained he hadn't called the police because he wanted to avoid a scandal and paid two detectives $5 to find her. His response seemed almost too calm to be believed.[7]

So Bicknese kept searching for his sister. Soon he discovered she hadn't gone to visit some close friends in nearby Kankakee, which he thought might be a possibility, and after he learned she was still not back after another check at her house, he went to the police.

Yes, Police Captain Hermann Schuettler agreed, the events did sound suspicious. Moreover, he had some information about Luetgert that added to his concern. While he knew Luetgert was a prominent member of the Chicago business community, he knew from neighbors' reports that Luetgert had had some violent arguments with his wife. In one incident, a year earlier, neighbors had reported seeing him shake his wife by the throat through the parlor windows of his Victorian mansion. When Schuettler investigated, he learned that Luetgert had become angry because Louisa had complained about his many affairs. A few days later, a neighbor reported seeing Luetgert chasing Louisa down the street, holding a revolver aloft, and yelling at her. But no one wanted the police to take any further action because they feared a scandal, so the police quietly let the matter drop. The wealthy and prominent commonly used this approach to conceal their problems in order to protect their reputation in the community.[8]

Eventually, after a series of violent quarrels, Louisa and Luetgert moved into separate quarters. Luetgert moved into a couple of rooms in the attached factory, and Louisa and other family members remained in the main house. Then, they lived mostly separate lives, much as did other wealthy people who had domestic problems, but remained together for appearance's sake.[9]

Perhaps their arrangement explained Luetgert's apparent lack of concern about his missing wife. Still, Schuettler found it curious that Luetgert had recently come to the station to report a lost dog and had asked the police to conduct an all-out search to find it. Even if he and his wife weren't close, why wouldn't he at least be as concerned about her as he would a dog?[10]

Still, Luetgert had a ready explanation to overcome Schuettler's concerns. He opined that Louisa had finally run away because of their domestic troubles and his recent financial difficulties, telling Schuettler that she had once threatened to leave him if he ever lost his money. So maybe she went to stay with some friends somewhere. Luetgert further said that he didn't want to report anything, because he really didn't know what happened, expected Louisa to come back, and most importantly, didn't want "any disgrace or scandal" because he was "a prominent businessman," and he felt such a scandal would hurt his family.[11]

Certainly, his concerns about a damaging scandal were true, Schuettler acknowledged. And despite any suspicions, Schuettler had no body and no evidence of any crime. So with no basis to charge him with a crime, Schuettler let him go.

Nevertheless, Schuettler pursued an investigation. First, he went with a few detectives to speak to neighbors, who soon confirmed the stories of Luetgert's fights with his wife and his wild sex life with many women. Then, after one detective theorized that Louisa had become upset by his actions and that subsequently Luetgert had drowned her in the nearby river, the police dragged the river. They also checked the alleys of Chicago. But they found nothing. Luetgert's cover-up was so good it left the police baffled about what happened to Louisa, and the local press described their fruitless search.[12]

Finally, though, the cover-up began to unravel after Frank Bialk, the former night watchman at Luetgert's factory, read about the police search and came to the police station to describe some suspicious activity there. "About ten days before," he reported, "Luetgert asked me to fire up the factory cooking vats." Bialk thought it a curious request since there was no processing work in the factory at the time. Then Luetgert had sent him away for several hours on two errands, while Luetgert remained to work at the factory. First, Luetgert directed him to buy some celery compound at a nearby drugstore, and after he returned with it, Luetgert told him he had to go back to get some Hunyadi water. To Bialk, it seemed as if Luetgert was trying to give him make-work errands to keep him out of the factory. Another odd circumstance was that when Bialk returned between errands, he found the door to the main factory locked, although it wasn't locked when he left, and he had to knock hard several times to get back in. But oddest of all was the strange-looking slime in front of the middle vat, which Bialk noticed before he left on his errands.[13]

After hearing Bialk's account, Captain Schuettler became even more suspicious. So on May 15, he returned to Luetgert's factory with a group of detectives to conduct a thorough search. Bialk and another employee, Frank Odorwosky, called "Smokehouse Frank," let them in. Schuettler noticed that the basement looked musty and grimy, and the heavy stench of butchered meat and sulfur chemicals filled the air. Along the way, Bialk revealed that one of the vats was used to cook sausage meat a few days earlier, and that several weeks earlier, a barrel of especially strong material, different from anything previously used at the factory, had arrived. Then Odorowky observed, "When I broke it up as Mr. Luetgert requested, it burned my hands."[14]

This revelation provided the beginning of the end of the

cover-up. Schuettler determined to find out what this mysterious substance was, and he and his men looked into the middle vat that had been used for cooking the sausage. They found it two-thirds full of a heavy, sticky brownish fluid, and Schuettler ordered his men to drain the vat. Using gunny sacks as filters, they began sucking out the fluid, and when they looked in the empty vat, they gasped in amazement at what they saw. Inside were several pieces of bone, a false tooth, and two old rings. One was a small badly tarnished friendship ring, the other a thick shiny ring with the engraved initials "L.L." Then, mixed in with the bone fragments, the detectives noticed two bent corset stays.[15]

When questioned about them, Luetgert seemed very cool, calm, and confident, protesting that these fragments were just animal bones. He acted like everything was perfectly ordinary, trying not to give away the cover-up.

However, Schuettler was not fully convinced. Were they really animal bones, or were they human? And how did the rings get there? Schuettler was convinced Luetgert had butchered more than animals. Yet, without any evidence to show that these were human bones or that Luetgert had brought his wife into the factory, he didn't have probable cause to arrest Luetgert. Besides, he knew Luetgert was a powerful member of society, someone he couldn't easily intimidate into talking. So he just quietly took the evidence from the vat to the police station for testing and directed the detectives to talk to other possible witnesses.

The evidence in the vat provided the break Schuettler needed to begin exposing the cover-up. The next day the police chemist reported that the bones were human, and he listed his gruesome findings: bits of a human third rib, part of the long humerus bone in the arm, and bones from a palm, a toe, and from the head and ear.[16] Though the forensic sciences were still in their infancy, they could establish these basic facts, which provided Schuettler the needed leverage to break through Luetgert's shield of respectability and power.

In addition, plain old-fashioned police detective work—going door to door to interview neighbors—turned up a few key witnesses. Three nearby neighbors said they saw Mrs.

Luetgert go into the factory about 1 p.m. with her husband, and one man said he heard a scream come from the direction of the factory that day. He hadn't reported it earlier because he thought it came from a neighboring saloon.

Finally, Schuettler felt he had enough evidence to arrest Luetgert, and on May 17, he and his men returned to the house to take Luetgert to jail. As they left, Luetgert protested mightily, determined to keep the cover-up covered: "I'm completely innocent. She just disappeared. I'm sure she'll turn up." But Schuettler didn't think so.

Meanwhile, the press was quick to report Luetgert's arrest—much as the press a century later eagerly reports crime and scandal, both helping and complicating the investigation. In this case, one result of the widespread press coverage was that people from all over the country began calling the press and police saying they had seen Mrs. Luetgert. One New Yorker, O.W.C. Crotty, who said he was engaged to Mrs. Luetgert before her marriage, claimed he had seen her in New York on May 7, buying a ticket to Europe, though the police quickly discovered she had bought no such ticket. Three other witnesses reported seeing her in Kenosha, Wisconsin, on May 3, 4, and 5.[17] Needless to say, such accounts helped to support Luetgert's cover-up and claims of innocence, particularly since in these early days of forensic science, the police couldn't tell if the bones they found came from a particular human. So if Louisa was in Kenosha, she couldn't be in the vat.

Thus, the police kept looking for additional evidence, and shortly before Luetgert's preliminary hearing, they found some circumstantial evidence supporting their theory from chemical expert Professor Delafontaine. After analyzing the sediment in the vat, Delafontaine discovered that it contained caustic soda and potash mixed with animal matter. Also, after pouring through the factory records, the police learned that two months earlier, Luetgert had ordered 325 pounds of crude potash and fifty pounds of arsenic from a wholesale drug firm, Lor Owen & Company. So the potash must have been the strong substance that had burned Frank's hands when he helped Luetgert break down the new chemical and put it in the vat.[18]

Meanwhile, despite the accumulating evidence, Luetgert continued to protest his innocence as he awaited trial in the city jail. He was held there without bail, despite his high social position, because this was a murder case. Again and again, he insisted that Louisa was still alive and he didn't kill her, and soon, he got some support from a flurry of claims that Louisa was elsewhere. One came in the form of a letter Chicago Alderman Schlake received on May 17 that was signed by "Louise Luetchert," who claimed she was living with friends in Chicago.[19] But was the letter really from Louisa? When the police took the letter to Louisa's brother Bicknese and sister Wilhelmina Miller for their opinions, they quickly dismissed the claim, saying that it wasn't her handwriting and that she didn't spell her name that way. So the police concluded the letter was simply a "clumsy fake,"[20] though they never found out if it was sent by one of Luetgert's supporters or confederates or just by a nut case or person inspired by all the publicity.

Yet, even if the police were convinced Luetgert killed Louisa, the big problem was whether the district attorney could prove it—a problem complicated by Luetgert's wealth and prominence. The prosecution was charging not only murder, but also that the murder was committed in a truly grisly method, and Luetgert still had the image of a respectable high society factory owner—a formidable obstacle to overcome. Also, the district attorney had to combat the defense's contention that Luetgert not only didn't do it, but also that Mrs. Luetgert was still alive somewhere.

A major difficulty, despite the bones and other materials the police had collected, was that this was still a completely circumstantial case. No one had actually seen Luetgert put Louisa in the vat, and the owner of the false tooth and corset stays found in the refuse could not be identified because there was no DNA or sophisticated dental or fiber analysis at that time. Plus, Luetgert's financial ability enabled him to hire the best defense experts, who lined up some expert witnesses to dispute all the evidence supporting the police theory.

The trial finally began on August 3 and continued for eight weeks. It lasted that long because of the heated battle of experts on both sides. Meanwhile, given all the publicity for a trial with a prominent defendant, an eager public followed the case closely.

District Attorney Deneen did his best to convince the jury of Luetgert's guilt. He called in one of Luetgert's maids, Annie Grieser, who identified the rings in the vat as Mrs. Luetgert's. He brought in several of Luetgert's lovers to show why Luetgert wanted to kill his wife. However, when he showed several love letters Luetgert had written from jail to one of the women, Mrs. Christine Feldt, she denied any intimate relations, which helped the defense.[21]

Finally, the trial came down to the battle of the experts. The prosecution side argued that the bones in the vat were human bones, that Luetgert had bought the potash and arsenic in planning the murder, and that the rings showed the human bones belonged to Mrs. Luetgert. But some defense experts claimed these were animal bones, and the defense brought in other witnesses who denied these were Louisa's rings. Also, some defense witnesses described seeing her in Wisconsin, and Luetgert's business partner testified that the unusual chemicals had been bought for some chemical experiments Luetgert was conducting on May 1 to improve the sausage-making process.[22]

So would Luetgert's cover-up strategy work? In the end, as often happens in these heavily defended cases against the rich and famous, the jury was hopelessly confused. After 38 hours, deliberations deadlocked—with nine jurors believing the prosecution case and three accepting the defense theory. Whereas the jurors supporting guilt were convinced by the three witnesses who saw Louisa go into the factory with Mr. Luetgert the night she disappeared, those supporting the defense were swayed by the witnesses who saw her in Wisconsin, and they weren't sure whether the rings in the vat really belonged to Mrs. Luetgert.[23]

Thus, the trial ended with a hung jury. Luetgert even asserted his innoncence in a sworn statement in which he stated:

> I did not kill my wife and do not know where she is, but I am sure that it is only a question of time until she comes home. . . . I am grateful for the public sentiment in my favor, and time will demonstrate that I am not only an innocent man, but a very grievously wronged man.[24]

But despite Luetgert's protestations of innocence, Deneen was determined to try Luetgert again, which not only kept Luetgert in jail for his next trial, but also thwarted his plans for stardom. A Chicago theater manager, who had produced a play based on Luetgert's story, had hoped to star Luetgert in the lead if he was acquitted.[25] But with Luetgert still in jail for another trial, that was no longer possible.

At the second trial, on February 10, 1898, the prosecution finally prevailed with a unanimous "Guilty!" verdict. Why the difference? Because often, by the second or third trial, the rich and powerful defendant has fewer resources. And sometimes the witnesses who previously supported the defendant or were afraid to testify against him feel freer to speak the truth after the outcome of the first trial has knocked away some of the defendant's protective armor. There are other examples of this in other chapters, such as in the Menendez brothers case in Chapter 8 and the Coppolino case in Chapter 2. In each case, the first trial ended in a mistrial or not- guilty verdict, but the second resulted in a conviction—and all the while the defendants continued to protest their innocence.

In this case, the prosecution gained an advantage when it was able to scare off two key witnesses who previously testified for the defense. One was William Charles, Luetgert's business partner, who claimed Luetgert was conducting innocent chemical experiments. The other was Mary Simering, the maid who denied she and Luetgert had an intimate relationship. They didn't testify the second time because after the verdict in the first trial, the prosecutor announced that he was going to ask the grand jury to issue indictments against these two witnesses for perjured testimony. So they refrained from giving false testimony again.

Another difference is that some witnesses turned against Luetgert, including some former lovers, who now spoke out against him. One was the a saloon keeper, Mrs. Agatha Tosch, who now testified that she saw Luetgert drinking beer in her saloon soon after his wife disappeared. She thought he responded oddly when she asked where his wife was; becoming pale and excited as he spoke, he replied, "I don't know. I am as innocent as the southern skies!" She thought the comment peculiar because if he didn't know her whereabouts, why claim innocence of any crime?[26]

Then, when Luetgert's mistress Mrs. Feldt took the stand, she pulled out the steamy love letters he had written and said Luetgert had given her $4,000 for safekeeping shortly before Louisa disappeared. Even more damaging, to gasps from the jury, Feldt testified that the day after Louisa vanished, Luetgert gave her a bloodstained knife without any explanation. Though the prosecutor had shown the bloody knife at the first trial, he hadn't had this dramatic testimony to make a convincing connection between the bloody knife and Louisa's death.[27]

Thus, taken together, the accumulation of evidence against Luetgert seemed more compelling, undermining his elaborate cover-up efforts. As a result, the second jury quickly returned with a guilty verdict, and the judge sentenced Luetgert to prison for life.

Even so, perhaps not believing he could be found guilty after being so powerful all his life, Luetgert laughed when the clerk read the verdict, as if he didn't regard it very seriously. Then, his attorney, Mr. Harmon, moved for a new trial, and as the deputies led Luetgert back to his jail cell, a crowd of reporters and friends surrounded him. Along the way, he confidently professed his innocence and expressed his surprise at the verdict, saying he was sure he would yet be acquitted. "I don't see how the evidence justifies such a verdict," he said, proclaiming, "One thing is sure—the Supreme Court will give me a new trial, and I shall be acquitted."[28]

Did Luetgert truly believe his cover-up might still work, or was he merely trying to put on a brave show of confidence? Whatever he thought or hoped, the Supreme Court did not take his case, and he was never retried. In the end, all his wealth, power, and influence didn't help. Instead, he died in prison, still protesting his innocence, though his cover-up had been clearly uncovered, affirming his guilt.

Concealing the Evidence in the Sea: The Case of Thomas Capano (Wilmington, Delaware, 1996–1999)

Skip ahead a century to 1996, and you have another rich and powerful cover-up case that parallels the Luetgert case in many ways. Like Luetgert, Thomas Capano had become very successful and prominent in his community, in this case Wilmington, Delaware, and he had a bevy of women besides a wife, though he later divorced her. He too was led to murder when a woman threatened to leave him, though the circumstances were different. Whereas Luetgert feared a scandal when his wife threatened divorce and wished to collect her insurance money, Capano wanted power and control when a former mistress sought to break off the relationship and marry another man. Like Luetgert, Capano arranged an elaborate scheme to cover up his crime, which stymied the police and FBI. And they too doggedly pursued him until the cover-up gradually came undone.

As in the Luetgert case, this case began when Capano decided he wanted to get rid of a woman who wanted to end her relationship with him. Like Luetgert, he took steps to conceal all traces of the murder. Capano similarly had a long history of trying to conceal things, much as Luetgert had tried to conceal his many affairs from a conservative Victorian society.

Capano, a former deputy attorney general and lawyer in a prominent Wilmington firm, was married until 1995 and had four children. He was also a member of one of the city's wealthiest, most powerful families—one that had built its fortune through extensive real estate holdings and construction deals that were initially made by his late grandfather, Louis J. Capano Sr., and then expanded by Louis Capano Jr., Thomas's father, who had three sons: Thomas, Louis III (also called Louie), and Joe. While Louie and Joe worked in the business, Tom went on to become a prominent lawyer.[29] Despite his prominence, Capano had much to conceal. For eighteen years he had been carrying out a secret affair with Debby MacIntyre, who hoped he would one day be free to marry her and didn't know that he was also engaging in a series of short-term, intense relationships with other women.[30]

One of these other women was twenty-seven-year-old Anne Marie Fahey, who, after working on his election campaign, became the scheduling secretary for the then governor of Delaware, Tom Carper, following his 1993 inaugural.[31] She was a tall, thin, attractive woman with a friendly manner and winning smile, though her weaknesses made her easy bait for a secret "other woman" relationship with a controlling married man. Besides having a low sense of self-esteem, a desire to please, and a willingness to take the blame and apologize at the slightest criticism, she was on a tight budget and suffered from anorexia. Though she sought to overcome it, her symptoms worsened when she became anxious and therefore she didn't want to eat.[32]

Tom Capano, then forty-four, met her in the spring of 1993, at a political fundraiser for a Democratic Party women's club.[33] She had walked over and introduced herself, and over the next weeks, his work as a lawyer for the Saul Ewing law firm sometimes brought him to the governor's office, where he passed by her desk and sometimes shared a few words.[34] In the late spring and summer, he took her to lunch a few times, and in the fall, out to dinner.

Though Anne Marie occasionally dated men her own age, she was soon drawn into a secret affair with Tom Capano. Part of the appeal was the intense attention he paid to her, wanting to know all about her and her everyday life, even encouraging her to share her problems and successes with him. As George Anastasia describes it in *Summer Wind*, though Anne Marie was eventually manipulated, controlled, and taken advantage of by Capano, initially she was captivated by his charm. She was "thrilled and excited by the attention of this suave, powerful, and sophisticated lawyer who was unlike anyone else she had ever met."[35]

Thus, even though she knew Tom was married, she was drawn to him, though simultaneously conflicted because of her strict Catholic upbringing. But Tom was a Catholic, too, and by early 1994 he had worn down her defenses and won her over, asking her to be his secret girlfriend. He even offered to pay for her to move into her own room, though she preferred to remain with her two roommates. Soon he began to buy her things to supplement her small $31,000 yearly salary as scheduling secretary, such as a dress for a family wedding and tickets for travel. Anne Marie understood that they had to keep their relationship secret because Tom was married and not planning a divorce. She rationalized that although he was unhappy in his marriage, he stayed because he cared so much for his four girls. As a result, she believed he desperately needed her to stem his unhappiness. However, she didn't know that he still had his mistress, Debby MacIntyre, of almost twelve years, and that he was still occasionally seeing a couple of other women from time to time.[36]

Thus, though Anne Marie hoped for marriage and children, knew this not possible with Tom, and felt conflicted over having a secret affair, she continued the relationship. She was drawn by a mix of Tom's charm and her loneliness, since she didn't have another steady relationship, and Tom had an ability to pull the strings at the right time to draw her back to him any time she seemed to be pulling away. He was especially good at appealing to her need to be needed, and he made her feel that he needed her there to keep him from succumbing to feelings of despair.[37] Thus, though he sometimes seemed overly possessive and demanding, she went along with him to keep him happy. The result was a setup for an increasingly dependent relationship, in which Tom became evermore controlling. For example, he told Anne Marie how to dress, and he ordered the wine and dinner for her without asking when he took her to fine restaurants in Philadelphia, where they wouldn't be recognized.

Even after Tom left his wife Kay after twenty-three years of marriage in the fall of 1995, he secretly continued his affair with Anne Marie, his nearly fourteen-year relationship with Debby MacIntyre, and his occasional flings with other women. It was like Tom was leading three separate lives, and enjoying the feeling of power and control he had over all these women. He liked being in charge, much as Luetgert had a century before.

However, everything changed when Governor Tom Carper played matchmaker and told a young man he had met, Mike Scanlan, a 30-year-old senior executive Vice President at MBNA America, about Anne Marie, thinking they would make a perfect match.[38] After a few dates, Anne Marie felt Mike was just the man she was looking for, and she decided it was time to end her affair with Tom. She was also determined to keep her relationship with Tom secret from Mike, fearing that Mike, a Catholic like herself, might end their relationship if he knew of her adulterous affair with Tom.[39]

Meanwhile, now that he was divorced, Tom bought an unfurnished house where he could live alone, where his four daughters, as well as Anne Marie and Debby could visit from time to time—though at different times, so they wouldn't find out about each other. But now Anne Marie had different ideas and told Tom she only wanted to see him on a platonic basis.[40]

Initially Tom was furious, falsely claiming he had left his wife for her. Then, when Annie Marie remained firm, he tried other tactics. He threatened suicide if she didn't return to him; took back some gifts he had given her for a time, such as a TV, clothes, and records; offered her a plane ticket for a trip to Spain; and repeatedly tried to set up a dinner date with her. But again and again, Anne tried to cool down the relationship, finding excuses to avoid seeing him. She continued an e-mail correspondence with him, however, hoping to gradually ease out of his life, thereby not hurting his ego or feelings.[41]

Unfortunately, Tom did not take Anne Marie's brush-off well; he continued to e-mail or call Anne Marie, pleading to see her again, telling her how much he loved and needed her, even as he continued to see Debby and a few other women. He also drove by her apartment from time to time to check up on her, and he called her repeatedly, even late at night. Eventually, Anne Marie stopped answering her phone and allowed her answering machine to screen her calls.[42] Tom became like a Sultan insulted at losing a single woman from his harem, and the more Anne Marie was determined to break away from him, the more determined he was to get her back.

Their opposing goals made for a deadly combination, though for a time in the spring of 1996, Tom's calls tapered off, leading Anne Marie to think that Tom was out of her life for good. She even wrote in the last entry in her diary that April: "I finally have brought closure to Tom Capano. What a controlling, manipulative, insecure, jealous maniac. Now that I look back on that aspect of my life, I realize just how vulnerable I had become."[43]

But in fact, the relationship wasn't over. At the end of April, Tom sent Anne Marie a series of e-mails claiming he had experienced a catastrophe in his life. His daughter, he falsely claimed, had suffered a brain tumor and was having surgery. Yet, despite her reservations, Anne Marie began talking to Tom again, hoping they could finally just be friends, and for a time, their e-mail exchanges were light and playful. Increasingly, though, with the help of some therapy, Anne Marie was learning to become more assertive, and she told Tom not to worry about her so much, that she needed some time alone to work on her problems, such as not eating enough.[44]

Unfortunately, Anne Marie's newfound assertiveness only made Tom more determined, and he bombarded her with food packages and other gifts and tried repeatedly to get her to join him for dinner. Finally, she did so on May 30, hoping he would understand that all she wanted now was a friendship. But once again, Tom used the opening to press for still more time together—urging her to have dinner out or at his house and to play golf together. But Anne Marie was more determined than ever to cut the cord. She refused any money he offered and sent him checks to pay back money he had already given her. Eventually, though, worn down by his persistence, she accepted one last offer for dinner on Thursday, June 27, the night before she planned to take the day off from work at the office while everyone else was at the state legislature for the end of the legislative session.[45]

That was the last night that anyone saw Anne Marie again, for after that dinner, she disappeared. After Mike and her family went to check on why they hadn't heard from her on Saturday night and failed to find her, they called the police. The police investigators, led by Bob Donovan, began by checking out Anne Marie's apartment and soon concluded that whatever happened to her didn't occur there. Though her things were uncharacteristically scattered around the apartment—for example, her shoeboxes were strewn about and her dry-cleaning bags were torn open[46]—there were no signs of violence and only her keys were missing.

Then, after checking her diary, e-mails, and letters written on Tom's law firm stationery, they quickly zeroed in on Tom as a likely suspect. These items showed an ongoing relationship in which Tom had sent Anne Marie cash, checks, gifts, and loans and spoken about dinners and evenings together. Yet a concluding diary entry for April 7, in which Anne Marie noted that she had at last "brought some closure" to her relationship, suggested that she was trying to end things.[47] She wrote:

> I've been through a lot of emotional battles. I finally have brought closure to Tom Capano. What a controlling, manipulative, insecure jealous maniac. . . . It hurts me when I think about that year. For one whole year, I allowed someone to take control of every decision in my life.[48]

That's why the investigators' first step was to speak with Tom. They contacted him at 3:30 a.m., rousing him out of bed, telling him they just wanted to talk to him about a missing person.[49] Initially, Tom acted like nothing was amiss, presumably hoping the investigation would just fade away. He appeared very calm and unflappable. He told them that he and Anne Marie had had a nice dinner at the Panorama restaurant in Philadelphia; then they had briefly come back to his house so he could pick up a package of groceries and a few other things for her. Then, he said he had taken her to her house, helped her take the package upstairs, put it on the kitchen counter, and returned to his house around 10 p.m. However, he mentioned one small fact that later helped to trip him up when investigators looked more closely at his story. He stated that he had stopped at the Getty's gas station along the way to get a pack of cigarettes,[50] though when investigators checked soon afterward, the attendant, who knew Capano,[51] said that Capano hadn't been there that night and that the station had closed at 9:30 p.m.[52]

At the initial interview, Tom also pointed out a number of reasons why Anne Marie might not be back for awhile. He suggested that Anne Marie could be unpredictable, something of an airhead, so that maybe she had gone off on her own for the weekend and would be back to work on Monday as usual. He additionally said that she planned to take Friday, the day after their dinner, off from work to go to the beach. He also explained that she had psychological problems, including suffering from depression, which he was helping her with.[53] Perhaps, he opined, she might even be suicidal, since she had talked about using pills to commit suicide in the past.[54]

In short, Capano's initial response was the first phase of

the cover-up—leading investigators to think that Anne Marie might have simply gone off on her own and that he knew nothing more. Presumably he thought that his solid reputation in the community would help the detectives believe what he said and not think he had anything to do with her disappearance. His initial denial was much like Luetgert's first suggestions to the police that his wife had simply run away.

Although his story was part of the elaborate cover-up he had set up to conceal what had really happened to Anne Marie that night, for now, his story seemed to satisfy the investigators; they took him at his word because of his highly respected position in the city and because they had no evidence to undermine his story. So they left, saying they would return with more questions. When they did two days later on Sunday, June 30, Tom led them on a walk-through tour of his house. Along the way, they noticed that it was filled with perfectly clean, new furnishings, and there was no sign of any struggle, no sign that Anne Marie had even been at his house—exactly the appearance that Tom wanted to present to the investigators.[55] As he led them out, he predicted that Anne Marie would probably turn up at work as usual on Monday.[56] But of course she didn't, and the investigation continued.

In a routine missing person's case, with no sign of foul play, no clear leads to follow, this might have been the end of the case. But given Anne's position in the governor's office and her parents' decision to spread the word about her disappearance to the press, the case soon went public, very public. Not only did the wire services and newspapers pick up the story, but also Anne Marie's brothers and sister soon were calling her friends and acquaintances to find out if they knew what might have happened to her. Meanwhile, the police began a door-to-door check of the houses around Anne Marie's house, and they searched the park across the street.[57]

Then, they received the first of the many tips that would lead them to focus on Tom Capano, much like some of the tips that led the police to zero in on Luetgert a century before. A key lead came when police contacted Michelle Sullivan after Anne Marie's sister told them she was seeing a psychologist. Sullivan said that Anne Marie had told her at one session that she was afraid someone would kidnap her or hire a third party to do that. Further, Anne Marie thought Tom Capano—a man she had previously said was repeatedly phoning her and stalking her—might do this.[58] Additionally, Sullivan said that on their last appointment on June 26, they were working on increasing Anne Marie's level of confidence, so she could successfully leave the relationship.[59]

Still more insight came when the police spoke to the waitress, Jackie Dansak, who had waited on Tom and Anne Marie at their last dinner together. [60] She told the police that the couple seemed to be very quiet and somber, barely speaking, and while Anne Marie appeared very unhappy, Tom acted very bossy. She claimed that they left around 9:15 p.m.[61]

So increasingly, the police were convinced Capano was involved with Anne Marie's disappearance. But how? So far, his cover-up was firmly in place, and their investigation was complicated by growing numbers of reports the police received from people who claimed to see Anne Marie in other places, as people learning of her disappearance in the media called in their sightings—much as people had reported sightings of Louisa Luetgert a century before. Although the police were able to quickly show these sightings were unfounded,[62] they were still at an impasse.

However, the wall of protection Capano had built around himself was gradually acquiring more nicks. For instance, when Anne Marie's hairdresser called the police to report that Anne Marie hadn't shown up for her June 28 appointment, she said that at her previous appointment, Anne Marie described how happy she was about the new man in her life, Mike Scanlan. Additionally, she said she was scared by the man she wanted to stop seeing, Tom Capano, because they had frequent arguments about ending their relationships, and she frequently found him waiting for her outside her apartment.[63]

Then, more help came from the FBI, who offered to assist on the grounds that Anne Marie's disappearance might be an interstate kidnapping because she had dinner in Pennsylvania and was taken back to Delaware. So now, Colm Connolly of the FBI joined Bob Donovan of the Wilmington Police on the case. As an initial strategy, he requested a pen register phone tap be placed on Tom's phones to show any local and long distance calls made from those lines after June 27.[64]

Meanwhile, as the FBI and police continued to investigate, Tom thought it was just a matter of time before the concern about Anne Marie would die down and he could go back to his life as normal, minus Anne Marie.

After four weeks, in late July, the police and FBI were still stumped; they had no body, no eyewitnesses, no blood, no weapon, no crime scene, and no sign of any struggle. They had only their suspicions that Capano, motivated by possessiveness or jealousy, had killed Anne Marie, which were based on a growing number of anecdotal accounts from Anne Marie's friends and associates describing the growing conflict between her and Capano. But this was not enough for probable cause to investigate Capano further.[65]

Then, as in the Luetgert case, they got the break they needed to begin unraveling the cover-up: information that Tom had bought a carpet. The break came on July 26, when Connolly and his boss at the FBI, Eric Alpert, were looking through Capano's credit card bills and noticed that he had made a purchase for about $300 at the Wallpaper Wearhouse, a wallpaper and carpet store.[66] It seemed like an odd purchase considering that Capano was only renting his house after his divorce, and when they went to the store to investigate, they learned he had bought an inexpensive Oriental rug.[67]

Another important piece of evidence came from Ruth Boylon, the woman who cleaned Capano's house every two weeks. She reported that he asked her to skip cleaning on July 8, and when she came in to clean on July 22, the large room by the kitchen had been completely changed. One sofa was gone, and in place of the fairly new, original carpeting was an area rug. She thought the change odd because the room had looked better before.[68] This information helped Connolly and Donovan to formulate a good theory of what happened, though they still had to uncover the missing evidence. In their view, as described by George Anastasia in *The Summer Wind*, "Capano must have removed the sofa and rug from his house because they had been tainted somehow. Most probably, they had been stained with blood."[69] And very probably he wrapped her body in the rug to dispose of it. Now if they could just find that rug and sofa.

Still more evidence came from another visit with Anne

Marie's psychologist, Michelle Sullivan, who thought that Anne Marie was unlikely to go willingly to Capano's house after their June 27 dinner. Sullivan suggested that Anne Marie's only likely reason for going to dinner with him was to break off the relationship—a goal of Anne Marie's that Sullivan hoped to help her reach by facilitating her to feel more self-esteem and confidence.[70]

Armed with this new evidence, Alpert wrote up a twenty-page probable cause affidavit explaining that the FBI and Wilmington police should search Capano's house on the grounds that he had probably killed Anne Marie there.[71] The search warrant was issued and took the cover-up another step toward its undoing.

Then, during an eleven-hour search of the house, they found evidence to show that the large room off the kitchen had been the scene of whatever happened to Anne Marie.[72] The evidence came in the form of a few dark brown specks that looked like blood, which could be tested against Anne Marie's DNA. They also discovered a number of cleaning and bleaching agents, including Carbona cleaner, used for removing bloodstains.[73] The local Wilmington paper, the *News-Journal*, garnered even more support when it described their search and printed excerpts from Anne Marie's diary about her conflicts with Capano and her relationship with Mike.[74]

Another crucial tip came from an employee who worked at the Capano & Sons construction company, run by Capano's father, Louis Capano Jr. The employee said that another employee had instructed him to empty the dumpsters on the company's grounds, which were only half full, before their regularly scheduled pick-up day.[75] The investigators thought the request to empty the dumpsters was curious. Was that to get rid of Anne Marie's body, or perhaps the missing couch or carpet?[76]

Meanwhile, as suspicions grew with the continuing investigation and reports in the media, Tom developed his own strategy to counter them. For example, after the intensive July 31 search of his home, he told friends and associates that he was being made a "scapegoat" in a case that had become politicized. He suggested that some high-level figures, such as Governor Carper and President Clinton, who had expressed concern and offered Carper his help, felt he made a convenient target.[77] Tom even went to a psychiatrist two times in August, though he gave two different explanations about the blood found in the large room at his house. One explanation was that the small amount of blood might have gotten there while he and Anne Marie were having intercourse; and the other was that the blood might have gotten there when he had an argument with Anne Marie over his urging her to get treatment for her anorexia. He said he tried to stop her from punching him, which resulted in her getting a bloody nose.[78] Yet, was he honestly seeking psychiatric help, or were the meetings with the psychiatrist a way to set up a witness who could later testify on his behalf?

Then, the prosecutors scored another win during the grand jury session that began on August 29 when the jury used its power to bring in reluctant witnesses, including Louis Capano Jr., his son Louis Capano III, and construction company employees, who now had to testify under subpoena.[79] At first, Louis sought to help his son maintain the cover-up by explaining that he had advised Tom to get rid of any of Anne Marie's belongings in his construction dumpster, so his wife Kay wouldn't find out about his affair with Anne Marie.[80] But even if, as investigators suspected, Louis Capano had lied, they felt they could use his false testimony under oath to press the truth from him later.[81]

Then, in November, another good lead surfaced when the search of the office of one of Capano's law partners revealed a time line written in Tom's handwriting for a day when he repeatedly met with his brother Gerry and dumped a loveseat someplace. Though the page with the time line was undated, the details suggested it was June 28, the day after Anne Marie disappeared, and investigators speculated that he had tried to hide the time line in someone else's office, expecting a search of his own office.[82] About six months later, when a lab report came back on January 3, 1997, stating that the blood in Tom's house matched Anne Marie's DNA, the investigators were even more certain there had been some kind of struggle in the big room off the kitchen, which Tom had sought to cover up.[83]

Yet, these bits of evidence were still not enough for an arrest, and Tom wasn't talking, protected by his lawyer Charles

Oberly, who chastised the FBI for conducting an investigation based on rumor and innuendo. He even suggested that Anne Marie was still alive and claimed that Capano continued to hope she would be found.[84]

But finally, the investigators, led by Donovan, Connolly, and Alpert, got their big break in the fall of 1997, when they put pressure on Capano's brother Gerry. They decided to do so because his name was mentioned many times in Tom's June 28 memo. The memo also included in a notation about driving to SH, which the investigators guessed was Stone Harbor, a site near the Atlantic Ocean. So they put Gerry under surveillance, planning to put pressure on him if he did anything illegal, and soon Gerry, who had a problem with drug addiction, did just that. Investigators suspected him of possessing and distributing cocaine and possessing a firearm, and they arrived at his house with a search warrant in early October. There, after finding that Gerry did possess cocaine and had some revolvers and shotguns, they invited him to cut a deal and tell them what he knew about the trip to Stone Harbor and Anne Marie's disappearance or else face jail time.

At first, Gerry kept silent, deciding what to do. But because he had been deeply troubled by what he had done to help his brother and had been having nightmares, he slowly began to crack.[85] Thus, a month later, on November 8, 1997, Gerry was finally ready to talk. He arrived with his attorney at the Wilmington Police Department and gave a statement. He described going to Tom's house on the morning of June 28. Tom met him there with a four-foot-long cooler with a chain and lock wrapped around it and a rolled-up rug. Then, as Gerry explained, they had gone to his fishing boat *The Summer Wind* at Stone Harbor, where he had motored out seventy miles to a 200-foot-deep area called Mako Alley, and Tom tried to dump the cooler in the water. But when it didn't sink, Gerry shot a hole in it with his shark gun, and when that didn't sink the cooler, Gerry returned to steering the boat. Meanwhile, Tom opened the cooler, removed something from it, and attached two anchors. After Gerry heard Tom vomit and the sound of a heavy splash, he went back to rejoin his brother, and just as he did, he saw a human calf and foot sinking into the ocean and a little blood coming out of the cooler.[86] He then helped Tom take the lid off of the bloodstained cooler, and they tossed the lidless cooler overboard. Though they imagined the cooler would fill with water and sink to the floor of the ocean, never to be found again, eventually, it bobbed back up without the body, where it was found floating in the water by the owner of a fishing boat, Ken Chubb. He figured he just needed to clean it up and add a lid, presuming that the pinkish bloodstains were just the result of fish that had been stored there. So he thought nothing sinister about his find for months,[87] until he heard the news that the police were looking for an Igloo cooler.

Gerry's story, if true, would be the key to breaking the cover-up because it showed what happened to Anne Marie's body, though not how she died. The investigators soon found corroboration for his story when they discovered that Tom had previously bought a large Igloo cooler back in the middle of April—two months before Anne Marie died, suggesting that he had been plotting to get rid of Anne Marie for some time. They also found intimations that the plan went back some months to early February, when Tom appeared to be setting up a story by borrowing $8,000 in cash from Gerry, telling him he needed it to pay off the boyfriend of a "crazy woman he had been dating" who was threatening him. He also asked to borrow a gun, asked Gerry if he knew someone who could "break someone's legs,"[88] and later asked Gerry if he could use his boat if this girl hurt his kids.[89] The investigators also found it curious that the day before and the day after Tom had gotten the money from Gerry he had additionally cashed two of his own checks for $8,000 and $9,000, and a week later he had paid back his brother. Why the odd transactions? In reviewing them several months later, Connolly and Donovan surmised that Capano might have been putting together some money to arrange for a hit on Anne Marie.[90] But why didn't he kill Anne Marie then? Perhaps because before June 27, he didn't have the opportunity to get rid of her, or he hoped to reconcile, making her murder unnecessary.

With Gerry's confession in place, Connolly had more leverage to put pressure on Tom's brother Louie to tell the truth, too, which Louie did. Through his attorney, Katie Recker, he described how Tom had claimed to him that Anne

Marie had been at Tom's house after dinner, where she slit her wrists and got a small amount of blood on the sofa while Tom was upstairs using the bathroom. But, Louie explained, Tom said he had taken her home still alive after that.[91] He continued to describe how, soon after, he and Gerry had dumped the sofa in the company's dumpster. And later, Gerry told Louie how he had helped Tom dump Anne Marie's body in the ocean, although Louie had kept that confidence and had continued to lie to protect Tom until he admitted the truth.[92] For example, he had lied at Tom's request when he had appeared before the grand jury.[93] But now that Tom's brothers were talking, Tom's cover up was at an end.

Accordingly, as Chris Barrish and Peter Meyer describe it in *Fatal Embrace*, once Connolly had the signed deals with Gerry and Louie Capano, he had enough to arrest Tom. Connolly arranged for them to testify to the grand jury on November 12,[94] and once they were, he and his boss Alpert gave the signal for the federal agents to arrest Tom.[95] The arrest came shortly after 10 a.m., as Tom was driving his brother Joe and Joe's wife to the airport. After the agents took him back to the U.S. attorney's office, Connolly, Alpert, and Donovan played the tapes for Tom and his lawyers, Charles Oberly and Joe Hurley, so they could hear Gerry confessing to what happened on the boat trip and Louie describing how he had gotten rid of the bloody sofa in his dumpster and how he had lied to the grand jury at Tom's request.[96] With the confessions on tape, Tom was faced with what might seem like the end of his cover-up—his own brothers, who had helped him for so long, had confessed what they knew.

But even after he was taken to jail, Tom still was determined to continue the cover-up by explaining away each bit of incriminating evidence with another lie. He said his brother Gerry was not to be believed and claimed that he had bought the cooler as a present for Gerry because he was a fisherman. Tom also found ways to continue to stay in contact and in control of those on the outside who he felt were still loyal to him. For example, he persuaded his ex-wife Kay to send checks to the commissary of some of the prisoners so he could use their phone time to make calls.[97]

Tom also worked on keeping his longtime mistress, Debby

MacIntyre, loyal to him, particularly because he didn't want her to tell investigators about a gun he had asked her to buy for him in early May 1997, about six weeks before Anne Marie disappeared.[98] A key reason for concealing his connection to the gun purchase is that its disclosure would be one more indication of premeditation, suggesting that he had shot her with this gun. Moreover, the purchase gave him a story he could use to point to another suspect. He could argue that Debby bought the gun for protection because of her fear of crime in the area. But she discarded the gun about two weeks before Anne Marie's disappearance because school had ended and, with two teenagers at home, she feared having a gun in the house. And initially that's the story Debby told to Connolly and the prosecution team.[99]

But could the prosecutors break through Capano's and his loyal witnesses' tangled web of lies? Fortunately, another big break came when Debby decided she couldn't testify for Tom with his manufactured story. Though Tom bombarded her with letters to make her feel guilty at her betrayal, like Anne Marie, Debby finally gained the courage to break free of his control and at last told prosecutors the truth—that she had bought the gun for Tom and had given it to him.[100] As she explained to them in May 1996, Tom had asked her to buy the gun, reluctantly she had done so with her own money, and he had never even reimbursed her for her purchase.[101]

Yet even with Debby preparing to be a prosecution witness, Tom wasn't ready to give up, thinking maybe he could change Debby's mind and keep her from testifying. To this end, he contacted another prisoner, Nick Perillo, about having a burglar break into Debby's house to not only take valuables but also to take or destroy some items they shared together so she would know who had sent the burglars. This way he hoped to discourage her cooperation with the prosecution. However, instead of helping Tom, Perillo turned Tom's plan over to the prosecutors.[102] So Tom's effort to shore up the cover-up backfired, as did his next scheme to pay $100,000 to a cell mate, Tito Rosa, to arrange to have not only Debby but also his own brother Gerry killed for betraying him. The plan backfired because that prisoner likewise went to the prosecutors and revealed the proposed scheme.[103] Eventually Tom was charged additionally with soliciting three crimes—the two hit jobs and the burglary.[104]

Still Tom came up with yet another scheme to get off—one that would be revealed at the trial. Tom didn't even tell his lawyers exactly what it was—only that Anne Marie had died in a "horrible, tragic accident," which he would explain at the trial.[105] The story would be still another effort at a cover-up, and just as Tom had manipulated others to go along with him, he was able to force his will on his lawyers, too. But would his strategy work this time?

Going into the trial, the prosecution seemed to have every advantage. They already had a clear time line for the cover-up, including credit card charges that helped to document every stage of the plan, from buying the carpet and cooler to dumping Anne Marie's body in the sea, though they had not recovered her body. They had strong circumstantial evidence putting her death in the large room off Tom's kitchen, where Anne's blood had been found and the original carpet and couch had been dumped and incinerated at Tom's father's construction company. They had also developed a strong case based on circumstantial evidence that Tom had probably shot her after she made it clear that she was not going to come back to him, that she was moving on.

But would that explanation convince the jury when faced with Tom's final ploy? The prosecution, led by Ferris Wharton, made a persuasive case that Tom had committed a premeditated murder by buying the cooler in advance and arranging for Debby MacIntyre to buy a gun for him. Further, Wharton argued that Tom had engaged in an elaborate cover-up, recruiting members of his family and others to help, and that Tom had lied about what happened. He pointed out how Anne Marie's own diary entries showed Tom's obsessive pursuit of her, as well as her growing determination to leave him, concluding with her last diary entry where she confidently wrote, "I finally brought closure to Tom Capano. . . . What a controlling, manipulative, insecure, jealous maniac."[106]

But when the defense presented its case, Tom was ready with his last cover-up strategy. His lawyer Joe Oteri began by describing all of the good deeds Tom had done to help out his family members and others, emphasizing his many acts of generosity. Oteri also pointed out how much Tom had helped Anne Marie with her own problems, including buying most of her clothes and providing her with plenty of food. As for the dinner on June 27, he explained that Tom had been trying to help Anne Marie with her anorexia problem, so no wonder the mood was somber and serious. And the cooler? Simply a gift to thank his brother Gerry for his nice acts toward Tom's daughters.[107]

Then came the pièce de résistance. Even though Oteri hadn't wanted Tom to testify and had never let a murder defendant testify before, Tom was determined to do so, certain he could turn on his usual charm and persuasion to win over the jury.[108] So, after swearing to tell the truth, he proceeded to lie and lie. Among other things, he sought to discredit his brothers, claiming they had lied themselves. For instance, he said that Gerry suggested he break the legs of the woman who was extorting him.[109] He claimed he had bought the cooler for his brother Gerry as a gift, since Gerry loved fishing.[110] He said the $25,000, which included his two checks and the $8,000 he borrowed from Gerry, was to help Anne Marie pay to get inpatient treatment for her condition, not to harm her, although she refused to take the money.[111]

He then explained the tragic "accident" that happened that night, while he and Anne Marie were at his house. As they were watching TV, there was a phone call he didn't answer, and shortly after the show, Debby burst in with a gun, using her own key to get into the house. When she saw Anne Marie there, she became hysterical, crying that she had been waiting for Tom to be free for so many years. He then saw her pull a gun out of her handbag, and as he told the jury:

> Debby was off the wall. She was not coherent. I tried to explain that Annie and I were friends, but she wasn't listening. She started to cry.[112]

As Tom tried to grab the gun to stop her, she shot Anne Marie. But it was "an accident," he insisted, and after they both unsuccessfully used CPR to revive her, he engaged in the cover-up to protect Debby, since Anne Marie was already dead.[113] As he appealed to the jury:

> It was the most cowardly, horrible thing I have ever done in my life. . . . I knew Anne Marie was dead. I was being selfish. I decided not to call the paramedics and the police. I wanted to protect myself and also to protect Debby.[114]

So he sent Debby home, telling her he would take care of doing whatever needed to be done, after which he engaged in a series of acts to launch the cover-up. He went to Anne Marie's apartment to drop off the groceries and otherwise make it look like she had been there that night.[115] Somehow, he explained, he was able to compartmentalize what he was doing, so he could function and do what he had to do.[116] Then, he returned to his apartment, put Anne Marie's body in the cooler, and got Gerry to help him dispose of the body, promising both Debby and Gerry that he would protect them and take the burden of what happened upon himself.[117]

In short, as his lawyer Joe Oteri concluded his argument, Tom had been devastated by Anne Marie's sudden death because he truly cared about her—it was a death due to a jealous woman who had become crazed at seeing Anne Marie in his apartment. Then, he had crazily tried to cover up the crime to protect his mistress, who had committed the murder. Later, he tried to cover up the cover-up in his effort to continue to protect her and his brothers who had helped out.[118]

But would the jury buy his defense? Would they believe Debby's denial that she had anything to do with killing Anne Marie, after she had previously lied to protect Capano? Or would the jury respond to the prosecution's summation that Capano had "lied and lied and lied—to his lawyers, psychiatrists, lovers and family" and had done so because he was guilty.[119]

In the end, after four days of deliberations, the jury came back with a resounding "guilty of first-degree murder" verdict, and when it came time to recommend a sentence, they recommended death. A key reason for their decision is that Capano's demeanor on the stand undermined his defense. Not only did they find him arrogant and ready to blame and trash everyone else, but also they found it hard to understand why it would take him two and a half years to reveal what happened if it really were an accident.[120]

Three days later, after a hearing to determine Capano's sentence, Judge William Swain Lee, agreed with the jury's recommendation.[121] In his remarks explaining his decision, he emphasized Tom's evil and malevolence, pointing out how his "selfishness, arrogance, and manipulativeness" destroyed two families—both Anne Marie's and Tom's own. As the judge pointed out, Capano's crime was not "a crime of passion but, rather, a crime of control": Although Anne Marie was no longer his lover, he could not allow her to escape from "his sphere of influence, control, and manipulation"; he couldn't allow her to reject him. So he "chose to destroy a possession rather than lose it."[122] Judge Lee even took into consideration Tom's failed cover-up in his remarks, stating that:

> The defendant fully expected to get away with murder and, were it not for his own arrogance and controlling nature, may well have succeeded. . . .
>
> He chose to use his family as a shield; make his brothers and his mistress accomplices; use his friends and attorneys for disinformation; attack the character of the prosecutor, make his mother and daughters part of a spectacle in an effort to gain sympathy. . . . He even bullied, berated and undermined the efforts of his own attorneys. . . .
>
> The selfishness, arrogance and manipulativeness of Thomas Capano destroyed his own family as well as the Fahey family. . . . He faces judgment because he is a ruthless murderer who feels compassion for no one and remorse only for the circumstances in which he finds himself. He is a malignant force from whom no one he deems disloyal or adversarial can be secure, even if he is incarcerated for the rest of his life.[123]

And with that, Capano's cover-up attempt finally ended and he was sent to death row, scheduled to be executed on June 28, 1999, three years after the day he tried to cover up the crime by throwing Anne Marie's body into the ocean.[124] As of this writing, he is still on death row at the Delaware Correctional Center near Smyrna, and his case is on appeal,[125] a process that is likely to go on for a decade. At one point his attorneys asked the Superior Court Judge T. Henley Graves to set aside his death sentence and convert it into a sentence of life in prison, though more recently, Capano has filed his own documents claiming that his lawyers provided ineffective assistance at his trial, so he should have a new trial or new sentencing. The irony is that because Capano chose to ignore the advice of his attorneys and repeatedly lied to them at the trial the attorneys have fought back, claiming that Capano refused to fully cooperate with them and involved himself in every decision about pretrial and trial strategy. Oteri even had to reveal the defense strategy of admitting that Fahey's death was due to an "outrageous, horrible, tragic accident" without knowing what that accident was.[126]

And so Capano's case drags on through the appeals process. At least the cover-up is over, though it survived as long as it did because of Tom's financial resources and connections, coupled with his own knowledge and determination. Yet, in the end, even his wealth and prominence weren't enough to buy off the jury and judge; they saw through his schemes.

CHAPTER 5

Family, Friends, and High Places

The power of family, friends, and one's status in society can make a big difference in the way the rich and famous are judged, affecting both the trial and its aftermath. It can play a role in getting the best lawyers and legal defense, as discussed in Chapter 7, "Legal Power." In addition, the image of high status and respectability can be a big factor that influences a jury to find a defendant not guilty, as shown in the Lizzie Borden case featured in that chapter.

But even when the wealthy are ultimately found guilty, their position and the support of powerful family and friends can affect how they are prosecuted, sentenced, or treated after their conviction—even when there is no mystery in who killed the victim.

One impact is that family members and highly placed friends can contribute to delays in the investigation. Another is that the police and prosecution can feel pressure to spend more time on a more careful investigation and to wait before making an arrest because they know they will be confronting a more formidable, well-funded defense. Also, family and friends of the wealthy can help a suspect avoid the long arm of the law, for example, by providing support to get out of the country, thus making it harder to investigate or prosecute. As a result, the case may just fade away.

Family, friends, and business associates can additionally appear as powerful character witnesses during a trial, helping to make the jurors more sympathetic to a defendant and more likely to acquit, even in the face of overwhelming evidence of guilt, as in the Borden case. There, the lawyers could point to not only the defendant's high status and respectable position in the community, but also to her strong support from highly respected and powerful family members as proof she couldn't have done it.

Jurors may also be more readily convinced of a self-defense claim, given the defendant's status or ability to cast aspersions on the victim, particularly if the victim comes from a lower social class. But even if jurors do think the person is guilty, they may be likely to convict on a lesser charge or decide on a lesser sentence, as in the Thaw and Cummings cases described in this chapter.

Then, too, in the event of a conviction, the defendant, because of his or her position and family influence, may serve a sentence under much better conditions than the average defendant, such as getting better and even private housing and receiving family visits, as in the Cummings case. The defendant may be able to get out of confinement more quickly, too, whether he or she spends fewer days in jail (Cummings) or negotiates a quicker release from an insane asylum (Thaw). Then, after the criminal proceedings are over, the defendant may be able to return to life in the protective cocoon of family, friends, and high society.

The downside of this special treatment is that such cases can anger the average person and the press, resulting in an outcry about the unfair consideration given to those with wealth and power. The public and press may even raise charges of corruption of justice by those in high positions, as occurred in the Thaw case. But after some weeks, as interest in the case and its outcome quiets down, the public's attention turns to something else.

As illustrated by the following two cases—one from the early 1900s, the other from the 1990s—the power of high position, family, and friends has a long history. In the sensational

Thaw case, Thaw's powerful family position helped to secure an insanity verdict; in the Cummings case, not only did the jury decide on a manslaughter verdict, but also her sixty-day sentence and special consideration in prison seemed like a slap on the wrist.

Getting Off Lightly: The Case of Harry Thaw (New York, New York, 1906–1908)

When Harry Thaw shot famed architect Stanford White at Madison Square Garden in 1906 over White's affair with Thaw's wife, former chorus girl Evelyn Nesbit, the case riveted America. There was no mystery; Thaw simply walked up to White, shot him point blank in the face, and walked out of the theater, where he was quickly arrested. But the case quickly opened up the world of high society high jinks, revealing White to be a lascivious debaucher of young women in his penthouse hideaway and Thaw to be the mad son of an elite family. Thaw's family millions enabled him to live a wastrel's life of luxury and get out of repeated scrapes, for example when his mother came to bail him out with her money and connections. Thaw's killing of White yeilded similar results; he was soon out of jail, based on his insanity plea. Subsequently, he spent little time in the mental institution where he was supposedly committed.

The story begins with Evelyn Nesbit's affair with Stanford White. Evelyn became a show girl at sixteen, soon after her widowed mother moved with her and her younger brother from an industrial slum north of Pittsburgh to a tenement in the New York slums in 1899. Her mother, nearly destitute, tried to find work as a dress designer.[1] But Mrs. Nesbit felt she might have a bright future by using her daughter's beauty to get into show business. Though Evelyn had little talent for singing or acting, Mrs. Nesbit took her around to producers and talent agents, and finally got some calendar artists and magazine illustrators to use her as a model.[2]

Evelyn's looks quickly made her very popular, and soon top illustrators of the day were sketching her, including Charles Dana Gibson, who sketched her as a "Gibson Girl" for one magazine cover. As a result, her image appeared in magazine covers and calendars around the world, and she became known as "the most beautiful woman in the world."[3]

At seventeen, Evelyn was hired to be one of six dancers in an ongoing variety show called *Floradora*, making her a "Floradora Girl." This role helped launch the extremely popular Evelyn into New York society. Not only did critics pour out their praise, but also ardent suitors appeared at the stage door wanting to meet her. For a time, she even dated and fell in love with the actor John Barrymore, though he had not yet gained fame and her mother thought him too poor to consider.

Then, another chorus girl in the show introduced her to Stanford White,[4] the best-known architect in America at the time. He was in demand as a designer of mansions of the New York elite, and he had designed some notable New York buildings, including the Washington Square Arch, the Century Club, and the second Madison Square Garden Building.[5] It was the beginning of a wild affair that would lead to murder.

Though White was married, he was an ardent womanizer and libertine, who cut a flamboyant figure in early New York, with his red hair, bushy mustache, and six-foot-two-inch, 250-pound frame. He began to show Evelyn the high life of New York, taking her to the best restaurants and the openings of Broadway musicals. He gave her expensive clothes and jewelry,[6] and he provided her and her mother with money, which he referred to as a "subsidy" to help develop her career in the theater.[7]

He also took her to the love nests he maintained at the Winter Gardens and at other apartments and houses around New York. But it was the Winter Garden apartment that would gain the most renown for its large room with a red velvet swing and mirrors covering the walls and on the ceiling. Often, Evelyn would sit on the swing, and White would swing her back and forth so he could watch as her skirts flew up.[8] One time, as noted in the court records, he took a photo of her posing in a revealing Japanese silk kimono on a bearskin and plied her with liquor; afterward, she woke to find she had lost her virginity.[9] But Evelyn didn't stay upset for long, and soon after she became White's public mistress. To give her the proper polishing, he enrolled her in an expensive finishing school. Then, he set her and her mother up in a New York apartment, gave her $25 a week for everyday expenses, and from time to time, bought her expensive furs, clothing, and jewelry. As Evelyn continued to pursue her career in musicals, White took her around the town and escorted her to fashionable resorts out of town, such as in Atlantic City and Saratoga.[10]

Then, Evelyn met Harry Thaw in 1901. Thaw, at thirty-five, was heir to the $40 million fortune of his father, William Thaw, who had built his wealth from investing in coke and steel plants in Pittsburgh. Though Thaw had left the money to his wife, Mary Copley Thaw, she lavished it on her son,[11] giving him about $80,000 a year in addition to the allowance left by his father. Early on, Thaw, sometimes called "Mad Harry," engaged in all sorts of strange behaviors. At home, he had anger fits in which he would suddenly tear the tablecloth from the table and kick food into the fireplace and at Harvard, he was expelled for "immoral practices," supposedly because he had sexually assaulted some other male students.[12]

In his twenties, he threw himself into a hedonistic life of pleasure, spending his fortune on show girls and prostitutes. One time he even treated over 100 "actresses" to a $400-a-plate dinner. He engaged in a variety of attention-getting stunts, too, one time taking over the wheel of a taxicab and driving it along Broadway until he smashed it into a department store's plate glass window. Another time, he rode a horse up the stairs of the elite Union Club.[13]

Thaw also spent his time and money abusing hundreds of women. At first, many of these women were of a similar social class, such as Ethel Thomas, who he initially lavished with great affection and attention, taking her on automobile rides and to the theaters and giving her flowers and jewelry. But one day, he revealed his sadistic nature when he took her to his apartment and hit her with a dog whip until her "clothes hung in tatters," as she described in a lawsuit against him, which Thaw's lawyers resolved with a financial settlement. After that, Thaw concentrated his attentions on lower class women who would be less likely to sue, and he found many of them by advertising for young girls to become theatrical stars. But once he lured them to his room he rented in a brothel under an assumed name, he stripped them, whipped them, and paid them off.[14]

After Evelyn met Harry in 1901, at the height of her fame as a chorus girl, he initially put on his usual chivalrous gentleman act. Even though she was known as Stanford White's mistress, Harry ardently pursued her, and her repeated rejections helped him fall in love with her. Finally, he offered to marry her if she would go with him on a tour of Europe. She agreed to go on the trip if her mother could go, and she took her mother along with her for the first few weeks. After that she and Harry stayed on for an additional few months. Thaw's money meant they could go to the most fashionable places, but at night, Harry privately let loose his sadistic nature, frequently tying her spread-eagled to the bed and whipping her.[15]

The experience led to the face-off between Thaw and White which ultimately led to murder. After Evelyn and Thaw came back from their trip, Evelyn did not marry Harry. Instead, she returned to White, not wanting to see Harry again. Upon hearing how Harry had whipped her, White told Evelyn to write up an affidavit and take it to the police. However, instead of going to the police, Evelyn took the affadavit to Harry and threatened to go to court if he did not honor her demand for a big settlement. Harry paid her even more than she asked, and oddly, instead of taking the money and running, Evelyn agreed to go on a second trip with him. After he attacked her with whips for a second time, she returned to the United States alone, again expecting to be finished with Harry.[16]

But this time, Harry pursued Evelyn, who was playing the lead in a new musical, *The Girl from Dixie*, and not only offered her more apologies, flowers, diamonds, but also promised both marriage and half of his money when he inherited his millions. Not sure what to do and hoping White might marry her, she went to him for advice, but White was unwilling to leave his wife and face the scandal that would occur at a time when having a discreet mistress was acceptable in polite society, but not divorce.[17] So Evelyn decided to marry Harry Thaw.

Yet, even though she married Thaw in April 1904, she continued to see White, going to his various love dens and hoping that he might eventually change his mind and want to marry her. But when White remained determined to maintain the status quo, Evelyn began playing on Harry's insane jealousy, telling him some details of her affair with White, such as describing the mirrored rooms and red velvet swing and how White had seduced her with liquor and taken her virginity. Why tell him all this? Because, according to Jay Robert Nash, in his profile of the Thaw case, "it is . . . possible . . . that she created those stories to goad Thaw into action, seeking retribution against a man who was by then escorting new show girls through his glittering night-life world."[18] Whatever her reason, Evelyn's tales were a prescription for murder, because soon Harry was so infuriated that he couldn't even speak White's name, referring to him as "The Bastard" or "The Beast." He told Evelyn to do the same, so she began calling White "The B."[19]

The triggering event finally occurred when White sent Evelyn a basket of roses as an apology for not being at his studio earlier that day when she had gone to meet him there. Certain that White was trying to take Evelyn away from him, Thaw took a pistol with him that night when he and Evelyn joined another couple for dinner and drinks and afterward went to the Winter Garden Theater atop Madison Square Garden to see a new musical comedy *Mamzelle Champagne*. Thaw placed the pistol under his heavy overcoat to conceal it.

After White arrived during the show, Harry stood up and strode around nervously for awhile, at first in the audience and then near White's table near the stage, glowering at him, though White paid him no attention. Then, as the final chorus began, with the chorus singing: "I challenge you, I challenge you, to a duel, to a d-u-e-l," Harry let loose his longtime pent-up anger and hatred against White. He fired two shots into White's face, and after White toppled to the floor, Harry shot him again. He fired a last shot into the floor.[20]

Needless to say, there was no mystery about what happened. As the audience turned into a chaotic mob, with women screaming and people rushing for the exits, Harry walked calmly toward the elevator and handed his gun to one of the theater guards, telling him that he was glad he had killed White, who deserved it because "he ruined my wife." At the elevator lobby, Evelyn rushed over and embraced Harry, saying, "Good God, Harry! What have you done?"[21] Despite her surprise, there is some indication that Evelyn might have known Harry planned to kill White at some point though she didn't know how. According to Albert Payson Terhune, who reviewed the musical for the *Evening World*, she had told Harry, "I never thought you'd do it that way!" and Harry replied that he had probably saved her life.[22]

In any case, shortly after that embrace, a police officer hired by the management arrested Harry. Now, Harry's high status and help from his mother made a major difference in how he was treated by the legal system and in the outcome of his trial. These factors also contributed to the ability of Harry and his legal team to smear White's reputation in the press, which helped his case, too.

After his arrest, when Harry was taken to the Tombs, the infamous New York City jail, he was treated like a special guest because of his money and status. He was provided with meals catered by Delmonico's, one of New York's finest restaurants, and given a fresh suit and underwear each day. He was assigned a more comfortable bed, and his butler came in to change the sheets each day. Though alcohol was normally forbidden, his physician prescribed a pint of champagne each day, supposedly to "settle his nerves," and he was able to visit with a number of regular visitors, including his wife Evelyn, who now presented herself as his loyal and devoted wife.[23] In addition, his mother and Evelyn now began to be seen together frequently, even though Mrs. Thaw had previously expressed a great dislike of Evelyn as a lowly showgirl. But with her son in jail, Mrs. Thaw lavished Evelyn with gifts and money, and promised her even more wealth after the trial, so she would stick by Harry to help free him.[24]

Harry's mother came to his support also by hiring five defense lawyers, including the noted Delphin Delmas from San Francisco. Additionally, she poured money into a press campaign to paint Stanford White as a lecher, libertine, rake, and satyr, who seduced young girls and married women.[25] The newspapers responded eagerly, as the case fascinated the public. They presented White as "an immoral beast who dressed in his tuxedo"[26] and victimized women, using his fame as an architect to take advantage of innocent virgins and other women in his pleasure dens. However, the public's fascination was accompanied by a public reaction against the rich generally. Previously, the rich had been viewed as upholders of righteousness and morality as well as esteemed for their good manners.[27] But White's murder triggered an outpouring of scorn that the wealthy were self-indulgent and corrupted by money and harbored libertine perverts behind the facades of their elegant mansions. And due in part to the PR campaign fueled by Mrs. Thaw's money, most of this scorn was directed toward White, even though he was the murder victim.

Harry's four-month trial finally began on January 27, 1907, with an unusual defense planned by this lawyers. They argued that he had suffered from temporary insanity because of a new mental disorder, "Dementia Americana," which, they maintained, afflicted only American males because of their belief that each man's wife is sacred. The disorder, they claimed, could lead its victim to feel an irresistible urge to kill someone violating this principle. Harry's lawyers brought in several noted psychiatrists to testify in support of this new malady. It was a defense made possible by the money of his mother, who announced publicly that she was spending more than $1 million to gain Harry's freedom.[28] Clearly, most defendants couldn't afford this kind of defense; nor could their families contribute this kind of money.

Besides the insanity experts, Delmas called on Evelyn to describe what she told Harry about how White had seduced her. Delmas hoped to show how Thaw became deranged due to what Evelyn told him, at a time when a woman's virtue was considered a matter of honor. Evelyn's detailed account was eagerly lapped up by the press. She related how she initially refused Thaw's offer of marriage because she had been "ruined by White,"[29] but did not mention anything about the sadistic whippings that had led her to refuse his proposal after their first trip to Europe. She also described the room with mirrors and the red swing where White had seduced her, telling the court that this was what she had told Thaw when he first asked to marry her. She further claimed that the affidavit she had once signed about Thaw's sadism was false, that she had been coerced into signing it and didn't know what was in the document.[30] In short, with the support of Harry's mother's money, Evelyn was now doing everything she could, even lying on the stand, to support Harry, and paint White, the victim, as the real villain.

District Attorney William Travers Jerome sought to counter this novel theory with several doctors who testified that Thaw was quite sane and pointed up the long time between Evelyn's confession of her seduction to Thaw and the crime. Jerome further got a sanity commission to find that Thaw was sane. But even if this theory might not provide legal grounds for claiming insanity, the prosecution's arguments proved no match to Delmas's powerful emotional summation, which lasted several days. It emphasized Thaw's state of mind when he heard of Evelyn's seduction and concluded with these powerful comments.

> What was the condition of his mind . . . when he saw the form, the hideous form of the man who had caused so much suffering to him and his wife . . .
>
> He struck as a tigress strikes to protect her young. He struck for the purity of the American home. He struck—and who shall say that if he believed on that occasion he was an instrument of God and an agent of Providence, he was in error.[31]

And in the end, Thaw's lawyers convinced enough jurors—five of them—to vote for an acquittal, resulting in a hung jury.[32]

But the prosecution's determination resulted in a second trial, which began on January 6, 1908. Again Mary Thaw's money bought Thaw the best defense, though this time, the lead lawyer was Martin W. Littleton. He also pressed for an insanity defense, but he sought to show that Harry was insane not only in committing the act but also before and that he suffered from a hereditary deficiency that predisposed him to this problem. And this time, after a trial that recapitulated much of the same testimony as in the first trial, including Evelyn's sad tale of seduction to Harry, the jury found him "not guilty on the ground of insanity at the time of the crime."[33]

However, rather than releasing Harry as he and his lawyers

and family expected, the judge committed him to go immediately to the New York State Asylum for the Criminally Insane at Matteawan, where he stayed for the next seven years. But again his mother came to his rescue, spending over $1 million over the next six years to get him adjudged sane so he would be released.[34] Among other things, she paid a team of attorneys and medical experts to argue for his sanity.[35]

In the meantime, Thaw's money and status bought him a fairly comfortable existence at Matteawan, much as it had at the Tombs. Unlike other prisoners who were committed to this facility, he was free to move about the grounds and even go outside the walls, and he was seen from time to time with Evelyn at some of the nearby clubs.[36] Sometimes, too, according to Evelyn, she bribed some asylum guards to let her spend the night in Harry's room, which is why she claimed that Harry was the father of the child she had while he was still in Mattewan and she was continuing to work the vaudeville circuit.[37] But was it really Harry's child? Both Harry and his ever-supportive mother denied it.

Meanwhile, with the continuing support of Harry's mother, Harry's lawyers continued to seek his release, filing numerous habeas corpus motions to show that Harry was not insane. Each time, Evelyn, as the loyal wife, would troop to the stand to tell her story at the court hearings to determine his sanity, though all the motions were turned down.[38]

Finally, after the sixth or seventh hearing, frustrated by the process, Harry escaped with the help of some abductors, presumably arranged through his mother, and fled to Canada. There, again, funded by his mother's money, a team of lawyers presented their case for his sanity to a court commission, and at last, in 1915, he was found sane, though the immigration authorities soon sent him packing back to America as an "undesirable alien."[39] Once back in the United States, after another brief legal skirmish to show that because he was a sane man he had a right to escape from the asylum, he finally was adjudged sane. After that, he quickly divorced Evelyn.[40] His mother had never liked her, so presumably, now that Harry was free and Evelyn's support as the loyal wife was no longer needed, his mother felt free to push Evelyn out of the picture.

Over the next few years, as Harry got into still more scrapes, his mother continued to be there with her money to bail him out. For example, in 1916, he was charged with beating a 19-year-old boy, Frederick A. Gump Jr. in a New York hotel, though charges were dropped when he paid off the Gump family with his mother's help. Soon after, though, there were other scrapes, and Harry was returned to Matteawan. But again he was released in 1922, and over the next few years, his mother continued to pay off the women and boys that he whipped to satisfy his sadistic desires.

In 1926, he had a brief reunion in Chicago with Evelyn, who was then singing in a small cabaret, and he saw her again in Atlantic City, where she was working in a nightclub. Evelyn was sufficiently encouraged by this last meeting that she told the press that they were going to remarry, and that Harry would now take care of their son, Russell.[41] But that was not to be. Harry soon went back to his playboy ways and never saw Evelyn again. Meanwhile, Evelyn continued on the nightclub circuit with her fading beauty, her glamour long gone.

As a postscript, Harry died of a heart attack in Miami in 1947 when he was 76. He never had to work at anything and was able to continue to live a wastrel's life because he always had the money from his mother and, after her death, he had his inheritance to rely on. As for Evelyn, after struggling in cabarets in Atlantic City during Prohibition, she took some small stage and film parts, but went on a downhill slide due to drugs and alcohol. Eventually, she retired to Southern California, where she painted seascapes, and died at 82 in 1967 in a Hollywood nursing home.[42]

A Slap on the Wrist: The Case of Susan Cummings (Faquier County, Virginia, 1997–1998)

Susan Cummings seemed an unlikely killer. Before she shot her former lover, polo player Roberto Villegas, Susan Cummings had always led a charmed, protected life. She and her fraternal twin sister, Diana, were the daughters of Sam Cummings, the international gun dealer who owned Interarms, the largest private arms company in the world, with gross annual sales of $100 million.[43] Susan and Diana spent their childhood in Monte Carlo, where their father moved soon after the twins were born to shelter profits from his multimillion-dollar company.[44] There they lived in luxury. They swam at a private beach, learned French as well as English, spent summers in a chalet in a Swiss mountain village, took riding lessons, and went to prestigious private schools.[45] Their father had little time for them because he was often traveling or worked in his private home office, but he taught them to shoot when they were five—a skill Susan later used in killing Roberto. As they grew up, Susan was more reserved, more retiring, and more comfortable around animals than people, unlike the outgoing, socially adept Diana. In high school, she was very much the tomboy; she wore no makeup or dresses and had trouble attracting a boyfriend.[46]

In the late 1970s, both Susan and Diana came to the United States when their father sent them to the all-girl Mount Vernon College. Soon after they graduated in 1984, he bought them a large 350-acre, million-dollar estate called Ashland Farms, with a large tract of surrounding woodlands. Whereas Susan moved into the big mansion, Diana moved into a smaller guest house a few minutes' walk down a path from the main house.[47] The setting was ideal for Susan because of her love of animals, and along with her sister, she spent her days involved in farming activities, including taking care of a stable of horses, several cows, and two dozen stray cats. From time to time, Susan sometimes attended the dinners and social events that were part of the Virginia horse culture, though her sister Diana, who loved socializing, went far more frequently.[48]

Then, in June 1995, Susan signed up to take polo classes at the Willow Run Polo School and took additional classes with Jean Marie Turon, a polo instructor from Argentina.[49] That June, when Jean Marie took some of his students to the Great Meadow polo arena to watch the professionals play in order to learn more about the game, she met Roberto Villegas, a friend of Jean Marie's.[50] Susan spoke to him briefly, and over the next few weeks, she ran into him at local polo events and barbecues.[51] Roberto found Susan attractive and liked her sincere interest in horses, and soon these meetings blossomed into a relationship. However, because Jean Marie was upset by some of the things Susan had done, such as underpaying him for the cost of her lessons despite her great wealth, he warned Roberto not to get involved with her.[52] But Roberto was strongly drawn to Susan and ignored Jean Marie's advice. At the time, Roberto was especially open to a new relationship because a four-year relationship with a girlfriend had recently ended over his transient polo player lifestyle. So he now wanted someone who shared his interest in polo.[53]

In turn, Susan was attracted by Roberto's good looks and star quality on the polo circuit. As Lisa Pulitzer describes in *A Woman Scorned*, her book about the affair and murder, Roberto was one of many polo players from poor backgrounds who came to the United States from Argentina seeking a better living. Once he arrived in Florida in 1991, a popular recruiting ground for polo players from Argentina, he found regular work, playing on the teams of the wealthy landowners who hired professional players and provided them with horses and accommodations.[54] Then, he gained some recognition when he competed in the United States Polo Association (USPA) tournament in Kentucky. Not only did his team win the prestigious President's Cup, but also Roberto was honored as the "Most Valuable Player" and his horse was recognized as the "Most Valuable Horse."[55] This recognition led to an invitation to participate on one of the teams in the newly established sport of arena polo in Fauquier County, Virginia—the Heart and Hand Team owned by Travis and Suzanne Worsham. Soon he was invited to the social functions hosted by the wealthy elite, who owned teams or attended the polo functions, and he became a "local celebrity."[56] No wonder Susan was impressed.

At the same time, his decision to join this elite team contributed to his breakup with his girlfriend, Kelli Quinn, and a fight over her decision to leave because she didn't want to keep traveling between Florida and Virginia. As a result of this fight, a report was filed with the police;[57] Later, Susan was able to use it in her trial for killing Roberto to support her claim that she had acted in self-defense because of his fiery temper.

But that was later. At first, Susan and Roberto's relationship flowered, unlike many of the short-lived flings between the wealthy women in the polo set and the polo pros. By late September 1995, they began going on dinner and movie dates, and Roberto's pro status and friendly, confident manner helped him get invitations to the social events put on by the wealthy and powerful in polo country.[58] Even though Susan was the one with social status, it was Roberto who helped her feel more comfortable in her own social world. During the winter, when he left to play polo for a wealthy team sponsor in Florida, she visited him there, and they kept in touch by phone and writing until he returned in April to Virginia for the 1996 polo season to work for the Cotswold Farm polo team. By now, Roberto had become the owner of seven horses, and he found a nearby farm to stable and graze them.[59]

Unfortunately, his relationship with Susan helped to undermine the very thing that attracted her to him—his success in polo. Their relationship caused him to lose his competitive drive and focus on being the best on the circuit. As a result, instead of going back to Florida in October for the 1996 winter polo season, Roberto stayed in Virginia to be with Susan. And instead of working out to keep up his skills and competing, he volunteered to help her with the many farm tasks at Ashland and at the nearby 800-acre estate she and her sister owned. Susan was delighted to have his help because, unlike most horse-farm owners who hire a full-time staff and despite her wealth, she was extremely frugal and only occasionally hired daily workers to help on the farm. However, his assistance set the stage for conflict, as it turned Roberto into a kind of unpaid menial laborer on her farm. Not only wasn't he paid for his long hours of hard physical labor, such as picking apples, clearing land, mowing grass, fixing fences, and gathering hay to feed the horses, but also he stayed in a small room, much like a migrant worker.[60] As a result, he had little time to practice playing polo. Another problem was that he had different ideas about how to treat the horses and was soon arguing with Susan about this. Whereas Roberto believed the horses needed regular strenuous workouts to remain in good competitive form, Susan felt they should be treated more gently and kindly, more like pets.[61]

Yet, despite Roberto's growing frustration, he went along with Susan's demands, and even moved his horses, some worth over $20,000 each, to Ashland, where Susan allowed him to board them and use them for competitions without the expense of feeding them or providing them with shoes and medicine.[62] One reason he did so was to help his own financial situation, since he was not earning his usual $4,000 a month as a professional polo player, but the deal gave Susan more control over his life and career—another factor that contributed to the growing conflict between them.[63]

An even worse decision came in late October, when Roberto suggested that Susan create her own team and that he would play on it. The result was that instead of paying Roberto his usual compensation, which would have netted him about $20,000, plus housing and board and care for his ponies, Susan paid only for his apartment and meals, clothing, care of his horses, team equipment, and the salary of a third player he recommended, Jean Marie. At the time of his murder, he was living in a $400 per month room with a private bath near Ashland—in a colonial ranch house owned by Virginia Kuhn, who lived in a smaller room across the hall—and once a month, Susan visited him there, as well as paid the rent. It was an odd relationship for a man from a South American culture, where the man is expected to be the head of household and provider. But Susan's wealth and position had turned him into a kind of paid servant rather than a true partner on the polo team, though Roberto was still too smitten with Susan to see this.[64]

Yet, the affair continued, even as tension mounted over the care and exercising of the ponies, and Roberto became increasingly dependent on Susan because he had no other source of income. At the same time, his performance in polo declined; he wasn't playing as well as usual and he felt the horses weren't getting enough exercise.[65]

Then, when Susan went to visit her parents in Monaco in July, after her father fell ill, Roberto had a chance to return to his old self and perhaps assess the relationship. As a result, according to Lisa Pulitzer, his friends noticed he was more relaxed, and he went out with several women while Susan was gone.[66]

By the end of July or mid-August, soon after Susan returned, her relationship with Roberto was increasingly in trouble. Close friends observed that they seemed more distant. And Susan told one friend, Jane Rowe, about her trouble with Roberto and her fears about what he might do. But was she really afraid? Or was this account part of a setup to prepare her defense for getting rid of Roberto, as the prosecution later claimed?

Then, one day in early September, a woman identifying herself as Jane Rowe called the Fauquier County Sheriff's Office on Susan's behalf, saying that Susan wanted to meet with an investigator about obtaining an order of protection against Roberto.[67] Why didn't Susan call herself, and was this call another part of this plan to set up a defense? It seemed suspicious because Susan never did follow through on getting the order of protection. Then, too, after she called and before the first meeting with an investigator, Susan drove to Pittsburgh with Roberto to go to a charity match, as if nothing were wrong with the relationship. As she drove the truck with the trailer with the polo ponies, Roberto sat beside her, letting her drive as usual[68]—another indication that Susan was still in control in the relationship, rather than needing an order of protection to protect her.

Trouble mounted on their return, however. Though Roberto was looking forward to playing for Argentina in "The Taste of Argentina" polo match the next day, Susan objected to him playing, claiming that the horses needed rest after their long trip to Pennsylvania and their workout in the competition there. Later that night, when he returned home, Roberto even told his landlady, Virginia Kuhn, about Susan's objections. Nevertheless, on Sunday morning, he got up and left for Ashland shortly before 8 a.m., ready to play.[69] Was he going there to insist on participating even after Susan turned him down the night before? Was that possibly the trigger for murder?

Whatever the cause, Roberto was killed an hour later in Susan's kitchen, and the case against Susan Cummings became local and then international news. A few minutes before 9 a.m., the sheriff's office got a call on their emergency line from Susan, reporting the shooting. "I need to report a . . . shot man and he's dead," she said and gave the Ashland Farms address at 8714 Holtzclaw Road.[70] Susan also mentioned that about a week before she had spoken to Sergeant Healy about

Roberto Villegas and said that Villegas had tried to kill her. But when the dispatcher asked, "Did you shoot him?" she said she needed to talk to her lawyer. After the dispatcher got some additional details about who she was speaking to, where the man was (on the floor of the second kitchen), and where the gun was (on the floor), she dispatched one of the deputies, Sergeant Cuno Anderson, to go to the house. She asked Susan to come to the front door to meet him.[71]

By the time Anderson arrived a few minutes later, Susan's sister Diana had joined her and stood behind her as she opened the door. Anderson saw blood dripping from some slashes on Susan's arm, but when he asked what happened she remained silent, not wanting to say anything until she spoke to her lawyer. He then asked her to turn around and handcuffed her. When he asked to see where the victim was, she led him through a maze of rooms in the main house to the small kitchen in the rear. In a narrow hallway by a pantry, he found a semi-automatic pistol on the floor and nearby two empty shell casings. As he walked down a few steps into a sunken kitchen, he saw Roberto's body lying in a pool of dark red blood, his legs outstretched like he had fallen forward after being shot. Anderson also noticed two bullet holes in the back of Roberto's red polo shirt, where the bullets had entered. And nearby was a small table with breakfast plates and a bag of pastries. There was no sign of a struggle; everything looked perfectly in order.[72]

Meanwhile, several other deputies arrived, and soon after, so did an ambulance with an emergency medical team. As part of crime scene investigation, one of the officers, Shawn Walters, took photos of the victim, the weapon on the floor, and the nearby shell casings.[73] The driver of the ambulance, Warrenton Rescue Chief William Grimsley Jr., also drew a sketch of the crime scene at the request of Sergeant Anderson, and a few days later, for reasons that are unclear, he drew an even more detailed drawing, which would become a matter of controversy at the trial because it differed from the pictures the sheriff's deputies took. Which was correct? Later, Susan's lawyers used the discrepancy to claim that the police had altered the evidence.[74]

Over the next few hours, the police continued to examine

the crime scene, took photos, obtained statements from Diana, and looked for nearby witnesses who might have heard something. They also took the sneakers Susan had been wearing when she first met the police at the door, since she changed her shoes to go to the station to be booked after her arrest. Around noon, once the officers had a search warrant, they carefully searched the interior of the house. Meanwhile, other officers arrested Susan and took her to the sheriff's office, where her lawyer, Blair Howard, who had briefly stopped by the house, waited for her.[75]

The next day at the bond hearing to permit bail, Howard presented the defense version of what happened. As he described it, recently the couple had ended their relationship, and Susan had met with an investigator at the Fauquier County sheriff's office, Sergeant Healy, because she was afraid that Roberto would hurt her. In fact, the day of the murder was the day she had arranged to meet again with investigators to seek a restraining order against Roberto. Howard also pointed out that Susan had scratches on her left arm and right cheek due to a confrontation with Roberto, and she killed him in self-defense, though he didn't explain how the confrontation began or how Susan was injured.[76] Howard further described Susan as someone who loved animals, and he called on two neighbors who were business associates of Susan and her sister to show that she was a responsible member of the community. One businessman, who rented 200 acres, described Susan as a "gentle and kind" woman who "loved animals"; the other, an owner of an excavating business, described her in similar terms.[77] These were both highly successful members of the business community, who Susan had come to know due to her position of wealth and status in the community as the owner of Ashland Farms.

In turn, these personal endorsements contributed to the low amount of her bond, which was unusual in a murder case and would be less likely in a case against someone without such a position and connections. At the end of a thirty-minute hearing, Judge Charles Foley released Susan on a $75,000 bond, and required her to give up her passport and firearms and remain in Virginia except for important business matters. The outcome might have been quite different had Roberto been the one who was accused. As some of his friends complained, Roberto might not have gotten bail at all.[78] As Lisa Pulitzer notes in *A Woman Scorned* of this seeming disparity:

> The judge's decision was met with mixed reaction. The friends of the heiress rejoiced at the news, believing that his decision to allow her to return to Ashland Farm was just.
>
> Yet, members of the polo set were deeply mournful of Roberto's passing and were outraged at the court's apparent disregard of their friend's unexpected and violent death.
>
> In light of the charges pending again her, many area residents were surprised at the modest figure the judge had chosen to set for bond.
>
> "If the tables were turned and it was the other way around, Roberto would be in jail now and there would be no bail," one irate polo player huffed under his breath.[79]

Susan's position also contributed to the sympathy she received from other members of the elite horse owner's community and in the press's relatively gentle treatment of her. There seemed to be a bias to want to believe her side of the story—that she had shot him out of fear in self-defense—the story that Howard told the press after the hearing: "I think she was scared to death. . . . She was frightened for her life. I think she did the only move when she was cornered that was available and tried to protect her life. We absolutely deny any suggestions that she murdered this man."[80]

Later, the explanation Howard would present in court was that Susan had gone downstairs, found Roberto in the kitchen with the croissants, and told him he had to leave, as she had requested he do the day before. But Roberto claimed he had to get ready for the game he planned to play in Maryland, whereupon Susan told him he could go, but couldn't take her horses. And that's when, as Howard asserted, Roberto became angry, pulled out a knife, and pressed it against her cheeks. Then, he slashed her arms, telling her that no woman would tell him what to do, and he would teach her a lesson. In response, she told him he could use the horses, but she still felt afraid. So she got the pistol from the kitchen cabinet, feeling that would help her control the situation. But, moments later, when she saw Roberto look at her angrily and start to rise from his chair to come toward her, she fired, feeling she was cornered in the small kitchen and couldn't run out without coming close to him. Then, she ran out of the kitchen, threw the gun on the floor, and called 911.[81]

Her self-defense scenario sounded plausible. But was that really the case? The police and prosecutors were coming up with a very different scenario based on the evidence they found at the scene. In their view, there had been no struggle, since everything looked in perfect order. Moreover, the position of the wounds on Roberto's body indicated that they had been fired from above. It also appeared that he had been sitting down and had toppled over after being shot from behind—not rising to come toward Susan, as she claimed. The police and prosecutors also believed the wounds on Susan's arms were self-inflicted because they appeared to be slashed in a straight pattern and were only surface wounds; if the wounds had been inflicted in a struggle, they would have been more jagged and deeper. The investigators also noted that the photos first taken of Susan for her mug shots showed no scratches or cuts on her face, suggesting those may have been added later.

Moreover, the police and prosecutors believed that Susan had been planning the murder some weeks before the killing and therefore planted stories about how she felt frightened by him. They felt even the call to the investigator to seek a restraining order was a ploy, as she hadn't followed through to obtain one. They also doubted her claim that Roberto was angered because she wouldn't give him the ponies, because the previous week, according to Roberto's friend, Jean Marie Turon, Roberto had asked to borrow several horses to participate in the "Taste of Argentina" competition.[82] So if he had already made arrangements to get other horses, why would his desire to participate in the competition be the basis of a fight, as Susan claimed? He had no need for her horses. Additionally, the investigators found that many of Roberto's friends said that he had told them he wanted to end the relationship; however, some others said that Roberto and Susan were considering going to Montana to buy land on which they could retire there in the future.[83]

Whatever the truth of who was seeking to end the relationship as it became increasingly rocky, Susan's friends seemed to have greater influence in gaining the media's attention to present Susan's side of the story—perhaps in part due to Susan's and their own high status. As a result, as described by Lisa Pulitzer:

> In the coming weeks, articles about the murder appeared in *The New York Times, The Washington Post, People*, and the tabloid magazine *Star*. In the stories, friends of the heiress defended her actions.[84]

Thus, with a little—or maybe a lot of—help from her friends, as well as her articulate lawyer, the spin in the popular media largely supported Susan's actions. She, rather than Roberto, the victim, was the one who was presented in a sympathetic light, and her high status, family, and friends helped to bolster this point of view—much like Lizzie Borden, featured in Chapter 7, had supporters rallying around her. Like Lizzie, Susan was presented as a meek, mild, shy, retiring, gentle person, and in this case, her love of animals helped to reinforce this image, making it seem that she couldn't possibly have done it. "Just look at her," was the charge of Lizzie's lawyer, and Susan's lawyer and supporters took much the same tack.

The defense also used the preliminary hearing as a means of getting out its message to the press and public, although it is unusual for the defense to present a case at that stage. Normally, the defense just listens to the prosecution's case against the accused, which is presented to show sufficient grounds to go to trial. But instead, Howard outlined the self-defense case he planned to present. Why? Because, the prosecution believed, he was doing so to "feed his story to the press,"[85] perhaps for the same reason the defense played to the press and public in the Lizzie Borden case—to create a broad support that might influence the jury, though in theory, the jury is supposed to be completely unbiased.

Another advantage of Susan's status and family connections is that they helped her lawyer, Blair Howard, get her bond modified by a motion to the judge, which enabled her to leave the country to travel to Monaco to visit her very ill father.[86] Normally, a defendant facing murder charges couldn't get a passport back to leave the country, and prosecutor Kevin Casey argued that Susan's departure posed a flight risk given the murder charges against her. Besides, he argued, why couldn't Susan simply talk to her father on the phone. But Howard argued persuasively that Susan and her sister could put up their $2.3 million farm as collateral to assure her return, and the judge agreed.

When the trial finally began six months later on May 6, 1998, the prosecution sought to argue the evidence, showing that Susan had shot Roberto four times while he was having breakfast at the kitchen table.[87] To support this theory, Casey brought in the medical examiner to testify that all four bullets had traveled downward and to the left as they hit Roberto's face and upper body and that Roberto had been seated rather than getting up to attack as Susan claimed.[88] Casey also brought in forensic pathologist Jack Daniel, who reviewed the photos of the wounds to Susan's arm and testified that the twelve to fourteen scratches were superficial, of similar length and depth, and typical of a self-inflicted wound.[89] Still another expert witness was state forensic scientist, Karolyn Tontarski, who testified that only a small amount of blood was found at the tip of Roberto's knife and nowhere else on the knife, which was inconsistent with the defense claim that he had slashed her over a dozen times.[90] Plus, there was no blood on his jeans, as there would have been if he had been standing. The prosecution even used a life-sized foam mannequin to show how Roberto had been seated at the table when shot from above.[91]

Yet, while the prosecution argued the scientific and medical evidence, the defense focused on Susan's story about how she feared Roberto and called on a string of friends and associates from the tony horse culture to show that Susan was a gentle, loving person, or to testify that Roberto had a violent temper and had "threatened and belittled her in public as their two-year romance soured" the previous summer.[92]

Though defendants often don't testify, Susan did, describing her desperate plight in an effort to gain the sympathy of the jurors. Susan described how Roberto was at first very nice and polite to her and was always smiling and attentive. But then she began to see his abusive side.[93] One time he got angry when she asked him not to use a hole puncher to punch holes in a saddle. He told her that no woman was ever going to tell him what to do and kicked her in the crotch. She additionally described his threats if she tried to leave him.

Finally she concluded with her story of how she feared for her life and shot Roberto that Sunday morning. She explained that she was "certain her polo player lover meant to kill her after he grabbed her by the throat and pressed a knife against her cheeks."[94] Then, after Roberto refused to leave her house, mocked her, and slashed her arm, she grabbed a pistol. Then, as he rose from a kitchen chair, she believed he was going to attack her, so she fired, shooting him four times. As she told the jury, "I acted in a moment of desperation, and it happened very quickly. Here was a man who I knew had a very violent temper who had threatened to kill me."[95] In fact, two weeks earlier, she had complained to the police of his death threats, stating that he told her he wanted to marry her and have children, and when she said she didn't want to do this, he said he would kill her.

As she went into more detail, she expressed herself very calmly, clearly, and articulately, using words to emphasize her fear, explaining that: "I was very fearful. . . . My heart was beating. I felt my blood rushing down. I felt extremely scared. I felt that my life was in danger. . . . I thought to myself . . . this man is going to kill me."

So why didn't she run? Because, she explained, she felt cornered in the small galley outside the kitchen, and even if she got out of the kitchen, she knew she would have to get through a maze of rooms before she could run out of the house and she was afraid she wouldn't make it. And so, as she came to the end of her testimony, she stated: "I started shooting and I don't know at what point I stopped. I acted in a moment of desperation. I never intended for Roberto to get shot. . . . I needed to get this man out of my life."[96]

Her testimony was followed by that of four character witnesses—a neighbor, a biology professor, a woman who boarded her horse at Ashland, and a veterinarian—who testified to her good, reputable character and her important role in the community. They variously described her reputation for honesty, her calm, gentle nature, her good reputation, and her love of animals.[97]

After that came a parade of witnesses who described Roberto's angry temper and who either had run-ins with him or observed him having arguments with Susan. For instance, one restaurant owner described how she witnessed a fight between Susan and Roberto in the parking lot of the restaurant, which ended with Roberto hitting her or throwing something at her before he drove off in his truck.[98] And one of Susan's friends, Elsa Acosta, who also owned horses, described how Susan and Roberto had an intense argument a few days before the murder and how at one point Roberto put a horse lead rope around Susan's neck, exclaiming "I'll kill her."[99] Although non-wealthy people can certainly find character witnesses to testify on their behalf, what was different here is that these friends and associates were for the most part wealthy business owners or part of the close-knit elite horse community, such as managers of the tony farms and restaurants.

In the end, as the prosecution and defense closing arguments made clear, the jury was left with two vastly different pictures of what happened that day. The prosecution had presented a clear case of premeditation based on the evidence from the scene of the crime—a man shot four times while eating breakfast at the kitchen table; and blood and photo evidence showing that Susan had carefully cut herself after his death to make it appear as if she had been in a struggle with him. Even the blood on her shoes indicated that she had walked close to the body in order to put the knife in Roberto's hands to make it look like he attacked her. Moreover, the lack of blood on his knife blade and just a small bit on the tip undermined her claim that he had attacked and slashed her with the knife. Plus, she had almost no blood on the sweatshirt she had worn that day, though she claimed she had gotten all those slashes on her arm from Roberto. Also, Roberto's lack of any motivation to attack—established by one of Casey's last rebuttal witnesses who stated that Roberto had no reason to fly into a rage because he had already arranged to borrow horses from Jean Marie Turon—didn't fit the crime either.

By contrast, the defense version ignored this evidence and chose to focus on Susan as a victim, using her testimony and the testimony of her character witnesses to show that she was a good person, whereas Roberto was a bad person with a bad temper who led Susan to fear for her life.[100]

In the end, Susan came close to being acquitted by the jurors who sympathized with Susan's plight and the poor treatment she claimed she received from Roberto, most of whom were female. Yet, questions about how she had received her wounds raised doubts about her claim of self-defense. Thus, the jury ultimately did decide to find her guilty—but not of premeditated murder, only for voluntary manslaughter, usually the charge for crimes of passion. Plus, the jury, which had the final say in how long she would spend in prison, gave her an extremely light sentence.

A major reason for the light sentence is the influence of Susan's family and position. Susan's sister and mother both appeared before the jury giving their pleas for leniency. First her sister described how she and Susan had shared a very close relationship, doing everything together, from sharing a business to living together. Then, her mother described their "wonderful relationship" in which Susan was always "very kind and nice and polite" to her parents, and she noted how much she loved animals.[101] Finally, to build on these supportive comments, Howard concluded with his own plea for leniency, emphasizing Susan's position in the community, equating the killing of Roberto with a mere mistake. As he put it: "She made a mistake. . . . That doesn't make her a bad person. That doesn't mean she's a person who should be removed from society."[102] While a non-wealthy defendant might also bring in friends and family members to attest to his or her good character, the difference here is the powerful influence of high-status family members, friends, and associates.

The jury's especially light verdict after finding her guilty of voluntary manslaughter, not murder, came on May 13, 1998, after eight and a half hours of deliberation over two days.[103] The sentence of only sixty days in the county jail and a fine of just $2,500 sent shock waves through the media and the public because it was such a lenient sentence given the crime of killing another person.[104] As one Internet commentator wrote:

> This would be the first known case in which the perp admitted killing the victim, was found guilty, and STILL got away with it. . . . It seems like an open and shut case . . . a guilty verdict for voluntary manslaughter . . . a sentence of 60 days in the county jail, and a fine of $2,500. So that's what a human life is worth. . . . It's a wrist slap guilty verdict.[105]

But Susan's confinement didn't last even for sixty days. With time off for good behavior, she served only fifty-one days, and those days were in relative luxury, courtesy of the county sheriff's discretion. Not only was Susan placed by herself in a single twenty-foot-by-eighteen-foot cell designed to hold six women, but also she was given her own private phone in the room. Moreover, whereas regular prisoners were restricted to thirty minutes of visiting time on weekends for up to three visitors, Susan initially was allowed far longer visits at any time, and her mother and twin sister visited her for several hours a day. Whereas regular prisoners could only eat jailhouse food, Susan was allowed to receive a sandwich and cookies, which her mother and sister brought to her.[106] And even before she began her jail time, the judge gave her a special privilege of waiting for several days so she could attend a memorial service for her father in Washington, D.C., whereas other prisoners are normally whisked off to jail right away.[107] Even Susan's lawyer, Blair Howard, was amazed by the light sentence, calling the result "unbelievable," as was the prosecutor, who pointed out that "Normally there would be a much more serious price to pay. . . . You could get five years in Virginia for killing a horse."[108]

The story of this special treatment soon made national headlines, after the *Washington Post* broke the story, describing Susan's "dorm-style room" with a telephone and relaxed visiting privileges.[109] In defense, Sheriff Joseph Higgs, who was in charge of the jail, explained that he had given Cummings her own cell because the other inmates caused "some unrest" on learning about her sixty-day sentence, when they got much stiffer sentences for lesser crimes.[110] So he feared they might harm her and moved her for safety reasons, and he sought to justify the special visiting privileges by claiming that Susan needed these to "take care of some paperwork" due to her father's death.[111] But given the press and public outcry, he soon stopped the special "royal treatment" that Susan was getting.

Still, after fifty-one days, she was out and able to return to Ashland and her life of wealth and raising thoroughbreds. Though many members of the polo circuit were "outraged and saddened" by the verdict and would not welcome her back, according to polo team owner Richard Varge,[112] Susan had gotten an extremely soft kid-gloves treatment due to her status and family connections, which contributed to the press, public, her jurors, and jailers seeing her in a sympathetic light.

It's a favorable bias that seemed to follow her at all stages of the criminal justice process and has been commented on by a number of observers of her trial. For example, in his TV series *Power, Privilege, and Justice*, which aired "A Scandal in Hunt Country" about the case, Dominick Dunne, a noted observer of the scandals and crimes of the rich and prominent, suggests that her trial reflected a "clash between hard evidence and social class."[113] And Paul Wright, editor of the *Prison Legal News* noted the very short sentence Cummings received (sixty days) for manslaughter compared to the sentences of other, less-fortunate offenders in the same jurisdiction: a man convicted of killing a cow was sentenced to nine months in jail, a woman convicted of shoplifting a back scratcher received 135 days, a car thief got five years, a purse snatcher got fifteen months, and a man who fired a gun into an empty house was sentenced to two years. Further, Cummings served only fifty-one days, and the other inmates housed at her jail were moved to other facilities during her stay so that she could have the women's section of the jail to herself. Guards noted that she received better treatment than any other prisoner they had ever seen, as she was afforded unlimited visits with family and friends, restaurant meals, and other privileges. Wright goes on in his *Washington Free Press* article to lament the impact of Susan's social class on the verdict and her privileged treatment in jail, noting that the criminal justice system generally gives the wealthy better treatment:

> The unspoken reality is that in America today there exist two systems of criminal justice. One is for the wealthy, which includes kid-glove investigations, lackluster prosecutions, drug treatment, light sentences and easy, if any, prison time. The other, for the poor, is one of paramilitary policing, aggressive prosecution, harsh mandatory sentences, and hard time. Wealth, and the political connections inherent to wealth, is the determining factor in deciding which system one gets. . . .
>
> Wealthy defendants frequently come from the same social strata and share friends and acquaintances with prosecutors. State prosecutors are all elected officials and as such they rely on campaign donations to get elected. The same goes for judges in most states. . . .[114]

In short, the Cummings case helps to support the prevailing perception that justice is blind when it comes to social class, position, and wealth. And the support one gains from one's family and friends—whether in the form of money and valuable gifts or connections with highly placed member of the community—help to tip the odds in one's favor at all phases of the criminal justice process, from arrest to trial to sentencing to serving time in jail.

CHAPTER 6

The Power of the Police, Press, Personality, and Politics

Sometimes the rich and powerful gain a big advantage by their high-status position, personal charisma, or political connections. These qualities and connections, in turn, can contribute to a positive bias in the press, a deference by the police, and a strong influence on the jury, who may be swayed by the press coverage (even though they are not supposed to be) or by the person's position. As a result, it becomes harder for jurors to think the person committed the murder, even in the face of compelling evidence, making an acquittal or mistrial more likely. Then, too, deference from the police investigating the case, as well as interference from the press covering a high-profile murder case, can undermine the early stages of the investigation.

For example, a large press turnout can disturb the crime scene, causing the loss of important evidence. Also, the police may treat a wealthy, powerful suspect with kid gloves, resulting in an inadequate interrogation in the beginning of the investigation in which the police don't ask the usually hard, in-depth questions. They don't probe for contradictions or follow up on responses that raise suspicions. Afterward, they may soon lose their opportunity to probe more deeply, often because the wealthy person quickly becomes lawyered up and protected by family members, friends, and other powerful community connections.

These various factors often lead to extended delays in the case, too. Sometimes delays occur because after an initially botched crime scene investigation, the police have to play catch-up to do interviews or search for crime scene evidence that was originally overlooked. Another reason for delay is that the police and prosecution know they will be under the microscope in high-profile cases because of the involvement of the press and high public interest. They also expect to be up against more powerful top attorneys. Therefore, they want to gather as much evidence as possible and they more carefully follow the book so that they build a stronger case and are less apt to lose motions to exclude evidence. Still another reason for delay in some cases is that the suspect has the funds and family support to leave the state or country, thus making pursuit of the case more difficult because the prosecution needs sufficient grounds to extradite and get the suspect back. Witness the twenty-five-year delay in bringing the Michael Skakel case in this chapter to trial.

Additionally, to recap some ideas presented in an earlier chapter, money helps the defendant buy attorneys and investigators who can engage in delaying legal tactics. Plus, the personal image of the defendant and his or her powerful family and social contacts contributes to different treatment by the press, police, and courts than that afforded the ordinary defendant.

Nevertheless, deference and legal delays can only go so far to favor the wealthy and prominent defendant; this golden glow can later fade, most notably if there is another charge against the defendant. Although the press and public may be supportive during the first case, if subsequent accusations lead to charges, public opinion and support may decline, such as in the T. Cullen Davis case discussed in this chapter. Likewise, if counterpressures mount, such as when victims or members of the press seek justice, public attitudes can change, and the often slow-to-react criminal justice system may take a renewed interest in a dormant case, as occurred in the Skakel case.

It is very difficult to separate these factors because they interact with each other. The suspect's wealth, position, community reputation, personal charisma and charm, and political connections individually or in combination play a part in influencing the press coverage, police treatment, length of the investigation and trial, and jury consideration of the case. At the same time, the press coverage and police treatment affect both the quality of the evidence obtained and how the jury considers the case. In general, all of these factors interact and combine together to favor the rich and powerful defendant, except for the relatively few cases where the press and public consider the person guilty from the outset, as in the Claus von Bulow case described in Chapter 7. But more generally, there is a propensity to not believe the wealthy person could have done it and give deference to his or her status and connections, as in the Cummings case, described in Chapter 5.

The following cases reflect these multiple themes. In the Cullen Davis case, Davis, one of the wealthiest members of Fort Worth society, was a kind of charming bad boy who was able to repeatedly get away with his antics because of his charm and political connections; however, his ability to charm began to wear thin after repeated criminal and civil legal scrapes. In the Michael Skakel case, powerful connections with the Kennedy family helped to discourage and delay the investigation and prosecution of a murder charge for over two decades, although the dogged persistence of the victim's supporters eventually got the investigation reopened, and Skakel was recently convicted.

Just how did these processes work to interfere with and delay justice? Here's what happened in these two cases.

Like Teflon:
The Case of Cullen Davis
(Fort Worth, Texas, 1976–1979)

Initially, it looked like an open-and-shut case for the prosecution, after a homicide occurred on August 2, 1976, at the mansion then owned by T. Cullen Davis on Mockingbird Lane in Fort Worth, Texas. Three witnesses said they saw Cullen Davis kill two victims and injure two others, including his estranged wife. But the prosecutor hadn't reckoned on Davis's ability to interfere with the investigation, charm the press, and influence the jury, as Davis was one of the richest men in Fort Worth. And later, Davis was able to turn on the charm, when he was accused in an attempted murder case.

The charges of murder and attempted murder against Davis exploded into the news soon after the first call came in to police from 4200 Mockingbird Lane, a 19,000-square-foot mansion that Davis had built at a cost of $6 million.[1] The mansion was a sleek, white, ultra-modern showplace, with twenty rooms on 181 acres, located in the exclusive southwestern side of Fort Worth, near the Colonial Country Club and golf course. Inside were expensive furnishings and equally expensive art and sculptures, which had been acquired by Cullen Davis's wife, Priscilla, a flamboyant platinum blonde who dressed like a vamp. She got to stay in the house after their marriage went hopelessly bad and throughout their continuous court fights.

Davis had met Priscilla in the mid-1960s, while they each were married to other people. Their passionate affair made headlines when Priscilla's then husband, Jack Wilbourn, hired a team of private investigators to break in on the pair. Davis's father had never liked the flashy Priscilla, and in August 1968, a few hours after his father died, Cullen married her.[2] She brought her "flash and trash" style into the marriage, which was a kind of big happy party filled with "drugs, sex, and country music," at the height of the Texas oil boom.[3] However, after a few years, as the boom itself went bust, the party ended and Priscilla filed for divorce in 1974, claiming that Cullen was "mean and abusive" to her. In response, Cullen countered that she was "a wanton adulterer who slept with, among others, a pot-smoking biker."[4] That was the context in which the murders occurred at Cullen's $6 million mansion.

The tragic events of the night of the murder—August 2, 1976—unfolded around 10:30 p.m. Priscilla, who still lived in the mansion, whereas Davis had to move out due to a restraining order issued in their nasty court fight, had gone out to visit friends with her current live-in boyfriend, Stan Farr. She left her teenage daughter Andrea at home, clicked on the security system, and left with Stan to join her good friend Bev Bass and Bev's boyfriend Bubba Gavrel for a night in town.[5] It was a night of celebration in honor of another one of Priscilla's court victories, despite having a pre-nup. The judge had granted her a two-month delay on the grounds that she wasn't emotionally able to face the divorce trial, along with an increase in support payments from $3,500 to $5,000 a month, plus an additional $52,000 to cover the upkeep of the mansion and her attorney's fees.[6]

Meanwhile, as Priscilla and her friends were out celebrating, shortly after 10:30 p.m., a killer dressed in black and wearing a black wig entered the mansion without any force, perhaps because Andrea recognized him and let him in. Once inside, he shot Andrea in the head in the wine cellar and lay in wait for Priscilla and Stan to return.[7]

When they arrived home shortly after midnight, Priscilla found the security system deactivated but didn't show much concern, presuming that either of her daughters, Andrea or Dee, who was staying at the mansion, might have done this. So Priscilla simply went in with Stan. Then, as she went to turn off a light at the top of the stairs to the basement, the man dressed in black suddenly appeared from the direction of the laundry room, said "Hi!" to her, and shot her just below her left breast, as she later told the police. Immediately, Priscilla thought the man was Cullen, and she called to Stan to go back, but it was too late. As Stan approached the door, the man in black fired through it. Stan briefly struggled with him but was fired at several more times, and with a last gasp and gurgle, Stan fell down dead.[8]

Then, as the man in black dragged Stan's body down the hall, Priscilla, who was still alive because the bullet missed her main artery, ran out the back door. But as she crossed the patio, she tripped and fell, and the man in black caught up with her. As he began pulling her back inside the house, still sure it was Cullen, she began pleading with him, telling him: "Cullen, I love you . . . I have never loved anyone else." Moments later, just as the man in black pulled her to the back door, he let her go, perhaps thinking she was too severely injured to survive, so he could finish dragging Stan's body into the basement.[9]

Meanwhile, as Priscilla struggled to get up and began running, Bev Bass and Bubba Gavrel drove up to the house. As they got out of the car, the man in black motioned for Bubba to follow him and led him along the walkway toward the well-lit door to the breakfast room, where Bev suddenly recognized him in the light and called out: "Bubba! That's Cullen." At that moment, Cullen turned around and shot Bubba in the stomach with his last bullet, shattering his spine and paralyzing him.[10] Seeing Bubba fall, Bev began running, afraid the man in black, who she thought was Cullen, would shoot her, too. As she later told the police, she even called back to him several times, "Cullen, please don't shoot me! It's Bev." But the man in black had no more shots left and stopped pursuing her. She ran out to the highway, where she flagged down a passing motorist, Robert Sawhill. He gave her a ride, and about a mile from the mansion, he pulled into a small convenience store, the Mr. M. Food Store, where they encountered a private security guard, A. M. Smedley, and told him what happened. Smedley then radioed his dispatcher to call the police. Shortly after that, Sawhill called the police and asked for an ambulance.[11]

Within a few minutes, two patrol officers, Jimmy Soders and J. A. Perez, arrived at the Food Store. Bev jumped into Soders car, telling him that her boyfriend had been shot and that Cullen Davis did it. Soders and Perez then drove back to the mansion with Bev,[12] but by the time they arrived, the killer had disappeared.[13]

Meanwhile, shortly before Sawhill and Soders placed their calls, Priscilla ran screaming to the door of a neighbor, Clifford Jones, yelling hysterically that she was Priscilla Davis, lived in the big house nearby, and that "Cullen is up there killing my children. He is killing everyone!"[14] So Jones, too, called the police, making the first of several calls that evening that came into police headquarters starting at 12:42 a.m. These were times that would become important later, when Cullen claimed he wasn't there, but fast asleep in bed.

Soon over a dozen officers were at the mansion. They quickly found Andrea's body in the basement, a bloody smear that might be a palm print on the basement door, and Stan's body in the hallway near the kitchen. They also noted that three witnesses encountered the killer—Priscilla, who was shot by him; Bev, who said she had seen Cullen shoot her boyfriend Bubba; and Bubba, who told the police after he emerged from surgery and they showed him a picture of Cullen that the killer was Cullen.

Given that three witnesses identified Cullen as the killer to the police and to others at the scene, including neighbors and medical personnel, this would normally seem to be an open-and-shut case. But Cullen soon used his charm and connections to call into question the identifications made by these eyewitnesses, and he put them on trial in the court of public opinion and the popular press. This "blame the victims and eyewitnesses" strategy, in turn, helped to influence the reaction of Fort Worth society and the jury.

So where was Cullen when the man in black was observed shooting people at the mansion? And could all three witnesses have been mistaken or lying? That's what Cullen and his attorneys sought to show. Cullen soon had an alibi in place, claiming that he was in bed at his girlfriend, Karen Masters's house at 12:40 a.m., so he couldn't be at the shoot-out at the mansion that was reported minutes later. Additionally, he claimed that the witnesses were lying in order to set him up because of his messy divorce battle with Priscilla.

According to Cullen's story, the first he knew of the murders was when his brother Ken called him around 4 a.m. at the home of his girlfriend, Karen Masters, to say he had heard about the murders. In response, Cullen's reaction was calm, cool, and collected. He calmly said he hadn't heard about the killings, and when Ken asked what he was going to do, he replied: "I guess I'll go back to bed."[15]

But Cullen had little time to do that because almost immediately, Officer Ford called to speak to him and told him to get dressed and go outside. When he did so at about 4:30 a.m., the house was surrounded by police cars, and Cullen was arrested. But before the police took him downtown to book him for murder and attempted murder, they asked to see the guns he owned. Cullen then showed them the five guns he kept in his Cadillac and the house, none of which was the murder weapon.[16] After this, they took him to jail and booked him based on what Bev told the police—that Cullen had met her and Bubba in the driveway, shot at both of them, and wounded Bubba. And later, after Priscilla and Bubba emerged from surgery, the police added them as eyewitnesses because they both identified him—Priscilla based on her initial encounter where she was shot, and Bubba after he saw Cullen's photograph, since he didn't know man in black's name.[17]

Yet, despite three identifications making Cullen the only suspect, Cullen soon used his connections, wealth, and reputation to outwit and outplay the prosecution. He was able to do so in spite of some of his statements to the police that made him appear guilty, such when he willingly went to police headquarters for initial questioning. When one detective asked him why so many people had to die at the mansion, he replied with this seeming confession: "Sometimes, a man don't need a reason." But his defense attorney was able to prevent the prosecution from using that statement against him because the police had not yet given him his Miranda warnings.[18]

Cullen was also able to take advantage of the three-week period when he was out on bail, before the prosecutors found a legal reason to charge him with a capital murder rather than the ordinary murder they first charged. The prosecutors were able to do this because Cullen had been barred from the mansion for two years by a restraining order due to the divorce proceedings. As a result, his alleged entry became a burglary because he had no right to be in the house,[19] and a murder committed during a burglary is considered a capital murder.[20]

However, before the prosecution filed the capital murder charge, Cullen used his time out on bail to make arrangements for handling his case, including using his money to buy a well-known, expensive top defense attorney—Richard "Racehorse" Haynes, who got his nickname when playing football in junior high. Among other things, Haynes had been featured in *Time* magazine as one of the top six criminal lawyers in the United States and had gained success in defending another high-profile, wealthy Texas defendant whose case ended in a mistrial.[21] In that case, plastic surgeon John Hill from Houston was accused of killing his wife after giving her poisoned French pastries and letting her die.[22] Haynes joined Phil Burleson, the other attorney Cullen had hired, to lead the defense.

Cullen additionally used his time out on bail to sway public opinion in his favor. Though Tarrant County District Attorney Tim Curry placed Cullen under constant surveillance, hoping Cullen might lead the police to the murder weapon or make a run for it as a sign of guilt, Cullen simply resumed his everyday life. Acting like nothing special had happened, Cullen went to his office every day, usually lunched at the elite Petroleum Club, and returned to his girlfriend Karen's house.[23] Those actions helped to build his public support, despite an initial uproar in the press and from outraged citizens calling in to complain about his very low $80,000 bail for murder,[24] given his huge wealth, even though that figure was twice the usual $40,000 bail in murder cases.[25]

A key reason for this growing support is that most people in Cullen's social set and the surrounding community couldn't believe that he had committed these murders. After all, because he was so rich, why would he kill anyone himself? Many questioned this because the very wealthy very often do hire hit men. Then, too, many people in the Fort Worth area believed that Priscilla had set up Cullen to frame him because of the well-known hostility between them.[26]

Thus, when Cullen's bail was revoked after the district attorney upped the charge to capital murder and he remained in jail for the next year awaiting trial, the defense continued use a PR strategy to gain continued public support and turn around any lingering negative public opinion by attacking the prosecution. To this end, the defense filed a series of motions and publicized these actions. Among other claims, the defense charged that the prosecution misused the secret grand jury process, harassed potential witnesses, illegally seized evidence, and made Cullen a victim of selective prosecution by charging him with burglarizing his own home. Further, they charged that the police hid their discovery of unidentified prints at the crime scene. The result of this pretrial aggressive defense was a series of favorable press headlines, such as "Murder Charge to Be Fought" and "Davis Claimed Not at Scene," which helped shift public opinion in Cullen's favor by the end of 1976.[27]

Meanwhile, he remained in the Tarrant County jail waiting for the trial to begin during these legal and PR efforts, but Cullen's wealth and connections afforded him special treatment in jail, much like in the case of Susan Cummings, described in the previous chapter. With Sheriff Lon Evan's permission, Cullen received hundreds of visits from business associates, and Evan defended these visits on the grounds that Cullen owned eighty-three companies and had to be able to continue his business, such as by signing papers and reviewing blueprints.[28]

Concurrently, Cullen used his local power and prestige to help discredit Priscilla and the other two witnesses in the media and in court by claiming that Priscilla was trying to pin the killing on him to get his money and put him in jail. So the defense strategy was to tarnish Priscilla and argue that Bev and Bubba had conspired with her to frame him. They also claimed that Priscilla's boyfriend Stan, who had been living in the house, was the real target of the killers. Why target him? One theory floated by the defense was that Priscilla wanted to end her relationship with Stan so that she could have a relationship with a young man she had met at a pot party. Another theory was that a drug dealer wanted to kill Stan because of a soured drug deal.[29] Such alternative theories were possible because there was little evidence in the case beside the three eyewitnesses' claims. To Cullen's advantage, the police had no murder weapon, no fingerprints or footprints belonging to Cullen at the crime scene, no bloody clothes, not even another witness who saw Cullen near the house before or after the time of the murder.[30]

The attack on Priscilla was at the core of the defense. One strategy was to present her as a drug abuser or addict and an oversexed, promiscuous woman. For example, the defense obtained an affidavit by David McCrory, then an investigator working for Cullen, in which he claimed he had witnessed Priscilla "buying drugs" and "snorting cocaine and heroin."[31] In addition, McCrory's affidavit accused her of being a "sexpot" who had many boyfriends before and after she filed for divorce. Further, the affidavit intimated that Priscilla may have engaged in group sex and taken her teenage daughter Dee to some parties, where Dee used drugs and participated in sex acts. McCrory additionally claimed that he was aware of "drug trafficking" in the house and thought the killings were "related to some kind of drug deal." He even claimed that Priscilla had warned him from her hospital bed:

> You have to keep your mouth shut. . . . If you keep your mouth shut, you will never have to worry about money for the rest of your life. I'll have at least ten million dollars when this thing is over with. Just remember, say it was Cullen who did it, because you know Cullen had to be behind it.[32]

Though this affidavit was unsigned and was never accepted into evidence, it was one more piece of purported trial evidence that leaked to the press after being carelessly left around, resulting in more pro-defense headlines, such as "Affidavit Indicates Pusher at Mansion" and "Mrs. Davis Allegedly Offered to Buy Silence," that could make their way to the jury. The potential fallout from the leak was bad enough, but making matters worse, the day after the stories hit the papers, McCrory went to the judge's office and told him that the claims in the unsigned affidavit weren't true.[33] His claim supported the possibility that this was a phony affidavit that was placed where it would be seen to further discredit Priscilla with the media and public.

An additional problem at the trial came about because of jury misconduct during the jury selection process. One of the sequestered jurors made several unauthorized phone calls when she was given permission to visit her terminally ill father, and she discussed the case in at least one call.[34]

As a result of these problems with local publicity and jury misconduct, Judge Cave declared a mistrial, and thereafter the case was transferred from Fort Worth to Amarillo, a smaller town in the north of Texas. But even with this change of cities, the atmosphere had already been shifted in favor of the defense because the rumors about Priscilla's involvement with drugs and sex orgies spread there as well, along with accusations of her lying and doing everything she could to get Cullen's money.[35] Cullen also gained a big advantage when the case was moved to Amarillo because it meant that there would be a more conservative jury, one that would be particularly critical of Priscilla as a drug-taking, cheating wife.[36]

The new trial was set to begin on June 27, 1977.[37] While Cullen remained in jail, he continued to receive special treatment here. He had a private cell with two bunks, a color TV, and, more often than not, catered meals. He wore a fresh business suit every day, and a deputy took him to frequent meetings with his chiropractor. One of his vice presidents visited every two days, bringing him the latest news of his network of corporations and documents to sign.[38] Other visitors included a group of housewives, who treated him as if he were a rock star, bringing him treats like pies and cookies. They even brought their children and grandchildren to the jail to meet him.[39]

The courtroom was still another arena for special privileges. During trial recesses, Cullen's supporters flocked around him, and he gallantly posed for pictures and chatted with them like a movie star celebrity. Plus, Cullen used the phone in the judge's outer office to speak to his business associates and make decisions for the company.[40] It was as if Cullen were the victim, not the accused in a murder case.

Another defense ploy was arranging for an illegal informer, a waitress at the Executive Inn, where the jurors were sequestered, to report what was going on in the jury room. She spoke to them and listened in on their conversations, then let the defense team know what they were saying.[41]

In addition, according to a *Fort Worth Star-Telegram* story that appeared in 2001, long after the case was over, Cullen paid off one of the prosecutor's investigators, Marris Howarth, code named "Eyes," to learn about the prosecution's strategy. As the story described, Cullen used Ray Hudson, the estranged father of Cullen's girlfriend, Karen Masters, as a go-between to contact Howarth, and supposedly, as Hudson claimed, Cullen paid as much as $25,000 in cash to Howarth for this tip-off. Then, Hudson funneled this information directly to Cullen to pass on to his lawyers. In effect, thanks to Cullen's wealth, the defense had a "mole inside the prosecutor's team,"[42] and the defense used this information to plan its strategy to counter whatever the prosecution planned to do.

Also, to help discredit Priscilla, Cullen paid for over a dozen lawyers, including the well-known Amarillo lawyer, Dee Miller, to increase rapport with the local jurors, and a second local lawyer, Hugh Russell, to investigate and assess each of the jurors being considered.[43]

During jury selection, Russell's goal was to find more conservative jurors who would "have no affinity for Priscilla and might even find her revolting."[44] He looked for solid citizens who would be so offended by Priscilla's fast and loose conduct that they would not believe her eyewitness identification and would believe she was willing to frame her estranged husband for his money so she could be free to pursue a wild, orgiastic, drug-addicted lifestyle.

Once the jurors were selected, Miller was chosen to win over the jury. The defense hoped he could sway them because he had close personal connections in town and all twelve jurors either knew him personally or knew of his reputation.[45] So selecting him was a subtle way to remind the jurors that Cullen was one of the good guys. To provide Cullen's out-of-city legal team with local support, Miller introduced them to the town's movers and shakers by taking them to events like Rotary Club luncheons, country club events, and meetings of the local bar associations. The strategy, as described by Gary Cartwright, in *Texas Justice*, was to make Cullen Davis and his lawyers seem like part of the local establishment, and to turn Priscilla into "the evil personification of *them*. In a reversal of normal trial roles, the defense would be identified with the establishment, and the state would come to be viewed as the outsider."[46]

Meanwhile, Priscilla's lifestyle with Cullen, which became even more exaggerated after their split, provided his lawyers with plenty of fodder. Priscilla had been born poor, and when they were dating and after they married in 1968, Priscilla had a flamboyant, flashy style. She dressed in skimpy, provocative outfits that immediately set her apart from the more traditional conservative style of the Fort Worth society women.[47] After she filed for divorce and remained in the mansion, while Cullen first lived in a motel and then with his new girlfriend Karen Masters, Priscilla invited an unusual cast of characters to live with her. Among them was former motorcycle racer, W. T. Rufner, and some of his friends.[48] After she evicted him, Stan Farr, a former Texas Christian University basketball player, moved in.[49] During the divorce case, Cullen's investigators and informants checking on her, including her own maid and gardener, described Hollywood-like events, such as "wild parties, shady houseguests, and broken furniture."[50] After Cullen's arrest for murder, the wild lifestyle continued.

These high jinks proved a great boon to the defense. The stories of Priscilla's drug use and wild behavior came up when she took the stand, and they were reported in the press, which eagerly followed the trial. Priscilla helped the defense, too, by her flashy appearance at the pretrial hearing. She arrived wearing a fancy outfit with frilly white lace and a dangling gold cross, and carried a Bible—an appearance that helped to turn the spectators in the courtroom, including some prospective jurors, against her. They saw her as a phony who was acting like she was sincerely religious with her cross and Bible, but clearly, because of her dress, was not.[51]

Later, during the trial, when Priscilla took the stand, Racehorse Haynes did an excellent job discrediting her personally and as an eyewitness. Besides making much of her loose and fast lifestyle, Haynes showed that many people who had lived in the mansion with her—some of them very sleazy characters—might have gotten in the night of the murder to do the killing. These characters included a former motorcycle racer, W.T. Rufner, and Larry Michael Myers, a convicted felon. Especially damaging was a color photo blowup of Priscilla posing with W.T. Rufner, their arms entwined around each other. Whereas she wore tight slacks and a low-cut halter, Rufner wore nothing except a red and white Christmas stocking. Although, Judge Dowling refused to allow the picture into evidence, everyone in the jury box could see it before it was covered up, and Haynes was able to talk about the picture to claim Priscilla had an intimate relationship with Rufner before her separation from Cullen, though she said she barely knew him at that time.[52]

The defense also zeroed in on Priscilla's extensive use of drugs, including Percodan, to suggest she might not have effectively recalled what happened the night of the murders. Then, after making the case that Priscilla was a "liar and tramp," the defense sought to show she had foreknowledge of the murders. They claimed that she knew something was going to happen that night, as shown by her statement to one friend that "something heavy's coming down." Then, after Stan was killed for revenge, the defense contended that Priscilla sought to cover it up for greed.[53]

Besides arguing these contentions in court, the defense leaked them to the press, and possibly some of the jurors. How? According to Cartwright, the defense lawyers left a damning memo on a table next to the exhibits that had already been admitted as evidence. Though this might have been left there by mistake, it could also have been left there to influence the reporters covering the case, who commonly checked what was on the table during recesses in the trial. When some reporters asked defense lawyer Burleson about the memo, he confirmed it was largely correct. From there, some jurors might have learned of it, perhaps those who were reportedly seeing unauthorized visitors and those who were receiving unchaperoned visits from their spouses.[54] This "leak to the jury" strategy was much the same as that used in the first Fort Worth trial that led to a mistrial.

Once again the prosecution anchored its case on the testimony of the three witnesses—Priscilla, Bev, and Bubba. They each stuck firmly to their story of seeing Cullen at the mansion, and the prosecution backed up this claim that the man in black was Cullen with assorted police and forensic evidence.

But again, Haynes' strategy was to ignore such evidence and claim the killings were set up by Priscilla to blame Cullen, and probably Stan was the intended victim. Haynes pointed out that Cullen had no financial motive to kill Priscilla because their prenuptial actually saved him money. Though the court ordered him to increase his payments to Priscilla to $5,000 a month, before the divorce proceedings, she had been spending $20,000 a month.[55] Haynes also emphasized how much Priscilla would gain if Cullen was found guilty. He described how Stan had built up $100,000 in debts from his business failures, which was a likely reason for his murder, and suggested that Andrea, Priscilla, and Bubba were likely "accidental victims" because they were at the scene at the time.[56] By contrast, Haynes suggested that the killer might be Horace Copeland, a businessman with a shady reputation for being involved in drug-dealing, who by now was conveniently dead.[57] As for Cullen, he was not involved, Haynes argued, presenting his alibi that he was in bed at Karen Masters's house at the time of the crime. To show this, Haynes called on Karen to testify that she had woken up at 12:40 a.m. to see Cullen in bed beside her, although the prosecution tried to raise doubts about her veracity, noting that she hadn't mentioned this incident at the grand jury or bond hearings.[58]

But despite all the prosecution evidence, after the longest and most expensive trial in Texas, the jurors came back in only four and a half hours with their "not guilty" decision on November 17, 1977. Cullen was so sure of the outcome that he had already made reservations to go skiing in Aspen, and a victory party had been in the works for weeks. Cullen even invited the judge and jury, as well as the media, after the verdict was announced.[59]

Why the quick acquittal? Some jurors felt there was reasonable doubt in the discrepancies in the times showing when different large expensive cars entered and left the mansion, or they felt the eyewitnesses could have been mistaken. Then, too, the defense had done such a good job of discrediting Priscilla that the jurors didn't give much credibility to her overall testimony, as the jury foreman told reporters. Because she had denied so many things about herself that later were shown to be true, maybe she was not to be believed about her eyewitness testimony either.[60]

And an especially influential factor was Cullen's wealth and status; the jurors felt it "unthinkable" to convict a man who was so rich and powerful. As the relative of one Amarillo millionaire at the victory put it: "Rich men don't kill their wives," to which juror Betty Blair agreed, saying: "It seems like if someone that rich wanted it done, he'd hire somebody."[61] The jurors couldn't imagine the possibility that Cullen might have wanted to be there to attack Priscilla himself.

Though the prosecution could have charged Cullen with another murder for killing Stan Farr and with assault or attempted murder for shooting Priscilla and Bubba Gavrel, the prosecution waited, deciding what to do, while Cullen remained free under a $1 million bond. The prosecution hesitated to bring these charges because of doubts of being successful,[62] doubts kindled when they couldn't gain a conviction in what seemed their strongest case—the murder of a twelve-year-old girl. If they couldn't win in that case, they felt they were not likely to gain a guilty verdict for the killing of Cullen's wife's lover, especially because in Texas lovers get little sympathy. They felt they had even less chance of mounting a successful case for assault or attempted murder.[63]

For legal and political reasons, District Attorney Tim Curry also decided not to immediately pursue the other three pending cases against Cullen. The bills for the first trial were already sky high—over $300,000 before the trial was moved to Amarillo—and he was up for reelection later that year. Then, too, the popular opinion continued to support Cullen, and, under Texas law, as long as Priscilla remained married to Cullen, she could not testify against him in Stan Farr's case. However, after her divorce trial was over, that could change. And possibly the prosecution could face a double jeopardy problem for additional prosecutions based on the same facts. Thus, for now, Curry waited, and in the end, didn't pursue any further charges against Cullen for what happened at the mansion.[64]

For his part, after the victory party and a skiing weekend, Cullen returned to his normal life as part of the elite world of Fort Worth and worked his way back into the social circuit. Priscilla, by contrast, didn't fare so well. Although she was still living in the mansion, she faced reduced payments for her nurses and bodyguards, and many of her old society friends shunned her or didn't come to visit anymore. But Cullen seemed blessed and exonerated as society opened up to him again. Though he had been dropped from the *Fort Worth Social Directory* while in jail, he was relisted, and over the next months, the local news features about him were largely praiseworthy, such as a spread of photos of him attending society events with Karen Masters. He was even featured in *D Magazine*, the city magazine of Dallas, as someone to watch in 1978, and one article praised him for his help in guiding the restoration of the downtown Continental Life Building while he was in jail. The magazine further suggested that now that Cullen was free, much might be expected of him in the future.[65]

But, even as Cullen was gaining reacceptance into his society life, he gave Curry a second chance to charge him with a crime—this time for attempted murder. Yet amazingly, Cullen again used his charm to slip free. The case was like déjà vu, and in brief, here's what happened.

Soon after acquiring a new company, Jet Air, Cullen hired David McCrory, the investigator whose leaked unsigned affidavit provided damaging claims about Priscilla, as an assistant to the company president. Then, in the summer of 1978, Cullen hired McCrory to do some investigative work on Bev, Bubba, and Priscilla's attorneys who were handling the divorce trial.[66] By August, Cullen felt increasingly frustrated by the slow pace of the trial, which was being handled by Judge Eidson, and David McCrory's work turned into something more than just conducting an investigation. Rather, as the prosecution charged, Cullen asked McCrory to kill over a dozen people on his enemies list, including Priscilla, Bev, Bubba, and the judge.[67]

The prosecution gained this information when McCrory reported the job offer to the FBI, and agents fixed him up with a wire on August 18 so that McCrory recorded his meeting with Cullen to discuss the hit. After Cullen asked for evidence that McCrory had successfully made the hit, McCrory gave him a photo of Eidson lying in the trunk of a car wearing a blood-soaked T-shirt, along with the judge's identification cards. On the tape were McCrory's words: "I got Judge Eidson dead for you," to which Cullen replied "Good" and handed him an envelope with $25,000 in cash. After that McCrory told Cullen: "I'll get the rest of them dead for you. You want a bunch of people dead, right?" to which Cullen replied: "All right."[68]

Yet, although Cullen was arrested, charged with soliciting murder, jailed without bond, and faced another trial, he managed still another Houdini-like escape in the face of seemingly solid evidence. This time, the defense went after McCrory as a proven liar in the past. Previously, as the defense showed, McCrory had stolen money from Cullen, had ongoing problems with the IRS, and had lied about those and other problems.[69] Whereas Cullen's first trial had been about demolishing Priscilla's credibility, this one focused on tearing down McCrory. What about the incriminating evidence on the tapes? Haynes simply sought to discredit this seemingly damning evidence. Cullen confidently claimed he was simply playing along with the FBI by trying to get evidence against McCrory for them on tape.[70] In addition, Haynes ridiculed the prosecution's claim that Cullen was willing to pay $1 million to have fifteen people killed, since the only evidence was McCrory's claim.

Unfortunately, the prosecution wasn't able to counter the defense and support McCrory's story with any of Cullen's fingerprints from the photo of the judge, which Cullen allegedly looked at, although the photographer had dusted the photo with fluorescent powder before giving it to McCrory to get prints. But any evidence got wiped away in the confusion of the arrest; the police officer fingerprinting Cullen had asked him to wash his hands, which would have removed any traces of the powder, and therefore any evidence that Cullen had touched this photo.[71]

The defense additionally intimated that Priscilla could have been involved in a conspiracy with McCrory to get Cullen to say what he did on the tape. When Cullen took the stand, he explained how he had thought he was cooperating with the FBI on instructions to play along with McCrory, though he had been duped. As Cullen described it, he believed his life was in danger, based on the advice of one of his security men. Then, he got a phone call from Jim Acree, who said he was a special agent for the FBI. Acree told him that McCrory and others were trying to frame him and suggested that Cullen "play along." So not wanting to take any chances, Cullen did.[72] As Cullen testified in court, Acree "said he had information that McCrory was involved in an extortion plot. He said, 'We think you are one of the victims. We want you to play along. That's the only way we can catch him. Follow his suggestions.' "[73]

Then, too, Cullen said he wanted to make the tape for the agent because he had been informed that Priscilla had "hired some people" to bump him off. He felt if he could prove that, this would be a great help for his divorce case, and the tape might show this. He also claimed he had told Karen about Acree's request to play along with McCrory, and James Stephens, a used-car dealer in Fort Worth, testified for the defense that he had seen David McCrory with Priscilla and Pat Burleson, a lawyer representing Cullen at his first trial, together.[74] Thus, his testimony was designed to show that Priscilla was behind McCrory's scheme to set up Cullen.

It was a brazen ploy, and the prosecution sought to discredit the story by bringing in Jim Acree to testify that he had not spoken to Cullen in August as Cullen claimed, although he acknowledged that he met Cullen and gave him four phone numbers where Cullen could contact him eight months earlier. Also, at that meeting, Acree said he told Cullen not to meet with anyone trying to extort anything from him, unless he told Acree in advance and Acree arranged to put him under surveillance.[75]

Ultimately, the case came down to whether the jury would believe McCrory's story or Cullen's, and after forty-four hours of deliberations and fourteen ballots, the jury couldn't come to a unanimous decision, leading the judge to declare a mistrial. The breakdown was eight for conviction, four for acquittal, and the reason some jurors held fast for not guilty was once again due to Cullen's wealth and charm. Though some jurors thought his story "pure fantasy," those that voted to acquit couldn't accept that a man with Cullen's money would "lower himself to having a judge killed."[76] Much like many jurors in the first trial, who couldn't believe a wealthy man would kill someone else himself, these jurors couldn't believe a wealthy man would target a judge.

Thus, once again, Cullen walked free, celebrating with a small victory party. Then, in April 1979, his marriage to Priscilla was finally dissolved as a no-fault lawsuit, enabling Cullen to keep most of his money and his mansion, while Priscilla received $3.4 million. Thirty days later, Cullen married Karen.

Meanwhile, the prosecution geared up to retry the case, convinced they had a strong case, despite the setbacks. Yet, again, Cullen got the best of them. Not only did he tell his story that he thought he was working for the FBI, but also he brought in a linguistics professor, Dr. Roger Shuy of Georgetown University, who analyzed the tapes and agreed that Cullen was "just playing along."[77] After only a few hours of deliberation, the jury found him not guilty for much the same reason that the four jurors in the previous case had voted to acquit; they found Cullen's story more credible than McCrory's, influenced in part by his wealth and reputation.[78]

So finally, Cullen was completely free; the prosecution dropped any further charges. However, his high-society lifestyle was soon to end. One reason is that soon after his acquittal, he formed a connection with Dallas evangelist James Robison, gave his life over to Jesus, and began holding religious meetings at the mansion. Then, having found religion, he sold the mansion for $32 million and bought a much smaller home in a middle-income section of Fort Worth.[79] Another reason his high-society life ended is that his $32 million fortune didn't last long; his companies suffered severely during the recession of the 1980s, and he lost over $40 million on bad real estate investments. Eventually, in 1986, he filed for personal bankruptcy, with debts of over $230 million.[80] But having found the Lord, he continued to fight for conservative Christian causes. Though potentially he could still be tried for the murder of Stan Farr, as of 2003, with Cullen in his late 60s, no prosecutor has sought to charge him, and even Cullen admits that he attained the outcome he did due to his wealth, enabling him to pay for what he needed in order to be found not guilty.[81]

Justice Delayed: The Case of Michael Skakel (Greenwich, Connecticut, 1975–2002)

From the discovery of 15-year-old Martha Moxley's body under a tree in the wealthy gated neighborhood of Belle Haven in Greenwich, Connecticut, the police investigation was flawed and members of the press and public trampled the crime scene. Furthermore, the investigative process was stopped by the lack of cooperation from one of the most powerful and wealthy families, the Skakels, when the murder weapon seemed to be one of their golf clubs and suspicion fell on one of their sons, Tom, the last person known to have seen Martha alive. It took over twenty-five years to finally convict their other son Michael for the crime after new evidence surfaced.

A major reason the case was finally revived and prosecuted successfully was the publicity and pressure due to Dominick Dunne, a writer dealing with high-society crime, and Mark Fuhrman, a former detective whose reputation was shattered during the O. J. Simpson case after he used the "n-word." Fuhrman wrote about the case in *Murder in Greenwich* after

Dunne gave him new information about the case, and the book sparked renewed interest. The case dramatically illustrates the way politics, the press, and personal power can both impede and then push forward the investigation and prosecution of a homicide.

The setting for murder was the fabulously wealthy, exclusive community of Belle Haven, a neighborhood of three dozen homes, where people live in large mansions surrounded by large tracts of land and belong to country clubs and yacht clubs.[82] It is also a gated community, protected by guard booths at all public accesses and patrolled by a private security force at all hours, so transient intruders gaining entry to commit murder are extremely unlikely.[83]

Then, on October 30, 1975, around 12:15 p.m., Martha's body was discovered under a pine tree only a few hundred feet from her parents' house. The discovery was made by one of Martha's schoolmates, 15-year-old Sheila McGuire, who lived nearby and was cutting through the Moxley's yard, a common practice in the area, to ask Martha if she wanted to go downtown.[84] Sheila was one of the few people in the neighborhood who wasn't aware that Martha was missing. Martha's mother, Dorthy, had already called the police shortly before 4 a.m., and around 10 a.m., had begun contacting friends and neighbors, including the Skakels, who lived across the road. When Dorthy rang the Skakels' bell, Michael answered the door looking "pale and disheveled, as if he were hung over and hadn't slept all night," and he told her Martha wasn't there, though, without checking with anyone else in the house.[85]

Before the police arrived and the investigation began, what was known of the previous night was that Martha, a popular bubbly 15-year-old, had gone out with friends to celebrate Hacker's Night, a local celebration held the night before Halloween. That Thursday night was also the beginning of a three-day weekend. After some high jinks on the streets, a party at the Skakel house began around 7:30 p.m.[86] For a time, Martha was in a car with both Michael and Thomas Skakel, who were both interested in her, listening to music and flirting with Thomas. Around 9:30 p.m., when the party broke up Michael drove off with his brothers, Rush Jr. and John, and his cousin Jim Terrian, and Martha continued flirting with

Thomas. Meanwhile two of her friends, Helen Ix and Geoffrey Byrne left to go home.[87] Whatever happened next to Martha became a mystery. Perhaps only the dogs in the neighborhood were aware something was happening, since from around 9:30–9:45 p.m. a number of dogs, though not the Skakel's dog, began barking loudly.[88]

About 12:15 p.m., Shelia found Martha's body under the pine tree, and shortly afterward the police arrived. From the start it was a botched investigation, made even worse by the arrival of the press, neighbors, and emergency personnel, who quickly trampled and contaminated the crime scene. Part of the problem was that the police department was badly inexperienced and lacked the knowledge or resources to deal with a violent crime scene. The investigation was further complicated because people in the community immediately suspected that an outside transient must have come in and killed Martha; they couldn't imagine that someone in the community could have done this. Thus, the police spent much time investigating these outside leads.[89]

As Mark Fuhrman describes the scene in *Murder in Greenwich*, based on initial police reports and interviews with retired detectives and others who were there, it was chaos. Among other problems, the police kept no crime scene log to indicate when personnel arrived and departed. Some major mistakes were also made by the first officers, juvenile officers Millard Jones and Dan Hickman, who arrived on the scene around 12:30 p.m. One of the most critical errors occurred when Jones went to the Moxley house to call headquarters. He didn't want to use the police radio because he didn't want journalists and others who might pick up news of the murder from their police scanners to spread the word and descend upon the scene. Accordingly, Jones instructed Hickman to remain with the body. But instead, Hickman returned to the car and put out a radio call for more officers and a medical examiner. As a result, by the time Jones returned to the crime scene, the news was already out, and in Hickman's absence, a dog was already there, licking the blood trail near the body, thus destroying some of the evidence.[90] And soon after, crowds of people descended, along with the first police investigators, including Captain Thomas Keegan, Steve Carroll, and Joe McGlynn.

As the investigators looked more closely at the body to determine what happened, they saw Martha lying on her right side, curled up in a semi-fetal position, under some overhanging pine branches that were close to the ground. She was still wearing the blue down jacket and turtleneck she had on the night before, but her blue jeans and panties were pulled down below her knees, though they saw no bruises on her buttocks or thighs. Her face was caked with blood, and bits of gravel were mixed in with the blood and under her skin, suggesting that she might have been dragged facedown from the driveway.[91] The investigators also found a golf club head and an eight-inch section of a club in the driveway, and another eleven-inch piece of the shaft near another pool of blood across the driveway near a dwarf Japanese elm tree.[92]

These findings suggested that the golf club was the murder weapon, a finding supported by the autopsy, which showed that Martha had been struck four times on the right side of the head with a heavy instrument, and one of these blows shattered her skull. The autopsy also showed she had been lastly stabbed in the throat, while she was lying on her side.[93] These various findings led Fuhrman to conclude that Martha was "beaten with the golf club and left for dead by the suspect," who later returned to hide the body. Then, when he found Martha still alive, he stabbed her in the neck with the shaft of the broken golf club.[94]

Though the search for the missing golf club or the set to which it belonged soon led to the Skakels, the police not only didn't use proper crime scene investigation procedures, but also they didn't follow-through with a search and fully investigate. Perhaps they didn't because they were either cowed by the Skakels' lack of cooperation or because they lacked experience in investigating homicide cases—a theme echoed in the other extensive accounts of the murder, such as *A Wealth of Evil* by Timothy Dumas and *Justice* by Dominick Dunne.

A major difficulty in the investigation is that the golf club handle was missing, so the police focused much of their effort on looking for it in the hopes of getting prints or blood from a suspect. But according to Fuhrman, the police had no need to find it because the pieces of the golf club that were found came from a relatively rare Toney Penna golf club, and within the next day or two they discovered not only that the Skakels owned the only such set in the neighborhood, but also that it was missing the six iron, which was the murder weapon.[95] Thus, the missing handle had little evidentiary value, and even if it were found, it could have been easily cleaned of any print or blood evidence. Moreover, the possibility that it was found but disappeared through a mistake or even a cover-up was proposed when the case was reinvestigated in the 1990s, after the first two officers on the scene—Hickman and Jones—both said they saw the shaft of a golf club projecting out of Martha's head.[96]

Another problem is that the police limited the scope of their investigation by assuming that Martha had been killed between 9:30 and 10 p.m., when the dogs were barking and Martha's mother Dorthy heard voices outside her window, rather than considering a longer time line—at least from 9:40 p.m. to 1:00 a.m., as suggested by the autopsy and witness statements. If they had, according to Fuhrman, this would have led the police to consider Michael Skakel a suspect early on.[97]

Instead, the police ruled Michael out right away because he had been at a neighbor's party from shortly after 9:30 p.m. until 11:30 p.m. So they looked at other suspects, and for a time they explored the possibility that a transient had come in from the freeway. However, this was an unlikely theory because Belle Haven was a heavily gated community, and many people out that night didn't see any strangers. Moreover, the lack of defensive wounds and savagery of the attack suggested that Martha was murdered by someone she knew.

Still another problem with the initial investigation is that the detectives didn't get a search warrant or conduct a careful search of the Skakel house, grounds, or vehicles once their search for the golf club led them to the Skakels, even though they soon learned that Thomas Skakel was the last person seen with Martha. Rather, they conducted a casual walk-through of the house based on the permission of Rushton Skakel, with whom they already had a friendly relationship. As a result, when Rushton later withdrew his permission once Thomas became a suspect, they could no longer search. Six months later, even after they got outside advice on how to conduct a homicide investigation from Gerald Hale of the Detroit homicide department, their request for a search warrant was rejected by Don Browne, the Connecticut state attorney.[98]

The investigators additionally failed to do a proper first interview and polygraph test with Thomas, as if they were giving him kid-glove treatment out of deference to the Skakel family. Their initial interview was an informal one, and when they gave him two polygraph tests on November 3 and 9, besides asking, "Did you kill Martha Moxley?" they didn't ask any probing questions, such as "What time did you leave Martha Moxley?"[99] If they had, his answers might have led them to question his initial story, which he later changed when a team of private investigators reinvestigated the case in 1991. But once Thomas passed the November 9 polygraph, the police turned their attentions elsewhere.

Why the great deference to the Skakels, which helped to undermine the investigation? Because, according to Fuhrman, the Greenwich police had an overly close relationship with this powerful family. As he writes:

> The Greenwich police worked for the Skakel family, literally. During their off-duty hours, they performed various side jobs—driving the Skakel children to school, parking cars during Skakel parties, running errands, and fixing problems for them. . . .
>
> Not only did the rank and file work for the Skakels, but their bosses were frequent visitors to the Skakel house, off duty and on.[100]

Perhaps, too, the police didn't want to press the Skakels too hard initially because they, like other community members, didn't want to think that any of the Skakels could be involved in a murder, given their position in the community, which included a link to the powerful Kennedy clan through Rushton's sister Ethel, who was married to Bobby Kennedy. Although there were rumblings among the neighbors that Rushton had a serious drinking problem and that the Skakel boys, especially Thomas and Michael, were known for wild behavior, the police did not seriously consider such factors in their initial investigation.[101]

In any event, according to the story of that night as reconstructed from interviews with Martha's friends and with Thomas and Michael Skakel and their older sister Julie, Martha and her friends Helen Ix and Geoffrey Byrne arrived at the Skakel house after their Hacker Night partying at around 9:10 p.m. There, they joined Michael in the Skakels' Lincoln where they listened to music, Martha and Michael in the front, Helen and Geoffrey in the back. Around 9:20 p.m., Thomas joined them and sat next to Martha, so she was seated between him and Michael.[102] As they sat together, Michael tried to feel Martha's thighs several times but each time she pushed his hands away, which possibly triggered feelings of jealousy in Michael, who was vying with Thomas for her. About 9:25, Rush Jr. and John Skakel came out and said they needed the car to take their friend Jimmy home; Michael joined them and they left.[103]

Then Helen and Geoffrey headed home, but Martha stayed behind with Thomas. Initially, Thomas told the police that he said good night to Martha at the front door at about 9:30 p.m. and went upstairs to do some homework, which included writing a paper on Abraham Lincoln. However, had the police checked with his teacher, they would have discovered she had assigned no such paper. Besides, Thomas was not a particularly good student and was unlikely to do homework on a Thursday before Halloween and a long weekend.

However, Helen and Geoffrey told the police five weeks later that as they left to go home about 9:30 p.m.,[104] they saw Martha and Tommy flirting and fall down together behind the bushes. Later, in the 1991 investigation, Thomas changed his story to admit that he had been playing around with Martha for twenty minutes until 9:50 p.m., when they engaged in mutual masturbation to orgasm. Regardless of what happened between Thomas and Martha during that twenty minutes, around 10:30 p.m., Thomas, dressed in the same clothes he had worn for dinner except for the tie, calmly joined Ken Littleton, a man hired just that day as the family's live-in tutor, to watch *The French Connection* on TV.[105] Ken had been at home unpacking and had not left the house that night, as he later told the police.

Meanwhile, before the police began to focus in on Tommy as a suspect, they pursued several dozen other leads that led to dead ends.[106] One was Ed Hammonds, a quiet loner who lived next door and was home alone that night watching TV. Before they cleared Ed as a suspect, they conducted a full search of his house,[107] interrogated him for hours over several days, and subjected him to two polygraphs[108]—not at all like the friendly, deferential questioning and informal search they had done at the Skakels.

Then, in mid-December, the focus of the investigation shifted after the two lead detectives, Jim Lunney and Steve Carroll, questioned the kids who were with Martha the last day. They heard reports of Tommy's "fierce temper,"[109] and on December 11, they heard Geoffrey and Helen's story that after they left Martha and Tommy to walk home, they saw both of them playing around in the bushes. Thus, the police now had a reason to turn their attention back to Thomas as a suspect. Possibly, they theorized, Thomas might have wanted to have sex with Martha, and after she refused, he hit her with the golf club and continued his attack with growing fury. They also discovered he had a history of emotional and disciplinary problems and felt that Thomas's psychological, medical, and school records might offer some clues as to why he might have snapped and later blocked out any memory of the murder.[110]

However, once their attention turned to Thomas, Rushton stopped cooperating and derailed their ability to further investigate his son. Though Rushton first gave the police an authorization to obtain Thomas's school, psychological, medical, and hospital records on January 16,[111] on January 22, he withdrew his authorization to gather any of Thomas's records, and he hired a lawyer, Manny Margolis, to represent Tommy. As a result, the Greenwich police investigation essentially ended because the primary suspect was no longer cooperating and the police did not consider Michael Skakel a suspect.[112]

The Greenwich police did make some effort for a time to look at other suspects, such as Ken Littleton, the tutor who moved in the night of the murder. They thought Littleton might be involved after he came to their attention due to his unusual behavior, which occurred because his life started to unravel after the murder. He became so disturbed by the investigation that he lost a teaching job at a private school, and he was arrested for four burglaries and several petty thefts he committed when he was drunk in nearby Nantucket in July and August of 1976.[113]

But despite Ken's personal problems, he had nothing to do with the murder and was ultimately cleared.[114]

The investigators also tried to get some help in April 1976 by meeting with two Detroit homicide investigators, Gerald Hale and John Lock, who helped them focus the investigation by giving them a profile of the likely killer: someone who "lives in the neighborhood and knew his victim" and is "a troubled young man with an explosive temper."[115] That profile led them to question many of the same people they had previously questioned, such as Helen Ix and Geoffrey Byrne, the last known people to see Martha alive, besides Thomas. After these interviews confirmed a crucial detail in the case—that Thomas and Martha were involved in sexual roughhousing—Hale and Lock recommended that they conduct a more formal search of the Skakel house. Perhaps even at this late date, the bloody clothes or missing golf club handle might still be found there. But when the police applied to Donald Browne for a search warrant, he denied it.[116]

Thus, the case went into a kind of somnolence until 1991—a "Decade of Silence"—as *Wealth of Evil* author Timothy Dumas describes it.[117] There was only sporadic police activity, such as tracing Littleton's activities until 1982 and investigating Geoffrey Byrne's mysterious death in 1980, which was possibly due to suffocation from a sinus problem, though his father Arthur Byrne opined that Geoffrey "willed himself to die," perhaps due to feelings of despair over Martha's murder.[118]

During this period, press coverage of the case was minimal, receiving just occasional mentions in other stories or wrap ups, such as when the *Greenwich Time* ran a feature article to mark the fifth year of the Moxley case two months before Geoffrey Byrne died. Meanwhile, local suspicions continue to swirl around Tommy Skakel. People whispered that he did it but got away with it, although Geoffrey came to his support in the *Greenwich Time* article, stating that he was sure "He didn't do it. . . . He's not the sort of person who could have done such a thing."[119]

Then, in 1991, a combination of forces revived the case. This time the power of the press put more pressure on the police to act, trumping the ability of the Skakels and their political supporters to close off information in the case.

The trigger was the William Kennedy Smith rape trial in Palm Beach in 1991, which became a media sensation because Smith was a nephew of the late president John F. Kennedy. The press attention to Smith revived interest in the Moxley case, because Tommy Skakel was a cousin of both John Kennedy Jr. and William Kennedy Smith.[120] Then, false rumors fueled interest even more, as the story spread among reporters covering the case that Smith had stayed overnight at Rushton Skakel's house in Greenwich on the night of Martha Moxley's death.[121] Though the rumor wasn't true, it led many reporters and others to wonder about the case, and Dominick Dunne used it as the basis for his novel, *A Season in Purgatory*, though he changed some details for libel reasons, such as making the murder weapon a baseball bat and calling the Skakels the Bradleys. When the book came out in 1993 and became a best-seller, the *CBS Evening News* did a story about how the book helped renew interest in the Moxley murder, which led to still more stories. And people in Greenwich began talking again about the case, too.[122]

Another major development occurred when the Smith case led to the very belated publication of an investigative piece by Len Levitt of *Newsday*. Levitt had been hired in 1982 by the *Greenwich Time* to do a follow-up story on the state of the Moxley investigation, but the story was never published—perhaps because it put the Greenwich police and the Skakels in a bad light. But after the *New York Post* published a May 1, 1991, story with the headline "Fla Case Revives Probe of Kennedy Kin in '75 Sex Slaying," the *Greenwich Time* felt pressure to print Levitt's extensive account of the case, which described the haphazard investigation by the local police.[123]

All of this media interest triggered State Attorney Donald Browne, who had previously turned down a request for a subpoena to search the Skakel mansion, to order a reinvestigation of the case. But now he appointed two state inspectors to head the investigation: Jack Solomon and Detective Frank Garr. At first, Rushton Skakel seemed willing to talk to the new investigators. He even invited them into his house, and after telling them he was convinced that none of his children were involved and that he shouldn't have listened to his attorneys who had told him to stop cooperating, he promised to set up meetings for them with all his children. But a day later, his attorney, Tom Sheridan, called to say that the investigators should talk to him if they needed anything. So again, the Skakels had shut down any voluntary cooperation with the police.[124]

Yet despite the Skakels' efforts to close out the investigators once more, the revival of media interest in Martha's murder due to Smith's trial and renewed whisperings about Tommy's guilt couldn't be ignored. Due to a lack of evidence, Thomas had never been charged with anything. Yet, he had spent much of his life under the shadow of guilt because he had not been cleared of the murder after Rushton had closed off further investigation. Such suspicions seriously impacted Thomas's social acceptance and work success. For example, after he transferred out of one private school to get away from the Greenwich area, he went to another private school in New York, but he had to leave because the parents objected to him being there. Then followed a fairly undistinguished academic and work life. He left Elmira College in New York before graduating in 1978 because of academic difficulties and briefly attended the New School for Social Research in New York in 1979 before dropping out. Then, he held a number of lower level jobs in various cities, eventually ending up as a kind of "errand boy around the office" for a company involved in trade with the Soviet government, Harco International.[125]

Thus, after the press interest not only led to a revival of investigative interest in the case along with a new focus on his son, Rushton decided to hire a private investigation firm, Sutton Associates, to either clear Tommy's name or give him the best possible defense in the event that he was guilty. As he told one Sutton Associates investigator, Billy Krebs: "If my kids didn't do it, I want my family's name cleared publicly. If they did do it, I want to prepare the best possible defense." But according to Dumas, Rushton was probably betting that the investigation would clear the family name.[126] Otherwise, why do it?

In their initial effort to clear Thomas, the Sutton investigators first sought to build a case against Ken Littleton by focusing on his other run-ins with the police and his whereabouts at the time of the murder.[127] This effort to implicate Littleton never went anywhere, however, because he wasn't involved in the murder. Instead, the case they developed soon pointed to Thomas, as well as Michael, never before considered a suspect, as prime candidates for committing murder. Why? Because after they asked former FBI colleagues to profile the killer, they learned he would share many of the same characteristics of Tommy and Michael Skakel. Among the qualities mentioned, he would be between fourteen and eighteen, live within easy walking distance of Martha's house, have the same socioeconomic status, and have regular interaction with her. Psychologically, the probable killer would "have experienced strong sibling rivalry tendencies, would have experienced behavior problems both at school and at home, and was under the influence of drugs and/or alcohol at the time of the crime." The report additionally included extensive medical and psychological data, doctors' reports, and interviewee statements, which suggested that both Tommy and Michael were prime candidates. As the report stated: "It seems that Tommy and his brother Michael were exceptionally difficult children who suffered from remarkably similar behavior disorders."[128]

This report was not what Rushton Skakel wanted to hear to clear the family name. As a result, after getting much of the report, Skakel paid off Sutton Associates for the work they had done so far, and instead of releasing this report to clear the family name or pursuing a defense strategy, he sought to bury the report. But a few years later, the report provided the key to restart the investigation in a new direction: it showed that Michael, not Thomas, was the most likely suspect—a fact long concealed by an inept police investigation and a wealthy family acting to protect its children from a full investigation of the case.

The bombshell hit after a seven-month lull in the case, after a CBS miniseries based on Dominick Dunne's *A Season in Purgatory* aired in May 1996. Before the show aired, the network publicized the show every day, explaining that it was "based on an actual crime in Greenwich, Connecticut," and newspaper stories discussed the real murder on which the miniseries was based. Then, seven months later, Dunne received a call from a recent college graduate who had worked for

Sutton Associates and helped put together the final report for Rushton Skakel. He was the one person working on the Sutton investigation who hadn't signed a confidentiality form. He had read Dunne's book, seen him on TV, and called wanting to meet him. When Dunne met him for lunch, the man impressed him as someone who had gotten emotionally involved in the story because of his sympathy for Martha Moxley and her mother. And now he was "outraged that justice would not be done, that money could make a difference even in a case of murder."[129]

The upshot of this lunch was that the man gave Dunne a copy of the Sutton report, which he had secretly kept. Shortly afterward, Dunne gave a copy to Frank Garr, one of the detectives appointed to continue to work on the case, though Garr had done little. Meanwhile, Dunne kept his own copy, and in 1997, he got a call from Mark Fuhrman's agent, Lucienne Goldberg. She called because Fuhrman, then mostly known as the cop who said the "n-word" at O.J. Simpson's trial and for his novel *Murder in Brentwood*, a best-seller about the case, was looking for a new project. He was hoping to find an unsolved murder and apply his detective skills to it for his next book.[130]

The timing was perfect. Though Dunne had been at the O.J. trial when Fuhrman took the stand, the two had never met. Now Dunne met Fuhrman for lunch and invited him to his house in Connecticut. There he gave Fuhrman a copy of the Sutton report, and they discussed the case. Soon afterward, Furhman met Dorthy Moxley, who was still eager to see justice done and a murderer apprehended for killing her daughter.[131] And the rest, as they say, is history.

Eagerly, Fuhrman pursued the project, though the police and many community members made it clear they didn't want him involved. For example, when he arrived in Greenwich in September 1997, he found it difficult to get any police cooperation. At first, Chief Peter Robbins, who had just taken over as chief of police in August, was unavailable each of the several times he called, and after Fuhrman appeared at headquarters and briefly spoke with Robbins, the chief told him he couldn't cooperate, though he would be glad to receive any information that Fuhrman wanted to provide. Fuhrman also found other officials and retired detectives who had worked on the case unwilling to talk. Many said they couldn't speak because they didn't want to "jeopardize the prosecution," though there hadn't been any prosecution in twenty-two years.[132]

But finally, Fuhrman found one retired detective, Steve Carroll, who had worked on the Moxley case for two years, who agreed to help him investigate. Still, it was tough finding people to talk, as Fuhrman and Carroll soon found out when they visited the crime scene in late September. At first, a housekeeper who worked for the McFee family now living at the Moxley house, said they could walk around the driveway and side yard where the murder had occurred. They returned soon after on October 3 and asked permission from Mrs. McAntee, who now lived there, to investigate further. But when her husband Robert arrived, he told Fuhrman to get out, and soon afterward he lodged a trespassing complaint against him. As a result, the lieutenant on duty, Lieutenant Dobson, told him to stay off both the old Moxley and Skakel properties or face trespassing charges.[133]

Despite this resistance, Fuhrman did find people willing to talk and obtain the original police reports. As documented in his explosive book *Murder in Greenwich*, these interviews, police reports, and the new evidence in the Sutton Report led him to zero in on Michael Skakel as the most probable killer. Meanwhile, in a parallel investigation, Len Levitt, the *Newsday* reporter, whose publication of the 1982 story for *Greenwich Time* was suppressed for so long, gained access to the Sutton Report and came to similar conclusions. And around the same time, Timothy Dumas wrote a more personal account of the case, from his viewpoint as someone who was born and raised in Greenwich and was fourteen when Martha Moxley was murdered.[134]

The surfacing of the Sutton Report and the reinvestigation was influential in triggering new interest in the case and leading to the call for a grand jury. When the Sutton investigators interviewed Tommy and Michael, they both changed their stories of what happened that night. Why? Perhaps because they knew that others, such as Helen Ix and Geoffrey Byrne, had been talking about that night, and perhaps because they realized what the new science of DNA, just coming into general acceptance, could reveal about the evidence found at the crime scene.

A critical change was that Tommy now said he last saw

Martha at 9:30 p.m. and went to do his homework. Though he still maintained he went inside to study and write his Lincoln paper, after which he watched TV with Littleton, he now admitted that he had engaged in sexual foreplay with Martha Moxley from about 9:30 to 9:50 p.m. before going inside. Yet, he insisted she was still alive when he left. As he told the Sutton investigators in 1994, when they interviewed him at the bed-and-breakfast he was now running in Stockbridge, Massachusetts, he engaged in an extended "kissing and fondling session which included mutual fondling." After that, they both masturbated each other to orgasm. Then, he left her and returned to his house, without changing his clothing or taking a shower.[135] His story was consistent with Littleton's original 1975 account of how Tommy came into the room to watch TV with him.

But whereas Thomas's changed story, as racy as it might be, helped to remove suspicion from him, Michael's changed story was strongly incriminating. Originally, he had told the police that he had gone to the party at Jim Terrian's at 9:30 and returned at about 11:20 p.m., went right to bed, and didn't wake up until the next morning. But now he described being on the Moxley property that night as a Peeping Tom and how he masturbated to orgasm on a tree near Martha's window.[136] Why tell this story now? Perhaps because the revived investigation and new DNA techniques might be able to place his blood or semen at the scene of the murder, and his story might be a way to explain away why either were there.

According to a description of Michael's statement by one of the Sutton investigators, Willis Krebs, Michael left his house between 11:45 p.m. and 12 a.m., soon after he returned home from the party. He passed the Moxley driveway, then approached a ground-floor window of a neighboring house to look at a woman who lived there. On previous occasions, she hadn't been wearing clothing, but now she was. So he walked back to the Moxley house, climbed a tree, and looked into the window of a room that he thought was Martha's. As he sat on a branch, he called "Martha, Martha," several times, got no response, and then masturbated to orgasm in the tree. After he climbed down, he stopped near a streetlight, where he felt "someone's presence" in the area where Martha's body was eventually found. Then, after he called out into the darkness and threw something at the trees, he ran back to his house, afraid of whatever might be in the darkness. Finally, finding all the doors in front of his house locked, he climbed to the second floor, crawled into his room through a window, and went to sleep. He estimated he was out of his house for about thirty to forty-five minutes, from about 11:45 p.m. or midnight to 12:30 a.m., when he returned home.[137]

This description of activities, once it came to light, was a major breakthrough. Not only did Michael no longer have an alibi, once the time line for Martha's murder was extended past 10 p.m., but also he placed himself all over the property at the time of the murder. Climbing into his bedroom window was also suspicious, since according to Fuhrman, several interviewees told him that the Skakels never locked their doors. So why go in the window? Possibly, Fuhrman theorized, Michael did so, because he had blood spatters on him from the crime and didn't want to be seen.[138] Thus, even if Michael did go to the party at the Terrians for two hours from 9:30 to 11:30 p.m., he still could have been back in time to kill Martha.

The Sutton report had even more incriminating evidence against Michael. Julie and John Skakel and a neighbor heard odd noises outside around 11:30 p.m. the night of the murder—about the time Michael returned home from the Terrian party. When Ken Littleton was interviewed, he described how Michael engaged in sadistic behavior and suggested that Michael might have used drugs. The psychological reports about Michael were damning, too. In one report, Dr. Sue Wallingford-Quinlan described him as suffering from "a severe agitated depression, a sense of being overwhelmed by a sense of evil and the futility of life." She also suggested that his personality had "borderline features," which characterize people who often engage in "reckless and self-destructive behavior," have "intense fears of abandonment," and may "react with inappropriate anger when they feel they have been abandoned." Such a person can easily switch from idealizing people to devaluing them, and responding to them "with anger and rage."[139]

Thus, the Sutton files suggested that Michael could have easily become very upset due to his longtime rivalry with Tommy, in general and over Martha. Although Michael had a relationship with Martha and was her boyfriend for a time, the report suggested that Michael now saw that Tommy was moving in on her and witnessed them engaging in sexual horseplay at 9:30 p.m. Fuhrman theorized that Michael could have easily snapped on seeing her making out with Tommy, particularly if he was already under the influence of alcohol and possibly drugs.[140]

Given this explosive evidence pointing to Michael as the prime culprit, it is no wonder that Rushton Skakel didn't want the Sutton Report released. But beyond the Sutton Report, there was even more evidence incriminating Michael. Some came from the private Elan School in Maine for adolescents with emotional, behavioral, or adjustment problems, where Michael was sent in 1978 after he drove the family jeep without a license and while he was drunk. Speeding, he nearly ran an officer down after the officer tried to stop him by the scene of an accident, and Michael crashed into a telephone pole. As part of the deal dismissing the case, Michael agreed to go to Elan for at least six months, and while there, Michael made some very incriminating statements. At his initial interview about why he was at the school, he said it involved a "girl with a golf club embedded in her chest,"[141] something that only the killer would know about, since this information wasn't released to the public. Then, too, one time Michael confessed to murdering Martha Moxley in a therapy session, though he quickly withdrew this confession. And later, a man who said he lived in the same house with Michael at Elan called the *Unsolved Mysteries* tip line in 1996 to say that Michael had told several people in group therapy that he had killed Martha with a golf club because he was drunk.[142]

Given all this new evidence, Fuhrman concluded his book with a list of reasons why he thought Michael Skakel was involved in Martha Moxley's murder, followed by his hypothesis of how the murder happened. In his scenario, Martha, Thomas, Michael, Helen, and Geoffrey are first listening to music, and Martha is between Thomas and Michael in the front seat. When Thomas puts his hands on Martha's leg, Michael becomes angry and jealous and feels abandoned by Martha. Then, as Michael drives off with Jim, John, and Rush Jr. to the Terriens, he sees Thomas and Martha making out and engaging in sexual horseplay by the driveway. At the Terriens, he becomes increasingly agitated, imagining Martha having sex with Thomas. Meanwhile, Fuhrman suggests, Thomas may have snuck Martha inside the house, and after seeing the *French Connection* chase scene with Littleton, he engages in more sex play with Martha in the guest room.

Then, as Fuhrman's scenario continues, when the car returns from the Terriens with John, Rush Jr., and Michael, Fuhrman imagines that a confrontation might have occurred between Michael and Thomas, who is trying to sneak Martha out of the house, which explains the 11:30 p.m. commotion heard by Julie and John Skakel and a neighbor. Then, as Martha leaves to go home, Michael grabs a golf club he has used to release tension before, feels a growing rage, and runs after her. After she tells him she doesn't want anything more to do with him and walks on, he chases after her again, and now is so enraged that he swings the golf club at her, killing her. Afterward, afraid of getting caught, he drags her body to hide it. When she appears to be still alive, he hits her again with the club and drives the jagged end of the broken shaft through her throat, while another part of the shaft falls by her head. Then, he drags her body to the pine tree, pulls down her pants and panties, masturbates to ejaculation, and runs back to his house. There he climbs in through the bedroom window to avoid being seen with blood on his hands and clothes, cleans up the last evidence of the murder, and goes to bed at 12:30 a.m.[143]

Is this how it happened? Whether it did or not, Fuhrman's 1998 book based on his carefully documented investigation, combined with the release of information from the Sutton Report and the Timothy Dumas book, originally called *Greentown*, triggered a wave of new publicity about the case. Once again, the long-dormant case was the talk of the nation, and true-crime devotees were eagerly looking into the case, such as noted in one enthusiastic June 6 review:

> For true-crime devotees, this is about as good as it gets. Two books dealing with the same murder, committed in 1975, and still officially unsolved today, a murder with all the spicy ingredients. A beautiful victim. A weapon that speaks of privilege and savagery. A location that places the murder among America's wealthy and careless elite.[144]

Thus, with renewed pressure from the press, on June 17, 1998, the state attorney's office, now led by State Attorney Jonathan Benedict, announced it was reopening the Moxley case, and soon after, Benedict applied for the appointment of an investigative grand jury. As a result, George N. Thim, a Bridgeport superior court judge, was selected to investigate both the case against Michael Skakel and the police investigation, and grand jury proceedings began July 10.[145] Over the next months, the grand jury called over fifty witnesses to testify, among them two witnesses from the Elan School, now in their late thirties, who were willing to testify that they had heard Skakel confess while he was at the school.[146] Though Rushton Skakel, now seventy-four, argued through his lawyers that he was unfit to travel or testify, the District Court of Appeals rejected his arguments.[147]

Ultimately, after hearing all the evidence from witnesses, among them witnesses who had spoken to the Sutton investigators or reported Michael's confessions at the Elan school, the grand jury issued an indictment, and Michael Skakel was arrested for murder on January 19, 2000.[148] Although he was charged as a juvenile because the murder occurred when he was fifteen, Benedict sought to prosecute him as an adult, which could carry a sentence of twenty-five years to life in prison.[149] The irony is that if Michael had come forward and been tried at the time of the murder, under the Connecticut statutes existing in 1975, he would have faced no more than two years in a juvenile facility.

Eventually, though, the transfer to an adult court was approved, and in the pretrial hearing, even more damaging evidence against Michael was released. John D. Higgins, one of the former students from the Elan School, said that Skakel had told him that "his memory of the night was hazy, but he remembered going through the family's golf clubs before the murder. Then, he said that he didn't know whether he did it [but] eventually said that he, in fact, did it." The other former student to testify, Gregory Coleman, said that Skakel told him he "bashed Moxley with a golf club after she refused to have sex." Then, especially damning, Coleman said Skakel bragged to him: "I'm going to get away with murder. I'm a Kennedy."[150]

In 2002, the trial finally got under way. A detailed review of the trial would largely repeat the story of the case already described in this chapter. In effect, the influence of the media, fueled by the Fuhrman and Dumas books, by Dominick Dunne, and by the Sutton Report leak, had conquered the confrontation with the police and the Skakels's political power. Dorthy Moxley herself recognized this when she called Dominick Dunne the night before Michael was indicted to express her appreciation, telling him: "You started it and I'll never forget." She also noted that among her angels in getting the investigation back on track were Mark Fuhrman and *Newsday* reporter Len Levitt, who used a leaked copy of the Sutton Report to publish his stories about the case.[151] The irony is that the Sutton Report, paid for by Rushton Skakel to clear his son Tommy's name, is what provided the impetus that led to Michael's indictment, and making the release of this report possible was the graduate student who came forward to release it because he felt an injustice had been covered up.

To some extent, the Skakels and Kennedys tried to come to Michael's defense, as when Robert Kennedy Jr. claimed that Dominick Dunne had a vendetta and that Mark Fuhrman was in it for the money in his attempt to convince a *New York Times* reporter that Michael was not guilty. Also, according to Dunne, a well-known author with ties to the Kennedy family told him that the Kennedys were urging a plea bargain to keep the case from going to trial, in part to avoid having the Kennedy named dragged into a murder case in which they weren't involved. Meanwhile, Michael and his lawyer, Mickey Sherman, pressed forward, certain he would not be convicted, and they denied any talk of a plea bargain to society columnist Liz Smith. At the trial, most of the Skakel family appeared to show their support, including Michael's four brothers, sister, and brother-in-law. Longtime suspect Thomas Skakel wasn't there except for one day, when the prosecution subpoenaed him to testify but didn't call him, so he didn't come to the courthouse. However, his longtime lawyer, Manny Margolis, attended regularly.[152]

The big question was whether Michael would get off this time. Would the power of his family connections, a decades-old case, and faded memories be enough for a not-guilty verdict? Or would the evidence against him sway the jury to guilty?

Among the most damaging testimony was the transcript of Michael's former Elan classmate Gregory Coleman, which was read into the record, since Coleman had died. In it, Coleman said that Michael confessed to killing Martha and said he would get away with it as a Kennedy. Also damaging was the testimony of John D. Higgins, who said that Michael told him he "must have done it; I did it." In addition to the highly damaging testimony from former Elon students Coleman and Higgins, a third former classmate, Elizabeth Arnold, came forward to describe how Skakel was close to tears as he explained how upset he was that his brother had stolen his girlfriend. She also said he had gotten very drunk and had a blackout that night.[153]

Still more evidence against Michael came when the prosecution found a former Skakel family driver, Larry Zicarelli, who testified how Michael cried on a trip to a doctor's office. As Zicarelli continued, Michael explained that he had done something very bad and had to either kill himself or get out of the country. Then, twice, Michael tried to run to the side of a bridge, and each time Zicarelli pulled him back. But Michael wouldn't tell Zicarelli what was wrong, only that if Zicarelli knew what he had done, he would never speak to him again.[154]

The prosecutor also made much of Michael's night peeper story and the accounts of Michael's childhood friends, who corroborated his crush on Martha. Additionally, the prosecution poked holes in Michael's credibility, showing that he had told different stories about which tree he had climbed. For example, he told one childhood friend, David Pugh, that he climbed the tree where Martha's body was found, but he told another friend, Michael Meredith, that the tree was right outside his window.[155] The significance of these discrepancies is that if Michael had really climbed a tree, he would know which one it was.

In response, Michael claimed that climbing a tree was a "coincidence" not related to Martha's murder and said he didn't initially tell about masturbating in a tree because it was embarrassing and might falsely incriminate him. As he explained, he didn't want his reputation damaged by people thinking him a Peeping Tom, and he felt he might be accused of Martha's murder, if people knew he was out that night.[156]

But in the end, the jury wasn't swayed by Michael's explanations in light of so much evidence against him. Thus, on June 7, 2002, after three days of deliberations, the jury found him guilty, and Skakel was sentenced to twenty-five years to life in prison.[157]

Thus, ultimately, after the pressure of the press and public opinion led to a grand jury indictment, followed by a preliminary hearing, a hearing to transfer the case to adult court, and finally a trial, the power of the press and the public triumphed over the influence of family connections and wealth. As a result, in a very public trial, covered closely by the press and Court TV, the many strands of evidence against Michael Skakel finally came out.

CHAPTER 7

Legal Power?

The rich, famous, and powerful not only have more resources to commit and cover up the crime, whether they do it themselves or hire someone, they also have the resources to better defend themselves. These resources provide many legal advantages. They have more money to hire the best legal power, which means having a top defense lawyer and, sometimes, a team of lawyers. They are more likely to gain bail, so they don't have to wait in jail while the case drags on—a plus because it is usually to the defense's advantage to prolong a case, allowing memories to dim and witnesses to leave or die. They can pay for private investigators who can ferret out exculpatory evidence that would otherwise not be revealed, even if the defendent really committed the murder. They have the funds for lawyers to bring numerous motions to exclude damaging evidence and testimony, change venue, and even just delay the proceedings, if that's to their advantage. Additionally, they can pay for more and better expert witnesses, as well as find more witnesses to testify on their behalf. Even their confident appearance in court, given their wealth and status, along with their top legal power, can persuade a jury to give them the benefit of the doubt.

All America saw the power of a strong legal defense in the O. J. Simpson case, where his defense team, led by top Los Angeles lawyer Johnnie Cochran, was called the "Dream Team." The result in that case, as is well known, was that O. J. was acquitted to the resounding echo of "If the gloves don't fit, you must acquit." The defense successfully undermined the seemingly powerful prosecution case that was built on extensive blood and DNA evidence and witness testimony. Though numerous polls at the time and in recent years have shown that about 80 percent of the U.S. population continues to think O. J. guilty—even Jay Leno has joked about O. J.'s purported search for the "real killers"—the general wisdom is that his lawyers so outshone the prosecution team that they got him off.

These formidable financial resources of the wealthy certainly make it possible to buy a better brand of justice. So whether guilty or not, the wealthy do much better than the average person. Alan M. Dershowitz, the noted appeals lawyer who gained Claus von Bulow's acquittal in his second trial, points that out in his book about the case, *Reversal of Fortune*. As he notes, von Bulow, a European aristocrat who married into a fabulous fortune, was able to spend more money than the state of Rhode Island did in prosecuting him in a case costing over $3.5 million to prosecute and defend.[1] Having this money was crucial, enabling him to bring in investigators, experts, and even a social research firm, which surveyed potential jurors to help select a jury not likely to favor the prosecution. As Dershowitz notes: "The American system of criminal justice . . . does provide a double standard for rich and poor. . . . The system *is* unfair—not because the wealthy can sometimes obtain justice, but rather because too often the poor and middle class cannot."[2] Alternatively, whereas a person from the poor or middle class might justly be found guilty and convicted, the wealthy person can go free.

As the following two cases nearly one hundred years apart illustrate—one from the late 1890s, the other from the 1980s—this pattern of getting better legal support has a long history. Ironically, in some of these cases in which the wealthy person gets off but is found guilty by popular opinion, an outlaw mystique develops around the person, turning him or her into a hero or heroine of pop culture.

Here's what happened in these two cases. The first was won in the courtroom, despite overwhelming evidence of guilt. The other resulted in a new trial and reversal of a guilty verdict, due to smart lawyering.

Law and Axes: The Case of Lizzie Borden (Fall River, Massachusetts, 1892–1893)

The story of Lizzie Borden of Fall River, Massachusetts, is well known. It permeated popular culture through the well-known but not-quite-accurate jingle sung by schoolchildren:

> Lizzie Borden took an axe.
> And gave her mother forty whacks.
> When she saw what she had done,
> She gave her father forty-one.[3]

This ditty not only attests to her guilt, though Lizzie was acquitted, but also it exaggerates the number of blows; whoever killed Lizzie's forty-two-year-old stepmother Abby, not her mother, hit her with nineteen blows and dealt her sixty-nine-year-old father, Andrew Borden, eleven blows. But irrespective of such inaccuracies, the jingle shows how popular opinion since the infamous trial is convinced that Lizzie did it; and public interest has inspired a small industry of literature and entertainment about the case—at least a half-dozen books, thousands of articles, several plays, and even a ballet.[4] Yet, despite the common wisdom, some of these books and other materials do take the position that Lizzie really didn't do it, even though the evidence collected by the police and the testimony in court suggests her guilt is almost certain.

Among the latter-day writers speculating that Lizzie really didn't do it and seeking to clear her name are Arnold Brown, William L. Masterson, and David Kent. In *Lizzie Borden: The Legend, the Truth, the Final Chapter*, published in 1991 (also reprinted in 1992), Brown argues that the real killer was Andrew Borden's mentally defective, illegitimate son, William, who worked as a butcher. He claims that Lizzie, who knew he did it, conspired with the local establishment to conceal his identity, participated in a rigged trial, and used part of the inheritance she and her sister Emma received to pay off the powers that be in town. Alternatively, William L. Masterson in *Lizzie Didn't Do It!*, published in 2000, suggests a number of possibilities, including any one of the many disgruntled customers, tenants, and business associates of Andrew. He thinks that any of these assassins might have been able to hide in the guest room, where one victim was killed. As for David Kent, in *Forty Whacks: New Evidence in the Life and Legend of Lizzie Borden*, published in 1992, he confesses that he doesn't have any idea who might have killed the Bordens, but he is convinced it wasn't Lizzie. Another writer, Victoria Lincoln, thinks it was Lizzie but tries to give her a mental illness defense. In *A Private Disgrace*, published in 1990, Lincoln states she believes the killer was Lizzie, but that she suffered from a sudden spell of temporal epilepsy. In still other scenarios, Bridget the maid might have done it, as she was in the house at the time of both killings; or maybe it was Lizzie's sister, Emma, if she could have returned from an out of town trip without being noticed and was familiar enough with the house to hide before her father returned.[5]

The books variously review, question, and reanalyze the original evidence, and in some cases, cite new sources, such as the diaries of relatives and neighbors who lived in Fall River in the days of the Borden murders. Some also question the conclusions drawn from the evidence that was collected, such as suggesting that the doctors and medical examiners might have made mistakes in assessing the time of death or proposing that some of the evidence might have been planted. One writer who presents the tragedy in comic book form, Rick Geary, author of *The Borden Tragedy: A Memoir of the Infamous Double Murder at Fall River, Massachusetts, 1892*, even compares the outcome of the Borden case to that in the O. J. Simpson case, pointing out that in both cases, a defendant of previously "unblemished reputation" is accused of a "ghastly double murder," to which there were no witnesses and the murder weapon was never found. But then, in both cases, after both maintain their innocence, hire the best attorneys, and are acquitted, "no evidence . . . points to any other individual, and the defendant remains under a cloud of suspicion."[6]

But whether or not Lizzie actually committed the crime, the legal power she was able to hire helped her gain an acquittal after she was charged and tried for murder. And apart from the Borden aficionados who still closely follow the case, what is not generally known is the important role her lawyers played in getting her acquitted in the face of very strong evidence of guilt. Just as O. J. had the funds to hire his Dream Team a century later, Lizzie as the daughter of one of the most powerful, if not the most powerful, family in Fall River, was able to hire the best. And just as O. J. did, she gained an outpouring of sympathy from the public and the media, in part helped along by her attorneys' influence with the press. The popular perception was that there was no way this refined, Christian woman who was active in church charity work could have committed such a horrendous crime, and Lizzie's lawyers played on this sentiment to help them win the case.

How were Lizzie's lawyers able to do such a masterful job? Her story shows the long tradition of how the rich and powerful can use the legal system to their advantage.

The murders occurred on a very hot day, August 4, 1892, in the Borden home in a well-to-do enclave of Fall River, a small city near Boston. Lizzie was a member of the ninth generation of the very powerful Borden family, which dated back to the arrival of John Borden, who came to Portsmouth, Rhode Island, from England in 1638. By 1714, the Bordens owned not only all of what came to be Fall River, but also they owned land in what would become other surrounding towns. During the nineteenth century, Fall River prospered with the growth of the textile industry, and it became a center of factories, mills, and foundries, making it the third-largest city in Massachusetts, with about 77,000 people. At the center of this thriving city were the Bordens. One was on "nearly every important corporate board," according to Robert Sullivan, who conducted a detailed legal study of the case and was once a justice of the Massachusetts Superior Court—the same court where Lizzie was tried. And one of the most prominent citizens was Andrew J. Borden, Lizzie's father. He had turned a small inheritance from his father and his successful undertaking business into a strong financial position, and he had gained a series of directorships in major companies in town, including the First National Bank, Globe Yarn Mill Company, Troy Cotton and Woolen Manufacturing Company, and Merchants Manufacturing Company.[7]

In short, Andrew Borden was a major presence in town, though he lived with his wife Abby and two daughters, Lizzie and Emma, in a fairly simple but stolid house on 92 Second Street, which was located downtown near city hall and his various business interests. The house consisted of two long floors, with a parlor, sitting room, dining room, and kitchen downstairs, and five large rooms upstairs—one for Mr. and Mrs. Borden, a connecting dressing room for Mrs. Borden, an adjacent room for Lizzie, a smaller room for Emma, and a guest room. Since the house had no hallways, one had to go through one room to get to another, and significantly, the outside doors to the house were normally locked, as were the doors to the second-floor bedrooms. This sense of a locked-in house, which would prove very critical at the trial, reflected Andrew's personal style, as a "dour, tightfisted-man" who was reserved, brusque, and even unfriendly. He brought that personal style to the atmosphere of the house.[8] It was a grim household, guided by a severe Protestant ethic, devoted to "making, hoarding, and cautiously spending money."[9]

Lizzie, then thirty-two, was unmarried and therefore considered a "spinster" at a time when women were expected to marry, and she lived a refined social life characteristic of women in socially prominent families. For instance, she went on a grand tour of Europe in 1890 with another woman of her class, and she was active in her church, the Central Congregational Church, which contributed to her respectable image. As a member of the church, she was involved in the Christian Endeavor Society, a participant on a missionary committee, and taught a class at Sunday school. She was a member of the Women's Christian Temperance Society, too. Such credentials and the family's high standing made it difficult for anyone to think of her as a murderess—a point that her lawyer would emphasize at her trial.[10]

Then, that very hot August Thursday, about 10:40 a.m., shortly after Andrew Borden returned home from work and lay down on the sitting room sofa for a nap, Lizzie Borden called up to the family's maid, Bridget Sullivan, who had a room in the attic, to say that someone had broken into the house and killed her father.[11] Before that fateful morning, everything in the household had seemed quite routine, though there were a few unusual occurrences. On the previous Tuesday, Andrew and Abby Borden had felt nauseous, though a doctor treating Abby said the problem was probably the result of eating meat that spoiled due to the heat. And Lizzie reported being sick on Wednesday; she told some neighbors she thought maybe the sickness was due to "unfit baker's bread" or to "some unknown person having poisoned the milk" after a farmer delivered it at dawn.[12] Then, that Thursday morning, after Bridget came downstairs to do her chores, unlocked the back door, and picked up the milk can, she, too, soon felt nauseous and went upstairs.

But otherwise nothing seemed unusual. Around 7 a.m., Andrew and Abby had breakfast, joined by a guest, John Morse, who had stayed overnight in the guest room. That Lizzie didn't join them was not unusual because Lizzie and Emma didn't get along well with their stepmother Abby and often ate by themselves. But Emma wasn't at this breakfast because she had left two weeks earlier to visit a friend, Mrs. Brownell in Fairhaven, Massachusetts, about fifteen miles away. Soon after breakfast, Morse left to visit a niece and nephew who lived about one-and-a-half miles away, and Andrew left to check over his various businesses.[13]

That left only Lizzie, Bridget, and Abby, Lizzie's stepmother, in the house. Around 9:30 a.m., after telling Bridget to wash the windows on the first floor, Abby told her she was going to put new pillowcases on the pillows in the guest room and went upstairs. Meanwhile, as Bridget washed the windows with a bucket and washcloth,[14] chatting briefly with a servant girl from the neighbor's yard and making several trips to the barn to get water, Lizzie remained inside the house. Perhaps she spent at least some of that time upstairs; as Bridget later told the police and testified at Lizzie's trial, she didn't see anyone in the downstairs rooms, yard, or back entrance, and she could see clearly into each room as she washed the windows.[15]

Around 10:40 a.m. Andrew returned home, where his next-door neighbor, Mrs. Kelly, saw him enter. He had some trouble getting his key to open the double locked and bolted door, and so Bridget let him in. Meanwhile, as Andrew entered, Lizzie was standing at the top of the front stairway on the second floor, next to the guest room, which was adjacent to her room. As she came downstairs to greet Andrew, she told him, while Bridget was still there, able to overhear her, that: "Mrs. Borden has gone out—she had a note from somebody who was sick."[16] Because the statement was not true, and no evidence of any note or sick person that Mrs. Borden visited was ever found, the statement was heavily targeted at the trial to suggest that Lizzie had a guilty knowledge of Abby's death.

In any case, Andrew briefly went up to his room, and around 10:50, he came downstairs and lay down on the large upholstered sofa in the sitting room to take a nap. Meanwhile, Lizzie began ironing handkerchiefs in the dinning room, as Bridget washed the last windows. After Bridget finished at about 11 a.m., she went up the back stairs to her room in the attic to lie down, still not feeling very well.[17]

About ten minutes later, Lizzie called up with the cry that would resound through history books: "Come down quick! Father's dead! Somebody's come in and killed him!"[18]

Within minutes, Bridget left the house to notify the family's doctor, Dr. Bowen, who lived across the street, and a neighbor, Miss Russell. Soon another neighbor, Mrs. Churchill, who lived behind the Borden house and noticed the sudden commotion, came over to help. So where was Lizzie when this happened? She said she was in the barn on an errand, as she told Mrs. Churchill, and when asked where her mother was, Lizzie said she did not know because Abby had left after she had gotten a note to see someone who was sick. Finally, after some discussion about who would go upstairs to check if Abby was there, Bridget and Mrs. Churchill went upstairs, and from the open door to the guest room, they could see Abby lying on the floor, near the bed.[19]

By this time, Dr. Bowen had arrived, and he examined the two bodies. He noticed that Andrew's face had been hacked, leaving numerous cuts. He counted eleven blows in all, and the first blow appeared to have been fatal. Besides the blood coming from the wounds, he saw some blood spots on the wall, nearby wall, and picture, but there was nothing on Andrew's suit to suggest any kind of fight or resistance. So clearly he had been attacked while he slept. As for Abby, she had nineteen deep wounds behind her head and a couple behind her neck and scalp, and her dark and congealed blood indicated that she had died earlier.[20] Later, it would be estimated that her death occurred about sixty to ninety minutes before Andrew's, although some modern-day revisionists have questioned whether there was such a long time delay between the killings—a significant point in arguing whether someone else could have gotten into the house and quickly escaped before being discovered. But the general view is that this delay occurred between the two killings.

In any event, based on the facts known at the time, if an outsider was the killer, the stranger must have been in the house without being seen before, during, between, and after the killings—a time when Lizzie and Bridget were both up and around. Moreover, the outsider would have had to get through both the outside and inside locked doors—a scenario that seemed unlikely to the investigators or at Lizzie's trial. Alternatively, if not an outsider, the killer must have been someone in the house. And since both John Morse and Emma had gone out for the day—John to visit relatives, Emma to a town about fifteen miles away[21]—and both had witnesses to back up their visits,[22] that left Lizzie and Bridget as the only people in the house. What about the illegitimate butcher brother? He was not mentioned in the police reports or evidence introduced at the trial. Additionally, no unhappy tenants, business associates, or customers of Andrew Borden were mentioned. There may have been some people passing by on the street from time to time, but there was no evidence that anyone got through the locked doors or was seen by Bridget as she cleaned the windows.

Meanwhile, as the doctor and neighbors were gathering at the house, the police were on their way. First to arrive was Officer George W. Allen, who ran from the nearby station house and entered the house through the back door because the front was locked and bolted. Then, he ran back to the police station for assistance. Soon a half-dozen more police officers were on the scene,[23] and they quickly reached the same conclusion as Dr. Bowen—that Abby had died significantly earlier than her husband. The police then searched for a possible intruder, but soon discounted that possibility, given the locked doors and movements of Bridget and Lizzie around the house.

Their suspicions were quickly aroused by Lizzie's behavior—both from their own observations and from their later interviews with neighbors. One reason for these suspicions was that Lizzie seemed calm and emotionless, as Miss Russell and Mrs. Churchill were with her in the kitchen, offering their sympathy and support. Oddly, too, while the officers were still searching through the house, Lizzie left the kitchen, returned to her bedroom, changed from the blue dress she had been wearing, and put on a pink or brown housecoat or dress, depending upon the account, and returned to the kitchen.[24] She also repeated her story of Abby's note to visit a sick friend to the medical examiner and some of the officers, though there was no sign of any such note in the house. And most suspiciously, Lizzie claimed she had gone to the barn loft to find iron sinkers for a fishing trip before returning to find her father dead. Supposedly, the trip would be on a church picnic the next weekend.[25] But when Inspector William H. Medley went up to the loft to investigate, he found it so stifling that he could barely breathe. Moreover, he noticed that the loft floor was covered by a coat of hay and other dust, which had no footprints or other signs of disturbance.[26] If that was the case, could Lizzie have really been in the barn during this time? Besides, her tale of going to find sinkers was a most improbable story because not only was there no iron in the loft and "an unbroken carpet of dust" that might have built up for months, but also the Borden girls were not known to go fishing or on church picnics. So it was "an obvious whopper!" to quote crime writer Martin Fido.[27]

Then, further evidence pointed to an inside job when the police searching the cellar found two hatchets and two axes with handles, along with a hatchet head attached to a recently broken handle that was dusted with ashes.[28] Presumably, the ashes had been used to scrub it clean.[29] Moreover, the police found that nothing seemed to be missing from the property of the victims or the household as a whole.[30]

Thus, early on, the police felt the killer couldn't be an intruder and quickly considered Lizzie their prime suspect. Even so, they initially hesitated to arrest her, given the prominence of her family. However, they were so certain she was the killer, not Bridget, that they allowed Bridget, who was afraid that an unknown murderer might come back to kill again, to leave the house to stay at a neighbor's house, after which she never returned to the Borden home.[31]

Over the next few days, the police continued to gather more evidence, which included sorting through the many tips and rumors they received due to the heavy press coverage and public fascination with the case. Crowds gathered in front of the house, while the police guarded the doors and kept out all but a few known friends and associates, and the murders became the number one discussion topic in town.

Meanwhile, acting completely innocent, Lizzie joined her sister Emma in placing an ad in the local Fall River *Herald* newspaper, which offered a $5,000 reward to "secure the arrest and conviction" of any person or persons causing the death of Mr. and Mrs. Borden. However, the ad didn't deter the police from focusing on Lizzie, and soon they had even more evidence of suspicious behavior—most notably Lizzie's attempt to purchase prussic acid, a lethal poison, a day before the murder, which she claimed was for cleaning a hat.[32] It was a purchase trumpeted in the Fall River *Globe*, which headed its feature article: "What Did Lizzie Want of Poison?"[33]

Then, though the police didn't know this during their initial investigation, Lizzie engaged in one of the most suspicious acts that would come out at the trial. She burned a dress.[34] It happened on Sunday morning, three days after the murders, soon after Miss Russell had made breakfast for Lizzie, Emma, and herself. Lizzie went to the stove with a blue dress and began burning it. When Emma asked what she was doing, Lizzie told her she was going to "burn the old thing" because "it's all covered with paint."[35] At the time, no one said anything to stop her, though the next day, after Miss Russell spoke to a Pinkerton detective, briefly hired by the Borden's family lawyer to do some independent investigating, she told Lizzie that he had asked about the dress and she shouldn't have burned it. She told Lizzie, "I'm afraid . . . the worst thing you could have done was to burn that dress," and Lizzie replied, "Oh, what made you let me do it? . . . Why didn't you tell me?"[36]

So why burn that dress? If there was nothing suspicious on it, such as bloodstains, why suddenly burn it? If Lizzie had the dress to show there were no bloodstains on it, that would have helped support her innocence, but the act of burning it contributed to a perception of guilt. Perhaps she might have initially hidden that dress on a hanger inside one of her other dresses so the investigating police wouldn't see it when they conducted their search, as one of the first women writing about the case, Victoria Lincoln, pointed out.[37]

In any case, by the next day, four days after the murder, the police still had not found any indication that anyone outside the Borden home was involved. In response, Judge Josiah C. Blaisdell of the Bristol County Second District Court called for an inquest to start the following day at the Fall River Police Station—an event that went on for the next three days. During this time, Judge Blaisdell called in various witnesses, including Lizzie Borden, and at the end of the inquest, he issued a warrant for her arrest. Lizzie was then taken to jail and arraigned the following morning in front of Judge Blaisdell, now the presiding judge at the preliminary hearing, who determined there was sufficient cause to hold her over for a trial. Over the next few months, the grand jury reviewed the prosecution case and in December issued three indictments against her—one for murdering her father, one for murdering her mother, and one for murdering them both.[38] Meanwhile, Lizzie awaited the coming trial in the Taunton jail. Although the outlook might have been bleak for her initially, her legal team, along with the growing public support they helped to generate for her, helped to turn things around.

The trial began on June 5, 1893, with the prosecution led by Hosea M. Knowlton, assisted by William H. Moody. They presented a solid case, showing how the evidence clearly pointed to Lizzie. Since the two deaths occurred about ninety minutes apart, it was doubtful an intruder could have hidden in the house during that time without being observed; it was also unlikely that an intruder could have gotten in to such a well-locked house. Only four people lived in the household, and two were away. Lizzie had lied that her stepmother had gone out, claiming there was a note. When a note could not be found, Lizzie further claimed that her stepmother might have burnt it. Lizzie alleged to be in the barn loft getting sinkers for a fishing trip, but Lizzie didn't fish, it was a stifling hot day, and the dust on the barn floor appeared undisturbed. Lizzie was known to not get along with her stepmother, and she acknowledged that to the police. In fact, some townsfolk were aware of the quarrels she had with her stepmother over the property Abby would inherit when Andrew died.[39] Plus, Lizzie had changed her dress soon after the police arrived and burned a dress three days later. Moreover, she had tried to get prussic acid a day before the murders, and people in the house had gotten sick, perhaps due to food poisoning, shortly before the murders. The prosecution even presented witnesses to show why no one saw any blood on Lizzie immediately after the crime, even before she changed her dress. They argued that little blood spatter occurred from the kinds of wounds that killed Andrew and Abby and that the killer could have stood behind a door when killing Andrew, thus avoiding the blood that did spatter in the room. Additionally, the prosecution brought in witnesses who testified about Lizzie's suspicious statements and behavior, such as her many comments about her mother going out to visit a sick person and her comments to Miss Russell about burning the dress. The evidence made the case seem like a prosecution slam dunk.

But even with that strong case against her, Lizzie had a powerful legal team behind her, along with a highly sympathetic public and press, who found it hard to believe a well-respected Christian woman from an elite family could have done such a crime. From the day the murders had occurred, Lizzie had been advised and then was represented by a top local attorney, Andrew J. Jennings. He was one of the most prominent citizens in Fall River, and his partner James M. Morton had been appointed to the Supreme Judicial Court of Massachusetts. For further assistance, Jennings turned to Melvin O. Adams, who had been an assistant district attorney in the Boston area before becoming a private practitioner. Additionally, heading up the defense team was George D. Robinson, a very well-connected and highly respected Massachusetts politician.[40] He was a former governor of Massachusetts for three one-year terms, from 1884 to 1887, and as governor, Robinson had appointed the judge trying the case: Justice Justin Dewey.[41] Today, such a cozy arrangement between a defense lawyer and a judge would probably not be allowed due to a conflict of interest, in that the judge might be expected to show bias in favor of the defense. In such case, either a new judge would be found or the lawyer would not take the case. But the trial went forward with this arrangement, and no one objected. And later, Dewey's rulings did seem to generally favor the defense.

Meanwhile, the circuslike atmosphere surrounding the trial, along with the support of the public and press, created a climate that could easily influence the judge and jury in the days before trials were moved or juries sequestered to avoid such prejudicial influence. Despite the evidence to be presented against her, Lizzie's support was growing, too. As Sullivan describes it in *Goodbye Lizzie Borden*, her supporters included "The Bloomer Girls" and other feminist organizations, the Women's Christian Temperance Union, and two influential reverends—the Reverend W. Walter Jubb and the Reverend E. A. Buck, who drummed up support for Lizzie from many other religious groups of different denominations.[42] In tones similar to those in the O. J. Simpson case a century later, the press reported how Lizzie's supporters berated the prosecution and the press for going after this "early middle-aged spinster" who was but a "helpless little girl."[43]

Ignoring such popular sentiment, the prosecution divided its case into three arguments for guilt. First, Lizzie was "predisposed to and had pre-determined" to kill the Bordens, as shown by the witnesses who would testify that she had a longstanding dislike of her stepmother and a fear of losing her inheritance. This established a motive. Second, Lizzie had the opportunity to kill both, including the strength and means, and only she alone had this opportunity. Third, her words and deeds after the murders showed a "consciousness of guilt." For example, she lied to prevent anyone from discovering the first murder (i.e., she said her stepmother had gone out because of a note about a sick friend); she lied about where she was during the murders (i.e., she claimed she had gone to the very hot barn to find sinkers); she lied and made inconsistent statements about her discovery of her father's body; and finally, she made some unusual statements and engaged in some unusual acts in the few days following the murder before her arrest.[44]

The first prosecution witness was an engineer who described the layout of the Borden house. Following this testimony, the prosecution took the jury to visit the house to show them firsthand where the murders occurred and why it would be difficult for any stranger to hide in the house. After that, John Morse, Lizzie's uncle, testified about his whereabouts during the time of the murder to show that he couldn't have done it. Bridget, the maid, described how she had been washing the windows, saw Lizzie ironing handkerchiefs in the kitchen, went upstairs to lie down, and heard nothing until Lizzie, then wearing a light blue dress, had called her to come downstairs because her father was dead.[45]

And so it went, witness after witness making a strong, powerful case for Lizzie's guilt. In fact, some witness testimony made it sound like Lizzie was setting the stage to kill and blame someone else for the murder; for example, Miss Russell, one of Lizzie's few close friends, testified how almost everyone in the house was sick two days before the murder, possibly from some baker's bread or milk, and that Lizzie expressed a general fear that someone might do something harmful. As Miss Russell related, Lizzie expressed fear that her father had an enemy because he was so "discourteous" and had much trouble with the men who came to see him. She also expressed fears that someone might break into the barn or do something else, though she didn't know what. In short, Lizzie either had a case of great paranoia, or she was sowing seeds to cast the suspicion away from herself. Then, Miss Russell described how Lizzie had burned a light-blue dress and had suggested that her stepmother might have burned the note that led her to leave the house.[46]

Still other testimony dealt with the wounds and blood, establishing the ninety-minute to two-hour delay between the killings by pointing out that Mrs. Borden's body was cool and the blood congealed, whereas Mr. Borden's body was still warm and the blood was still red. Such testimony also showed that the killing could have been done without covering the killer in blood.[47] Then, in an effort to establish the murder weapon, Moody brought in three doctors as witnesses to show how the wounds could have matched the head of the handleless hatchet found in the cellar.[48] Still other witnesses from the neighborhood, about a half-dozen of them, were brought in to show that no one saw any strangers enter or leave the Borden house.[49] About the only damning evidence the defense was successful in excluding was Lizzie's unsuccessful attempts to purchase the deadly prussic acid from two different drugstores, which she couldn't get because it was only sold by prescription.[50]

All in all, the prosecution presented an extremely strong case against Lizzie, and even the defense offered little to rebut all of the evidence that pointed to guilt. Even so, Lizzie's lawyers were able to combat what otherwise might have seemed like an open-and-shut case. They did so by largely ignoring the evidence and playing up Lizzie's good character, as well as getting some help from the judge.

One defense strategy was to use witnesses to testify about Lizzie's long-standing good reputation, as well as her participation in religious and charitable activities, in order to suggest that she couldn't have committed these horrendous crimes. Additionally, the defense sought to undermine the credibility or contradict the testimony of the prosecution witnesses. Another ploy was to allude to the many strange people seen in the neighborhood of the Borden's home to imply that an intruder did come in. But without any evidence that any one had done so, the defense was essentially using a "smokescreen technique." As Sullivan notes, the witnesses were referring to "vague and unidentified persons and . . . events that could not reasonably be in any way associated with the fact of the crimes."[51] Moreover, such people might be normally present on a busy city street during the day. Yet, this approach helped to distract from the strong evidence of the prosecution.

Especially effective, too, were Robinson's showy final arguments. He presented himself as a country lawyer, who appealed to the jurors' appreciation of "noble causes," including "patriotism, God, motherhood, the protection of womanhood . . . the sanctity of the home . . . and . . . the acquittal of Lizzie Borden."[52] At the same time, while establishing a strong rapport with the jury, he ignored or distorted much of the prosecution's evidence. He even suggested that the Fall River police had been "discourteous" in questioning Lizzie, a grieving woman, on the day of the murder, so soon after her "great bereavement,"[53] even though such questioning was precisely the proper police procedure. Likewise, Robinson ignored the medical testimony that explained why there might be little blood on the killer and emphasized the lack of blood on Lizzie. He suggested that Bridget, as well as Lizzie, had heard about the missing note directly from Abby, when, in fact, Bridget was only reporting what Lizzie had told her about the note.

Robinson then effectively played on the sentiments of the jurors with his dramatic conclusion: "To find her guilty, you must believe her to be a fiend! Does she look it?"[54] Just "look at her," he appealed to the jury.[55] And, of course, the respectable, demur Lizzie, who looked like the perfect Christian woman in her tight Victorian dress, did not look the fiend. His summation was an effective counter to the prosecution's emphasis on looking at the evidence.[56]

But perhaps what was most unusual and helpful for Lizzie's case was Judge Dewey's charge to the jury, which might be due to his close relationship with Robinson. As Sullivan points out in his analysis of the trial transcript, Judge Dewey's "opinion that the jury should acquit Lizzie shone unmistakably through the words of his instructions. A judicial direction to find Lizzie Borden Not Guilty marked Justice Dewey's charge from beginning to end."[57] The judge even suggested how the jurors might weigh the evidence, when he remarked on Lizzie's sterling, positive character, which involved "active benevolence in religious and charitable work." Further, he observed that in some cases, having such a character "may raise a reasonable doubt of the defendant's guilt even in the face of strongly incriminating evidence."[58]

Judge Dewey additionally undercut the evidence the prosecution produced to show Lizzie's long-standing conflict with her stepmother by saying, "Imputing a motive to the defendant does not prove she had it." He even suggested other reasons why the note from Abby might have disappeared after a stranger killed her. Perhaps, Judge Dewey speculated, the killer might have found the letter or note with her and then might have had a "reasonable and natural wish to remove that as one possible link in tracing himself."[59] Yet, why should an unknown outsider have any knowledge of the note or expect the note to have any link to the crime? Clearly, the judge was giving his own theory to support Lizzie's claim of innocence, though such speculations on the evidence went far beyond the usual instructions on how to assess the evidence given by a judge to a jury. Instead, Judge Dewey was acting more in the role of a defense attorney than a judge in making this argument.

Even further benefiting the defense, Judge Dewey advised the jury to look at Lizzie's numerous inconsistent statement about where she was and what she did when her father was murdered with caution, since such oral statements could be "subject to much imperfection and mistake." In addition, he urged the jurors to subject the prosecution's medical evidence about the time of death, murder weapons, Lizzie's physical ability to commit the crimes, and presence of blood to "careful scrutiny." In fact, Judge Dewey even undermined the value of the prosecution's evidence when he observed that medical experts sometimes "manifest a strong bias or partisan spirit in favor of the party employing them."[60]

In short, Judge Dewey essentially knocked down the whole prosecution's case in his charge to the jury. But why? Perhaps he was strongly biased by his close connection to Robinson, who had appointed him to the bench. As a result of the combination of that charge, the powerful character evidence presented by Robinson, and Robinson's persuasive country charm, Lizzie's legal team won the day. Within a few hours, at 4:30 p.m., the jury returned with its "Not guilty!" verdict, followed by a great cheer in the courtroom and out in the streets.[61]

So Lizzie returned to her home in Fall River, vindicated in court. Soon afterward, though, the case was revisited by both the press and the public. As a result, the general consensus soon was that Lizzie really had done it, despite her acquittal.[62] As people came to realize, besides her hostility to her stepmother and her fear of losing property she might otherwise inherit to Abby, Lizzie was the only person with the opportunity to commit both crimes. Significantly, too, she acted after the crime like someone with guilty knowledge, and she had enough time to clean up any remaining traces of blood on her clothing after killing her stepmother (about ninety minutes) and after killing her father (about fifteen minutes before telling Bridget). And when she burned the dress, claiming it was paint, she could have destroyed any other evidence.

Thus, while Lizzie's legal defense had been brilliant, her acquittal couldn't keep the public from deciding that she had done it, as expressed in the famous children's rhyme that she "took an ax and gave her parents many whacks."[63] In fact, one early version of the rhyme is more explicit in describing how she did it:

Lizzie Borden took an axe
And gave her mother forty whacks.
Then she stood behind the door
And gave her father forty more.[64]

Given this harsh public sentiment against her, it's no wonder that after the trial Lizzie lived mostly as a recluse for the rest of her life. She used her inheritance to move with her sister Emma to a new house in a fashionable section of Fall River.[65] Once the tide of public opinion turned against her, so did her former supporters from the clergy and so did the Fall River elite. She was no longer welcome in their society, and even their children were forbidden to speak to her.[66] As a result, she lived a mostly quiet isolated life for the next thirty-four years until she died at home in 1927. However, she did make some occasional trips to other cities, such as Boston and Washington, D.C.; she also had an interest in the theater and developed a close relationship with the well-known actress Nance O'Neill and some other popular entertainers of the day. However, it would seem that many of the stories of the wild parties she gave are simply exaggerated or gossip, according to Robert Sullivan's investigation of her later days.[67]

Turnaround: The Case of Claus von Bulow (New York, New York, and Newport, Rhode Island, 1980–1985)

The Claus von Bulow case is generally treated as a murder case in the literature of well-known murder cases even though the victim is still alive. However, for all practical purposes, the victim, after nearly two decades of being in an irreversible coma that was possibly the result of a shot of insulin, is treated as if she were dead. Only the final distribution of the assets of her estate awaits her actual death. Legally, the case was prosecuted as an attempted murder case, though at any point, it could have become a murder case had the victim died during the trials. Thus, I have included it here, particularly because it illustrates so well the ability of the wealthy to obtain the best legal representation. In this case, that meant beating the odds of a conviction at the first trial by winning the right to appeal, winning that appeal, gaining a new trial, and overwhelming the prosecution with a brilliant defense.

The case became one of the most closely watched trials of the rich and powerful. The setting was the exclusive high-society world of New York City and Newport, where Claus and Martha "Sunny" von Bulow lived in luxury. In New York they had an elegant co-op, with a suite of rooms attended by servants, and in Newport, they had a twenty-room mansion, Clarendon Court, which looked like the palace of a king. It had stately rooms, a large pool, and beautiful gardens, and it was furnished with expensive antiques. It was also the scene of gala society parties, with hundreds of elegantly dressed guests, waited on by eager-to-please servants, while an orchestra played.[68]

Most of the money for this lavish courtly lifestyle came from Sunny, a wealthy heiress and the only child of George Crawford, founder of the Columbia Gas and Electric Company. He was worth three-quarters of a billion dollars at his death when Sunny was four, and he left his money to her.[69] When Sunny first married in her twenties in 1957, she married into royalty, marrying Prince Alfred Edward von Auersperg. He had become a sports instructor after his family fell on hard times, though he still had blue-blooded credentials. But his limited income didn't matter, since Sunny's money provided for a luxurious lifestyle. They had two children, Princess Annie, nicknamed Ala, and Prince Alexander, called Alex. But Sunny wanted to end the marriage after eight years because she had grown tired of Prince Alfie's affairs with other women, as well as his big-game hunting trips to Africa, and wanted to live in New York. In the meantime, two years before the marriage ended, in 1964, she had met Claus von Bulow at a London dinner party, and shortly after her divorce from Prince Alfie, they married in 1966.[70]

At the time that they met, Claus was a high-society bachelor, primarily due to his position as an assistant to J. Paul Getty, for whom he flew all over the world. He had aristocratic roots through his mother, Joanna, who was the daughter of Fritz von Bulow, a wealthy descendant of the von Bulow family in Germany. She had married his father, Svend Borberg, a Danish playwright and theater critic, and divorced him when Claus was four. After the Nazis occupied Denmark at the beginning of World War II, Joanna fled to London, where Claus grew up. After he graduated from Cambridge with a law degree, he served for eight years as a barrister under the highly respected barrister Quintin Hogg, who later became Lord Hailsham.[71] Though Claus had a relatively modest salary when he worked for Getty—$120,000 a year, perhaps about $500,000 today—he had been acquiring other sources of wealth through investments and art purchases.

Still, his own wealth was dwarfed by Sunny's, and that became a key issue in the ensuing attempted murder trials. Her great wealth raised the question of motive. Did Claus try to kill Sunny for her money, rather than divorce her, so he could continue to live a luxurious lifestyle and marry Alexandra Isles, the glamorous society woman and soap opera actress he was seeing?

For the first ten years of their marriage, everything seemed fine. Claus had left Getty's employ to move to New York to be with Sunny, and he became essentially her full-time escort in the high-society life. Though Sunny also had a reclusive nature that made her draw increasingly inward over the years, initially she seemed to thrive in enjoying the high-paced society lifestyle. It was a life of traveling around the world, going to and giving fabulous parties, visiting galleries, and collecting antiques. Claus and Sunny also had a child together, Cosima.[72]

But although Sunny had the money, to a great extent their social life revolved around seeing and entertaining Claus's friends. For example, at their frequent dinner parties in their Fifth Avenue New York co-op, the guests were Claus's friends, and Sunny's old friends found it harder and harder to reach her.[73] But outwardly, Sunny seemed to defer willingly to Claus's control, just as she had with Alfie's domineering style in her first marriage. The presumption of male dominance was fostered by both men, who had been raised in the European tradition where men are in charge in a relationship.

Sunny also felt comfortable letting Claus take charge because she had a somewhat retiring, shy personality; she was more comfortable doing things at home, whereas Claus was the outgoing, social one. So gradually, she dropped out more and more from the social circuit, though she still appeared at many of big events. Sunny now spent much time at their Newport mansion arranging flowers and swimming to keep fit, and Claus became active in many Newport associations, such as the Preservation Society and Cliff Walk Association.[74] He also became an active member of the exclusive Knickerbocker and Union Clubs in New York—the Knickerbocker being the setting for the turn-of-the-century Molineux case, described in Chapter 1, in which Molineux felt an affront to his honor by a rival for the woman he loved and tried to poison his rival only to kill someone else.

Then, in the 1970s, strains began to develop in the marriage. One reason is that Sunny became increasingly reclusive and resistant to accepting invitations. Though she still liked to travel, her ideal entertainment was having dinner at home with her husband or children and then playing a board game or watching TV. By contrast, Claus continued to enjoy the social whirl of parties, and increasingly bored and frustrated, he felt like an appendage to his wealthy wife.[75] He even complained to Sunny's now-grown children, Ala and Alex, that he was beginning to feel like a "cheap gigolo." He said that he was losing the respect of his business associates and Newport neighbors, who thought of him as a "parasite sponging off his wife."[76]

So gradually, Claus and Sunny began drifting apart. In some versions of the story, Sunny began drinking, using drugs, and eating too many sweets, contributing to a decline in her health (according to Alan Dershowitz's version based on some witnesses). In others, she became increasingly displeased that Claus wasn't working, wanted him to find high-level work, and did not drink, use drugs, or eat to excess (according to William Wright and Jay Robert Nash, based on other witnesses supporting the prosecution case). At the same time, Sunny lost interest in having sex with her husband,[77] possibly after the birth of her daughter Cosima in 1974 or possibly nine years earlier, according to other sources.

It was in that context of growing problems in the marriage that in 1978, Claus met Alexandra Isles at the Knickerbocker Club. She was a 33-year-old divorced socialite and actress who appeared on the TV soap opera *Dark Shadows.* Before meeting Alexandra, Claus had had occasional flings with other women and had been seeing a New York prostitute, Leslie Baxter. But now he became seriously in love with Alexandra.[78] He was attracted to Alexandra when they first met not only because was she younger than Sunny, but also because she had an active social life in New York. He was also impressed that Alexandra was independently raising her young son, as well as pursuing an acting career.

Claus began by asking her out to lunch and dinner, and after several months, they began an affair. Two months later he asked her to marry him, though he told her it would take some time for him to diplomatically get out of his marriage with Sunny. How long? Alexandra made it clear she didn't want to be a secret mistress, and eventually she gave him an ultimatum: she would give him six months, until October 1979, to divorce Sunny or else she would leave him. This way, everything could be settled and they could all be together "as a family by Christmas."[79] Then, when he didn't meet this deadline, she gradually phased out seeing him, and when they did see each other, the tension between them grew over him not being free.

Then, Sunny suffered her first coma on December 26, 1979, which the prosecution later suggested was triggered by Alexandra's demand for Claus to get free of Sunny by Christmas.[80] At the time, the crisis was treated simply as a medical emergency, in which Sunny, near death, was rushed to the hospital. She recovered, and after a period of recuperation, returned to her high-society life, which included giving some parties, despite her preference for spending quiet time at home. However, after Alexandra gave Claus still another ultimatum to divorce Sunny, Sunny experienced a second coma around Christmas just a year after her first coma—this time on December 20, 1980. Because two comas in a year was highly unusual, the circumstances of Sunny's first coma were revisited in a more sinister light.

Among other things, Sunny's longtime maid, Maria Schrallhammer, who had been with her since her first marriage to Aflie von Auersperg, claimed that during the first coma, she had seen Sunny lying in a state of unconsciousness for most of the day, while Claus sat beside her, seemingly unconcerned, reading a newspaper. When Maria told Claus she was concerned and urged him to call a doctor, he at first resisted, saying nothing was wrong and Sunny was simply asleep. But finally, when Sunny's breathing began to sound like a death rattle, he called for help about 6 p.m. Soon her longtime doctor, Dr. Janis Gailitis, arrived and saw her turning blue, triggering a desperate race to the emergency room to revive her.[81]

Why did Claus wait so long before calling? At his second trial, Alexandra, no longer his mistress, testified that he had waited as long as he did because he hoped for Sunny's death. As Alexandra explained, von Bulow had called her after the first coma while she was at her mother's house in Ireland and told her that he had lain on the bed beside his wife for hours waiting for her to die. However, at the last minute, he wasn't able to go through with it and called the doctor.[82]

Yet, some accounts suggest that when he talked to Sunny's friends about her drinking and depression, von Bulow had been setting the stage to claim that Sunny had caused her own coma by drinking too much, and she either overdosed or tried to commit suicide.[83] According to some of Sunny's friends, Claus began telling these stories of Sunny's drinking problem in July 1978, three months before he met Alexandra Isles. He even told Sunny's family doctor, Richard Stock, that Sunny was "having a problem with the bottle," and Stock entered this information into the medical record without checking to confirm its validity.[84]

But were these stories true? It's not certain; even as von Bulow spread these stories, other friends of Sunny's saw no signs of alcoholism. One concerned friend even tried to find out the extent of Sunny's drinking by telling Sunny about her own struggles with alcoholism. She thought Sunny might admit any such problem, but Sunny did not. Sunny even passed up the wine served at lunch for a glass of milk. So the friend left their get-together convinced that Sunny really didn't have a problem, and she was puzzled that Claus should be suggesting that she did.[85]

For now, though, the strange circumstances surrounding Sunny's first 1979 crisis were unreported, in part because the wealthy generally want to keep any personal problems quiet, and there were only suspicions. But the second coma a year later triggered Claus's two step-children Ala and Alex to launch a private investigation into what happened in both comas. The revelations from this private investigation led to a further investigation by the police, which resulted in two trials and lingering suspicions by many that Claus did it. Even if he was acquitted after a successful appeal from a guilty verdict in the first trial, many held lingering suspicions that Claus really was responsible. In the second trial, his lawyers were able to outlawyer the prosecution because Claus had the money to pay for them to achieve this result.

How did his legal team do it? At the first trial, the evidence against Claus seemed overwhelming, leading to a quick guilty verdict, after which both the media and public took that view that he did it—the view shared by William Wright in his book *The Von Bulow Affair*, Jay Robert Nash in his high-profile homicides collection *Murder Among the Rich and Famous*, Dominick Dunne, and others. But after Claus hired a new high-power lawyer, Alan M. Dershowitz, and his team of student assistants, his lawyers turned that verdict around with new evidence and a new spin on the evidence and testimony already presented. True justice? Or just very good lawyering, since von Bulow could pay for the best? The questions still remain, but here's how Dershowitz was able to turn the verdict around.

In the first trial, Maria, Sunny's maid, had provided critical evidence. She spoke about her growing suspicions when Claus had not been willing to call for medical help for his wife right away. Then, she noticed a suspicious-looking black leather bag, about four inches by seven inches long, which Claus was carrying. When she looked into the bag, she found a number of prescription drug vials, including one made out to Leslie Baxter, who turned out to be a New York prostitute. Maria wondered particularly about two strange-looking vials, one containing white powder and the other yellow paste. She asked Sunny's daughter Ala about them, and then together they told

Alex, Ala's brother. He was curious about them, too, and so Alex and Maria took them for testing by Sunny's longtime doctor Dr. Stock. The powder and paste turned out to be two ordinary drugs used as sedatives: secobarbital and Valium. But they weren't in their usual pill form, which seemed odd. Yet, not wanting to cause a scandal, Alex and Ala kept silent, not telling anyone outside of the family about their suspicions.[86]

Meanwhile, other suspicious developments were occurring, as the prosecution pointed out in their case, such as when Sunny told a few family members and friends she was considering divorce. She said she felt she was restraining Claus, since he was with her much of the time, was financially dependent on her, and didn't have a successful career of his own. So, to alleviate the mounting tension between them, she set up a $2 million irrevocable trust for Claus with the help of Morris Gurley, the Chemical Bank trust officer for herself and her mother, and she provided that the $120,000 yearly interest on the trust would go to Claus.[87]

Then, in April, Sunny woke up, feeling extremely weak and her speech was slurred. Concerned, she went for medical testing, and after a week, the tests showed she had a reactive hypoglycemia, resulting in a very low blood sugar level. The condition would be made worse by eating sweets because that would lead her pancreas to release even more insulin to counteract the sugar, thus lowering her blood sugar level even more.[88]

Meanwhile, Claus's affair with Alexandra continued, and he got an apartment in New York to show her that he was taking steps to break from Sunny. At the same time, Sunny was becoming more reclusive, seeing fewer people, and accepting fewer invitations, afraid to do anything to trigger another coma. However, Alexandra was getting restless, and in November, when it seemed that Claus was not really living in his New York apartment, she fled to Washington, D.C., determined not to see him anymore. But Claus pursued her there, proclaiming his love and promising to marry her "right away."[89]

Presumably, a divorce might have been a readily available solution. Ironically, over the Thanksgiving weekend, Sunny told her son Alex that she had decided to divorce Claus. Yet she wouldn't tell Alex why, only that it was something "too horrible to tell." Meanwhile, that same weekend, Maria found the small vial with insulin in Claus's black bag, which would prove critical for the prosecution. Still suspicious about Claus, she made the discovery after she asked Alex to come with her to search for the black bag, which they found in one of Claus's closets. Inside, she noticed a small glass vial labeled "insulin," and she asked Alex: "What for insulin?"[90] Yet, thinking insulin was just another medicine, Alexander paid little attention to it at the time.

Then, Sunny strangely collapsed on December 1. She had been having headaches for days, and therefore decided to stay in bed that day. That night, just before Claus called 911, Maria saw Sunny lying on a blood-soaked pillow with a small wound on the back of her head. Sunny was rushed to the hospital, where she was diagnosed with aspirin toxicity. After a day of delirium and slurred speech, she returned to normal, and after a few more days in the hospital, she returned home.[91]

Then came the final coma. Claus suggested giving Maria a few days off, and he, Sunny, and their daughter Cosima headed for a weekend at Clarendon Court in Newport. As Maria helped Sunny and Cosima with their bags, she noticed the black bag inside a large white canvas bag. Inside the black bag, she saw several syringes and vials, including one that was marked "insulin."[92]

At first, though, all seemed normal for a family holiday weekend over Christmas. The family spent the day decorating a Christmas tree, and at dinner, though Sunny complained of a headache, she skipped the main course but had ice cream with caramel sauce for dessert. Maybe that was not a good idea, given her reactive hypoglycemia condition. But Sunny seemed fine as she planned to go to a movie with Claus and her son Alex. Yet, as they waited for Sunny to get her coat, Alex found the conversation with Claus odd. As he described in court, Claus told him he was not "comfortable with his life," since he felt that "he was living off Sunny" and he thought most of the people in Newport felt this way, too.[93]

After Claus, Sunny, and Alex returned from the film shortly after 9 p.m., Claus went to work in his study and Sunny went into the bathroom, changed into a dressing grown, and joined Alex and Cosima, in the library. As they talked, Alex noticed that Sunny's speech began to slur. Then

Claus appeared and asked Sunny if she wanted anything. She asked for a cup of chicken soup, her voice becoming weaker and weaker. After she drank thc soup, she became too weak to even hold the glass of ginger ale she had been drinking. Alex helped her into bed, and after Claus came into the bedroom, Alex went out for a drink. Around 5:30 a.m. when Claus woke up, Sunny was still asleep.

About 11 a.m., the crisis began. After Claus spent an otherwise ordinary morning taking a walk, reading the paper, and having a few phone conversations, he found Sunny sprawled on the floor, her head under the toilet, and her nightgown pulled up above her underpants. He quickly called a doctor, and a few minutes later, a lieutenant from the fire department arrived, along with an ambulance that took Sunny to the Newport Hospital. Soon afterward, Sunny went into cardiac arrest. The doctors stabilized her breathing, and then Dr. Gerhard Meier, the doctor on duty, gave her several pushes of glucose over about twelve hours on the theory that the glucose would increase a low blood sugar level that might be causing her unconsciousness. But instead, her sugar level went down, which was later discussed at the trial as a sign of the presence of insulin.

Sunny never regained consciousness. Though she was transferred to another Boston hospital, the Peter Bent Brigham Hospital, where she could be treated by doctors with expertise with comas and blood sugar problems, her coma was irreversible.[94]

Meanwhile, as Sunny lay in the coma, the suspicions of Maria, Alex, and Ala grew, and their actions led to the first trial. One cause for suspicion is that without knowing about the black bags or Alexandra Isles, the doctor in charge of Sunny's care, Harris Funkenstein, a well-known neurologist, came to believe that Sunny had been injected with insulin.[95] Also, Maria, Alex, and Ala found it suspicious that a few days after Sunny arrived at the hospital, Claus urged the family to remove her life support system, after the doctors said this was an option to consider now that she was unable to breathe without help and would remain in a vegetative state. But other family members refused.[96] Alex and Ala also found it suspicious that Claus kept up the campaign to remove her life support, arguing that the high costs would mean major cutbacks in living expenses, though this wasn't true since Sunny's trust had plenty of money.

Their suspicions led Alex and Ala to launch an investigation with the help of Richard Kuh, a lawyer in private practice, who had once been the assistant New York district attorney for eleven years. After describing their suspicions, they asked him if they could conduct a private investigation without involving the police or creating a scandal. Kuh said they could, and a few weeks after speaking to Maria and hearing her story, Kuh arranged for one of his investigators, Edwin Lamberg, a retired New York police officer, to accompany Alex to look for the suspicious black bag at Clarendon Court when Claus wasn't home. Alex and Lamberg brought a locksmith with them because the closet where Maria had found the bag was locked, though they found a key on Claus's study. After searching through the closet, they found a large black metal box under a shoe shelf and in it a small black bag. Inside the bag, they found some bottles of pills, liquids, and three hypodermic needles, two still in their plastic wrappings, while the other needle was loose and looked like it might have been used.[97] This find proved to be the evidence they needed to begin building the case against Claus.

After Alex took the bag to Kuh, who showed it to his brother, a New York doctor, Kuh suggested that Alex take a sampling of the drugs and the used needle to the family's doctor for further testing, which Alex did. He place the drugs and needle in a manila envelope and brought them to Dr. Stock, who had them tested at the Bio-Sciences Laboratories. When the results came back six days later, they showed that the bluish white powder contained amobarbidol, the blue liquid contained a mix of Valium and amobarbidol, and most telling, the needle had a high concentration of insulin. Immediately, given the other suspicious circumstances surrounding Sunny's coma, Stock called Kuh and advised him to call the police or he would.[98]

By the end of February, Sergeant John Reise of the Rhode Island Police was on the case, along with a prosecutor, Stephen Famiglietti, from the Rhode Island Attorney General's Office to monitor his progress. After Reise heard the stories of Alex, Ala, and Maria and reviewed Sunny's medical records, he began interviewing numerous witnesses.[99] Among them were doctors, former servants, and others who knew Sunny, as well as Leslie Baxter, the prostitute whose name was on the Valium prescription found in Claus's black bag.[100]

By mid-April, Reise felt he had strong enough evidence that Sunny's two comas were caused by an injection, that the needle in Claus's bag was stained with insulin, and that Claus had a powerful motive to want his wife dead: he was in love with another woman and would inherit many millions if Sunny died. He went to interview Claus, telling him that he was a suspect, while two other officers searched the house. Before they could search the closet, however, Claus locked the door. Reise also found a powerful expert witness in Dr. George Cahill, a director of research at the Howard Hughes Medical Institute, who was one of the top blood sugar experts in the world. Looking solely at the medical evidence of Sunny's rapid drop in blood sugar after she was given a series of glucose pushes, he concluded she must have been given a "sugar-eating agent," namely insulin.[101]

In June, a grand jury began reviewing the evidence Reise had collected, as well as calling their own witnesses, and after a few days, the grand jury concluded there was enough evidence to indict von Bulow for injecting his wife with insulin. Word of indictment, issued on July 7, was picked up by the press, turning the von Bulow case into big news.[102]

Claus, soon released on $100,000 bail, had two top criminal lawyers defending him—John Sheehan and Herald Fahringer.[103] He also had the luxury of almost two years out on bail after the trial was postponed until January 1982 at the request of the prosecutors, who wanted more time to assemble their case based on expert witness and medical testimony. But in this first trial, Claus's lawyers, Sheehan and Fahringer, were outgunned. Not only was von Bulow up against the state, but also Alex and Ala were providing additional funds for investigating the case and finding witnesses. As a result, the case, with strong circumstantial evidence and Maria Schrallhammer as the star witness, was compelling. Maria was especially convincing as she described her growing suspicions when she saw Sunny experience two comas and found the vial of insulin in Claus's black bag.[104]

The prosecution also presented a compelling case with its

medical evidence. One high point was showing how a lab had found evidence of insulin on the loose needle in the bag. They additionally presented testimony from Dr. Cahill, who expressed certainty that Sunny's comas were caused by insulin injected into her body, based on the fact that her blood sugar continued to drop even though she was given substantial amounts of glucose.[105]

Other compelling evidence came from the story of banker, Morris Gurley, whose testimony showed that Claus had a very strong motive to murder his wife. He explained that upon Sunny's death, Claus would receive about $14 million under her will, which included Clarendon Court, the New York apartment, control over various charitable gifts, and a fixed income from various trusts, whereas he had brought relatively little capital into the marriage. But if he and Sunny divorced, he would receive far less, only about $120,000 a year from the irrevocable trust and a much smaller cash settlement. Also persuasive was the testimony of Alexandra Isles, who testified about their affair and about their continuing relationship even after Claus was accused of killing his wife. In fact, in January, a month after he told her his wife was in an irreversible coma, Claus and Alexandra went to Nassau with her eleven-year old son Ada. Just two months later, in March, the three of them traveled to Florida with Claus's daughter Cosima, who had split with Ala and Alex to support her father. Only after Claus was indicted in July and on her lawyer's advice did Alexandra stay away from him, except for a brief Christmas visit.[106]

It was powerful stuff, and the defense was unable to counter it with their alternative possibilities approach. Especially damaging was the testimony of their supposed star witness, an exercise instructor named Joy O'Neill, who said that she had given Sunny private instruction for five days a week and that Sunny advised her to give herself injections of insulin or vitamin B so she could eat whatever she wanted. The defense strategy was to use O'Neill's testimony to show that any insulin in Sunny's blood was injected by Sunny herself, perhaps as a self-destructive act if she was depressed about her husband's infidelity and possible divorce. But it turned out that Joy had only taught Sunny a few times and not during the year 1978, when she claimed the conversation about insulin occurred. So that revelation ruined her credibility. Another problem for the defense was that Claus's lawyers didn't effectively explain why Claus seemed so unconcerned about his wife's first coma, and they confused the jurors with their multiple-choice defense that the comas could have been triggered by many things, such as eggnog, amobarbital, aspirin, a low-body temperature, an ice-cream sundae with caramel sauce, or a sudden, unexplained disease.[107]

In short, the state's case boiled down to whether von Bulow administered insulin to kill his wife on two separate occasions, considering he had the motive—to get the woman he loved and Sunny's money—owned the black bag with insulin on the needle, and was the only person in the house who knew how to give injections or had access to needles and syringes. Plus, there was no evidence that Sunny had any problems with either alcohol or drugs, apart from stories spread by Claus, which seemed further proof of his guilt in that he appeared to be spreading false stories about Sunny to cast blame on her for her own death.[108]

Thus, given the power of the prosecution case, in short order, the jury found Claus guilty in this first trial, and he was sentenced to thirty years—ten years of imprisonment for the first attempt on Sunny's life, twenty years for the second.

But Claus fought back, and he was able to use his money and legal team to turn the tide, leading to his new trial. His ability to finance a strong appeal, with the help of top appeals lawyer Alan Dershowitz, made all the difference. To fund this, von Bulow drew on his funds from his trust and the sale of some artwork and some investments. Additionally, he gained help from his rich friends, which may have included a contribution from J. Paul Getty. The result of this renewed legal effort was a very unusual reversal, occurring in only about 5 percent of all murder and attempted murder appeals. This enabled him to have a new trial, which in turn resulted in an acquittal. How did he do it? In *Reversal of Fortune*, which was later turned into a film featuring Glen Close, Jeremy Irons, and Ron Silver, Dershowitz describes how good lawyering made all the difference and put a totally different spin on the evidence.

Dershowitz's strategy was to show that the same facts that might lead Claus to want to kill his wife—his loss of love for her and his affair with Alexandra Isles—might lead Sunny to self-destructive, suicidal behavior. Also, Dershowitz sought to undermine the web of circumstantial evidence the prosecution had built.[109]

A first important step was getting bail for von Bulow by writing up a strong bail application before the sentencing proceedings, scheduled for May 7, 1982. As a result, before von Bulow began serving time, Judge Thomas H. Needham permitted to him to remain free on $1 million bail while he pursued his appeal. Shortly after Dershowitz arranged this release, von Bulow dropped his former lead council, Fahringer, who had given a weak performance. As a replacement, Dershowitz added a local Rhode Island lawyer, John "Terry" MacFadyen, so that his team included someone local to increase rapport with the jury. Then, Dershowitz looked carefully at the various legal grounds for overturning a verdict, such as if any prejudicial judicial errors occurred or if the judge admitted any improper, irrelevant, or prejudicial evidence. Dershowitz also brought in a team of law school students to help with research, creating several teams of students to examine different issues and prepare briefs on these topics.[110]

One critical legal issue was whether the evidence obtained from the private search by Alex and the private investigator was legal, since that produced the most important physical evidence in the case. If Alex and Ala had gone to the police, the police wouldn't have been able to conduct a search without a warrant. As a result, Dershowitz considered questioning whether a wealthy family could avoid having to be subject to the usual police procedures by hiring their own "private police" who would not be subject to the exclusionary rules that applied to the police for improper searches based on constitutional considerations. It might have been a compelling argument for excluding the bag, though Dershowitz ultimately decided for strategic reasons that it was best not to push this argument; a person who is guilty usually wants to keep evidence out, and this approach would make von Bulow seem guilty. Rather, he felt it was more persuasive to argue that crucial exculpatory evidence wasn't brought in, most notably the notes of the interviews that Rich Kuh, the lawyer the family hired to investigate, had conducted with key witnesses, including Maria.[111] So the Kuh notes became the centerpiece of Dershowitz's arguments in his appeal.[112]

Dershowitz then began getting leads for potentially useful evidence that could be used if a new trial was granted to show von Bulow's innocence, though some leads proved to be red herrings. For instance, he considered using Truman Capote, a writer famed for writing about people in high society, who described how Sunny had shown him how to inject vitamins and amphetamines, and had even recommended and sent him a book called *Recreational Drugs*.[113] Also, Dershowitz initially considered using David Marriott, a man in his twenties who worked in some print shops in the Boston area and claimed to know an interior decorator Gilbert Jackson, who supplied Alex with drugs and needles and sometimes brought these items to Alex himself. If true, these claims would help to undermine Alex's credibility. As proof, Marriott claimed he had supporting evidence from a priest, Father Magaldi, who he had seen for counseling. The priest seemed to corroborate his story, claiming that David had told him about these deliveries. Unfortunately, these stories of David and the priest were later discredited, and Dershowitz decided not to use Capote as a witness because he had his own credibility problems, among them being an author with drug problems.[114]

By contrast, Dershowitz's strongest exculpatory evidence came when he decided to look more closely at the contents of the black bag, which provided the most damning evidence, so he could question its validity. When he did, he found major weaknesses in the state's case. For example, he found that when the search of the bag was conducted, all of the items found during the search were put together for convenience. But there was no record of what was found in the bag and what was outside it. Then, too, a prescription label on one of the vials was made out to Martha von Bulow, linking her to the bag. He also found an expert, Dr. Robert Shaler, director of serology for the chief medical examiner in New York, to testify that the needle could not have been injected, but must have been dipped into a solution, since it had encrusted insulin on it, but no traces of human tissue or blood from an injection.[115]

More supporting evidence came when Dershowitz requested a retest of the BioScience lab test for insulin on the needle. This time he found that two experimental washings with amobarbital, Valium, and saline solution but no insulin, came back with false positives. These results raised the possibility that the needle that was allegedly the murder weapon was not injected into Sunny and didn't have any insulin on it either. Additionally, Dershowitz's team looked more closely at the conclusive testimony of the prosecution's expert witness, Dr. George Cahill of the Harvard Medical School, who opined that a patient who didn't rebound after receiving two glucose pushes would probably have been injected by insulin. But as they discovered, the hypothetical did not apply because there had only been one glucose push within an hour, not two as in the hypothetical.[116]

In short, in framing an appeal, Dershowitz gathered expert testimony to counter the many experts brought in by the state. It's hard to know whose opinions were the most accurate in making a case for guilt or innocence in this battle of scientific experts. But with the funding provided by Claus and his supporters, Dershowitz, with his team of students, was able to build a powerful alternate case for innocence by finding new evidence and supportive experts to show that Claus had been wrongly convicted.

The first barrier was getting through the appeal, and Dershowitz's strategy, after studying the judicial opinions of each of the appeals judges, was to show not only that von Bulow's trial was full of technical legal errors, but also that von Bulow was factually innocent. Although a defendant's actual innocence is not supposed to be an issue in an appeals hearing, in fact, the justices are concerned with it. Thus, Dershowitz combined the evidence pointing to von Bulow's innocence at the original trial and the evidence gathered since then with the technical arguments about legal issues. Among other things, Dershowitz emphasized that Sunny had ingested a high level of alcohol, aspirin, and sweets; that the search and seizure of the black bag was improperly done and should have been excluded; that Kuh's notes of his interviews with critical witnesses were not available to the defense; and that other important tests, such as for fingerprints on the black bag, hadn't been done. Dershowitz also included affidavits from several witnesses who had seen Sunny when she had become very intoxicated and described how she drank a great deal, leading her to lose control and slur her speech.[117]

It was a masterful performancc, argued before the court on October 17, 1983, and in his motion for a new trial, filed on October 18, 1983, Dershowitz even suggested that von Bulow might have been subjected to a frame-up. As he put it in his new trial motion, the newly discovered medical evidence showed that the alleged murder weapon, which Alex found in the black bag, could not have been injected into Sunny. Rather, as his new trial motion stated ominously:

> Instead, it was "dipped into solution" . . . and . . . may not have contained insulin at all. This new evidence raises precisely the specter of a frame-up that the State itself said would require an acquittal: namely, that the evidence used to convict Claus von Bulow was "planted" in order to convict an innocent man.
>
> But whether or not it can definitely be proved that Alex sought to "frame" his stepfather, any single one of the new facts . . . would be sufficient to warrant a new trial.[118]

It was a powerful argument, and that was the tack Dershowitz used in the second trial—that von Bulow was innocent and had been wrongly convicted based on a flawed investigation and evidence. The appeals court decision granting a reversal and new trial came down on April 27 and ordered another trial on two grounds. One was that the defense had not been given copies of the original Kuh notes; the other was that the state police should have had a search warrant when they sent some pills found in the black bag out for testing.[119]

Thus, now Claus had his second chance in the new trial, which began in January 1985. In the battle of the witnesses and experts, Dershowitz was able to undermine the state's case against von Bulow. Especially critical were the Kuh notes, in which Dershowitz found some discrepancies that called into question exactly what Maria saw in the bag and when. Kuh's notes and Maria's trial testimony indicated that when she had opened the bag after Sunny's first coma, she found Valium, several prescriptions, and bottles in the black bag. But there was no mention of her finding any insulin or syringes in the bag. However, after Sunny's second coma, Maria said she had seen these items, leading her to talk to Alex and Ala about what she found. In the trial, she said she had seen the label for insulin and asked about it. But in her interview with Kuh, she said the labels had been scraped off, so she couldn't have read the name on the label. As a result, Dershowitz theorized that she had later remembered what she had seen differently, as a result of her discussions with Ala and Alex, in which they felt a growing suspicion of Claus.[120] As Dershowitz wrote of this breakthrough:

> Every important part of Maria's trial testimony concerning the post-Thanksgiving sighting was thus specifically contradicted by Kuh's notes of what she said when her memory of the events was freshest—about two and half weeks after the coma—and before there was any family theory into which the Thanksgiving sighting of insulin and the syringes neatly fit.[121]

Thus, for Dershowitz, gaining access to these notes proved the key to undermining the prosecution case, leading him to challenge the insulin theory. As he described the new legal strategy:

> We would provide that Maria and Alex had *not* seen insulin and syringes in the black bag after Thanksgiving. We would prove that Sunny's blood did not contain high levels of insulin. We would prove there was *no* insulin on the needle found in the black bag in January. And we would prove that the prosecution's doctors were *wrong* in concluding that exogenous insulin had caused Sunny's coma.[122]

It was a strategy that proved effective for Dershowitz and his team, working with Thomas Puccio, a recently retired prosecutor. They pointed up inconsistencies in Maria's testimony about when she had seen any insulin in the black bag. They showed how Dr. Janis Gailitis, who saved Sunny's life after her first coma, had told the prosecution that the coma could have been caused by factors other than insulin, though the first jury never heard this. They got Dr. George Cahill to acknowledge that factors other than insulin could have been responsible for the second coma.[123]

They even brought in Alexandra Isles, no longer Claus's mistress, to describe how Claus had told her that he had seen Sunny drink a lot of eggnog and take a Seconal before her first coma, and that he had watched her lying unconscious, hoping she would die. Ultimately, though, he couldn't go through with it and called a doctor, saving her life. Additionally, they brought in other experts and witnesses to support their contention that Sunny had been taking drugs or alcohol and to demonstrate that there could not have been any insulin on the needle because any residue would have been "wiped clean when the needle was extracted."[124]

In short, Dershowitz and his team sought to show that whereas Claus might have been guilty of "unhusbandly behavior" in not responding quickly to his wife's first coma and cheating on her with a mistress, he did not cause her death by injecting her with insulin. Instead, they suggested, Sunny's coma was self-induced either through an accident or a suicide. Also, Dershowitz decided not to put Claus on the stand in order to keep the emphasis on the medical testimony that showed there could not have been a crime.[125]

The result was that this time, after two days of deliberation, the jury found Claus not guilty on June 7, 1985.[126] Thus, with the help of good lawyering, Claus was able to gain a reversal. But was he really innocent or just able to buy this result?

Despite the not-guilty verdict, the results were highly controversial, and many were still unconvinced, especially because of Claus's reactions after the trial. For example, Dominick Dunne went to Newport a few days after the trial, and he found that the "battle lines between the pro– and anti–von Bulow factions remained drawn, and seemed possibly even fiercer than ever."[127] Also, Dunne found it telling that von Bulow announced to the media in New York that he would go to visit Sunny, now lying at the Columbia-Presbyterian Medical Center, for the first time in four years to show his "continuing love for her," but even though he was in New York for two weeks after the acquittal, he never followed through.[128] Then, the day after getting back his passport, he left for London with the new woman in his life, Andrea Reynolds. They spent one day together there before

Reynolds flew to Switzerland to visit her father. After von Bulow visited friends in London, they met again in Italy. Their romance, however, soon cooled.[129]

But regardless of von Bulow's actual guilt or innocence, his case dramatically illustrates the power of the rich and wealthy defendant to use the legal system. Claus had the money to pay for the best lawyering and he got the best. As Dunne observes:

> A rich person on trial is very different from an ordinary person on trial. The powerful defense team assembled by von Bulow for the second trial so outshone the prosecution that the trial often seemed like a football game between the New York Jets and Providence High. Outsiders versed in legal costs estimated that the second trial cost von Bulow somewhere in the neighborhood of a million dollars. Besides Thomas Puccio and Alan Dershowitz, the Harvard law professor who won the appeal, four other lawyers, two of them from New York, attended the trial. Von Bulow even hired his own court stenographer, because the court-appointed one could not turn out transcripts fast enough to suit the defense.[130]

So yes, in this case, having the money to hire a team of good lawyers made all the difference. Whether von Bulow injected his wife with insulin or not, Dershowitz and his team were able to undermine the basic premise of his guilt with their team of experts and witnesses. Was he really innocent? At this point, it would seem, no one but von Bulow will really know, much as in the case of many other celebrated rich and powerful defendants charged with homicide. Even the movie made about his story leaves the answer to what happened in a limbo, as noted by film critic Roger Ebert in his film review on October 10, 1990. After seeing the movie, he wrote, "I am no closer than before to a clear idea of who did what, or why. That is the charm of the movie. Something terrible happened to Sunny von Bulow on that winter day 11 years ago, and nobody knows exactly what it was."[131]

CHAPTER 8

When Rich Kids Kill

In the last few decades, killings by kids of all ages have increased, and the age of kids arrested for murder has become younger and younger. The age for treating a kid as a juvenile in the criminal justice system has dropped, too—commonly down to younger than sixteen, or even younger than fourteen or fifteen in some states. As a result, prosecutors can charge the juvenile as an adult at a younger age—or ask the judge to do so—so that the case is removed from juvenile court. This trend to treat younger and younger juveniles more severely is a response to the growing perception of kids as a danger, along with rising crime statistics for juvenile crime. It's a perception reflected in the media by stories about gangs of predatory teenagers in the inner cities and occasional horror stories of misfit teenage boys who have struck back at their tormenters, such as at Columbine High School in Littleton, Colorado, or have plotted to do so, such as in Elk Grove, California.

What of rich kids? How are they any different? Just as homicide among the rich and powerful is much rarer and so more newsworthy, so it is when rich kids kill. There are relatively few such cases, and they commonly evoke extensive media coverage when they occur.

Another major difference is the sense of arrogance, challenge, and planning that occurs in some of these crimes. When any juveniles kill, they often are doing it for the sheer thrill of killing, like a game or sport. They may seek the rush of power and the feeling of being clever at outwitting the police. Such killings are a little like the initiation rites in some teenage gangs that demand a death of a random victim as the price of entry. However, killings by the rich are not done as a part of a gang, but by one or two teens, and they involve careful preplanning, such as in the Leopold and Loeb case featured in this chapter. Moreover, rich kids have more resources to put into their plotting and planning, so they can create a more complicated, hard-to-solve case, such as by renting rooms or cars or by getting special equipment to commit the crime, as did Leopold and Loeb.

One reason that some rich kids kill their parents is the opportunity to gain large sums of money, along with the freedom to spend it and live a more independent life. This may seem a surprising motive, since these rich kids are already living a luxurious lifestyle—one characterized by private schools, fashionable clothes, and other perks of wealth. But they also may feel hemmed in by their parents' rules and expectations that go along with living a wealthy lifestyle, such as doing well in school, choosing a prestigious career, or dating and marrying the socially correct kind of person. But with their parents out of the way, the rich kids who kill can become free to live as they want, using their parent's money to continue the wealthy lifestyle they have learned to enjoy. That's what happened in the Menendez brothers case. They wanted their controlling parents out of their way and wanted their money.

Still another theme in these rich kid cases is the search for establishing one's identity and showing off one's ability by breaking with parental strictures for behavior or striking out at one's parents. Although this effort to create one's sense of self and stretch boundaries is part of everyday adolescence, being brought up with wealth can provide more opportunities to explore further (as in the Leopold and Loeb case) or can create a sense of entitlement that helps to justify a parental homicide and avoid or reduce guilt (as in the Menendez case).

I have chosen the following two cases from different time periods—one from the early part of the century and one from more recent times—to illustrate these patterns.

Can We Do It? The Case of Nathan Leopold and Richard Loeb (Chicago, Illinois, 1924)

The Leopold and Loeb case shocked the nation when it occurred in 1924 in Chicago. It first came to public attention when the body of 14-year-old Bobby Franks was found stuffed into a culvert under a bridge in a wooded park. Just as the body was discovered, Bobby Franks's father received a call from a "Mr. Johnson" asking for $10,000 in ransom for the safe return of his son. The discovery of the body foiled the kidnapping plot, and over the next week, the news media turned the search for Bobby Franks's killer or killers into a nationwide whodunit, as both the police and the press looked for leads.

The discovery of the killers within a few weeks through a series of obvious clues, including a pair of horn-rimmed glasses dropped by the culvert, shocked the nation. They were the least likely killers—two graduate students at the University of Chicago, 19-year-old Nathan Leopold and 18-year-old Richard Loeb, both from wealthy Jewish families. They had killed simply to show they could do it. Both had been influenced by Nietzsche's superman philosophy and considered themselves above the law. They had planned and carried out the crime as an intellectual exercise to show their brilliance and cunning in creating the perfect crime where they wouldn't be caught—and, moreover, would even gain $10,000.

At the time, the big question that swirled around them and became the centerpiece of their defense by famed lawyer Clarence Darrow was whether they were insane or mentally disturbed. This psychological analysis subsequently became a central part of a novel based closely on their story titled *Compulsion*, whose author, Meyer Levin, looked at their actions through Freudian lenses. For example, he suggested that perhaps the chisel used to kill Bobby Franks was a phallic symbol, and perhaps the crime reflected an acting out of "unconscious conflicts from childhood traumas" that led to the killings.[1]

Today, we would be more likely to see their acts as the result of the development of an antisocial personality (also called a sociopath or psychopath), who is "anti-social, aggressive, highly impulsive," and feels "little or no guilt" for his or her actions.[2] As Gilbert Geis, a criminology professor at the University of California, Irvine, and Leigh B. Bienen, a senior law lecturer at the Northwestern University School of Law, write: "The best understanding today is that Leopold and Loeb killed Bobby Franks purely for the excitement, a monstrously daring adventure made more exhilarating by the necessity to avoid being caught."[3] They killed essentially for the "experience," much as they might "kill a spider or fly," as their lawyer Clarence Darrow would say of them.[4] And today, the development of such a personality seems less a sign of mental illness than a problem of our times. Due to problems of insufficient socialization, a growing number of kids from all economic groups feel no compunction of killing; their only concern is getting caught.

The Leopold and Loeb case is the perfect example of such a kill-for-thrills murder, one committed for no other reason than the emotional thrill and intellectual challenge of successfully doing it and getting away with it, without feeling any guilt or remorse. The case also illustrates how committing a murder as a challenge can represent an escalation from committing less-serious crimes, much as occurs with serial killers who commonly start with nonlethal acts of violence, then graduate to murder. That's what happened in the Leopold and Loeb case. Initially, Leopold and Loeb engaged in a series of petty thefts and burglaries for excitement—not for money, since they already had plenty of this—before graduating to murder.

Both Nathan Leopold and Richard Loeb were born to very wealthy Chicago families. Nathan's father, Nathan Sr., began to make his money in the shipping, iron ore, and copper business. Then, he set up a box and carton manufacturing business, Morris Paper Mills.[5] The business thrived, and by the time of the murder, Nathan's two older brothers, Mike and Samuel, worked with their father in the business. The family lived with servants in a large three-story home in the Kenwood area on the South Side of Chicago—an upper-income neighborhood characterized by large mansions.[6] Richard Loeb's family lived in this area, too. Loeb's father was a top executive at Sears, Roebuck and Co., and his family showed off their wealth in their large South Side mansion and in a glamorous summer estate in Michigan.[7]

Both boys also had a background of prep schools and high achievement, before they came together at the University of Chicago to create their partnership in crime. Loeb attended the University of Chicago Laboratory School, also known as U-High, a prep school affiliated with the university. He graduated in 1923 from the University of Michigan at seventeen, before going on to the University of Chicago to do postgraduate work in history. While at the University of Michigan, he was a member of the Zeta Beta Tau fraternity, a connection that would later prove significant in his spree of crime and murder with Nathan Leopold. Meanwhile, Leopold attended the other popular prep school for the wealthy families in the area—the Harvard School. He graduated from the University of Chicago at eighteen and enrolled in law school. On the side, he pursued a hobby he had enjoyed since childhood—ornithology—which took him to the woods and marshes around Chicago, where he shot birds and gathered specimens for his collection of over 3,000 birds.[8]

In the fall of 1923, Leopold and Loeb were drawn together not only by their common backgrounds and high intellects, but also by their complementary personalities. Among the many qualities they shared, as biographer Hal Higdon describes it, is that both were "dark . . . slight . . . Jewish . . . wore their hair slicked back in the Valentino 'sheik' style . . . [and] both dressed well, wearing suits and ties to classes . . . were wealthy . . . lived in imposing houses in the same neighborhood . . . drove expensive cars . . . drank . . . [and] smoked."[9] At the same time, the differences in their personalities helped bring them together and complete them, so they became "the sum of those personalities." Whereas Loeb was outgoing, friendly, and social, Leopold tended to be antisocial, arrogant, and not very well-liked, though some friends at law school who studied with him appreciated his scholastic abilities.[10]

Leopold and Loeb's friendship soon turned into a mutual

exploration of criminal activity, fueled by excitement and their philosophical musings about Nietzsche's philosophy. Just as criminality commonly increases for many types of crimes, such as moving from small thefts to larger ones, so Leopold and Loeb started small. In the beginning, it was as if they were experimenting, enjoying the thrill of getting away with small, low-risk adventures. Then, inspired by success, they moved to another level. For example, at a hearing after his arrest, Leopold described how he and Loeb had been involved in various criminal activities before the murder:

> They were all on occasions when we were together on either an actual criminal adventure or a would-be criminal adventure. One, specifically, was the robbery of the Zeta Beta Tau house in Ann Arbor. Another was the time—the two times—that we attempted to break into the house at Hubbard Woods to steal some liquor. In each case I was armed. And on at least one occasion—perhaps two or even three—when we went out on trips to steal Electrics, to break plate glass windows, I was carrying a gun.[11]

In short, though extremely bright, high-acheiving graduate students from wealthy families, Leopold and Loeb were fascinated by crime. These criminal activities were like an exciting release from their otherwise ordinary, conventional, respectable, well-dressed lives. Encapsulated by their family's wealth, they had everything they could want; so this was their way to break out of a cocoon of boredom—a problem that sometimes afflicts rich kids. As writer John Brophy observes.

> Leopold and Loeb were, or affected to be, bored by life. They were able to buy almost anything they wanted and they believed they understood those things which are not purchasable with money because they had read about them and discussed them. Boredom is an impasse into which the children of the very rich are always liable to find themselves heading.[12]

But beyond being bored and seeking excitement, given their high intelligence, they found a source of inspiration and support for their activities in the writings of German philosopher Friedrich Nietzsche and his notions of the "superman," who was a superior being. As explained by Dr. William A. White, one of the psychiatrists (then called "alienists") testifying at the Leopold and Loeb trial, Leopold had been impressed by Nietzsche's notion of the superman or "übermensch" who was "not bound by the rules that govern ordinary people." He was so enthralled by this concept that in discussing this idea with one of his law school professors, he argued that supermen should not be responsible for their acts, though he misinterpreted Nietzsche's philosophy, which claims that a true superman would be so superior, that he "would not be tempted to acts of evil."[13]

Initially, Leopold explored Nietzsche's doctrines, then shared these ideas with Loeb. As Leopold interpreted this philosophy, it gave them the green light to do whatever they wanted to do, including embracing a hedonistic philosophy. This rationale also, as psychiatrist White explained at the trial, led them to engage in a lifestyle "devoted to complete and absolute selfishness," one with no place for emotions or feelings where "the intelligence reigns supreme," so the only crime that an individual can commit and be held responsible for is a "mistake of intelligence."[14] And so, having adopted this perspective, Leopold viewed both himself and Loeb as supermen, who were so superior, they were not bound by ordinary human laws.[15]

Thus, they were able to justify murder for thrills and excitement by giving it an intellectual cachet. Yet, despite the intellectual patina justifying their action, the thrill-seeking behavior of Leopold and Loeb that led to murder had been developing since childhood, according to the Hulbert and Bowman report, a 300-page report of a psychiatric study of the boys commissioned by their defense attorney, Clarence Darrow. As the report described, both had complementary fantasies that brought them together to seek even more thrills through crime.[16]

Loeb, in particular, seemed to be especially drawn to crime since he was eight or nine, when he stole money from a boy who lived next door and hid it under the roof of a backyard playhouse. He felt no guilt. Rather, he very much enjoyed knowing he had taken the money and where he had hidden it, while his victim remained ignorant. At around the same age, after he and another boy began a lemonade stand, he buried the toy cash register with their money. Soon he began shoplifting for thrills, too. He didn't care about using the articles or about the value of the articles taken; rather the exciting thrill is what that motivated him. A number of times he stole from relatives, too, such as taking a $100 Liberty bond from a brother, and taking some bottles of liquor from a second cousin and his uncle.[17]

Meanwhile, Leopold had his own early childhood history of petty thefts, such as stealing some stamps from a friend's stamp album, taking some of his brother's ties to trade for cigar bands, and taking fruit from a Greek restaurant.[18] Though he didn't have as much of an early crime and thrill-seeking background as Loeb, the propensity was there.

Then, in 1921, when Leopold was a junior and Loeb was a sophomore at the University of Chicago, they participated in their first criminal plot together and were bound together by another personal dynamic that helped fuel their escalating series of crimes—Leopold's sexual attraction to Loeb, coupled with Loeb's desire for a partner in crime. As described in the Hulbert and Bowman report, this initial criminal venture began when Loeb invited Leopold to join him for a weekend at the family's summer estate in Michigan. On the train, they set up their first con—a system for using signals to cheat at bridge—and then they had their first homosexual encounter in the Pullman berth. Apparently, it was initiated by Leopold, who felt "attracted to Loeb as a lover," and Loeb reciprocated primarily because he saw Leopold as "an accomplice for his acts of petty thievery."[19]

Thereafter, their adventure in crime began. It started small, as such adventures generally do, then gradually escalated. Initially, they stole some pipes in a downtown department store. Then, they made off with a tennis trophy from a hotel. Soon after, they stole a Milburn Electric car from a garage, using the keys from Loeb's mother's car. They were chased by a truck from that garage, crashed the car into a pole, and escaped. A month later they stole another Electric car and parked it near a restaurant while they ate dinner. When the police came asking for the car owner, they calmly denied owning it. They also drove around town throwing bricks at the windshields of parked cars and through store windows. One time, the excitement of this activity was heightened when one of the cars was occupied by a couple making love in the back seat, and the man shot at them as they sped away. Sometimes they turned in false fire alarms, and they began to set some real fires too, once to a shack on a vacant lot and at least twice to larger buildings.[20]

From thefts and vandalism, they graduated to burglary and found planning the crime especially enjoyable. Though their first burglary attempts didn't succeed—the first because their car engine was too noisy, so they just drove around the area; their second because they failed to break a window, so they abandoned the effort—they enjoyed the planning process so much that they planned more.

One burglary that proved especially significant because one of the items they stole was connected to their later murder, was from the Zeta Beta Tau fraternity house at the University of Michigan at Ann Arbor. Because Loeb had been a fratenrity member, he already knew the house layout. Committing a burglary there also appealed to them because Leopold and Loeb liked the idea of being able to discuss the crime with some of the victims that Loeb knew. The night of the burglary, they crept in at 3 a.m., carrying pistols, wearing masks, and carrying rope in case anyone might interrupt them.[21] But no one did. While everyone slept, they took a variety of small items, including watches, money, fraternity pins, and fountain pens.[22] And most significantly, they took an Underwood typewriter, which they later used to type the ransom notes in the Bobby Franks case.[23] The following weekend, when Loeb was in Ann Arbor visiting friends, he had a long talk with one of the victims, Max Schrayer, about what happened, pressing Schrayer with numerous questions to learn what happened. Schrayer even showed him the list of stolen items he had put together for the police, which included the Underwood typewriter.[24] This interest in the victim's response was much like that of other criminals, like an arsonist who returns to see the response to his fire—like a craftsman enjoying admiration for his handiwork. After this, several more burglaries followed.

Perhaps a reason for Leopold and Loeb's continued success with these petty crimes is that Chicago in the early twenties was experiencing a serious crime wave and was at the height of prohibition, illegal drinking, and gang warfare.[25] Thus, police resources were stretched thin, and minor crimes were not given much attention. In turn, their initial success, coupled with their fascination with crime, led them to plan what they considered the ultimate criminal challenge—a murder, which would become the Bobby Franks case. They made their decision on what crime to commit and how to do it as if they were conducting "a scientific experiment," eventually deciding that "the apex in crime was kidnapping, murder, and the collection of ransom."[26]

Yet, for all their studious planning, their activities before the crime seem like the actions of crooks in a movie caper, seeking to hide their trail through a series of false identities and drops. And later, their actions created a paper trail that provided more overwhelming evidence of their guilt. The setup began on May 7, 1924, when Loeb withdrew $100 from his account at the Hyde Park State Bank. He next drove downtown to the Morrison Hotel with Leopold. While Leopold waited in the car, Loeb registered under the phony name of Morton D. Ballard from Peoria, Illinois, took a suitcase with books to the room, left the books there, and rejoined Leopold in the car. Next, back at the Hyde Park State Bank, Leopold, pretending to be Ballard, used the $100 Loeb had withdrawn to open up an account under Ballard's name.

Two days later, on May 9, Loeb withdrew $400 more from his own account. Afterward, he and Leopold drove to the Rent-A-Car company, where Leopold, again posing as Ballard, went in to rent the car, while Loeb went to a nearby restaurant and cigar store to wait by the phone.[27] When the salesman called to check references, Loeb, posing as Louis Mason, responded with glowing praise. As a result, Leopold was able to rent the car, and when he returned, with the car a few hours later, he asked the salesman to send an identification card to his hotel, so he wouldn't need to provide references the next time he wanted to rent a car.[28]

Unfortunately, there was a glitch at the hotel, the first of many such glitches, which helped to unravel Leopold and Loeb's perfect crime. When Loeb returned to the Morrison

Hotel, planning to get his suitcase of books, pay the bill, and ask the clerk to hold his mail, he discovered the suitcase was no longer in his room. Afraid that the maid might have been suspicious because he hadn't used the bed and that she kept the suitcase, he abandoned his plan and didn't pay the bill. Instead, to have a place to get their mail, Leopold, again posing as Ballard, went to the Trenier Hotel, told the clerk he had planned to register, but didn't, and asked that clerk to hold his mail. Then, Leopold called the Rent-A-Car company to explain that he was staying at the Trenier Hotel instead of the Morrison Hotel and to request that they send the mail there.[29]

About two weeks later, on May 21, Leopold and Loeb put the next phase of their plan into action. They had decided to pick a random victim and determined it should be a young boy from a wealthy family that would be willing to pay ransom. They also already had a gun and a chisel used in a previous burglary, and had already typed out a general ransom note addressed to "Dear Sir" on their Underwood typewriter—the one taken in the University of Michigan burglary—thinking the stolen typewriter wouldn't be traced to them.

Their next step was to get a car and find their victim. To start the plan in motion, at 7:30 a.m., Leopold picked up the family red Willys-Knight car from the Leopolds' chauffer, Sven Englund, went to his law school classes, and met Loeb at 11 a.m. to get the rental car they would use. They drove to the Rent-A-Car company and parked several blocks away, while Leopold, posing as Ballard, rented a similar but dark blue Willys-Knight car. Then, after a stop for lunch, they drove back to Leopold's house, Leopold in his car, Loeb in the rental car, where they met Englund at the garage. Leopold explained that he needed to transfer some equipment from his own car to his friend's car, and after doing so, he asked Englund to fix his squeaky brakes.[30]

Now, thinking they had carefully concealed their identity by using a rented car obtained under a false name, Leopold and Loeb headed to the Harvard School, where Leopold had once been a student, to look for their victim and parked about a block away. At first, Loeb got out and talked to one prospective victim, nine-year-old Johnny Levinson, who attended fourth grade with Loeb's younger brother. But Johnny said he was on his way to play baseball, and after an instructor at the school stopped by to greet them, Johnny went on his way, very nearly a victim, but for chance.[31] So Loeb rejoined Leopold in the car to wait.

A few hours later, they spotted another likely prospect when fourteen-year-old Bobby Franks, who had been umpiring for the game, left to return to his home, which was about three blocks away. He was the perfect victim—the son of a wealthy businessman, Jacob Franks, who had made his money as the head of a pawn brokerage business, the Franks Collateral Loan Bank, and subsequently became the president of the Rockford Watch Company. Additionally, Jacob Franks was a part owner of the Elgin Watch Case Company and an investor in real estate. Bobby was also a very convenient victim because the Franks lived down the street from the Loebs. It seemed like it would be easy to lure him into the car, especially because, from time to time, he had played tennis with Loeb on the tennis court at the Loebs' house.[32]

Minutes later, as Bobby Franks walked along the street and another boy, nine-year-old Irving Hartman, Jr., stopped nearby to look at some flowers, Leopold and Loeb drove by in their rented Willy's-Knight. It is not certain who was driving, however, because this was never made clear at the trial. But very possibly it was Leopold, since Loeb knew Bobby and could best lure him into the car. By the time, Hartman looked up from his flowers, Bobby Franks was in the car and on his way to his doom.

The story of what happened next is quite well known. Either Leopold or Loeb, though most probably Loeb if Leopold was driving, struck Bobby on the head four times with the chisel and stuffed rags in his mouth to suffocate him.[33] Then, Leopold and Loeb drove to Eggers Woods, a forest preserve by Wolf Lake, where Leopold had previously gone looking for birds. There, rather than burying the body, they pushed it into a culvert—a sewer or drain crossing under an embankment—thinking this would be a more convenient, less messy way to get rid of the body in an out-of-the way place where it wouldn't be discovered. However, that decision proved to be a major miscalculation. They also took off Bobby Franks's clothes, attempted to pour hydrochloric acid over his face to make him less recognizable, and threw the chisel in the marsh.[34]

Then, they drove home, pleased that this first phase of the plan had gone so well, although Leopold later discovered he had dropped his glasses near where they hid the body. But he figured he could always explain that he had been looking for birds in the area, so not to worry. Now it was time to launch the kidnapping phase of the plan, and they mailed the "Dear Sir" letter, which they had already prepared, to Bobby Franks's father to arrive the next day by special delivery. The letter was the one they had carefully typed on the Underwood, and it advised the victim's father that his son had been kidnapped, but was currently "well and safe." So he needn't worry as long as he carefully followed their instructions and did not contact the police or a private agency. As the letter instructed, he should obtain $10,000 in old bills in certain denominations ($2,000 in $20 bills and $8,000 in $50 bills), to be placed in a cigar box or cardboard box. Then, he should wait at home with the money and be ready to respond to telephoned instructions about where to deliver it. Otherwise, the letter warned, "death will be the penalty," and it was signed "George Johnson," another of the aliases that Leopold and Loeb had concocted for their caper.[35]

After setting the plan in motion, Leopold and Loeb returned to their daily activities, congratulating themselves on their brilliance in carrying out the successful execution of the plan. Now they deemed themselves truly worthy of the "superman" designation. But the plan was already starting to unravel. The unraveling began when Tony Manke, a Polish immigrant working for a corn products company, finished his work on the night shift and walked along a path by a single railroad track that crossed over the culvert. When he glanced down, he saw two bare feet sticking out of the culvert pipe. Just then a railroad crew on two handcars directed by Paul Korff arrived, and he waved for them to stop. As Manke pointed down to the projecting feet, Korff thought someone might have drowned. He jumped into the water, and with the help of his crew members, dragged Franks's body out of the culvert and placed it in a tarpaulin to take out on one of the handcars. Then, before leaving, Korff looked around to see if the boy might have left some clothes in the area, perhaps if he had drowned while swimming. Though he and his men found no clothes, since Leopold and Loeb had taken them away, Korff noticed a pair of eyeglasses on the ground, which he picked up and put in his pocket. When a police squad car arrived soon afterward to pick up the body, he turned the eyeglasses over to the police. Though the police would later find many clues that could have led them to Leopold and Loeb, the eyeglasses would turn out to be the first big break in the case. Ironically, after the police took the body to Stanley Olejniczak's funeral home, his wife thought the glasses belonged to the dead boy and put them on his head.[36]

For now, though, Leopold and Loeb were savoring their clever plan, and they paid no attention to the two lead items in the Chicago *Daily News* that day, which would soon be connected. One was a story about a kidnapped boy from a wealthy family; the other was about a dead boy found in the culvert, who probably had drowned. Seeing these two stories, city editor Alvin Goldstein thought maybe the two boys were one in the same, and he asked a reporter to take Jacob Franks's brother-in-law, Edwin M. Gresham, to the funeral home to see if he was right.[37]

Around 2:30 p.m., as Gresham went to the funeral home to check, Leopold or Loeb phoned the Franks, posing as George Johnson, and instructed Mr. Franks to go to a certain drugstore with the money, telling him that a Yellow Cab would be coming to pick him up. But Mr. Franks not only didn't remember the address due to being in a state of shock, but also, by the time the cab arrived, Gresham had called him to break the grim news that the dead boy was his son. So Franks sent the cab away. Meanwhile, expecting Franks to turn up at the drugstore, either Leopold or Loeb called the phone booth there an hour later, at 3:30 p.m., asking if a Mr. Franks was there. But a porter sweeping the floor who answered the call said no he wasn't, and when Leopold or Loeb called again five minutes later, the store owner, Percy Van de Bogert, answered and told him no, no one in the store matched that description.[38]

Yet, even though the kidnapping phase of the plan appeared not to work any longer, Leopold and Loeb seemed unconcerned because the money was of less interest than the excitement of doing the act. The story of the kidnapping, discovery of the body, and the police investigation fascinated Chicago and the nation over the next week, and Leopold and Loeb became fascinated themselves. They were eager to lap up every bit of news, especially when the police were following leads in the wrong directions in the beginning of the case. They were like serial killers who felt empowered by destroying their victim and playing a winning cat-and-mouse game with the police.

For a time, Leopold and Loeb seemed to be very much enjoying themselves and feeling smart and powerful, as they spoke to others about the crime no one else knew they had committed. For example, on Thursday, after the late afternoon paper reported the discovery of Bobby's body, Leopold and Loeb went in to the corner drugstore near the Harvard School to buy a copy and saw one of the school instructors there, Mott Kirk Mitchell. Loeb commented to him about the terrible thing that happened to "poor Bobby Franks," noting that Bobby had frequently played tennis on the Loeb tennis courts. Then, for several minutes, Leopold and Loeb talked about the crime with Mitchell. Later, Leopold went home, and Loeb joined a group of reporters and curiosity seekers in front of the Franks home, down the block from his house. There, he asked others about the crime and condition of the body, and he even gave his opinion on the punishment that should be given to whoever committed such a "terrible crime," stating that "whoever committed the crime should be strung up."[39]

Loeb also enjoyed closely following the case as the intensity of interest in the case grew. With nearly $20,000 pledged for tips leading to the capture of the killer or killers by the Franks, the police chief and two morning papers, the *Tribune* and the *Herald*, tips began pouring in to the police. Loeb even initiated his own "investigation," such as when he stopped by the Zeta Beta Tau fraternity house at the University of Chicago on Friday afternoon. He invited the campus correspondent Howard Mayer, and two *Daily News* reporters, Alvin Goldstein and James Mulroy, to join him to look for the drugstore where a caller had tried to contact Mr. Franks. The four of them then drove around in Mayer's car checking drugstores. Eventually, when they arrived at the Van de Bogert &

Ross drugstore and the porter and pharmacist reported that they each had received a call, Loeb excitedly told Mayer that now he had a "scoop," and he raced back to the car calling out ecstatically: "This is the place! . . . This is the place!"[40]

After the reporters contacted their editors, called the police, and told the police officer who arrived what they found, they drove on to the coroner's inquest. On the way, Loeb picked up several newspapers, saying he was going to bring them to his mother. Then, as they spoke on the ride, Loeb revealed his cynical, remorseless nature when Mulroy, seated next to him, asked if he had known Bobby Franks and wondered what he was like. Loeb responded: "If I was going to murder anybody, I would murder just such a cocky little son of a bitch as Bobby Franks."[41] It was a strange comment, and it would later be used with other evidence to show the cold-blooded way that Loeb and Leopold chose and killed their victim. For now, though, no one suspected either Loeb or Leopold, although Loeb's remark indicated how much he viewed the homicide and ensuing investigation as part of an intellectual game, allowing him to feel superior to the victim, as well as the initially puzzled cops.

Yet, already, the inquest provided some important clues. First, after finding four wounds to the head caused by a sharp instrument and signs of suffocation following a violent struggle, but no signs of sexual abuse, Coroner Oscar Wolff concluded the killer was probably not a sexual "pervert." Secondly, Wolff thought the killer or killers were well-educated, because the ransom note was written in such "perfect English." Further, he thought that the killer or killers were probably familiar with the area where the body was found, since it was in an obscure out of the way location.[42]

Initially, though, the police went off in the wrong direction, focusing their search for suspects on three teachers at the Harvard School, including Mott Kirk Mitchell, who spoke to Leopold and Loeb the day after the murder. One reason for this focus on Mitchell is that some police were still thinking the murder had been committed by a pervert, and Mitchell had effeminate qualities. Much wasted police effort also went into fielding the many tips coming into police headquarters, including some from obvious nuts, such as one that announced: "I am the murderer and kidnapper of the Franks boy. When you get this letter I will probably be a dead man. I intend to commit suicide. I am very sorry I did that inhumane piece of work. A sorry man."[43]

In turn, as the newspapers trumpeted the latest daily developments, Leopold and Loeb continued to follow the news closely, enjoying their clever handiwork. Sometimes, seeming to thrill in the potential danger, Loeb even toyed with the idea of revealing himself, such as on Saturday night, three days after the murder, when Leopold and Loeb went to a nightclub with University of Chicago classmate, Abel Brown, and their dates. When Brown introduced Loeb to another person at the club, Loeb commented after shaking hands: "You've just enjoyed the treat of shaking hands with a murderer."[44] While Brown passed off the remark as Loeb's offbeat sense of humor, it was a telling comment, showing how Loeb was enjoying being on the edge.

Meanwhile, as much as Leopold and Loeb prided themselves for their cleverness in crafting a crime that drew so much attention, the clues were mounting. For example, the Morrison Hotel had kept the Rent-A-Car company's letter authorizing Mr. Ballard to rent a car without further identification, along with the suitcase of books that Loeb had abandoned.[45]

More clues came when the police began to investigate who might have visited the forest preserve near Wolf Lake and obtained information on who had bought the glasses found at the site. After a game warden told the police that Nathan Leopold came to look at birds there, the police roused him out of bed on Sunday around 11 a.m. and invited him to accompany them to the station. During the interview they simply asked some questions about his visits there and whether he wore glasses, though they didn't ask to see them. After Leopold explained he had been to the area about five or six times that year, including Saturday and Sunday, May 17 and 18, with his friend George Lewis, and that he had been going there for six years, the police felt Leopold's answers seemed "so ready" and his demeanor "so innocent," that there was no need for suspicion. Then, too, given Leopold's wealth and social status, they didn't think he would have any motive to kidnap anyone for money.[46]

So Leopold returned home feeling no need for concern, and later he picked up his girlfriend Susan Lurie and took her out for a day of canoeing, after which they relaxed on the grass, as if it was just another ordinary day. Leopold even took his law exams the next day and easily passed them.[47] Though he didn't have the same fascination with following the case as Loeb, he felt equally smug and assured he would get away with it.

Then, on Thursday, May 29, eight days after the murder, the police got their big break when they discovered who might have owned the glasses. The discovery came after State Attorney Robert E. Crowe's assistant, Joseph P. Savage, visited a few optical companies and found the company that sold them—the Almer Coe company—because of the slight diamond mark on the lenses. Though the prescription and frames were common, the frame hinges were only made by the Bobrow Optical Company in Brooklyn, and Almer Coe was the only distributor of frames with these hinges in the Chicago area. So now it was just a question of looking through the sales records, and 54,000 records later, the company found three purchasers of the frames, one of them by Leopold.[48]

As a result of this discovery of Leopold's purchase, two detectives—Sergeant William Crot and Frank A. Johnson—arrived at his home and brought him to the La Salle Hotel in downtown Chicago for questioning by Robert E. Crowe, his assistant Joseph Savage, who had traced the purchaser of the glasses, and John Sbarbaro. The questioning soon began to undermine Leopold and Loeb's careful façade. After asking a series of questions, the investigators took Leopold back to his house to see if he could find his glasses, and when he couldn't, he acknowledged that the glasses at the culvert were his and said he could have dropped them there while looking for birds. He further explained that he probably lost them when he was with his friend George Lewis on May 17 or 18, perhaps because he left them in the breast pocket of his suit and didn't realize they were there, since he hadn't worn them for a month. The explanation sounded plausible, but the investigators pressed on, first getting Leopold to demonstrate how the glasses might have fallen out when he picked up his coat. Then, they pressed Leopold to remember what he had done the day of the murder, refusing to be satisfied with his vague recollections. After all, they urged, they were only asking him to recall what happened on a day about a week before when a nearby neighbor had been killed.[49]

In response to this growing pressure, Leopold finally told the cover story he and Loeb had prepared to provide an alibi for that day if they were pressed to talk about it. As this story went, he explained that he had been with Richard Loeb, first to look for birds. Afterward, they picked up two girls and drove them around, though he only knew their first names, Edna and Mae. He said he had been hesitant to tell a story that would involve his close friend with the police, but now, he was willing to admit it, answering their questions about that day freely and calmly. Plus he answered many other questions, such as about his ability to type and how he had been closely reading up on the case in the newspapers.[50]

Although Leopold seemed to have ready answers and appeared quite calm, the investigators pressed on, turning the interview into an interrogation of a possible suspect until 4 a.m. Meanwhile, as Crowe, Savage, and Sbarbaro continued the questioning, the two detectives who had picked up Leopold, Sergeant Crot and Sergeant Johnson, went back to his house to search more carefully. They not only picked up his typewriter and some samples of his typing and handwriting but looked through his red Willys-Knight.[51]

Meanwhile, as the investigators questioned Leopold in one room of the hotel, the police brought in Loeb for questioning in another hotel room. Initially, Loeb, like Leopold, held up well, claiming he had been with Leopold the day of the murder, and told the story about the two girls, though at first he said they had gone their separate ways around dinner time. But during a break in the questioning Loeb, who now had been moved from the hotel to a cell in a police station, got a message in his cell, which Leopold sent through one of his reporter friends. In the message, Leopold told him to tell the truth about the girls, and after that, Leob told their previously prepared cover story. [52]

Both were held for further questioning. Soon their cover story broke down, as other evidence surfaced that tied Leopold and Loeb to the crime, due in part to the help of reporters, who were doing their own investigation of this high-profile case, most notably Alvin Goldstein with the *Daily News*. After he learned that Leopold had participated in a small study group of freshman law students, he got copies of the dope sheets typed on Leopold's typewriter, which the students used to help prepare for exams. Perhaps they might be the same as the typing on the ransom note, he speculated. In reviewing the dope sheets, he noticed that some of the notes were typed on a different machine and learned that Leopold had used a portable typewriter for those. To determine if the typing was the same as on the ransom note, his newspaper contacted an expert from the Royal Typewriter Company, H. P. Sutton, who confirmed that it was from the same typewriter. At once, the newspaper turned the evidence over to State Attorney Crowe, though again Leopold had an innocent explanation. This time he calmly explained that though he might have once used the typewriter, he didn't own it, and the detectives who returned to search his house couldn't find it.[53] Leopold and Loeb had planned for this possibility, too, had already dumped the typewriter in the marsh.

Then, more evidence turned up from the story told by Leopold's chauffeur, Sven Englund. He described how Leopold had brought his car to be fixed the day of the murder, saying the brakes squeaked, and he had worked on the car to fix the brakes, while Leopold and Loeb left in another car. But in their story about picking up two girls the night of the murder, both Leopold and Loeb had claimed they used Leopold's red Willys-Knight.[54]

Given this mounting evidence, Crowe's assistants questioned Leopold and Loeb even more intensely in separate rooms, telling them what evidence they had, and finally Loeb confessed. After learning of Loeb's confession, in which he said that he and Leopold had planned it, Leopold confessed, too.[55] In their confessions, they outlined their months of preparation, leading up to their plan to kidnap a victim they already knew who had a wealthy father because such a victim would be easier to capture, and his or her father would be able and willing to pay the ransom. They further explained how they had worked out various plans to collect the ransom, eventually deciding to give the victim's father instructions through a series of notes leading him from one place to another until he got on a train. Then, the plan was for him to throw the box with the ransom at a certain place, near to where they would be observing. This way, they could get the box if it landed as expected, or if not, perhaps because the police had been contacted, they could escape.[56] They spent several days walking around the railroad tracks to select the drop point—another sign that they enjoyed the intellectual challenge of all this planning.

Yet the one thing that remained unplanned and left to chance was the victim's identity, which they determined randomly. The victim would in effect pick himself by "pure accident," as Leopold told Crowe in his confession.[57] Then, step by step, Leopold and Loeb in their confessions described exactly what had happened that fateful day, including how they burned most of Bobby Franks's clothes in the basement of Loeb's house and cleaned the bloodstains from the floor of the car so their role in the crime would never be discovered. Two days later, Leopold and Loeb even led investigators to the lagoon where Loeb had thrown the typewriter and the keys, which he had pulled off with a pair of pliers.[58] Why tell so much now? Perhaps they revealed all these details because just as Leopold and Loeb had enjoyed the intellectual challenge of plotting their crime, now that they were discovered, they gained a similar gratification in showing off how carefully they had plotted their scheme.

Thus, now that the investigation was over, with the killers revealed and the plot explained, the major question left was, why? That was the big question plaguing the press and the public after the news of the killers splashed across the front pages of newspapers around the nation the next day. Especially shocking was the pure randomness and senselessness of the crime. Why should two privileged boys from wealthy families, who already had money and position, want to kidnap and kill for no reason other than the thrill of killing?

The general popular reaction was total shock. People considered Leopold and Loeb "monsters" and called for their death. Their families were devastated, and the Jewish community felt a deep anguish, since the boys and their families were an integral part of the Chicago Jewish community.[59] At the same time, the absolute senselessness of the crime contributed to the public's fascination with the case, leading it to be called the "Crime of the Century." As Gilbert Geis and Leigh B. Bienen note in their book *Crimes of the Century*, "the absence of a sensible motive for the killing of Bobby Franks, the stunning intellectual abilities of the killers, the great wealth and high standing of their families, and their 'different' (that is, Jewish) cultural heritage contributed to the most intense public attention ever to be focused on a murder in the United States."[60]

There seemed little in the way of a defense, other than to plead insanity or appeal for mercy, and that's what Clarence Darrow decided to do, after he was hired by the Leopold's and Loeb's families to defend them, in what the newspapers dubbed "the million-dollar defense."[61] Then sixty-seven, Darrow was the most famous criminal defense attorney of the day, noted for his folksy charm that helped him to win over the jury. But in this case, Darrow felt he had little chance to appeal to the jury because the murder of Bobby Franks was so horrendous and the proof of guilt so absolute.[62]

Thus, rather than fight the charges or use an insanity defense, which would have required a jury trial, Darrow had Leopold and Loeb plead guilty to both offenses with which they were charged—first-degree murder and kidnapping for ransom—either of which could bring the death penalty.[63] He felt a judge would be less ruled by emotion and more forgiving. Then, in a three-month hearing over the penalty, Darrow argued before Judge John R. Caverly to spare their lives.[64] His strategy was twofold—first, in order to avoid an insanity case, which would require a jury hearing, he argued that the crime was due to a "malfunction of their mental functions,"[65] and second, he appealed for mercy based on the youth of the two defendants.[66]

According to Hal Higdon, this twofold strategy was a novel legal maneuver; "never before had evidence of a defendant's mental condition been offered to lessen a sentence."[67] But Darrow argued that when a defendant pled guilty, the judge had the discretion to impose the sentence and examine witnesses "as to the aggravation or mitigation of the offense." Accordingly, Darrow wanted to offer evidence of the defendants' mental condition "to show the degree of responsibility they had." Also, he wanted to present evidence of their youth and have their guilty pleas taken into consideration "as grounds for mitigating the punishment."[68]

The prosecutor, Robert E. Crowe, still insisted on presenting the damning evidence he had collected against Leopold and Loeb, which included calling 102 witnesses to testify, even though Darrow was willing to stipulate to all of this evidence.[69] Crowe wanted to get all this evidence in to emphasize the horror of the crime, and Judge Caverly let him do so. Afterward, Darrow finally had his chance. To show Leopold's and Loeb's mental disturbance, he played up the senselessness of the crime, arguing that this indicated their faulty nature, that they were mentally abnormal.[70] In his summation he argued:

> Not for money, not for spite, not for hate. They killed him as they might kill a spider or a fly, for the experience. They killed him because they were made that way. . . .
>
> Are they to blame for it? There is no man on earth who can mention any purpose for it all or any reason for it all. It is one of those things that happened; and it calls not for hate but for kindness, for charity, for consideration.[71]

Then, arguing for mercy based on their youth, he pointed out that:

> We have all been young, and we know that fantasies and vagaries haunt the daily life of a child. . . . Here are two boys who are minors. The law would forbid them making contracts, forbid them from marrying without the consent of their parents, would not permit them to vote. Why? Because they haven't that judgment which comes only with years, because they are not fully responsible.[72]

In the end, it was Darrow's argument for youth that won the day. Judge Caverly ignored the extensive psychiatric testimony that Darrow had presented to show the mental dysfunction that led to murder. Instead, he was most impressed by the young age of Leopold and Loeb.[73] He noted that:

> In choosing imprisonment instead of death, the Court is moved chiefly by the consideration of the age of the defendants, boys of eighteen and nineteen years. . . . The court thinks it within his province to decline to impose the sentence of death on persons who are not of full age.[74]

So, with that, the case of Leopold and Loeb was over, and Caverly gave them each terms of life plus ninety-nine years. Over the next few years, there was much debate about various theories to make sense of their killings. The media portrayed Leopold and Loeb as monsters who thought they were supermen because of their interest in Nietzsche's writings. Then, after a few more years, the search for an explanation turned psychological, looking for clues in their faulty upbringing, in sexual perversion, or in unconscious conflicts from childhood traumas.[75]

But probably the best explanation is that they were sociopaths—antisocial personalities who felt no guilt or remorse for their acts.[76] Today, this is a phenomenon that needs no explanation of insanity. Its causes lie more in problems of socialization, social controls, and the lack of development of a conscience, which has become something of a plague in today's media-driven thrill-seeking culture. Probably other contributing factors were Leopold's and Loeb's high intelligence, arrogance, and wealth, along with the influence of Nietzsche's philosophy, which contributed to their sense of entitlement and led them to feel they could be above the law.

After sentencing, Leopold and Loeb were sent to different prisons at Statesville and Joliet, respectively, though after a few years, in 1932, they were able to work together on various prison projects at Statesville. Both were model prisoners, but Loeb was killed in 1936 when another prisoner, James Day, stabbed him in a shower. One possible reason is that Loeb stopped helping Day financially after the prison cut the size of the allowances prisoners received from their families; another is that Loeb had offered Day money to engage in a homosexual liaison. Day told various stories of why he stabbed Loeb.[77]

For much of his time in prison, Leopold took a leading role in contributing to improved prison conditions, including organizing the prison library, setting up a correspondence school for prisoners, and doing research on predicting parole success. He also volunteered in a malaria experiment. Eventually, he gained enough support from political leaders, academics, and criminal justice officials that he was paroled from Statesville on March 13, 1958, after serving slightly over thirty-three years of his sentence. He then moved to Castaner, a Puerto Rican village in the mountains, where he worked as an X-ray technician for the Church of the Brethren. Later, he got a master's degree in social medicine at the University of Puerto Rico, published a book on ornithology, and taught mathematics at the university. He even married in 1961.[78] Essentially, his later life became almost like an atonement for what he had done.

Give Me Liberty and Money: The Case of Lyle and Erik Menendez (Los Angeles, California, 1989–1996)

Three quarters of a century later, the case of Lyle and Erik Menendez shares much in common with the Leopold and Loeb case. Two rich kids engaged in an especially brutal murder, had no sense of guilt and remorse, and did their best to cover it up. When the evidence proved overwhelming, they argued mitigating circumstances as a defense. And like Leopold and Loeb, they had the money to pay for the best legal defense. Yet, whereas Leopold and Loeb chose their victim by chance for the thrill of killing, Lyle and Erik chose their parents, both for their money and to be free of their tight control over their lives. They wanted the money and the freedom to spend it on a luxurious wealthy lifestyle, without the influence of their controlling father, who ran his family as he did a successful corporation.

Just like the Leopold and Loeb case, the Menendez case burst into public attention as a mystery, though it, too, was soon solved. The murder occurred on a warm evening in Beverly Hills on August 20, 1989. Jose and Kitty Menendez were relaxing in their large white Mediterranean-style $3.5 million mansion. Jose, dressed casually in shorts and a shirt, and Kitty, wearing a sweatshirt and jogging pants, were sitting on the sofa watching a thriller on TV. Their sons, Erik, 18, and Lyle, 21, had gone out for the evening, so they were alone.[79]

About 10 p.m., Erik and Lyle drove up, stopped near the mansion, and got two shotguns out of the trunk. They walked to the front door, where the normally set alarm was off and the gates were open. This allowed them to easily walk in with their guns and proceed down the hall to the family room without either of the guard dogs barking. Jose and Kitty didn't have a chance. As soon as Erik and Lyle got to the family room, they began firing. Several shots hit Jose including his elbow and right arm, and one blew off his head. As Kitty began running, several shots hit her in the leg, arm, thigh, and left breast, bursting one of her lungs. When she still wasn't dead, though mortally wounded, the brothers ran back to the car, reloaded their shotgun with birdshot, and returned to shoot her in the head.[80] Altogether, they fired about two dozen shots, including shooting both Jose and Kitty near the left knee to suggest a mob hit. Afterward, they carefully picked up the shell casings left by the rampage.

Then, their mission accomplished, Erik and Lyle drove away, and returned home a little after 11 p.m., where they saw the bodies of Jose and Kitty lying where they had shot them. As Erik gazed at the bodies, almost hypnotized by what he and Lyle had done, Lyle called the police. It was 11:47 p.m., and he sounded truly hysterical, as he sobbed out his story to the dispatcher, crying: "They shot and killed my parents." Then, he explained how he didn't hear anything, since he just came home with his brother. A few minutes later, Beverly Hills patrol officers Michael Butkus and John Czarnocki arrived, followed by Sergeant Kirk West and a team of police to search the house. Meanwhile, Erik and Lyle continued to act hysterically. For example, when Butkus and Czarnocki approached the house, they ran out and fell down on the street, yelling over and over: "Oh, my God, I can't believe it."[81]

It was a convincing performance, and initially, Lyle and Erik seemed the least likely suspects. Instead, the initial investigation, headed by top homicide detective Les Zoeller, known for his persistence on tough cases, focused on the many different people who might have wanted to kill Jose and Kitty—and there were many because Jose had a history of being a very tough boss who had fired many people, accumulating many enemies in both his business and personal life.

Though Lyle and Erik were not yet suspected, the police at the scene were certain this was not just a random murder, because the way the victims were shot showed a deep hatred for them. But so far, the police had no weapon or suspect, and no evidence seemed to have been left behind at the scene. When the coroner's investigator, George White, wrote his report he concurred, noting that the victims were either "acquainted with their killers" or this had been a professional hit. Significantly, there had been no forced entry.[82]

Meanwhile, as Zoeller and other police continued to investigate the crime scene, Lyle and Erik were taken to police headquarters, where detective supervisor Sergeant Thomas Edmonds questioned them, though more as witnesses than suspects. Whereas Lyle was quite calm, as usual as the strong, controlled older brother, much like his father in personality, Erik was quite shaken up, often sobbing at times. As he asked his questions, Edmonds pieced together a chronology of what the brothers said they had done that day, which sounded like a fairly routine day. Among other things, Erik had practiced tennis; the brothers had spent some time at the mall; and they had gone to see the film *Batman* in Century City, after they found the lines too long for a James Bond movie *License to Kill.*[83] When later asked if they had their ticket stubs, they said they had thrown them away.[84] They also had plans to meet a friend, who had recently moved to California, at the Cheesecake Factory. But when they drove home to get Erik's ID, they encountered the murder scene, and Lyle claimed he saw and smelled clouds and gun smoke in the air. Zoeller thought that odd because the first cops to arrive hadn't seen any smoke. Still, Zoeller didn't yet suspect Lyle or Erik, and simply asked Lyle if he thought anyone might hate his parents enough to kill them. Lyle suggested it might be the mob, perhaps because his father "wouldn't cooperate with such activities."[85] Finally, near dawn, the interviews came to an end, and the investigators told the brothers they were free to go.

Surprisingly, the investigators hadn't given them a gunshot-residue test to show if they had recently fired a weapon.[86] Perhaps if the investigators had, that test could have dramatically shortened the investigation. But for now the Menendez brothers weren't suspects. Perhaps the investigators did not give them the test because they viewed them as the grieving sons of wealthy parents, and they didn't want to seem insensitive and offend them. The police even let the brothers enter the mansion when they returned after the interviews, though it was a restricted crime scene, surrounded by yellow tape, so the brothers could get their tennis rackets, which they both needed as serious tennis players who participated in competitive play.[87]

Another reason that it took the police so long to suspect the Menendez brothers is that outwardly, the family had a picture-perfect life. Jose had come to the United States from Cuba in 1953 with virtually nothing. But with a good head for figures and a concern for the bottom line, he had worked his way up. In 1986, he came to International Video Entertainment, a company in deep financial trouble, and he helped it become the largest independent video distributor in the nation. Jose also combined the company with several others he purchased into a new company called LIVE Entertainment, based in Van Nuys. As Ron Soble and John Johnson, authors of *Blood Brothers* note, by the time Jose was killed in 1989, the company's revenues had grown in just three years from $40 million to $400 million. Jose's wheeling and dealing was, in fact, so successful that he had put together an estate worth $14 million by the time of his death.[88] It was $14 million that Lyle and Erik stood to inherit.

Yet Jose's aggressive, off-putting nature was such that the investigators at first looked to his business associates, employees, and ex-associates, who might have turned lethal because of the way Jose treated them. Ironically, while Jose was inspired by the power of positive thinking and success teachers like Og Mandino, he readily stepped on others as he worked his way to the top. As Soble and Johnson describe him:

> He could be brutal in business, especially with people he felt were not giving the same percentage of their souls to the company each day that he was . . .
>
> His temper was legendary, as was the sarcastic, belittling tone of voice he adopted when dealing with someone he was convinced was incompetent. He didn't mind humiliating people in public either, where others could watch the unfortunate victim being disemboweled by a man with a surgeon's touch.[89]

No wonder Jose had acquired many enemies as he rose to the top, any of whom might be a suspect. But what the investigators didn't initially realize is that his image as a family man hid the fact that he treated his sons in much the same controlling, demanding way as his employees and business associates. He wanted the best for his sons, too, and he was determined to mold them into well-educated citizens. That's why he sent Lyle off to Princeton and turned the family dinners into sessions to debate important issues. Also, he placed a great importance on his son's tennis achievements. He sought to mold them into tennis pros, sometimes accompanying them to tennis tournaments and coaching them on how to improve their game.[90]

Unfortunately, a major problem with Jose's ambitions for his sons is that neither Lyle or Erik were particularly good students. Lyle had even been suspended from Princeton for one year for plagiarism, after he turned in a report that looked similar to another student's in Psychology 101.[91] Moreover, the brothers were only middling tennis players, and probably didn't have the ability to become the best that Jose hoped for them. Thus, Jose was continually putting the boys down and making them feel they weren't good enough, at the same time that he urged them on to be the best they could be, regardless of their ability or level of desire.

Initially, though, the investigators didn't know about these family dynamics, so apart from looking at Jose's associates and employees, the investigators pursued the theory that the murder might be a mob hit. Erik even helpfully suggested that one possibility could be Noel Bloom, a pornographic films distributor, previously associated with the Bonanno crime family. Supposedly Bloom hated Jose after a business deal went bad, though Bloom denied he had anything to do with the murders. This mob theory was obviously a good way to deflect attention from themselves, and Lyle and Erik used their fear of the mob to explain why they moved from hotel to hotel in the days after the murder.[92]

Early on, though, the police became skeptical of a mob hit because the murder didn't have the corresponding characteristics. Among other things, mob hits did not usually occur in the home, and the crime scene was more of a massacre than the usual quick and clean mob killing, typically done with one shot in the back of the head. Also, a mob assassin wouldn't normally kill the wife. Nor would a mob killer carefully pick up all the shell casings, as he would want to get out quickly after the murder.[93] But even if many Beverly Hills police officers suspected the Menendez brothers from the beginning, even from the first night, as a few officers told crime writer Dominick Dunne after the brothers' arrest, at first there was no proof. These officers had only their early gut reactions.[94]

The brothers soon helped to provide that proof, however, starting with the way they acted after the murders. Their behavior at the funeral service, held on August 28, a week after the murders, was telling. Lyle, rather than seeming grief stricken, appeared very cool, collected, and without emotion, though in an impressive eulogy, he spoke of his parents in fond, glowing terms, emphasizing how they raised him and Erik with love and devotion—a stark contrast to the reality of Jose driving them relentlessly to success.[95]

Suspicious, too, were the changes in the brothers' lifestyle within a few days of the murders, a result of their newfound freedom. For instance, Lyle dropped his plans to finish college and decided on a business career, whereas Erik decided not to go to UCLA and focus on a tennis career.[96] But perhaps more suspicious than anything was their shopping spree that began a few days after the murders and went on for months. As Dunne describes it: "As new heirs, they embarked on a spending spree that even the merriest widow, who had married for money, would have refrained from going on—for propriety's sake, if nothing else—in the first flush of the mourning period. They bought and bought."[97]

Among other lifestyle changes, the brothers moved around from one luxury hotel or apartment to another, claiming they couldn't bear to stay in their mansion and they feared a mob hit. Eventually they rented adjoining luxury apartments in Marina Del Ray for about $2,500 a month.[98] They also went shopping for jewelry only four days after the murders, spending over $11,000 on Rolex watches. Plus, Lyle bought himself a silver Porsche for $64,000, and Erik purchased a new Jeep Wrangler. Then, to help create his new image as the successful business entrepreneur, Lyle began acquiring a flashy new wardrobe, spending thousands for shoes, undergarments, suits, ties, and shirts.[99]

Meanwhile, as Erik worked on pursuing his tennis career, which included hiring a $50,000-a-year tennis coach, Lyle began setting up his new business, Menendez Investment Enterprises, with plans to fund it with the money obtained from the final estate settlement. He planned to go into "real estate investments, show-business productions, shopping centers, stocks and bonds,"[100] essentially stepping into the role of the father he hated, so much so that he killed him. To start the business, he bought a fast-food restaurant, Chuck's Spring Street Cafe, in Princeton that sold chicken wings to students. He invested $550,000, using a $300,000 bank loan as a down payment, with plans to change the name to Mr. Buffalo's.[101]

All of these activities helped to suggest a clear motive for the crime—that the boys wanted to be free of their parents control, so they could do what they want, which included skipping a university education, changing career paths, and living a lavish lifestyle.

Another very suspicious activity was erasing a computer file that might have been Jose's new will, which Jose began rewriting in the summer of 1989, only weeks before the murder, after he and Kitty received some bad news about Lyle's behavior. Besides being on academic probation for bad grades at Princeton, Lyle was put on disciplinary probation, as well, after he threw a party for his brother and some friends at the student center and some pool tables were damaged. In addition, Jose and Kitty learned that Lyle's driver's license had been suspended and that the family's privileges at the fancy Beden Brooks Country Club had been suspended after Lyle took a friend for a ride in a cart on the golf course and damaged some of the greens. For Jose, such behavior was unacceptable after all his efforts to turn the boys into responsible citizens, so he and Kitty threatened to cut them out of the family will that had been written back in 1980 before Jose became wealthy. Under its terms, if either Jose or Kitty died, the money would go to the other, but if they both died together, Lyle and Erik would inherit everything. While Jose and Kitty had made this threat to change the will from time to time for a couple of years, now they became serious, and in June, Kitty began to work on creating a new will on the computer in her bedroom.[102]

Shortly after the murders, during an inventory of the house, Lyle found out about this change, when one of the relatives who came to Beverly Hills to express condolences checked the computer and found three file names that he wondered about: "Erik," "Lyle," and "Will." Though the relative couldn't open the password-protected files and knew nothing about Jose's plans to rewrite his will, when he told Lyle and Erik about these files, they became concerned. Though an electronic draft of a new will wouldn't be legally binding, since a will has to be signed and witnessed, Lyle may not have realized this, and he acted immediately to get rid of the file. He flew back from a tennis tournament in Queens, New York, on August 30, and when he couldn't open the files himself, he called a computer services firm run by Howard Witkin. After Witkin found the files unreadable, since they had been corrupted, Lyle asked him to erase the whole disk, claiming he wanted to get rid of any personal family information on the computer because he wanted to sell it. So Witkin completely erased the data.[103]

However, rather than keeping quiet about this very suspicious action to get rid of the files, Lyle soon told an old friend at Princeton, Glenn Stevens, that he had erased everything because he "could only lose" if a new will were discovered, since he and Erik inherited everything under the old will. Then, Lyle made the mistake of mentioning his friend Glenn Stevens to two reporters, Ron Soble and John Johnson, who were writing about the case for the *Los Angeles Times*, when they asked the brothers for the names of their closest friends so they could learn more about the family. When Soble and Johnson called Glenn, he told them about the computer and his suspicions, turning on his old friend because Lyle seemed so "blasé" about the murders. Glenn was also feeling hurt because Lyle, who had once been his "best buddy," now seemed too busy to spend much time with him. Then, when Glenn called lead investigator Les Zoeller to describe his discussion with the reporters, he passed on Lyle's story about erasing the computer along with his suspicions.[104]

These revelations, in turn, contributed to other developments that ultimately gave the police the necessary evidence to make an arrest. The case blew open on October 24, when Zoeller went to visit Erik, who was still in Beverly Hills, while Lyle was back East in Princeton. He began by telling Erik that the *Los Angeles Times* reporters were suspicious of the brothers and were going to write an article based on these suspicions. When Erik tried to remain cool, Zoeller said he had his suspicions, too, ever since Lyle and Erik hadn't been cooperating and returning the investigators' calls. Then, Zoeller struck pay dirt when he told Erik that he knew Lyle had erased the will and that he had heard that the two brothers hadn't been getting along. In response, Erik expressed his concern that Lyle was spending too much money and was becoming too bossy and manipulative, just like their father had been. Yet when Zoeller wondered if Lyle was involved in the murders and might have hired someone, Erik coolly said no, and that Lyle would contact the police when back in town.[105]

When Zoeller left, he still didn't have enough evidence to arrest the boys, despite his growing suspicions. But the meeting left Erik feeling panicky, so he called his therapist, Jerry Oziel, a few days later, leading to a fateful meeting on Halloween, October 31, which would unravel the case.

When he made the call, as later revealed in court, Erik told Oziel he wanted to talk and drove over around 4 p.m. But since he was very tense and edgy and didn't want to talk in the office, they went downstairs, walked around, and sat on a park bench for awhile chatting. On the way back to the office, Erik spoke about "how great a man his father had been" and "how much he missed his mother." Finally, he dropped his bombshell: "We did it. We killed our parents."[106] Then, he began unloading all the details he had kept to himself. As he told Oziel, a week before the slayings, he had seen a movie on TV called *The Billionaire Boys' Club* about how a group of wealthy young men from Beverly Hills had become involved in murder due to greed. After he invited his brother Lyle to watch the movie, they saw parallels with their own lives, and were especially intrigued when they saw how one of the boys seeking to gain the family fortune put out a contract for a hit man to kidnap and kill his father. Since they were already afraid that Jose was going to write up a new will to disinherit them and hated him because he had been so domineering and controlling over their lives, the movie helped to inspire them to kill. Though they didn't really want to kill Kitty, they felt they had to murder her, too, not only so they could inherit the money, but because she was a very unhappy woman.[107]

At this point, Oziel suggested that Erik should invite his brother Lyle to join them, and about ten minutes later Lyle did, though in the meantime, Erik told the therapist more of the plot. He described how they had bought the shotguns and after the murder, picked up the shell casings, changed out of their bloody clothes, hid them in a dumpster, and threw the guns into a canyon in the Hollywood Hills by Mulholland Drive.

Meanwhile, while Lyle was on his way, Oziel invited his then girlfriend Judalon Rose Smyth, a thirty-seven-year-old former actress, to listen in by the door because he had a concern for his own safety, given what Erik had just told him. He expected her to listen in confidence, but several months later, on March 5, after she had a falling out with Oziel, she contacted the Beverly Hill police, and told them about what she had heard, leading the police to finally arrest Lyle and Erik.[108]

What Smyth heard was dynamite. As she later testified in court, she heard a very angry Lyle scream at his brother: "I can't believe you told him! I don't even have a brother now! I could get rid of you for this! I hope you know what we have to do! We've got to kill him and anyone associated to him."[109] After Erik sobbed that he couldn't stop Lyle from doing whatever he had to do and exclaimed: "But I can't kill anymore," Erik ran out of the office in tears. Moments later, Lyle raced out past Smyth to the elevator, Oziel just behind him, where he told Oziel that Erik shouldn't have done this, adding: "We'll just have to take care of this."[110]

Alarmed by this exchange, Oziel stayed at Smyth's house for awhile and told his wife and kids to leave their house, afraid of what Lyle might do.[111] Yet, he didn't call the police right away, in part because of his concern about patient-therapist confidentiality and his fear for the safety of himself and his family if he said anything.[112] Instead, Oziel arranged additional meetings with Lyle and Erik, telling them he might be able to help them explore their family history to understand why they hated their parents so much, which might help their case in court. When they met with him again, he began taping these sessions, including one on December 11, which would become a major issue at their trial. Though the brothers briefly considered killing Oziel because he knew too much, they decided against it, fearing it might look suspicious if their therapist died soon after their parents had died.[113]

For now though, the brothers' secret was safe with Oziel, and they continued to live their new lives of freedom and luxury, unaware of how their behavior was leaving a trail of suspicion that would later be used against them.

The breakthrough came when Judalon Smyth called the police on March 5, less out of a concern for justice in the Mendenez case and due more to a falling out with Oziel. He had been letting Smyth stay at his house with his wife and kids on a temporary basis, since she was feeling lonely and scared and suffering from bouts of depression. However, when he learned that she had been talking with his daughter about replacing his wife as her mother, he ordered her to leave their house.[114] As a result, Smyth was out for revenge, and she spoke to police detectives for six hours, describing how she had been at Oziel's office, where she overheard the boys tell him that they had killed their parents and then they had threatened to kill Oziel if he told anyone. She also told the police that Oziel had made tape recordings of his sessions with the boys,[115] and that the brothers had bought the guns at a San Diego sporting-goods store.[116]

Although the police had some doubts about her credibility and felt her testimony would probably not be admissible in court as hearsay because she had overheard the conversation through the walls but wasn't directly present, her lead was enough to provide probable cause for a search warrant. Then, once the police had the tapes with the brothers' confession and threats, they could use Oziel as their witness to what happened in the session.

Thus, based on what Smyth reported, two days later, on March 6, a team of detectives and officers appeared at Oziel's office with a search warrant and a court representative, called a "special master," to help determine what tapes they could appropriately take. Though Oziel protested the search, based on therapist-patient confidentiality, his argument was one he would have to make later in court. For now, though, the police had their warrant to search, and they soon found over a dozen tapes in Oziel's safe-deposit vault. Though technically they were supposed to only take the tapes and put them in sealed evidence containers, they listened to a few of them[117]—an issue that would later come up in court, along with the confidentiality issue, on whether the tapes were admissible.

Based on Smyth's story and the tapes they heard, around 1 p.m. that afternoon, several police cars rolled up to the Menendez mansion, just as Lyle was pulling out of the driveway to go to lunch with two friends. After blocking his exit, the police arrested him and took him to the L.A. County Men's Central Jail. There he was formally booked on "two counts of suspicion of murder," and put in a jail cell.[118]

Erik didn't learn the news of the arrest until the following morning because he had been playing, though not very well, in a tennis tournament in Israel. After making a few calls to relatives and a lawyer, Erik realized he had to leave Israel as quickly as possible. He did not want to be arrested abroad where conditions were likely to be far worse than those in an American jail and court system with its constitutional protections. After returning to the United States and meeting with some relatives in Miami, he called the Beverly Hills police to tell them he was turning himself in. When he arrived, four detectives met him, handcuffed him, and booked him into the same jail with his brother on the same suspicion of murder charges.[119]

The arrests sparked a media frenzy, intensified even more because this happened in Beverly Hills, a part of the L.A. entertainment and media capitol of the world. Perhaps all this attention contributed to the brothers' sense of self-importance.

When they appeared in court on March 26 for their first hearing to enter their plea to the charges, they still had their cool, cocky arrogance, despite being in jail for two weeks, for they were still the self-assured rich kids who felt protected by their wealth and ability to make and break their own rules. As Don Davis described in *Bad Blood*, calling them "boys" as the defense and media commonly referred to them:

> When the boys entered the hearing, it was as if they either did not know about the possibility of a death sentence, or weren't worried about it, or just didn't care. . . .
>
> The brothers had been in jail for two weeks, but neither looked nor acted as if anything were amiss. . . . They wore their arrogance that day on the sleeves of their dark, tailored sports coats, and sauntered into court as if they were thinking of buying the place.[120]

In time, though, that attitude disappeared. As the weeks turned into months and then years, that snappy arrogance gradually was replaced by a more submissive, cultivated preppy boyish look, and they wore casual sweaters and slacks, not suits. While they were worn down by their days in jail, their lawyers coached them to maintain this innocent look to help jurors better identify and empathize with them as just two kids.

One reason the court case dragged on for so long is the battle over the tapes. The prosecution desperately wanted them in as evidence to show that the brothers had confessed, while the defense wanted them out for the same reason, and argued privilege and confidentiality between a patient and psychotherapist to exclude them.[121] The hard-fought legal battle went on for three years, since at first Judge James Albracht admitted the tapes on the grounds that Oziel reasonably believed the brothers constituted a threat and could "disclose the communications to prevent a danger."[122] But eight days later, the Second District Court of Appeals reversed his ruling, after which the prosecutors and defense launched a series of appeals and counter-appeals. In the end, some of the tapes were allowed in on the grounds that Lyle had threatened his therapist, giving Oziel sufficient cause to feel that his life, as well as that of his wife and children, was at risk, thereby overcoming the privilege.[123]

While the case was in legal limbo and the brothers remained in jail, they and their lawyers—Jill Lansing for Lyle, Leslie Abramson for Erik—maintained their innocence. They had a good chance of prevailing, for without the tapes, the prosecution had only a circumstantial case against them.[124] And as the case dragged on, neither Lyle nor Erik mentioned any sexual abuse or molestation by their parents, nor had they ever mentioned it to any friends or relatives or to Oziel in their therapy sessions.

But once the prosecution got permission to use the tapes, including one with the confession, and made Oziel its star witness, the defense strategy changed from claiming innocence. For now it was hard to refute the confession and details of the crime, which the brothers provided in their own words. So now they acknowledged that, yes, they had killed their parents, as Leslie Abramson told the judge in a pretrial hearing on June 9.[125] But they claimed they acted in self-defense because they thought their parents were going to kill them if they didn't act. And they had a good reason for their fear because their father had been molesting them for years, and when Lyle stood up to Jose, telling him the abuse of Erik had to stop, Jose threatened to kill them.[126] Supposedly, Lyle had this confrontation with his father a few days before the murders because Erik had suddenly told him about this abuse, which had been going on for twelve years. Lyle was so disturbed by this revelation because his father had molested him, too, from the time he was six and until he was eight years old.[127] As Lyle testified in court:

> I thought we were in danger. I felt he had no choice. He would kill us. He'd get rid of us in some way, because I was going to ruin him.[128]

So why not simply leave? Because, Lyle testified, their father had the power to find them wherever they tried to hide, and because they felt they couldn't speak to the cops, because they wouldn't believe them.[129]

Did any of this really happen? The prosecution's position

was this was a completely fabricated story designed to explain the killing once they could no longer deny they did it. But the defense went to great lengths to shore up this theory with gripping testimony by both Lyle and Erik about how they had long wanted to keep this horrible secret from anyone, including their friends, relatives, and therapist, because it was so humiliating and upsetting to admit. That's why they had said nothing. Additionally, the defense brought in a stream of over fifty witnesses, including coaches, teachers, friends, and experts, who spoke about the damaging effects of such sexual abuse.[130] The defense also cited recent legal cases that supported abuse victims who struck back and killed their abusers, even when not under an imminent attack.[131]

It would seem this new defense strategy had its origins in the spring of 1992, while the battle of the tapes was still raging. That's when the defense attorneys brought in Santa Monica attorney Paul Mones, who specialized in defending children who had killed one or both of their parents and wrote a book, *When a Child Kills*, about some of his cases. According to Norma Novelli, who regularly visited Lyle from mid-June 1990 until his trial ended in 1993 and later documented their conversations in *The Private Diary of Lyle Menendez*, Lyle told her how Paul first visited him in March, 1992. At this meeting, Lyle told her, Paul described the types of abuse that children suffer from their parents, and for the first time, Lyle hinted to her that his father had sexually abused him. To demonstrate this, he pointed to a photo of himself and his father in the *Los Angeles Times Magazine*, claiming that the photo showed his father with his hand on his crotch. But did it really show that? Novelli thought the picture looked like a "normal family photo."[132]

Still, the defense was committed to this abuse claim, as Leslie Abramson told Judge Stanley Weisberg, at a June 1993 hearing, when she stated: "We will present evidence that our clients believed themselves to be in danger of death, imminent peril, or great bodily injury when their parents were shot."[133] To justify this fear, the defense strategy began trashing the parents as child abusers and molesters—not only in the trial court, but also in the court of public opinion—and Abramson was the most visible public face for this strategy.

For example, three days before the start of the trial before two juries—one for Lyle, the other for Erik—Abramson gave an interview to the *Los Angeles Times* in which she described how Lyle and Erik's parents raised them in a "training camp" or, even worse, a "concentration camp" atmosphere. Not only did Jose molest Lyle from when he was six to eight years old, but also he had been molesting Erik up until the time of the shooting.[134] In graphic detail, in frequently sobbing testimony, both Lyle and Erik detailed what they allegedly experienced. They claimed that Jose forced them into a variety of perverse sexual acts, such as forcible oral copulation, sodomy, rape, and the use of assorted household objects, such as needles, tacks, and knotted ropes, which Jose engaged in to satisfy his lust and his need to control and manipulate others.[135]

When Lyle took the stand toward the end of the defense case, he provided even more graphic descriptions. For example, he described how, when he was six, Jose began to talk to him about how sex between men was part of the bonding process. Then, between the time he was six and eight years old, he claimed Jose came to his bedroom two to three times a week after sports practice, where he "massaged and fondled him" and showed him how to do the same to him. Sometimes, Lyle said, his father used a toothbrush and shaving brush on him, and one day he raped him.[136]

Once Lyle had finished testifying, Erik detailed his own sexual abuse saga. He said that Jose played several types of sexual games with him, among them "knees," in which Jose performed oral sex while kneeling, and "rough sex," in which he stuck needles, tacks, and pins into Erik's backside and thighs. Sometimes he forced Erik to have anal intercourse with him.[137]

Then, having demonstrated the nature of the abuse from Lyle and Erik's testimony, the defense brought in a battery of experts to show how a long history of abuse could lead to murder.[138] Among them was Dr. Ann H. Tyler, a child abuse expert from Utah, who testified that "a lifetime of psychological abuse had left Erik Menendez immature and naïve." She also discussed how repeated abuse can lead to "learned helplessness," where victims believe they lack the will to do anything, so they "cannot flee an abusive situation."[139]

So was this torturous tale true or was it a fabrication to evoke sympathy? And did thc jury find it credible? In answer to the first question, most probably it wasn't true. Even Lyle's regular visitor Norma Novelli didn't believe the molestation story, pointing out that Lyle came up with the story "long after he confessed," and he had never mentioned it before. As she stated in her book: "We had talked about every subject you could imagine for a couple of years, and there was no mention of molestation."[140] Moreover, on the Oziel tape, when Lyle and Erik knew they were being taped as they explained their killings, they made no mention of abuse, incest, or molestation.[141] Plus when Oziel described the characteristics of a sociopath, the brothers readily agreed, saying: "We're sociopaths" or "We'd be in that category."[142] And one characteristic of a sociopath is an ability to lie and manipulate without any guilt.

Although this abuse defense might seem outlandish and implausible, the prosecution made the big mistake of not trying to refute it, which turned the Menendez trial into a trial of Jose and Kitty. The prosecution did not seek to counter this defense because they were so sure this far-fetched abuse story was unbelievable and that their evidence for murder for the $14 million inheritance and freedom from controlling, demanding parents was so compelling that a rebuttal was not needed. But it was necessary because the prosecution's lack of a counter to the abuse story left the door open for the jury to feel some empathy for the defendants, and both juries deadlocked. While some jurors on both juries thought the brothers were guilty of first-degree murder or part of a conspiracy to commit such a murder, others thought they might be guilty of second-degree murder, voluntary murder, or not guilty at all of any charge, resulting in two hung juries.[143]

Perhaps Pierce O'Donnell, a high-power attorney commenting on the Novelli conversations with Menendez expressed it best, describing this as a defense engineered by Lyle Menendez to subvert justice, given that the evidence of guilt was so overwhelming.[144] But unlike the plea-for-mercy defense offered by Darrow to spare the life of Leopold and Loeb, the brothers' strategy, if successful, offered the possibility for a full acquittal. It provided a chance to get away with murder and resume their life of freedom without their parents and obtain whatever was left of their inheritance. As O'Donnell put it:

> The prosecution mounted a weak and ineffective rebuttal that largely ignored the main thrust of the defense: the defendant's mental state due to the supposed abuse. In my opinion that was a fatal mistake.
>
> In retrospect, we can see that the jurors were almost brainwashed. After the sexual abuse and psychological torture claims were repeated so many times, and defense experts were allowed to testify (incredibly!) that they believed the allegations were true and that the long-term abuse excused the crimes, the unsubstantiated charges took on a life of their own, gradually becoming fact and then the basis for juror sympathy.
>
> It was a brilliant strategy, flawlessly executed. As effective as the defense lawyers were, the major credit must go to Lyle Menendez. There is no doubt in my mind that he was the Grand Architect of the Defense who pulled the strings and wrote the script. Any doubt about this was resolved by his candid statements in his conversations.
>
> As we can now see, the subversion of justice began once the trial judge let in the parent-bashing evidence.[145]

In the end, however, justice prevailed when the Menendez brothers were retried in a prosecution that began October 11, 1995. At this point, the brothers had been in jail for five years, and their estate was gone, much of it spent on their defense, as well as high living and bad business deals before their arrest. Thus, in the new trial, both had to turn to the public defender for their defense, arguing indigence. However, Leslie Abramson continued to defend Erik, but for a lower fee as a court-appointed attorney. And this time, the single jury hearing both cases returned its first-degree murder verdict on March 20, 1996, and Lyle and Erik were each sentenced to two consecutive life prison terms without the possibility of parole.[146] Though Lyle and Erik still tried to argue sexual abuse, only Erik took the stand to testify, and this time, most of the jurors did not believe the story. Why not? As juror Lesley Hillings told a Court TV interviewer it was "because there were inconsistencies in Erik's story which left doubt in jurors' minds. Also, some jurors felt that either one of the brothers could have left the home at any point and chose not to. Some felt Jose Menendez did not seem the type of person that would do that."[147] Moreover, the Oziel tape was compelling, showing evidence of premeditation, and the jurors did not believe that the Menendez brothers ever feared for their lives at any time.

As of this writing, both Lyle and Erik are still in prison, Lyle at the California Correctional Institution at Tehachapi and Erik at the California State Prison in Sacramento County. It is an ironic coda to their youthful plan to gain both freedom and money by killing their parents because now they have neither. Also they now receive little public attention, as the almost-celebrity status gained during their first trial has faded despite the A&E special *The Menendez Brothers*, which aired on March 10, 2004, while I was writing this chapter.

CHAPTER 9

Losing It

Although wealth provides many protections, some of the wealthy do "lose it" in various ways, and this can lead to murder.

One way to lose it is to fall on hard times while trying to keep up a public show of still being wealthy, as in a family with long line of wealth. Such a heritage breeds a sense of entitlement or arrogance; one feels privileged and "to the manor born," so the loss of this cachet can be especially painful and lead to a downward emotional spiral, as in the case of the Wardlow sisters, from an old aristocratic family.

Another way to "lose it" is by becoming increasingly eccentric, which can lead to family estrangement, increasing social isolation from others, or to mental disturbance. Certainly, eccentric and mentally unbalanced behavior can occur for anyone from any social class. However, the wealthy can use their economic and social position to further magnify and exaggerate these problems. For example, they can support a fantasy or personal quirk with their wealth, as did Howard Hughes in his later years, when he retreated to a penthouse suite in Las Vegas and protected himself from contact with people who might have germs with an army of personal bodyguards. In some cases, such personal quirks, magnified by wealth, can lead to murder, as in the du Pont case, profiled in this chapter, or in the more recent Robert Durst case, where the heir to a family fortune was found living in a seedy rooming house as a woman and was accused of murdering a neighbor and chopping up the body. Eventually, he was acquitted on the basis of self-defense in a surprise verdict that stunned even the defendant, though he is still in jail because of other charges of interfering with the prosecution by disposing of the body.

Plus, in some cases, the very wealthy have been found living double lives that have led to murder—sometimes because of the fear of exposure, as in the Capano case profiled in Chapter 4. And sometimes these double lives lead them to become mixed up with shady characters involved in an underworld of crime, drugs, and prostitution, such as in the Phil Spector case now working its way through the courts, in which Spector was accused of shooting Lana Clark, a former actress and nightclub hostess, who had come to his home in the early morning hours on January 23, 2004.

Once the eccentric, disgraced, prodigal, or otherwise straying family member is accused of murder, these cases often become big media stories because of the public fascination with people with wealth or from wealthy families who have gone wrong and done wrong. There is an intrigue about such cases, and watching them unfold is like watching a morality play. There is a common, erroneous perception that the wealthy are not supposed to have such problems, so when they do, there is a popular satisfaction in seeing the high and mighty humiliated or brought down to size. It is as if the accusation serves to remind the wealthy that that they are not above the rules of society and that justice will catch up. As described by Dominick Dunne, a frequent chronicler of the wealthy and privileged in trouble: "As a wise man in publishing once whispered in my ear when I first started to write, 'There is nothing the public enjoys reading about more than the rich and powerful in a criminal situation.' "[1]

The press and public are eager to read such stories, but commonly, the families and relatives of the accused wealthy or once-wealthy family member rally together and do their best to protect that person, in part to protect the family name and reputation. In some cases, that means funding or contributing to the defense. In other cases, they turn out in force to show their support—as in the Skakel and Cummings cases described in previous chapters.

The following cases illustrate how losing it can lead to murder and show the long history of such cases. The Wardlow case comes from early in this century; the du Pont case from the 1990s.

From Southern Aristocracy to the Streets of New Jersey: The Case of the Wardlow Sisters (East Orange, New Jersey, 1909–1911)

The story of the Wardlow Sisters is like a southern gothic story and features weirdly eccentric sisters from a long aristocratic tradition, who had seen better days before they ended up accused of murder. The case began after Virginia Wardlow called the police to report an accident on November 29, 1909, in East Orange, New Jersey, a quiet residential suburb across the river from Manhattan. At the time, the primary means of transportation in the area were horse and wagon, the New York-New Jersey Ferry, and the Lackawanna Railroad.

When Sergeant Timothy Caniff took the call at 4:40 p.m., he heard a quiet well-spoken voice asking if he could send over a coroner because there had been an accident. But the county had no coroner and Caniff couldn't reach the county physician, so he sent the physician's assistant, Dr. Herbert Simmons, who walked from his nearby office to the Wardlow's home, a two-story gray frame house with a small attic. Virginia Wardlow, the oldest of the three Wardlow sisters, lived there, and like her other sisters, she dressed totally in black, so when together, they looked like three crows covering their beaks with black veils.

Virginia greeted Dr. Simmons on the porch. A tall, thin woman, she looked a little like a witch with her long black cape that touched the ground and her heavy black-veiled face. She invited him in and led him upstairs through a hallway to the second-floor bathroom. When Dr. Simmons opened the door and entered, he saw the nude body of a woman crouched in a half-filled bathtub, her head bent over her knees into the water, her left hand holding a washcloth. As her lifted up her head, he saw what had been a beautiful woman with long brown hair, perhaps in her mid-twenties. Then, on a pile of clothing on the floor, he noticed a note pinned to one piece of clothing.

It seemed to be a suicide note, but, as the police would wonder later, was it? Had this woman really committed suicide or had someone killed her? The note, written in clear strong handwriting, read:

> Last year my little daughter died; other near and dear ones have gone before. I have been prostrated with illness for a long time. When you read this I will have committed suicide. Do not grieve over me. Rejoice with me that death brings a blessed relief from pain and suffering greater than I can bear.[2]

When Dr. Simmons asked who the woman was, Virginia explained that she was her niece, Ocey Snead. As she described, Ocey had slipped into a deeply despondent state after her first child and husband died during the past year. Virginia also noted that Ocey had a sick four-month-old son in a hospital in Brooklyn and had been in poor health for some time.

Still, Dr. Simmons was suspicious after he asked when the body was found, and Virginia said she had found it only a short time before she called the police station. But Dr. Simmons could tell the woman had been dead at least 24 hours, and when he asked about this, Virginia explained that Ocey had asked her to start a fire in the kitchen to heat some bath water for her. Then, knowing Ocey wanted to take a nap, she went away leaving her undisturbed.[3]

However, Dr. Simmons was suspicious, since Virginia's explanation didn't fit the facts. He was also puzzled by the lack of furniture in the house, though Virginia explained that she and her sisters had only settled there temporarily. Even so, it seemed mysterious that a large house should be so empty, bleak, and without heat on a chilly November day. As a result, when Dr. Simmons called the police station, he reported the case was an apparent suicide but that the circumstances were suspicious, and he suggested that a detective should come by.

When Sergeant William H. O'Neill arrived, he similarly suspected something was wrong as he inspected the house for clues. As he walked around, he noted that the first three rooms on the second floor were entirely empty, except for a single silk maternity gown hanging on a hook in one closet. In the fourth small room, he saw a narrow cot where Ocey slept before she died, and nearby, a barrel used as a dressing table had several empty cans of evaporated milk, a package of cereal, and bits of orange peel—sure signs of abject poverty. Yet, a long black silk gown and pretty shoes hung near the cot, suggesting that Ocey had once been affluent. The downstairs was similarly empty, except for a few pieces of improvised furniture, such as a dining room table made from a packing box and a plank top. When Sergeant O'Neill wondered about the lack of beds, Virginia told him she slept on the floor. The two women thus appeared to be living in dire poverty with no sign of the affluent life they had once led.

And for now, Virginia was saying nothing of these better days. Rather, she stated that she and Ocey had been living in East Orange for ten days, and before then, in the Flatlands section of Brooklyn on East 48th Street and Mill Lane. She told him they had come here for Ocey's health to nurse her, though the empty house and cold New Jersey weather seemed like the last place to come for such a purpose.

Thus, suspicious at this strange story, Sergeant O'Neill took Virginia to the station to talk to Chief of Police James Bell, but she told him little more, even though he held her for the night as a material witness. It was the beginning of a case that would become stranger and stranger as the weeks went on, showing how eccentric Virginia and her other sisters had become after their fall from privilege.

The coroner's autopsy showed that Ocey had not only drowned in the bathtub, but was already near death, as she had been suffering from starvation and weighed only eighty pounds when she died. Then, detectives began getting reports from neighbors that the house was dark most of the time. Another piece of the puzzle came when a cabbie described driving Ocey and her aunt, Virginia, to the house. When they arrived, he helped Ocey, who seemed very weak and ill, into the house, and referred the aunt to Dr. Charles E. Teeters. Yet, when the doctor came to the house and examined Ocey, Virginia was able to convince him that there was no problem, and he wrote up a health certificate stating that Ocey was in "normal health" though "weak and inclined to bronchitis."[4]

Tracing back in their history, before they lived at the Flatlands address in Brooklyn, Detective O'Neill discovered from the New York City hotel registers that three months before in August, Virginia had checked them into the exclusive Brevoort hotel. But after a brief spat with a clerk who said her room payment wasn't enough, she and Ocey had moved to a two-family brick house in Brooklyn, which neighbors called the "House of Mystery."[5] And apparently Ocey's starvation problems had already started; one neighbor, Mrs. Ethel Moore, reported that when she assisted at the birth of Ocey's second child, she heard Ocey, who seemed quite thin, complaining that she was being starved to death. When O'Neill visited the house, he found it, too, was almost empty of furniture, like the house in East Orange. He found only a few remnants of broken furniture and clothing and a few cans and boxes of groceries.

So what was going on? Gradually, O'Neill pieced together a story about how Ocey, then in her mid-twenties, had moved in with her twenty-four-year-old husband, Fletcher Snead, about a year and a half earlier. A few months later, the three sisters dressed in black had joined them. Several months after that, in March 1909, Fletcher had left, and Ocey had her baby in August. At that time, a doctor, William Pettit, had prescribed improved nutrition and medicine for Ocey's weakened condition, but none of his instructions were followed, because, as one of the sisters, probably Virginia, told the doctor, they couldn't afford to do so because they had to use all their money to pay the premiums on Ocey's insurance policies, which were worth about $20,000. Meanwhile, the family continually seemed to have financial problems. They were nearly evicted several times for nonpayment before they managed to pay their rent, but eventually, they were evicted in early November. That's when they put their belongings into storage, moved to Brooklyn, and put Ocey's child in a Brooklyn hospital, St. Christopher's, where the child remained in ill health.

Then, strangely, Virginia Wardlow had brought in a sickly looking Ocey to see a lawyer, aptly named William Fee, to draw up a new will for Ocey. As Fee told O'Neill, Virginia thought the existing will might be considered invalid because it didn't mention Ocey's baby. After he drew up the will, leaving $500 to Ocey's son and the remainder of her estate to her grandmother, Martha Eliza Wardlow, who was appointed executrix and guardian, Ocey quietly assented and signed the will.[6] So why would there be such a will, if Ocey and the sisters were living in poverty?

As O'Neill returned to East Orange with the results of his Brooklyn investigations, he was suspicious of what he had learned, convinced that Virginia Wardlow, who was Ocey's caretaker in her final days, had starved and drowned her for her money. Though Virginia claimed the drowning had been a suicide, he felt the insurance policies and will showed a motive, even though the estate was supposedly left to the grandmother.

When he returned to the police station, O'Neill found even more evidence of foul play when Detective Harry Riker described finding a bundle of documents in the cellar. Among them were Ocey's life insurance policies leaving money to her grandmother, yet there was no pen or ink in the house, raising questions of how the suicide note was written. And Virginia had claimed she had lit a fire for Ocey's bath, but there was no sign of any fire in the kitchen stove for many weeks, and no towel in the bathroom for drying oneself after a bath. So the suicide story didn't add up.

Though Virginia denied neglecting a relative and claimed that Ocey could have dried herself on her petticoat, the police were skeptical, and Chief Bell recommended charging Virginia with murder, convinced she had carried Ocey to the tub, threw her into the water, and held her down until she drowned.[7]

So the next day, Virginia was formally arraigned at city hall in East Orange, as an eager crowd of press and members of the public filed into the council chambers to watch. Her arrival caused a sensation because her appearance seemed so bizarre—a little like when Michael Jackson went to a 2004 hearing on child molestation charges and stood on a car dressed in black as if he were at a concert performance. When

Virginia stepped out of the closed carriage, she was wearing her black cape and veil, a detective at either side, looking like a ghostly apparition from the dead. When she approached the bar, at first she refused the recorder's request to lift her veil to be identified, but finally did so, as he read the murder complaint. Then, she quickly put it down again, and an officer led her back to the patrol wagon to return to her cell in Newark. Her strange appearance captivated the public, and the next day the *New York Herald* blared out the news: "Arrest Aunt of Bathtub Victim: Charge Will Plot."[8]

In time, the police arrested her two sisters, as well, and over the next year, until their January 1911 trial, the police sought to gather more evidence to explain who the sisters were and why they might have murdered their niece Ocey. The investigators followed a trail of papers through several states and Canada, with some help from other police agencies and the press, as readers who had met the Wardlow sisters came forth as witnesses, relating their strange encounters with them. One was Brooklyn lawyer Julius V. Carabba, who described how Virginia arrived with one of her sisters and a very sick Ocey asking him to alter the will Fee had prepared, saying it hadn't been properly witnessed. After he took a quick look at Ocey and advised them to quickly get her to a doctor, they protested that they couldn't afford it. When the two sisters went downstairs to look for a pen, Ocey whispered to him that she was dying, and asked him to draw up the will to give her property to her infant son and grandmother, not as they might instruct him. Subsequently, when Carabba suggested getting the grandmother's consent to make them the beneficiaries of the will, they objected and left. And he never did draw up a new will.[9]

Meanwhile, detectives checking in several cities in the North and South uncovered a maze of insurance policies on Ocey's life, starting in 1900, when she was fifteen. In that year, they found seven policies, taken out with twenty- and thirty-year endowments, and discovered loans taken out on all of the policies, which had reached their borrowing limit. Suspiciously, the insurance company officials reported that many duplicates had been issued for lost policies and many reassignments were made from one family member to another—

all signs of a family in growing financial trouble—as well as documents that could easily be misused. Additionally, the investigators found that in many New York City banks, Ocey's insurance policies had been deposited as security for loans.[10]

Thus, it appeared that from all these manipulations that Virginia and her sisters had kept the seven policies, valued at $24,000—about several hundred thousand dollars today—alive for a decade. But now it seemed the policies could not be used for any more financial dealings, except in the event of Ocey's death, whereupon the funds would go to her eighty-four-year-old nearly blind grandmother, and after her death, to Virginia and her sisters.

So where was this grandmother? What happened to Ocey's mysteriously missing husband? Had there been some foul play? And where were the other two sisters? To find out, the detectives followed various leads back into the sisters' history. One lead was the name of Ocey's baby, David Pollock, the name under which the sisters had stored all sorts of furniture, trunks with clothing, family records, and newspaper clippings. Another lead was a New York drugstore proprietor who called to say that a strange woman in black had left a big package of papers with him for safekeeping. When he brought them to police headquarters, the police discovered these were family records that showed that the sisters came from an aristocratic southern family that descended from a long line of aristocrats.[11]

As the police now discovered, the sisters were daughters of a South Carolina supreme court justice, David Lewis Wardlow, who was part of a southern family clan that included church leaders, merchants, lawyers, bankers, surgeons, and public officials. The family roots went back to the Anglo-Saxons, who had come to Scotland when the Normans conquered England, and their name was even in the history books during the tenth-century reign of Alfred the Great. Then, in the eighteenth century, seeking religious freedom, the family had emigrated to the United States and became part of the old southern gentry.[12]

But apparently, the family—or at least the sisters' part of it—had fallen on difficult times, as the records in the trunks and packages showed. After they left the South, they had first stayed in upscale expensive hotels like the Brevoort; then they moved to more medium-priced locations; and finally, they relocated to the last two nearly empty houses the police had searched.[13]

Then, a Manhattan address on one bill led Detective O'Neill and Riker to a housekeeper, Mrs. Cathleen Bond, who told them about one of Virginia's sisters, Mary Snead, and an elderly grandmother, who were living in the basement in a nearly bare room with no food. When the investigators arrived, Mary was cloaked in black, like her sisters, and the grandmother was wizened, frail, and nearly blind, as she huddled in a corner of the room.[14]

When they questioned her, Mary filled in more details. She explained that Ocey had been born to her sister Caroline, then the wife of a colonel in the Confederate Army, who, after the Civil War ended, worked as a tobacco inspector for one of the big merchandise houses of New York, which exported its merchandise to Europe.[15] Then, when Ocey was sent to the South to be educated as a proper southern lady, Ocey met and married Mary's son Fletcher in 1906. About a year later, they moved to New York, where they had their first child, though he died after just two days. Soon afterward, Fletcher went traveling for several months, and Ocey received a message that he was dead. However, he later turned up in Canada, but Caroline kept this information from Ocey. Meanwhile, after Fletcher left, Ocey, in ill health and despondent, thought she was going to die and asked for a lawyer to make her will. But as Mary tried to convince the detectives, Ocey hadn't been starved or mistreated, so Virginia was completely innocent of any charges.[16] Mary also had an explanation for the sisters' mysterious seclusion. Since they were people of "breeding" living among not particularly well-educated working-class people, they did not think others would find it "congenial" to mingle with them."[17]

Thus, despite their financial decline, the sisters were still trying to cling to their past high status, even if they had to live without furniture or food. Their background was certainly impressive, as the detectives discovered. The three sisters had been born shortly before the Civil War, and after attending good schools, all had become teachers in private schools for women, at a time when there were no co-ed schools. In 1892, Virginia had even advanced to become the president of Murfreesboro's Soule Female College, a small, exclusive women's college near Nashville, Tennessee.

Odd things began to happen after Virginia's sisters joined her at the school. Mary, a recent widow, was the first to arrive with her three sons, including Fletcher, and she began teaching at the school. Then, in 1901, Caroline Martin, recently widowed, arrived with her daughter Ocey. Suddenly everything began to change. The college stopped paying its bills on time. Ocey, who had been a lively girl, suddenly had extended illnesses and spent most of her time in her room, and Caroline took out the first insurance policy on her for $7,000. The girls enrolled at the school were suddenly moved from room to room without any reason, and the three sisters wandered around the school dressed in black, like three odd witches. Their strange behavior unnerved the students and other faculty members, such as when one student woke up one night and saw the sisters chanting something as they passed by the stove in her room. Although the next day the sisters claimed they had just come to investigate something burning in the stove, their behavior was scary, and over the next months, students began deserting the school, while money problems at the college increased. Eventually, a committee of trustees threw the sisters out of the school, later gave up repairing the school's tarnished reputation, and sold off its property.[18]

A similar upheaval occurred when Mary Snead began teaching at Christiansburg, Virginia. Within a few months, her sisters Virginia and Caroline were there, and soon after Caroline took over direction of the school, it went downhill. Again classes were shifted around oddly, and the sisters wandered the corridors dressed in black. Then, a fire mysteriously erupted in the room of Mary's twenty-eight-year-old son, John, after his nightclothes caught fire. A few hours later he was dead, and, because his bedclothes had been drenched with kerosene oil, rumors of foul play spread through the school. Though no criminal charges were filed, the town gossiped about what had really happened, especially because his aunts had heavily insured him and he had recently reassigned a policy on his wife, in a sanitarium for ill health, to Virginia Wardlow.[19]

Such background information helped to further convince O'Neill, Riker, and the Essex County prosecutor that Ocey's death was not suicide but murder, and that not only was Virginia involved, but also her sisters were accomplices. The grand jury set up by the prosecutor was convinced, too, and brought murder charges against Virginia. A key factor leading to these charges was the suicide note, after handwriting expert William J. Kinsley, who had handled almost 1,000 cases of questioned documents, agreed there was an apparent forgery. He pointed out that the body of the note was written by someone who held the pen obliquely and wrote the letters close together, but in the signature, the letters in the word "Snead" were far apart and the lettering was much finer.[20]

So Virginia remained in jail awaiting trial. Meanwhile, the police continued to watch Mary in Manhattan, and other detectives tried to find the older sister Caroline. She was hard to locate because she had been traveling since Ocey's death, and she paid her fare in cash on the train, so the depot window had no record of her ticket purchase. The search turned up a strange background for Caroline, too. Among other things, the city superintendent had recommended her for retirement as a principal at a New York public school because she was "mentally incapacitated."[21] The detectives heard reports that she had mistreated her second child, a son, who reportedly died of spinal meningitis, although some former pupils and teachers claimed he fell down a long flight of stairs and died of his injuries. Also curious was that just before Caroline and her husband Colonel Martin moved to New York, their mansion near Louisville, Kentucky, mysteriously burst into flames and burnt to the ground, after which they collected $22,000 in insurance. Despite rumors of wrongdoing, the insurance company paid them, and no criminal investigation was conducted.

Another suspicious circumstance was that Colonel Martin died suddenly when he and Caroline were living in a rundown Victorian boarding house in Manhattan. A neighbor heard a loud crash, then found the Colonel semiconscious on the floor and groaning. Yet, Caroline lounged nearby on the bed, seemingly unconcerned, while Ocey cried hysterically, until Caroline glared at her, saying "Remember." Ocey quickly fell silent, looking dazed and scared.[22] It also seemed strange when New York City lawyer Maxwell Hall Elliott reported that Caroline borrowed money from him every six months on her pension to pay off insurance premiums.

This new evidence suggested that Caroline was behind the scheme to kill Ocey for the insurance money, even though she wasn't present, and perhaps she even had some strange power over her sisters. But where was Caroline? She finally turned up on December 14, after the police issued a call in the press for information on her as a material witness. A hotel clerk at a seedy New York hotel on West 49th Street near Broadway, in the heart of the theater district, called to say she was staying there, and that's where the detectives found her. Yet, the police were frustrated in their efforts to arrest her. They didn't have enough evidence to hold her for a New Jersey case without any proof she had been there, and there was no New York case against her. Caroline also wouldn't open the door to talk to them.

But after Caroline fled the hotel to avoid their questions, the police got help from some of the reporters crowding into the hotel lobby. A group of reporters climbed up a fire escape to her room, where one newspaperman found a black tin box she had left behind. Inside were clippings about Ocey's death, hotel receipts showing where Caroline had been since Ocey's death, and more importantly, three suicide notes by Ocey written in the same handwriting as the note found at the scene of her death. The three notes were like practice attempts for the note found by her body, in which the writer talked about feeling despair after her little daughter died and a long period of sickness and suffering.

After the reporters called the police about their find, the police had what they needed to arrest Caroline. East Orange Prosecutor Wilbur Mott issued an arrest warrant for her, and Detective O'Neill and a New York detective went to pick her up.

This third arrest marked the beginning of the end for the Wardlow sisters. Though Caroline told her favorite reporters that the case against her and her sisters was the work of the "big interests who want to cheat us out of our money"[23]—a conspiracy of the police, lawyers, and insurance companies—their case went to trial. Caroline and Virginia were accused of directly killing Ocey with premeditation and malice aforethought, while Mary Snead was accused of being part of the murder conspiracy.

Ironically, Virginia's end came much like Ocey's did. After the trial was postponed twice—once when she fell ill of an intestinal disorder and again when the prosecutor suffered from sunstroke on a vacation—Virginia, already thin and ill, stopped eating and starved herself to death. By August 10, she was dead.

Still, the prosecution pursued charges against the remaining two sisters, though in September, Caroline's lawyers fought back to get the charges dismissed. They argued in a hearing that she was insane, describing her gradual descent from eccentricity to insanity over the years, and Caroline seemed to confirm this allegation when she testified. She ranted on about being the victim of a conspiracy and complained that the court was bribed and "all efforts were being made to railroad her to prison." When her black bonnet fell off during her tantrum, she ranted even more wildly.[24]

Caroline's behavior didn't convince the judge of her insanity, however. Instead, the judge concluded that while she might be insane to some degree, given her highly excitable, irritable, and hysterical behavior, she still seemed to have a "keen alert mind, a remarkably good memory . . . and a pretty clear comprehension of the whole case" against her.[25] Thus, the charges against her stood.

The trial finally got underway on January 9, 1911, but it was quickly over. Caroline entered a plea of guilty to manslaughter, and the judge sentenced her to seven years in the New Jersey State Prison. Ironically, when she arrived, she had to take off her black cape, glove, and veils to wear regular prison clothing. After a year, she really did become insane, suffering attacks of stupor followed by hysterical outbursts, and she was transferred to the State Hospital for the Insane, where she died after an attack of stupor on June 20, 1913.

Her manslaughter plea ended any further proceedings against Mary Snead, since her lawyer argued that there was no accessory to manslaughter crime. So Mary Snead went free and returned with her son Albert to his ranch in Colorado, where she lived the rest of her life in obscurity. Her other son Fletcher, who had been Ocey's husband, disappeared into Canada.

So the strange case of the Wardlow sisters, who fascinated the public with their ghoulish black dress and odd behavior, was over. Their effort to hang onto their wealthy aristocratic past had turned them into the three eccentric women reminiscent of three black crows or witches, and now they were either dead or had flown away.

The Grand Delusion: The Case of John Du Pont (Newtown Township, Delaware, 1996–1997)

Whereas the Wardlow sisters became increasingly eccentric and two of them turned to murder because they were losing their money, John du Pont became increasingly eccentric and eventually killed because he had too much money. His vast wealth contributed to his creating his own fantasy world where he made the rules. He became more and more isolated from people, more and more delusional and paranoid. And no one stepped in to stop his descent into madness because he was paying the bills and no one dared challenge him. Then, one day on January 26, 1996, he totally snapped, killing one of his closest friends and confidants. His reason? Because in his delusions, this person became a threat. Here's how his huge fortune helped fuel his fantasy world, until it collapsed that day in January.

The case exploded into public consciousness with the murder of David Schultz, an Olympic gold medalist who helped John E. du Pont, the 56-year-old heir to the $80 million du Pont Company fortune, run his program for world-class athletes. There was little mystery about the shooting; the only question was why.

At the time of the murder, John was driving a Lincoln Town Car with his bodyguard Pat Goodale seated beside him. Just before that, they had met for about a half-hour at John's mansion to discuss a project involving du Pont's 400-acre Foxcatcher estate in Newtown Square, located about fifteen miles from Philadelphia. When the meeting ended, John invited Pat to ride with him around the grounds while he looked at the damage caused by the winter storms.[26]

On the way to the car, John picked up a camera, bird book, and .44 magnum revolver with a nine-inch-long barrel. As they drove around the estate, they turned into the driveway of the stone farmhouse on Goshen Road, where Dave lived with his wife Nancy and two children. Dave had been working on his car radio in the snow-covered driveway and had just shouted for his wife to come out and listen when John drove up.[27] As Dave, half-in and half-out of the car stood up and smiled, John picked up his gun, reached out of the window, and shot Dave point blank. After Dave fell to the ground, John shot again.

Moments later, Nancy ran out of the house, saying: "John, stop," and when he pointed the gun at her, she fled back into the house and called 911. When she stepped outside to tell John the police were coming, he pointed the gun at her again, whereupon Pat jumped out of the car, ran up to the porch, and told Nancy to call the police, after which she called them again.[28]

Meanwhile, as Nancy told the operator to send the police to Goshen Road and Pat tried to stop the bleeding, John drove off. But the reason for the shooting was so far a mystery. As Pat later told the police, he had no idea why John should suddenly shoot Dave, nor did Nancy, except that he was "insane," as she told the dispatcher.[29]

Within a few minutes, the paramedics arrived, along with the police, but it was too late. Dave was already dead. Meanwhile, John retreated to his mansion, in the center of the 800-acre Foxcatcher Farms estate. The mansion, modeled after Montpelier, the home of James Madison, had once been owned by John's grandfather and had over forty rooms on three floors, plus a large basement and attic. Once he arrived, John holed up in the first-floor library, which was built in the 1950s as a bomb shelter and was the ideal place for a long siege. It looked something like a windowless vault, was stocked with food, and could only be accessed by entering the combination on the lock on the door.[30]

As John dug in for the coming standoff with the police that

would last for two days, news of the murder spread, and soon several teams of police from Newtown Township and surrounding counties were on the property. Eventually, about 100 officers from the police, SWAT team, FBI, and state law enforcement units set up a command center at the Newtown Square Fire Station, and a small city of news vans, satellite trucks, reporters, and cameramen was established on the scene. Though the police called on the assistance of relatives, friends, and John's longtime trusted attorney, Taras Wochok, to persuade him to leave, nothing seemed to budge him out of his library redoubt for the next two days.[31]

A big problem in convincing him to come out is that John was delusional and paranoid, acting at times like the ruler of a country under siege. He also appeared to shift among several different personalities as he communicated with the police, primarily through Georgia Dusckas, a sports psychologist, who was his executive assistant and the last employee to leave the mansion, though John asked her not to go. She used her cell phone to call back and forth to relay messages between du Pont and the police.[32]

His delusions were very apparent. At one point, when he ordered the police to contact his lawyer, he told them that he was a "Bulgarian secret agent who had diplomatic immunity" and insisted that they should "notify the Bulgarian embassy" or they would face certain "chaos."[33] John also insisted that one of his favorite Bulgarian wrestlers, Valentin Jordanav, should come visit him, and when he asked that other wrestlers join them, he even suggested that Dusckas should "invite Schultz up" to participate, too, showing he was totally out of touch with what he had just done.[34]

The next two days were like a scene from an action movie. Police sniper teams with about seventy-five officers spread out in front of and behind the mansion, as well as at the kennel, powerhouse, and Foxcatcher National Training Center for wrestlers. Still other officers were stationed at the exits of the many tunnels for the heating and electrical systems that sprawled through the house.[35]

Due to du Pont's delusional state, the siege dragged on and on. At one point, du Pont identified himself as the Dalai Lama, asked the police to address him as "His holiness," and told them to remove the floodlights they had put up around his property because they were "desecrating holy land." At other times, du Pont said he was Jesus Christ or the president of the United States. The efforts of relatives, friends, and Wochok were not enough to snap him back to reality or persuade him to come out.[36]

But finally, the police found a way to entice him out: they turned off the heat and the mansion became colder and colder in the freezing January weather. Du Pont asked that the heat be restored, but the police refused to send over a maintenance man to fix the boiler. Du Pont next offered to fix it himself if the police would let him go to the boiler room outside the mansion. After some negotiation in which the police got his assurance that he wouldn't take his gun, because they didn't want anyone getting hurt, du Pont left the mansion. Once he did, a team of officers surrounded him and ordered him to surrender. Then, they grabbed him, tackled him to the ground, and made the arrest.[37]

The capture was the end of the standoff and the beginning of a long slog through the court system to discover why du Pont had committed murder, whether he was insane, and what to do about it. The police first took du Pont to be booked at the Delaware County Prison, and normally, after booking, he would be transferred into the general prison population. But as was often the case, du Pont refused to cooperate with anyone else's rules. He refused to answer any of the usual intake questions, which included information about his background, medical history, and whether he had any personal safety concerns about being placed in certain areas of the prison so the staff wouldn't put him there. But du Pont refused to say anything, even if for his own benefit in his placement in the prison. As a result, without this required information to determine his placement, the prison officials couldn't move him out of his cell in the Health Services area. So du Pont remained there in isolation for the next eight months, and his condition further deteriorated. He stopped shaving and wouldn't allow his hair to be cut, so he soon look like a wild man. He also became thinner because he refused to eat most of the food the prison served, except for some tea and crackers.[38]

Ironically, du Pont's huge fortune contributed to his unstable mental condition, which led to murder. His wealth led him to feel he was not bound by the rules, so he never sought treatment for his condition, nor did anyone tell him he needed to get treatment. In addition, du Pont experienced a series of family losses that contributed to his emotional upset and isolation. Furthermore, he failed to be good enough at the few things he wanted to accomplish, such as becoming a success at swimming. But his money allowed him to keep pursuing these activities. Because he contributed generously to organizations, they let him participate anyway, and some sportsmen even let him win competitions to keep his support coming. But ultimately he was a failure because he was not good enough, which weighed deeply on him. After his mother died, he became increasingly isolated and irrational, and his eccentricity, his employees, and the wrestlers he funded protected him from recognizing and getting treatment for the growing madness that consumed him.

Initially, though, du Pont seemed to have everything. He was born in 1938 to William and Jean Austin du Pont, heirs to the du Pont chemicals fortune. When he was two, his parents separated, and his father largely abandoned the marriage, leaving Jean to raise John. Though John, in his teens, occasionally joined his father on duck hunting trips, William mostly ignored him, preferring to focus on his new wife, with whom he lived on a du Pont estate in Bellvue, Delaware, and pursued a life centered on racehorses and tennis.[39]

Unfortunately, in raising John on her own, Jean repeatedly gave in to his every whim, setting the stage for him to grow up as a self-centered bully. John and his mother lived alone in the large du Pont mansion, since John's older sisters and brother were away at school and then left to form their own families, and therefore Jean indulged him without boundaries, as described by Carol A. Turkington, a psychological journalist, in examining his psychology:

> She was simply unable to deny the boy anything. . . . While it was quite clear she doted on him, it is also true that she neither disciplined him nor showed him any outward signs of physical affection.[40]

This upbringing set the seeds for later disaster. John grew up living a lonely, undisciplined life in a huge mansion, where he could do whatever he wanted. Yet he felt a deep sense of abandonment by his "absent father, distant siblings, and physically unresponsive mother." As a result, he grew up being "arrogant, willful, and stubborn," although very shy, withdrawn, and emotionally vulnerable.[41] The childhood friends he had mainly were the children of the hired help, most notably Hubert Cherrie Jr., the son of his mother's chauffeur, a retired Philadelphia cop.[42]

As a teenager, John went to the elite Haverford School in Philadelphia, where he was first drawn to swimming and wrestling. For him, these sports were a way to gain acceptance, as he had few other skills. Besides being a poor student, he had a stutter and short attention span and was awkward around other people.[43] He also developed a passion for collecting objects of natural history, including fish, birds, and especially shells. Eventually, his collection became so large, with millions of specimens, that he turned it into the private Delaware Museum of Natural History, which was completed in 1972 with funds from the $80 million inheritance left to him when his father died.[44]

As much as he tried, du Pont never gained the success he wanted in sports, though his money became a way of compensating by supporting other athletes. It also compensated for his difficulty in social relationships, setting his stage for his later mental decline. For example, after graduating from the Haverford School at nineteen and briefly attending the University of Pennsylvania, John went to the University of Miami, where he became a member of the varsity swim team from 1962 to 1963, and graduated in 1965. Then, he joined the Santa Clara Swim Club, hoping to continue competing. However, though he worked hard and practiced regularly, his coach George Haines, could tell he didn't have the talent to become a top competitor. Yet John liked being around athletes, so Haines let him continue swimming and put him in lanes where he wouldn't interfere with the competitive swimmers. In appreciation, over the years, du Pont contributed about $500,000 to Santa Clara Swim Club.[45]

Then, in the mid-1960s, unable to become a great swimmer himself, John focused on joining the U.S. Olympic pentathlon team, where there were fewer competitors. He had the advantage of setting up his own training facilities at his Foxcatcher Farm estate, as well as hiring top coaches to help him develop the five skills in the pentathlon—swimming, shooting, running, fencing, and riding and jumping horses.[46] Though he won against little competition in 1965 in Australia, he finished next to last, in twenty-first place, among the competitors seeking to join the 1968 Olympic team.[47]

Given his poor performance, rather than trying to further compete, he decided to use his money to become a "patron and benefactor" to top athletes. Thus, in the early 1970s, he began the first of a series of programs to develop world-class athletes—the Foxcatcher Swim Club. He brought in his former Santa Clara coach George Haines to train the athletes, which helped to attract many eager recruits from around the country.[48]

But the seeds for mental illness were already there in John's heavy drinking. He began to show up at the pool drunk from time to time and reacted with rage when Haines tried to discuss the problem. Despite his occasional efforts to sober up and stop drinking for awhile, something would occur that would trigger him to start up again, such as when he was faced by a disappointment.[49] For example, he began to drink again when the U.S. team did not participate in the 1980 Olympics in Moscow because of a boycott by President Jimmy Carter to protest the invasion after the Soviets invaded Afghanistan.[50] After that, John disbanded the entire swimming program.[51] Over the years, his continued drinking was a major factor in his mental decline.

Another factor in his decline was his growing social isolation and his feelings of alienation. He began to feel he was being persecuted and wasn't even safe on his own estate, and by his thirties in the 1970s, he "became increasingly withdrawn, more painfully shy, and lonelier than ever," according to Carol Turkington.[52] Though outwardly he was engaging in socially worthwhile activities, such as creating his natural history museum, opening a shooting range on his estate for the police, and letting the police use his helicopter to transport evidence,[53] he was gradually retreating socially and engaging in odd behaviors. For example, he developed a kidnapping phobia, and for protection, had a twelve-foot-high steel fence topped with barbed wire installed around his estate. He also now required visitors to go through an electronic-card access system at the front gate, and he began to turn down most social invitations.[54]

Yet, through the 1980s, despite his drinking problems and growing isolation, John still seemed fairly normal. He even got married briefly in 1983 to a twenty-eight-year-old occupational therapist, Gale Wenk, who he met when treated for a hand injury.[55] The nuptials were celebrated with a festive reception for 500 guests at the Vicmead Hunt Club in nearby Delaware.[56] But within six months, the marriage was over, in part due to his heavy drinking, paranoia, and violence when he got upset and drunk. For example, soon after they married, John warned Gale to watch out for being ambushed by varying the way she went anywhere. He began pushing and shoving her in drunken rages. He threatened her with his ability to do anything because of his wealth and connections. And one day he told her that he could kill her, bury her in a swamp on the property, tell the police and papers he had done it, and not "spend a day in jail" because of his "influence in law enforcement and political connections, as John du Pont."[57] Another time, when Gale asked him to turn down the music on a radio station playing patriotic music, he held a gun to her head and accused her of being a Russian spy. He told her that the fate of Russian spies was to be shot and threatened to blow her "brains out."[58] Needless to say, Wenk soon moved out.

Then, in 1985 and 1986, du Pont shifted his interests to the triathlon—an endurance sport that combined long-distance swimming, road cycling, and running a marathon—and to wrestling.[59] This interest in wrestling led him to set up the programs that would begin his relationship with David Schultz, who became his close friend and later his victim. Initially, he contacted Villanova University and pledged $5 million for the school's new basketball center if the school carved his name above the door, which led to the opening of the du Pont Pavilion there in 1986. Soon after that, he offered to fund a new wrestling program at the school, which opened in the summer of 1987, and he brought in Dave Schultz's younger brother Mark to work as one of his assistants. Meanwhile, as the Villanova program went forward, du Pont began setting up the Foxcatcher National Training Center for Olympic athletes on his estate for top swimmers and wrestlers, which was completed in 1989, and he established a wrestling club called Team Foxcatcher. His money helped to smooth the way to getting top wrestlers for the teams. As an enticement, he gave USA Wrestling a $100,000 donation, and he offered wrestlers free housing and thousands of dollars in salaries and bonuses.[60]

Yet, by the end of 1987, things began to deteriorate. John was drinking more heavily, and wrestlers and faculty members reported seeing him intoxicated at various times.[61] Then, he had a traffic accident, which led Villanova to break its ties with him despite his money. The accident occurred when du Pont was driving back to his estate from Villanova and hit a flagman, Lonnie Harris, who was trying to stop traffic for a cement truck driver. After Harris tumbled onto his hood and fell to the ground, du Pont tried to lift him up, saying "You're not hurt that bad," and introduced himself as the wrestling coach at Villanova. But he left after five minutes, before the police or an ambulance arrived. Though du Pont's insurance paid about $15,000 and he paid a nominal fine, Villanova found the incident embarrassing. It was the final straw after a series of other problems, such as a legal complaint by wrestler Andre Metzer that du Pont made homosexual advances to him and grabbed his testicles at the Foxcatcher Wrestling Center. So the incident provided a good reason to terminate the wrestling program.[62]

Meanwhile, du Pont reportedly began to use cocaine, making him hyper and jumpy.[63] Most significantly for John's fragile mental state, his mother died on August 9, 1988. He had been extremely close to her, and her death, more than anything, triggered his mental deterioration over the next few years. Her death was so traumatic, according to Bill Ordine and Ralph Vigoa, because "she was John's mother, his wife, his best friend, his sister," as his lawyer, Taras Wochok, put it.[64] And her death, according to Turkington, "severed the last tenuous thread that kept John tethered to sanity." Then, with that thread broken, John's "uncertain hold on reality" slowly slipped away, and triggered his "descent into madness."[65]

After John went through a period of deep mourning, it initially appeared that he had overcome her loss by throwing himself into his wrestling program. A few days after she died, he moved back into the mansion from a small house, where he had lived on the grounds, and brought four wrestlers to live in the house with him. Then, he focused on building up the Foxcatcher wrestling team.[66] He even brought in David Schultz, then considered the top wrestling trainer in the world, to help coach the team.[67]

Yet, under this veneer of seeming normality were increasing signs of delusion and paranoia. From time to time, John's speech wandered. He complained he saw things move that weren't moving, including the walls, books, or the whole house.[68] He asked national wrestling champion Jack Cuvo to help him look for animals and ghosts in his bedroom, and when Cuvo helped him go through his bedroom, some bullets fell out of John's pockets. At other times, he claimed bugs from outer space covered his body, and he cut himself with a knife to tear them out.[69]

However, for a variety of reasons, no one confronted John about his growing madness. He didn't want to acknowledge his problems and he had the money to pay for people to go along with his whims. Whereas some people went along with his delusions to humor him and avoid his anger, others did so to stay on his payroll as wrestlers or security guards.[70] For instance, when John became concerned there were secret tunnels and trap doors in his mansion, he got his security guards to obtain X-ray equipment to take X-rays of the columns and walls of his house, as well as seventy-five feet underground. Though the guards were skeptical they would find anything, they went along with the search.

Some of his delusions were particularly bizarre. He believed that the geese and swans in the ponds on his estate were trying to hypnotize him. He thought the timers on the exercise machines in his gym could take him back to another time period.[71] And at times he thought a mist was trying to take over the house, and he set up a camera in the hopes of recording this.[72]

To stop the madness, John's longtime lawyer Wochok set up a meeting with psychiatrists at the Institute at Pennsylvania Hospital to see if John could be committed involuntarily, since John didn't recognize his problems. But ultimately, Wochok decided not to act, considering that John hadn't hurt anyone else yet, and he didn't seem to be a danger to himself; so far he was taking care of himself and hadn't threatened to commit suicide.[73]

So the situation continued, with du Pont growing steadily worse, until his delusions led to murder. The wheels were set in motion when John convinced David Schultz to join his wrestling faculty. David's younger brother Mark had left after one year in 1988. John provided David, his wife, and his two children with their own small farmhouse on Goshen Road on the grounds of the estate.[74] As John's delusions grew worse, David became a calming voice who helped to remind John that his delusions weren't true.[75] David also acted as a mediator and peacemaker. For example, after John appointed him as coach for the Foxcatcher team, he fought to keep John from unfairly dismissing the wrestlers or argued that the well-known wrestler Valentin Jordanov should get a higher salary. Then, too, Schultz helped to open doors for John to the wrestling world in Eastern Europe because he had so many strong connections there.[76] Unfortunately, as du Pont became increasingly dependent on Schultz's friendship and support, the risk was that once he doubted that friendship, the sense of betrayal, even if delusional, would trigger a rage that might even lead to murder, which is what seems to be what happened.

Du Pont experienced a further break with reality the fall in 1994 when he began reading about Eastern religion. He decided that he was the Dalai Lama and began telling everyone around him that he was.[77] After a trip to Bulgaria in late 1994, where he went to an award ceremony and met the president of Bulgaria, he began to claim that he himself was the Bulgarian president.[78] Yet ironically, even as du Pont became madder, the wrestlers were doing well. In 1994, six of the ten World Championship Wrestlers were from the Foxcatcher team, and five won World Championships in 1995.[79] In turn, this apparent success, along with du Pont's money, contributed to keeping the growing danger under wraps. Since du Pont's huge wealth was paying for everything, there seemed little reason to disturb the arrangement, though a less wealthy person might by now have been committed.

Then, in 1995 and early 1996, several more events further fueled du Pont's paranoia and directed his hostility toward David Schultz. One incident occurred in October 1995, when two fires broke out on the estate—one in a small house, another in the powerhouse and greenhouse near the mansion.[80] Another incident occurred after du Pont got into a conflict with one of his wrestlers, Dan Chaid, and had Dan evicted from the estate in October, shortly before the two fires. But Dan didn't leave, and when du Pont found him working out the day after the fires, he threatened him with a gun, telling him to get off the farm. Dan did leave this time, though when he returned in November to retrieve some property he left behind at David Schultz's house, du Pont again confronted him there, this time very drunk and raving, and du Pont fell hitting his head. Though several witnesses observed the encounter, du Pont later thought he might have been attacked by a member of the Russian mafia, and his lawyers filed a complaint with the police claiming Chaid hit him with a baseball bat.[81]

Whatever the reality of what happened that day in November, it led to du Pont's deepening distrust of David Schultz. In the past, Schultz had always been there to protect him, but now he wasn't.

Thus, du Pont began to distrust Schultz and even feared being around him. As a result, despite a tradition of inviting David Schultz and his wife for Christmas dinner at the mansion, he called David on December 23 and told him not to come for dinner this year. Then, in early January, he told David not to go to an important training camp held by USA Wrestling in Chicago, though David had already arranged to attend.[82]

By January 26, the day du Pont shot David, the tension between the two men was so great that Schultz was already thinking of moving on. However, he decided to stay, perhaps because he felt du Pont was just going through his usual paranoid mood swings, and like other wrestlers, he was hoping to stay through the 1996 Olympics. But now the tension had built to a final explosion, and perhaps some of du Pont's antagonism toward Schultz was fueled by jealousy. Du Pont may have resented him because Schultz was so loved by the fans when he wrestled in Russia and had a wonderful loving family.

As psychological journalist Carol Turkington describes the coming denouement:

> Some of the wrestlers suggest that, as du Pont became more disoriented, he turned against Dave Schultz, the one man among all the wrestlers who did the most to help him. . . .
>
> Some of the wrestlers suggest that John may have begun to resent Schultz, who was everything John du Pont was not: an internationally beloved athlete, respected by everyone he met. And Dave Schultz had what John du Pont could not buy, not for all the du Pont millions: a devoted family who loved him just for himself.[83]

So tension was already at a high level when a few events in mid-January triggered the shooting. One was a trip du Pont made to California on January 17–18 to buy a rare stamp from British Guiana for nearly $1 million. When he returned, he confided in two maintenance staff employees, Walter Fitzgerald and Terry McDonnell, that he knew someone on the farm was threatening him and that the trip had confirmed his suspicions.[84] More trouble came when a violent windstorm on January 19–20 and a big rainstorm on January 24 caused extensive damage on the grounds. On Thursday, January 25, du Pont seemed even more unnerved when he was working out for the first time after his November fall and head injury, and he told one of the wrestlers that someone was "playing games" with him and his "life could be in jeopardy."[85] Later that night, he told his longtime personal assistant Georgia Dusckas that he feared going to New York with some of the wrestlers because that trip might be the third strike against him, after the fire in October and the November incident at David Schultz's house.[86] In short, in his paranoia, du Pont was already connecting various events in his head as signs of looming danger and imagining Schultz at the middle of it.

Then, even more ominously, on that same Thursday night, January 25, when John attended a party at one of the wrestler's house, he saw David and his son Alexander playing on the deck with pop bottles and a three-foot-long small piece of plastic to create a bottle rocket, and possibly he saw them shoot it off a few times. Though the device was an ordinary children's toy, in du Pont's mind they had a bazooka, and given his growing tension with David, his delusion may have led him to wonder in fear that David might be planning to use this "bazooka" against him.[87] And perhaps his anxiety was further fueled after John, who already had delusions about the Russian Mafia and dangerous Russian spies, had seen Schultz dressed up in a Russian outfit at the party for Bulgarian wrestlers before they left for New York.[88] After this event, seeing David with the "bazooka" seemed even more sinister.

Thus, the stage was set for disaster the following day, January 26, when John went to pick up Pat Goodale, who had helped to set up the security systems for the estate and was helping to supervise the restoration of an old airplane.[89] As they drove around, John saw David working on his car, and seemingly without reason, fired the fatal shots. Yet in John's mind, fueled by his paranoia and delusions, he seemed to believe he did have a good reason, though it was the product of distorted, unreasonable thinking. Or maybe he was just hopelessly insane and snapped.

These were the arguments du Pont's team of a dozen defense attorneys would use over the next year of court battles, after he was arrested and charged with first-degree murder. His mental state became the basis of his defense, since two eye-witnesses at the scene saw du Pont shoot David point blank without any provocation. Later, however, du Pont offered several other explanations himself. One was that Schultz didn't really die and there had been no tension between them; so why didn't Schultz just come over and visit him. Another was that Schultz had been shot by a body double who looked just like du Pont and had escaped. But obviously, these were not scenarios his lawyers took seriously. Instead, the only real options were whether du Pont could claim the killing was voluntary manslaughter on the grounds that he unreasonably believed he was threatened by Schultz, leading him to kill in this deluded self-defense or whether he could be judged not guilty on the grounds of insanity. Then, too, the defense argued that du Pont was not competent to stand trial, which drew out the legal process even longer. Ultimately, though, he was tried for first-degree murder, along with a number of other lesser charges, including third-degree murder, voluntary manslaughter, and involuntary manslaughter.[90]

Because du Pont had an estimated $250 million share of the E. I. du Pont inheritance, he was able to spend far more on his defense than the prosecution—$2 million versus $500,000.[91] Yet much of his lawyers' work simply delayed the case with thousands of pages of documents and dozens of petitions and motions, most of which were denied. One motion, for example, was to allow du Pont to leave his jail cell to get papers from the estate so that he could show that he had nothing to do with Schultz's killing and that he was "the Dalai Lama, a citizen of Bulgaria, and a government official for the United States and other countries."[92]

His lawyers also were unsuccessful in repeated requests to obtain bail, in part because du Pont had so much money that no amount of bail could keep him in the country, and because, as the prosecution argued, he refused to cooperate with prison authorities and had refused to surrender after the murder for two days. However, his lawyers successfully arranged for him to have a neurological examination at his expense at the University of Pennsylvania Medical Center to determine if his abnormal behavior over the past few years might have an organic cause, possibly due to his history of heavy drinking.[93]

Thus, before the trial, long delays resulted from the competency argument, and just as du Pont was unwilling to cooperate with regular prison procedures, which included a routine physical examination, so he was uncooperative in court. At his first hearing after his arrest, for example, one of his lawyers, Richard Sprague, advised the judge that du Pont did not understand the charges that had been read and was not answering anything.[94] But did du Pont really not understand? Or was his behavior a continuation of his long pattern of not following rules and doing what he wanted, made possible by his great wealth and an upbringing by a mother who indulged his every whim?

The motions and petitions went on and on, causing more and more delays. Even when his lawyers suffered a turndown by the judge, they appealed to the superior and supreme state courts. Sometimes, they even appealed their rejected appeals, so they had proceedings simultaneously at all court levels.[95] After all, du Pont had plenty of money to pay for all this legal maneuvering.

Meanwhile, as the legal volleys went on, du Pont continued to tell his delusions to his lawyers and the psychiatrists they hired, Dr. Philip Resnick and Dr. Robert Sadoff. In explaining why David Schultz was shot, he still spoke of himself as the Dalai Lama, and he described a convoluted plot by U.S. government officials in Washington that developed after they were angered when he and Schultz went to Russia, and Schultz carried the Russian colors, while he carried the Bulgarian colors. Supposedly, du Pont believed, these officials decided to get rid of both of them, and after they killed Schultz, they tried to "pin the murder" on him by using a double that looked like him.[96]

The defense, in turn, used such outlandish stories to support their contention that du Pont was not only insane at the time of the murder but incompetent to assist in his own defense. Du Pont's appearance, too, contributed to their arguments for insanity and incompetence, whether he planned this or not, because over the weeks of court maneuvering, he looked more and more like a mad wild man, letting his hair grow and refusing to cut his beard. After some weeks, he looked much like the eccentric and mad Howard Hughes in the last years of his life.

In response, the trial judge, Patricia Jenkins, arranged to have du Pont evaluated by a team of specialists at the Norristown State Hospital to determine his competence to stand trial. Eventually she determined he was competent because he seemed to adapt well to life at the hospital. Whereas he had not cooperated well in jail, there he became quite cooperative. He mixed with other patients, took his medications, and ate without resistance, though he had claimed he subsisted on only tea and crackers at the jail (though he got some extra food from his lawyer).[97] So, at long last, the long-delayed trial was scheduled to begin on January 21, 1997, in Delaware County, almost a year after Schultz's shooting.

Because there was no question who did it, du Pont's defense lawyers argued for insanity, based on the M'Naghten rule, which had previously been used in an insanity defense in Pennsylvania and has a long history going back to 1843 in England. According to this rule, the basic test for insanity is that the person has such a defective reason due to a disease of the mind that he doesn't know "the nature and quality" of his act, or if he did know it, he did not know he was doing anything wrong.[98] Or more precisely, to cite the description of the test given in *Black's Law Dictionary:*

> The standard . . . to determine whether a person is sane is did the defendant have sufficient mental capacity to know and understand what he was doing, and did he know and understand that it was wrong and a violation of the rights of another; to be "sane" and thus responsible to the law for the act committed, the defendant must be able to both know and understand the nature and quality of his act and to distinguish between right and wrong at the time of the commission of the offense.[99]

As evidence, his lawyers argued that his mental condition had deteriorated after his mother's death in 1988. They provided many examples of how he acted strangely, including his belief he was the Dalai Lama and other high-and-mighty leaders. They described how he told friends about his belief that someone was out to assassinate him. They brought in six psychiatrists to point out that he suffered from schizophrenia and was "mentally unbalanced and could not be held responsible for his conduct."[100] They also attempted to show he was a paranoid schizophrenic who didn't know what he did was wrong.[101]

The defense strategy was to show du Pont as a "pitiable, lonely, friendless, familyless victim,"[102] whose paranoid fears were intensified by his security team, which included Pat Goodale, who had been in the car with him that fateful day. They pointed out how many people had gone along with his bizarre security concerns, such as his fear that wrestlers were sneaking into the house and moving the walls around. To support their position, they even used Nancy Schultz's own statement that "he's mentally insane," which she gave to the police shortly after the murder when they asked her to describe du Pont.[103] Additionally, they sought to show that du Pont only shot the man he thought was a threat to him, which is why he didn't shoot Pat Goodale, seated beside him, or Nancy Schultz, when she came over to the car, though he pointed a gun at both of them.[104]

In the end, the prosecution was able to overcome the insanity defense by showing du Pont did know what he did was wrong. Among other things, they cited his three-day standoff with the police to show that he knew the shooting was wrong was aware he could be arrested for what he did. Moreover, he had asked for his attorney over 100 times during the standoff, showing that "he was fully aware of the nature of his act and the need for legal representation."[105] As a result, after hearing from forty-three witnesses and deliberating for seven days, the jurors found du Pont guilty, but not of first-degree murder; instead they found him guilty of third-degree murder and mentally ill,[106] meaning he "acted with malice, but without a premeditated intent to kill."[107]

After the verdict, du Pont was returned to the Norristown State Hospital until his sentencing three months later, with a possible penalty of ten to forty years. When he returned for sentencing in May 1997, he was clean shaven and looked quite ordinary. After David Schultz's family members argued for the stiffest sentence, describing du Pont as a "self-absorbed, arrogant, narcissistic bully accustomed to buying his way out of trouble," as Schultz's mother put it, du Pont's lawyers pleaded for mercy.[108] Du Pont even apologized, making his first ever statement in court, stating: "I finally concluded that on January 26, 1996, I was ill. . . . I wish to apologize to Nancy Schultz and the children for what happened and wish them all the best in the future. I wish to apologize to my friends, family, and athletes for any disappointment I might have caused them."[109]

But his words were too little, too late. The judge sentenced du Pont to thirteen to thirty years in prison, an especially long sentence for third-degree murder in Pennsylvania, and he was sent to Cresson State Prison in western Pennsylvania. Initially, he was put in the isolated mental health unit, where he was only allowed to visit with his lawyers, but eventually he was moved into a single cell in the general prison population.[110]

The sad tragedy of this case is that du Pont's fortune contributed to his spiral of madness, and it also kept anyone from stepping in to stop his delusions by getting him help. Carol A. Turkington makes this point in her epilogue to his story. As she writes:

> It appears that what his friends and fellow athletes witnessed was the gradual disintegration of an extremely fragile, lonely man, whose wealthy and eccentric lifestyle cloaked the symptoms of what appears to be serious mental illness. . . . In du Pont's case, his wealth allowed him to live out his grandiose illusions in a way that helped him sustain his fantasy world for many years and even make substantial contributions to the real world at the same time. . . .
>
> Ultimately, however, his need to control the fantasy collided with reality . . . and . . . in middle age, a series of profound life stresses . . . pushed him over the line separating eccentricity from pathology. . . .
>
> He appears to have turned against the one man most able to give him what he so craved: friendship, acceptance, love . . .
>
> Du Pont's wealth bought him the indulgence of acquaintances, neighbors, and colleagues. It brought him the dubious gift of "protection" from the professional help he needed.[111]

Conclusion

As the previous chapters have illustrated, when the rich and powerful kill, their motives, methods, ability to defend themselves, and other factors are often quite different from those who are neither rich nor powerful. This is not to say that, in some cases, the wealthy don't engage in some of the same practices as do the non-wealthy. For example, a wealthy man gets in a fight with his wife, pushes her down the stairs, and then tries to cover it up by staging a crime scene—a case from the Palo Alto area that was in the Bay Area papers some years ago. Or as another example, a wealthy man uses his power of persuasion to get his teenage daughter to kill for him and uses her love and guilt to cover up the case.

But there are many other cases where the rich and famous do it differently because they have the money, resources, connections, and lifestyle that lead to major differences. For instance, they have the resources to more easily hire a hit man to kill for them, as well as the connections to find one more discreetly, such as among the less privileged staff members on a golf course, as in the Blackthorne case. They have the family connections, as well as the money, to mount a more aggressive, spirited defense, as many of these cases illustrate, such as the Thaw and du Pont cases. They have a greater ability to gain help in staging an elaborate cover-up, such as in the Capano case, where not only family members but also the successful family business played a role in concealing evidence. They may be able to get special consideration by judges and corrections officials in sentencing and serving their time, such as in the Cummings case.

Sometimes, too, they can get better press coverage—or are better able to manipulate the press and public reaction—because of their status and position in the community, as in the Lizzie Borden case, which then, though it's not supposed to, can bias the jury in their favor. They also have the resources to hire teams of expensive lawyers, investigators, and experts, so they might ultimately succeed in an extended and expensive appeal, as in the von Bulow case, or get a verdict for a reduced charge, such as the guilty but insane third-degree manslaughter verdict in the du Pont case. And with their family and political connections, they may be able to even get away and obtain very long delays in the criminal justice process, as in the Davis and Moxley cases.

Though I have emphasized just one of these themes in profiling each of these cases, many of these elements run through all of them. That's because of the intermingling of factors, such as having money, family connections, political influences, and better lawyers, investigators, and experts, combined together in a single package.

Another commonality in these rich and powerful cases is that they share the intensity of extensive press coverage—sometimes even a frenzy of attention—which by itself helps to make these cases different from the run of the mill murder cases, although some of those may also capture the popular imagination and become the center of media attention. Some of these cases involving newly famous but not previously rich people may also provide the defendant with a newfound clout to obtain a team of high-priced lawyers and investigators, as in the Scott Peterson case. There, the media interest turned an otherwise ordinary middle-class man into a famous defendant with a high-powered attorney, Mark Geragos, after the case garnered high-profile attention by the unique circumstances of a Christmas Eve mystery involving a missing woman with a winning smile, a secret mistress, and a body and fetus that washed up several months later. Sometimes, too, the high status of the victim can lead to headlines, though the killer is not wealthy or prominent, as in the killing of fashion designer Gianni Versace by a wanna-be rich hanger-on. But for the most part, the average murder case gets much more limited coverage, whereas the rich and powerful case is a magnet for the press once a wealthy and prominent person becomes the suspect or the victim.

This high level of media attention is not just due to the appeal of today's celebrity culture. Ever since the rise of the mass media in the mid-1800s—first with the rise of the penny press in the 1840s and then with the mass production of photo images in print in the 1870s and 1880s—this fascination with the misdeeds of the wealthy and prominent has existed. At the same time, the rich have always been able to use their resources to better protect themselves at all stages of the justice process—from the discovery of the missing or murdered victim to their arrest and court trial.

No wonder the popular view is that the rich can buy a better brand of justice in the country. They are right. Generally, the rich can. They have the resources and connections to better plan, carry out, and cover up their crimes—or to hire the help they need to do it. They are better able, with their resources, to protect themselves from investigators, such as by not responding except through their lawyers. However this strategy can backfire if someone is suspected, but might be innocent, such as when the Ramseys immediately brought in lawyers after the police suspected one or both of them of killing their daughter Jon Benet. The perception in the public mind was immediately that they were guilty—a perception that still lingers today, reflected in the occasional tabloid stories about how or why one or both of the Ramseys did it. Recently some new information and a reanalysis of the evidence held by the police has suggested that perhaps the killer might have been an intruder who entered through a basement window, though this new theory is still being debated. But if the Ramseys were guilty, their money and legal approach did result in no case ever being filed against them.

In writing this book, I have used one or two examples to illustrate each theme, and in many chapters I have used a case from early in the century, along with a more modern case from the 1970s or later, to show how these themes are enduring. For example, the Lizzie Borden case from the 1890s and the Thaw, Luetgert, and Hazzard cases from the early twentieth century variously show the power of position, family, reputation, and money to affect the criminal justice process, then as now. Also, this early period has had its share of wealthy eccentrics, who have slipped from being eccentric and making up their own rules into murder, sometimes accompanied by madness, as in the Wardlow case.

Certainly, there are many more cases I could have chosen, and many of these might make for a future follow-up book. But I had to limit the number of cases in order to provide in-depth analyses. Also, I left out some cases simply because they are so well known that they don't need another book about them, such as the O. J. Simpson case from 1994, which has had at least thirty-three books written about it, including humor books. (Among them was a book on what was in O. J.'s notes that he scribbled in the courtroom, and one I wrote myself titled *Cooking with O. J.*, in retrospect a rather tasteless book, featuring real recipes with humorous copy based on the names or news items from the trial, such as "Kato Kaelin Flakes" for breakfast.) Today, the O. J. case could stand for many of these themes, such as the power of celebrity to influence a jury and hire the best legal team to put the prosecution on trial rather than the defendant. But I felt the case is too well known for still another summary and analysis.

I also did not include some of the most recent cases in the news that are still being resolved in the courts, such as the Robert Durst case. He is the wealthy defendant living in a seedy part of Galveston, Texas, who recently was acquitted of killing his neighbor, Morris Black, whose body was found chopped up in bags floating in Galveston Bay—though Durst is still in jail on other charges for chopping up the body and interfering with the police investigation. News came out about his dressing like a woman, and investigators are looking into whether he might have killed his wife, who disappeared two decades ago, and whether he might be involved in the more recent death of Susan Berman, a longtime friend. She was killed after the police reopened the investigation into his wife's murder and hoped to question her about it, on the theory she might have helped Durst cover up the crime. And recently, about a week before writing this, *48 Hours* aired a special called *The Robert Durst Story.* However, even though Durst might have been a good candidate for inclusion in the "Losing It" chapter on wealthy eccentrics, I felt his case was too much in the recent news and too unresolved to include it. Another example of such an unresolved case is the charge that music impresario Phil Spector shot and killed Lana Clark, a onetime actress working as a hostess, in his mansion. Is it murder or a tragic suicide, as Spector claims? The case is still working its way through the courts.

I additionally eliminated any organized crime murder cases, as noted in the introduction, because these arise out of that special lifestyle and are typically ordered as the ultimate punishment when someone is disloyal, fails to pay money, or reneges on a deal. So they are in a class by themselves and even merit their own book.

It's hard to know whether there are really more rich and powerful killers than in previous years, or if we are more aware of these cases due to the media in today's celebrity-driven culture or due to better forensic and investigative techniques for obtaining evidence, resulting in charges in what would otherwise be unsolvable cases. Then, too, there might be more rich killers today due to a generally higher standard of living, resulting in proportionately more killers that might be classified as rich and famous.

Whatever the case, a true crime industry has developed since the 1980s based on writing about these cases and featuring them in TV investigative reports. As a result, I have had to be more selective in choosing recent cases out of a larger pool of cases, whereas these earlier cases were more often anomalies, which helped to turn them into the press sensation of the year. But in recent years, there have been a number of these cases to choose from, and many of the most high-profile cases have had not one, but two, three, or even more books about them, each one a slightly different take on the same basic facts in the police and court reports and the day-to-day news record.

But whether these selected cases are more recent or from decades ago, they illustrate how homicide among the rich and famous does differ in style, motives, investigation, trial, and in other ways, given the different lifestyle and culture of those who are wealthy and prominent. From using more quiet, gentile methods, like poisoning, as in the Roland Molineux case, to staging a near perfect cover-up, like Thomas Capano did to getting help from friends and associates, like Allen Blackthorne did, these killers and their killings are often different. So is their typically long trek through the legal system to defend themselves once suspected or accused made possible with the help of the greater funds available to them from themselves or their families, such as in the long drawn-out Moxley and du Pont cases. As the discussion has illustrated, these defendants often have not one, but two, three, even a team of high-priced lawyers, arguing motion after motion, such as to keep out evidence and testimony—and to keep the accused killer out on bail, too. Sometimes the approach works, as in the Cummings case, but at other times, the killers' great wealth works against them, such as when du Pont remained in jail because the prosecution and judge were so afraid that no amount of bail would be enough to keep him from fleeing the country, given his huge fortune and history of extensive travel to other countries.

The book has also illustrated how these murders may arise out of the classic personal motives for homicide, such as over money, jealousy, and a desire to leave a terrible marriage. But at the same time, the amount of money involved is vastly more than in an everyday case, and the wealthy have more power to act on their feelings of anger or sadness at being rejected or to take action in response to a desire to reject and get rid of others. They additionally have more wealth and power to help them better strategize how and when to eliminate the person who has offended them or stands in their way.

These cases have also illustrated the great difficulties investigators often encounter in investigating the crimes of the wealthy and powerful. Although these homicides share many of the same barriers to investigation as other cases (such as when no one is willing to talk, little evidence is at the scene, and an uncooperative suspect is protected by a lawyer), these cases often have even more investigative barriers. Among them are the more unusual and harder-to-detect methods (such as the poison in the Coppolino case), the access to more unusual or protected places for concealing the body (such as in the vats in the Luetgert case), and the money and clout to keep a cover-up and alibi scheme in place (such as in the Blackthorne case, which included helping one crucial witness stay in Mexico for two years). Then, too, some cases have reams of documents, motions, and petitions for prosecutors to deal with (such as in the du Pont case), making these prosecutions even more difficult, time-consuming, and costly.

The high level of press and public interest can complicate these cases, too. Eager journalists and members of the public can contaminate the crime scene (a big problem in solving the Skakel case), whereas public opinion and the appearance and position of the defendant can subtly sway the jurors in favor of a defendant (as in the Lizzie Borden case and the von Bulow appeal, though jurors are not supposed to be subject to such influences).

In conclusion, then, yes, homicide among the rich and powerful can be very different—not always, but very often, because their wealth and prominence helps shape the way they kill. Additionally, the way the police, prosecution, public, press, and criminal justice/legal system respond give the wealthy and prominent defendant an advantage at all stages of the criminal justice process. So, to expand upon what F. Scott Fitzgerald once said of the very rich: They "are different from you and me," because "they have more money." Perhaps one might also say that the rich killers are different from others when they kill because they have more money. As a result, they not only may kill differently, but may be able to buy a better brand of justice because they have more money. It's the common wisdom, but yes, it's true, as I have sought to illustrate with the cases in this book.

NOTES

Chapter 1

1. Albert Borowitz, "Packaged Death," in Johathan Goodman, ed., *The Christmas Murders: Classic Stories of True Crime* (New York: Sphere Books Ltd., 1988), p. 51.
2. Borowitz, p. 52.
3. "Molineux Murder Indictment Fails," *New York Times*, April 13, 1899, pp. 1–2.
4. Borowitz, pp. 52–53.
5. Borowitz, p. 53.
6. Jay Robert Nash, "Molineux, Roland B.," in *Bloodletters and Badmen* (New York: M. Evans and Company, 1995), p. 438; Borowitz, p. 57.
7. Nash, "Molineux, Roland B.," p. 438.
8. Borowitz, p. 59.
9. "Molineux Guilty in First Degree," *New York Times*, February 11, 1900, p. 5.
10. Borowitz, pp. 59–60.
11. Borowitz, pp. 56–57.
12. Borowitz, pp. 57–58; Nash, "Molineux, Roland B.," p. 438.
13. Borowitz, pp. 57–58.
14. Borowitz, p. 60.
15. Borowitz, p. 60.
16. Borowitz, p. 60.
17. Borowitz, p. 61.
18. "Molineux Murder Indictment Fails," pp. 1–2.
19. "Molineux Murder Indictment Fails," p. 1.

20. "Molineux Murder Indictment Fails," pp. 1–2.
21. Borowitz, p. 61.
22. Borowitz, p. 62.
23. Nash, "Molineux, Roland B.," p. 439.
24. "Molineux Guilty in First Degree," pp. 1–5.
25. Borowitz, p. 63.
26. Borowitz, p. 64.
27. Borowitz, p. 65.
28. Borowitz, pp. 65–66.
29. Roland Burnham Molineux, *The Room with the Little Green Door* (New York: G. W. Dillingham, 1903), p. 132.
30. Molineux, pp. 184–189.
31. Molineux, pp. 243–263.
32. Borowitz, pp. 66–67.
33. Theo Wilson, *Headline Justice: Inside the Courtroom: The Country's Most Controversial Trials* (New York: Thunder's Mouth Press, 1998), p. 121.
34. Jay Robert Nash, *Murder Among the Rich and Famous: Celebrity Slayings that Shocked America* (New York: Arlington House, 1983), p. 156; Wilson, p. 122.
35. Nash, *Murder Among the Rich and Famous*, p. 157.
36. Nash, *Murder Among the Rich and Famous*, p. 156; Wilson, p. 122.
37. Wilson, pp. 129–130.
38. Nash, *Murder Among the Rich and Famous*, p. 157.
39. Nash, *Murder Among the Rich and Famous*, p. 157; Wilson, p. 122.
40. Wilson, p. 122.
41. Wilson, p. 123.
42. Nash, *Murder Among the Rich and Famous*, p. 158.
43. Nash, *Murder Among the Rich and Famous*, p. 155.
44. Wilson, pp. 123–124.
45. Wilson, p. 124.
46. Nash, *Murder Among the Rich and Famous*, p. 159.
47. Wilson, p. 129.
48. Wilson, p. 131.
49. Wilson, pp. 126–127.
50. Wilson, p. 127.
51. Nash, *Murder Among the Rich and Famous*, p. 160.
52. Nash, *Murder Among the Rich and Famous*, p. 160.

53. Wilson, p. 128.
54. Nash, *Murder Among the Rich and Famous*, p. 160.
55. Wilson, p. 127.
56. Wilson, p. 127.
57. Nash, *Murder Among the Rich and Famous*, p. 160.
58. Wilson, p. 131.
59. Wilson, p. 132.
60. Nash, *Murder Among the Rich and Famous*, pp. 160–161.
61. Wilson, p. 134.
62. Wilson, p. 128.
63. Wilson, p. 128.
64. Wilson, p. 129.
65. Wilson, p. 128.
66. Nash, *Murder Among the Rich and Famous*, p. 162; Wilson, p. 136.
67. Wilson, p. 139.
68. Wilson, p. 140.
69. Wilson, p. 139.
70. Nash, *Murder Among the Rich and Famous*, pp. 163–164.

Chapter 2

1. Gregg Olsen, *Starvation Heights* (New York: Warner Books, 1997), p. 23.
2. Olsen, pp. 7–10.
3. Olsen, pp. 10–13.
4. Olsen, pp. 190–196, 224–227.
5. Olsen, pp. 197–202, 118–121.
6. Olsen, pp. 23–29.
7. Olsen, pp. 38–39.
8. Olsen, p. 39.
9. Olsen, p. 43.
10. Olsen, p. 47.
11. Olsen, p. 49.
12. Olsen, p. 50.
13. Olsen, p. 51.
14. Olsen, pp. 51–59.
15. Olsen, p. 66.
16. Olsen, p. 67.
17. Olsen, p. 73.

18. Olsen, p. 79.
19. Olsen, p. 81.
20. Olsen, pp. 85–87.
21. Olsen, pp. 85–93.
22. Olsen, pp. 97–101.
23. Olsen, pp. 101–102.
24. Olsen, pp. 126–132.
25. Olsen, pp. 137–139.
26. Olsen, pp. 140–141.
27. Olsen, pp. 147–149.
28. Olsen, pp. 158–159.
29. Olsen, p. 159.
30. Olsen, pp. 182, 188.
31. Olsen, pp. 187–188.
32. Olsen, pp. 197–201.
33. Olsen, pp. 334–335.
34. Olsen, p. 367.
35. Olsen, p. 383.
36. Olsen, pp. 384–385.
37. Martin Fido, *The Chronicle of Crimes* (New York: Carroll and Graf, 1993), pp. 240–243.
38. Leonard Katz, *The Coppolino Murder Trial* (New York: Bee-Line Books, 1967), p. 9.
39. Katz, pp. 9–10.
40. Paul Holmes, *The Trials of Dr. Coppolino* (New York: New American Library, 1968), pp. 36, 42.
41. Holmes, pp. 44–45.
42. Katz, pp. 10–11.
43. Eugene B. Block, "Trials in Contrast," in *The Fabric of Guilt* (Garden City, NY: Doubleday and Company, 1968), pp. 97–98.
44. Holmes, pp. 28–29.
45. Holmes, pp. 29–30.
46. Holmes, p. 119.
47. Holmes, pp. 48, 120–122.
48. Katz, pp. 12–15.
49. Block, pp. 96–97.
50. Holmes, p. 24.
51. Block, pp. 96–97.
52. Holmes, pp. 26–27.

53. Holmes, p. 27.
54. Katz, p. 53.
55. Block, p. 98.
56. Block, p. 100.
57. Holmes, pp. 54–56.
58. Katz, p. 20.
59. Holmes, p. 53.
60. Holmes, p. 77.
61. Holmes, p. 57; John D. MacDonald, *No Deadly Drug* (New York: Fawcett Gold Medal, 1968), pp. 404–415.
62. Katz, p. 30.
63. Holmes, p. 75.
64. Katz, p. 21.
65. Katz, p. 22.
66. Katz, p. 22; Block, p. 102.
67. Katz, p. 22; Block, p. 102.
68. Block, p. 102.
69. Katz, p. 31.
70. Holmes, pp. 89–90.
71. Katz, p. 99.
72. Katz, pp. 99–112.
73. Katz, p. 115.
74. Katz, p. 124; Block, p. 105.
75. Katz, p. 125.
76. Block, p. 106.
77. Block, pp. 107–108.
78. Block, pp. 107–108.
79. Block, p. 109.
80. Holmes, p. 277.
81. Block, pp. 110–111; Holmes, p. 284.
82. MacDonald, p. 560.
83. Holmes, p. 288.
84. MacDonald, pp. 561–562.
85. MacDonald, p. 562.

Chapter 3

1. Ann Rule, *Every Breath You Take* (New York: Pocket Books, 2001), pp. 34–61.
2. Rule, pp. 72–73.

3. Rule, pp. 79–81.
4. Rule, p. 492.
5. Rule, pp. 77–79.
6. Rule, pp. 81–83, 88–91.
7. Rule, pp. 91–95.
8. Rule, pp. 96–100, 102, 106.
9. Rule, p. 111.
10. Rule, pp. 124, 136, 146.
11. Rule, p. 181.
12. Rule, pp. 122–123.
13. Rule, pp. 138–141.
14. Rule, pp. 142–143, 145.
15. Rule, pp. 192–193, 184–188.
16. Rule, p. 224.
17. Rule, pp. 226–228.
18. Rule, pp. 232, 244, 247.
19. Rule, pp. 255, 258.
20. Rule, pp. 259–260.
21. Rule, pp. 267–269.
22. Rule, pp. 270–271.
23. Rule, pp. 283–285.
24. Rule, pp. 313, 322.
25. Rule, pp. 329, 336–337.
26. Leonora Minai and Jounice L. Nealy, "Court Releases Prosecutors' Documents in Bellush Case," *St. Petersburg Times*, June 23, 1998.
27. Times Staff Writers, "Chronology of Events," *St. Petersburg Times*, July 7, 2000.
28. Rule, pp. 345, 358–364, 368.
29. Times Staff Writers, "Chronology of Events."
30. Times Staff Writers, "Chronology of Events."
31. Rule, pp. 381, 409–411.
32. Rule, pp. 310, 412.
33. Leonora Minai, "Blackthorne Portrayed as Bitter, Vindictive," *St. Petersburg Times*, June 16, 2000; Rule, pp. 368–369, 455, 465.
34. Rule, pp. 421–425.
35. Minai, "Blackthorne Portrayed as Bitter, Vindictive."
36. Minai, "Blackthorne Portrayed as Bitter, Vindictive."
37. Rule, p. 481.

38. Rule, p. 486.
39. Rule, pp. 488–491.
40. Rule, pp. 513–514, 527–528.
41. Minai, "Blackthorne Portrayed as Bitter, Vindictive."
42. Rule, pp. 550–551, 620–621.
43. Rule, pp. 550–551, 620–621.
44. Leonora Minai, "Blackthorne's Conduct Erased Jurors' Doubts," *St. Petersburg Times*, July 8, 2000.
45. Minai, "Blackthorne's Conduct Erased Jurors' Doubts."
46. William R. Levesque, "Two Life Sentences, Daughter's Hatred," *St. Petersburg Times*, November 3, 2000.

Chapter 4

1. Martin Fido, *The Chronicle of Crime* (New York: Carroll and Graf, 1993), p. 103; "Another Luetgert Murder?" *New York Times*, May 19, 1897, p. 1.
2. Jay Robert Nash, *Bloodletters and Badmen* (New York: M. Evans and Company, 1995), pp. 403–404.
3. "Another Luetgert Murder?" p. 1.
4. Nash, pp. 405–406.
5. "Luetgert Jury Disagrees," *New York Times*, October 22, 1897, sec. 5, p. 1.
6. Nash, pp. 403–404.
7. Nash, p. 405.
8. Nash, p. 404.
9. Nash, p. 404.
10. Nash, p. 405.
11. Nash, p. 405.
12. Nash, p. 405.
13. "Luetgert Jury Disagrees," sec. 5, p. 1.
14. "Luetgert Jury Disagrees," sec. 5, p. 1; Nash, p. 404.
15. Nash, p. 405.
16. "Luetgert Jury Disagrees," sec. 5, p. 1; Nash, p. 405.
17. "Luetgert Jury Disagrees," sec. 5, p. 1.
18. "Luetgert Jury Disagrees," sec. 5, p. 1.
19. "Luetgert Case in Chicago," *New York Times*, June 18, 1897, sec. 2, p. 2.
20. "Luetgert Case in Chicago," sec. 2, p. 2.
21. "Luetgert Case in Chicago," sec. 2, p. 2.

22. "Luetgert Jury Disagrees," sec. 5, p. 1.
23. "Luetgert Jury Disagrees," sec. 5, p. 1.
24. "Luetgert Jury Disagrees," sec. 5, p. 1.
25. "Luetgert Jury Disagrees," sec. 5, p. 1.
26. Nash, p. 406.
27. Nash, p. 406.
28. "Luetgert Is Convicted," *New York Times*, February 19, 1898, pp. 2–3.
29. George Anastasia, *The Summer Wind: Thomas Capano and the Murder of Anne Marie Fahey* (New York: Regan Books, 1999), p. 8.
30. Ann Rule, *And Never Let Her Go: Thomas Capano: The Deadly Seducer* (New York: Pocket Books, 1999), pp. 60–85.
31. Katherine Ramsland, "Missing Person," in *The Rise and Fall of Thomas Capano*, Court TV's Crime Library, www.crimelibrary.com/notorious_murders/classics/capano/1.html, p. 1.
32. Rule, pp. 91–95.
33. Anastasia, p. 18.
34. Rule, pp. 121–123.
35. Anastasia, p. 14.
36. Rule, pp. 121–142.
37. Rule, pp. 163–175.
38. Anastasia, pp. 152–154.
39. Rule, pp. 186–190.
40. Rule, pp. 198–201.
41. Rule, pp. 205–207; Anastasia, pp. 167–202.
42. Rule, pp. 208–210.
43. Rule, p. 240.
44. Rule, pp. 243–248.
45. Rule, pp. 268–271.
46. Ramsland, "Missing Person," p. 1.
47. Ramsland, "Missing Person," p. 3.
48. Anastasia, p. 21.
49. Anastasia, p. 34.
50. Rule, p. 284.
51. Rule, pp. 282–288.
52. Anastasia, pp. 34–36, 39.
53. Ramsland, "Brothers United," in *The Rise and Fall of Thomas Capano*, p. 1.

54. Rule, pp. 282–285.
55. Rule, pp. 287–288.
56. Rule, pp. 287–289.
57. Rule, pp. 291–292.
58. Rule, pp. 293–298.
59. Anastasia, p. 77.
60. Anastasia, p. 191.
61. Rule, pp. 296–298.
62. Rule, p. 305.
63. Rule, p. 311.
64. Rule, pp. 321–325.
65. Rule, pp. 332–339.
66. Anastasia, p. 75.
67. Rule, pp. 340–341.
68. Rule, pp. 341–342; Anastasia, pp. 75–76.
69. Anastasia, p. 76.
70. Rule, pp. 342–343; Anastasia, p. 201.
71. Anastasia, pp. 77–78.
72. Anastasia, p. 79.
73. Rule, pp. 348–352.
74. Rule, pp. 352–353.
75. Ramsland, "Brothers United," p. 3; Chris Barrish and Peter Meyer, *Fatal Embrace: The Inside Story of the Thomas Capano/Anne Marie Fahey Murder Case* (New York: St. Martin's Press, 1999), p. 172.
76. Rule, pp. 356–358.
77. Anastasia, p. 91.
78. Anastasia, pp. 93–94.
79. Rule, pp. 364–365.
80. Barrish and Meyer, p. 202.
81. Anastasia, pp. 96–99.
82. Rule, pp. 376–379.
83. Rule, p. 382.
84. Rule, p. 384.
85. Ramsland, "Brothers United," p. 3.
86. Rule, pp. 394–399; Anastasia, pp. 162–164; Ramsland, "Gerry Breaks," in *The Rise and Fall of Thomas Capano*, pp. 1–3.
87. Ramsland, "Gerry Breaks," p. 3.
88. Anastasia, pp. 178–179.

89. Rule, pp. 396–400.
90. Anastasia, pp. 179–180.
91. Rule, pp. 402–404; Barrish and Meyer, pp. 233–234.
92. Barrish and Meyer, p. 234; Rule, pp. 404–405.
93. Anastasia, p. 213.
94. Anastasia, p. 212.
95. Barrish and Meyer, pp. 234–235.
96. Anastasia, pp. 212–213.
97. Rule, p. 431.
98. Anastasia, pp. 185–187.
99. Rule, pp. 433–438.
100. Rule, pp. 447–457.
101. Ramsland, "The Fall Guy," in *The Rise and Fall of Thomas Capano*, p. 3.
102. Rule, pp. 461–472; Anastasia, pp. 243–245.
103. Ramsland, "The Fall Guy," p. 3.
104. Rule, pp. 473–479.
105. Anastasia, pp. 250–251; Mary Allen, "Lawyers Call Capano a Difficult Client," *The News Journal*, January 17, 2004, www.delawareonline.com/newsjournal/local/2004/01/17lawyerscallcapa.htm.
106. Rule, pp. 489–497.
107. Rule, pp. 497–500.
108. Ramsland, "Capano's Defense," in *The Rise and Fall of Thomas Capano*, p. 1.
109. Ramsland, "Capano's Defense," p. 1.
110. Barrish and Meyer, pp. 321–333.
111. Barrish and Meyer, p. 327.
112. Anastasia, pp. 261–262.
113. Barrish and Meyer, p. 325.
114. Anastasia, p. 262.
115. Ramsland, "Capano's Defense," p. 2.
116. Anastasia, p. 263.
117. Ramsland, "Capano's Defense," p. 2.
118. Rule, pp. 580–601.
119. Ramsland, "The Last Word," in *The Rise and Fall of Thomas Capano*, p. 1.
120. Ramsland, "The Last Word," p. 1.
121. Rule, p. 642.
122. Rule, pp. 661–662.

123. Anastasia, p. 286.
124. Rule, pp. 669–671.
125. Mary Allen, "Capano Contests Sentence," *The News Journal*, September 10, 2003, www.delawareonline.com/newsjournal/local/2003/09/10/capacontestss.htm.
126. Allen, "Lawyers Call Capano a Difficult Client."

Chapter 5

1. Jay Robert Nash, "1906: Harry K. Thaw: The Millionaire Murderer," in *Murder Among the Rich and Famous* (New York: Carroll and Graf, 1983), p. 20; "Pictures of a Tragedy," *Smithsonian Magazine*, February 1999, http://www.smithsonianmag.si.edu/smithsonian/issues99/feb99/object_feb99.html.
2. Nash, pp. 20–21.
3. Marvin J. Wolf and Katherine Mader, "1906: Mad Harry, Evelyn, and the Beast," in *Rotten Apples: True Stories of New York Crime and Mystery 1689 to the Present* (New York: Ballantine Books, 1991), p. 153.
4. Wolf and Mader, pp. 21–22.
5. Wolf and Mader, p. 154.
6. Wolf and Mader, p. 154.
7. Nash, p. 22.
8. Wolf and Mader, p. 154; Nash, p. 22.
9. Wolf and Mader, p. 154; Nash, p. 24.
10. Wolf and Mader, pp. 154–155; Nash, p. 24.
11. Terrence Flint, "Murder at Madison Square Garden," in Art Crocket, ed., *Celebrity Murders* (New York: Pinnacle Books, 1990), pp. 154–155.
12. Wolf and Mader, p. 155; Nash, p. 24.
13. Wolf and Mader, pp. 155–156; Nash, p. 24.
14. Nash, pp. 26–27; Wolf and Mader, pp. 156–157.
15. Nash, p. 27; Wolf and Mader, p. 158.
16. Nash, p. 27; Wolf and Mader, p. 158.
17. Nash, p. 28; Wolf and Mader, p. 158.
18. Nash, p. 28.
19. Nash, p. 28; Wolf and Mader, p. 159.
20. Nash, pp. 29–30; Wolf and Mader, pp. 150–160.
21. Nash, p. 31; Wolf and Mader, p. 160.
22. Nash, p. 31; Wolf and Mader, p. 160; Flint, pp. 164–165.

23. Wolf and Mader, p. 161; Nash, p. 35.
24. Nash, pp. 35–36.
25. Wolf and Mader, pp. 160–161; Nash, p. 33.
26. Nash, p. 33.
27. Nash, pp. 32–33.
28. Martin Fido, "Society Sex Scandals Behind New York Killing," in *The Chronicle of Crime* (New York: Carroll and Graf, 1993), pp. 120, 122.
29. Flint, p. 167.
30. Flint, pp. 168–169.
31. Flint, pp. 171–172.
32. Nash, p. 37; Wolf and Mader, pp. 161–162; Flint, p. 167.
33. Flint, p. 172.
34. Nash, p. 38; Wolf and Mader, p. 162.
35. Nash, p. 38.
36. Flint, p. 173.
37. Wolf and Mader, p. 162.
38. Flint, p. 174.
39. Flint, p. 175.
40. Wolf and Mader, p. 162.
41. Nash, p. 39; Wolf and Mader, p. 162.
42. Nash, p. 40; "Pictures of a Tragedy," p. 5.
43. Lisa Pulitzer, *A Woman Scorned* (New York: St. Martin's Press, 1999), p. 39.
44. Pulitzer, p. 56.
45. Pulitzer, pp. 56–65.
46. Pulitzer, pp. 63–66.
47. Pulitzer, p. 67.
48. Pulitzer, pp. 67–69.
49. Pulitzer, pp. 72–75.
50. Pulitzer, p. 83.
51. Pulitzer, p. 88.
52. Pulitzer, pp. 85–86.
53. Pulitzer, p. 88.
54. Pulitzer, pp. 89–95.
55. Pulitzer, p. 94.
56. Pulitzer, pp. 94–95.
57. Pulitzer, pp. 95–97.
58. Pulitzer, pp. 98–99.
59. Pulitzer, pp. 105–109.

60. Pulitzer, pp. 106–107.
61. Pulitzer, p. 107.
62. Pulitzer, pp. 106–109.
63. Pulitzer, p. 108.
64. Pulitzer, pp. 109–113.
65. Pulitzer, p. 118.
66. Pulitzer, pp. 119–120.
67. Pulitzer, pp. 120–121.
68. Pulitzer, p. 121.
69. Pulitzer, pp. 122–124.
70. Pulitzer, p. 1.
71. Pulitzer, pp. 2–9.
72. Pulitzer, pp. 10–15, 136–137.
73. Pulitzer, pp. 15–17.
74. Pulitzer, pp. 17–19.
75. Pulitzer, pp. 132–143.
76. Jacqueline L. Salmon, "Polo Match Turns Sour," *Washington Post*, September 9, 1997, p. A01.
77. Pulitzer, pp. 164–165.
78. Pulitzer, p. 165.
79. Pulitzer, p. 165.
80. Salmon, p. A01.
81. Pulitzer, pp. 144–148.
82. Pulitzer, p. 167.
83. Pulitzer, pp. 174–175.
84. Pulitzer, p. 174.
85. Pulitzer, p. 180.
86. Pulitzer, p. 183.
87. Pulitzer, p. 187.
88. Pulitzer, p. 194.
89. Pulitzer, p. 195.
90. Pulitzer, p. 197.
91. Pulitzer, pp. 197–198.
92. Associated Press, "Heiress Testifies Shooting Came After Weekend of Threats," *The Shawnee News Star*, May 9, 1998, www.news-star.com/stories/050998/new_shooting.html (accessed February 2004).
93. Pulitzer, pp. 205–206.
94. Associated Press, "Heiress Testifies Shooting Came After Weekend of Threats."

95. Associated Press, "Heiress Testifies Shooting Came After Weekend of Threats."

96. Pulitzer, pp. 206–210.

97. Pulitzer, pp. 210–211.

98. Pulitzer, pp. 212–216.

99. Pulitzer, p. 219.

100. Pulitzer, pp. 222–228.

101. Pulitzer, pp. 228–232.

102. Pulitzer, p. 232.

103. "Heiress Gets 60 Days for Killing Boyfriend: Convicted of Manslaughter, Not Murder," *San Francisco Chronicle*, May 14, 1998, p. A6.

104. Pulitzer, p. 233; "Mike's Comment of the Week," Interscan Corporation, June 12, 2000, www.gasdetection.com/MDS/m061200.html (accessed February 2004).

105. Ibid.

106. "Luxury Life for Prison Queen: Cell of Splendor for Rich Killer," Tabloid News Services, May 5, 1998, www.tabloid.net/1998/05/22.

107. Pulitzer, p. 235.

108. Anne-Marie O'Neill, "Jail Break," *People*, June 1, 1998, p. 115.

109. Jennifer Ordonez, "In Jail, Heiress Has Privileged Existence," *Washington Post*, May 21, 1998, p. A01.

110. "Luxury Life for Prison Queen," p. 2.

111. Pulitzer, p. 236.

112. O'Neill, p. 116.

113. "A Scandal in Hunt Country," *Dominick Dunne's Power, Privilege, and Justice*, CourtTV.com, www.courttv.com/onair/shows/dunne/episodes/scandal.html.

114. Paul Wright, "The Crime of Being Poor," *Washington Free Press*, no. 65, September/October 2003, www.washingtonfreepress.org/65/crimeBeingPoor.htm (accessed February 2004).

Chapter 6

1. Gary Cartwright, *Texas Justice: The Murder Trials of T. Cullen Davis* (New York: Pocket Books, 1994), p. 4.

2. Cartwright, p. 38.

3. Mark Gribben, "Priscilla and Cullen," in *T. Cullen*

Davis: The Best Justice Money Can Buy, Court TV's Crime Library, www.crimelibrary.com/notorious_murders/not_guilty/t_cullen_davis (accessed February 2004), p. 2.

4. Gribben, "Priscilla and Cullen," p. 3.
5. Cartwright, pp. 98–99.
6. Cartwright, p. 96; Steven Naifeh and Gregory White Smith, *Final Justice* (New York: Onxy/The Penguin Group, 1994), p. 139.
7. Gribben, "A Man Don't Need a Reason," in *T. Cullen Davis*, p. 2.
8. Cartwright, pp. 100–101.
9. Cartwright, pp. 101–102.
10. Cartwright, p. 104.
11. Cartwright, pp. 104–106.
12. Cartwright, p. 107.
13. Gribben, "Murder at Mockingbird Lane," in *T. Cullen Davis*, p. 4.
14. Cartwright, p. 103; Gribben, "Murder at Mockingbird Lane," p. 4.
15. Cartwright, p. 109.
16. Cartwright, p. 110.
17. Gribben, "Murder at Mockingbird Lane," p. 4.
18. Gribben, "A Man Don't Need a Reason," p. 1.
19. Cartwright, p. 113.
20. Gribben, "A Man Don't Need a Reason," p. 1.
21. Thomas Thompson, *Blood and Money* (New York: Dell, 1976), p. 276.
22. Gribben, "Racehorse Haynes," in *T. Cullen Davis*, p. 1.
23. Cartwright, pp. 116–117.
24. Naifeh and Smith, p. 166.
25. Cartwright, p. 113.
26. Cartwright, p. 117.
27. Cartwright, pp. 202–203.
28. Cartwright, p. 141.
29. Gribben, "Trial Within a Trial," in *T. Cullen Davis*, p. 2.
30. Cartwright, p. 125.
31. Naifeh and Smith, pp. 205–206.
32. Naifeh and Smith, p. 206.
33. Naifeh and Smith, p. 207.
34. Cartwright, p. 142.

35. Naifeh and Smith, p. 209.
36. Gribben, "Cullen on Trial," in *T. Cullen Davis*, p. 1.
37. Cartwright, p. 147.
38. Cartwright, p. 214.
39. Cartwright, p. 214.
40. Cartwright, p. 215.
41. Gribben, "Trial Within a Trial," p. 1.
42. Gribben, "Eyes," in *T. Cullen Davis*, p. 1.
43. Cartwright, pp. 164–165.
44. Cartwright, p. 165.
45. Cartwright, p. 169.
46. Cartwright, p. 170.
47. Gribben, "Priscilla and Cullen," p. 1.
48. Naifeh and White, pp. 114–116.
49. Cartwright, pp. 9–10; Naifeh and Smith, p. 124.
50. Naifeh and White, p. 131.
51. Cartwright, pp. 174–175.
52. Cartwright, pp. 180–183.
53. Cartwright, pp. 183–185, 190–192.
54. Cartwright, pp. 191–192.
55. Cartwright, p. 239.
56. Cartwright, p. 240.
57. Cartwright, pp. 272–276.
58. Cartwright, pp. 251–257.
59. Gribben, "Innocent by Reason of Wealth," in *T. Cullen Davis*, p. 1.
60. Cartwright, p. 304.
61. Cartwright, p. 307; Gribben, "Innocent by Reason of Wealth," p. 1.
62. Cartwright, p. 309.
63. Gribben, "Cullen Tempts Fate," in *T. Cullen Davis*, p. 1.
64. Cartwright, pp. 317–319.
65. Cartwright, pp. 321–323, 325.
66. Cartwright, p. 332.
67. Gribben, "Cullen Tempts Fate," p. 1.
68. Gribben, "Cullen Tempts Fate," p. 2.
69. Cartwright, pp. 339–342, 355.
70. Gribben, "Cullen on Trial," p. 3.
71. Cartwright, pp. 370–372.
72. Cartwright, pp. 394, 409, 413–414.

73. Cartwright, p. 415.
74. Cartwright, pp. 415–416, 427–428.
75. Cartwright, p. 439.
76. Cartwright, p. 453.
77. Cartwright, p. 461.
78. Gribben, "Cullen Tempts Fate," p. 4.
79. Cartwright, pp. 463–464.
80. Gribben, "Texas Justice," in *T. Cullen Davis*, p. 1.
81. Gribben, "Texas Justice," p. 2.
82. Dominick Dunne, "Trail of Guilt," in *Justice* (New York: Three Rivers Press, 2001), p. 400.
83. Mark Fuhrman, *Murder in Greenwich* (New York: Avon Books, 1999), p. 9.
84. Fuhrman, p. 19.
85. Fuhrman, p. 17.
86. Fuhrman, pp. 6–9.
87. Fuhrman, pp. 10–12.
88. Fuhrman, p. 13.
89. Fuhrman, pp. 24–25.
90. Fuhrman, pp. 81–83.
91. Fuhrman, pp. 84–86.
92. Fuhrman, p. 91.
93. Fuhrman, pp. 106–114.
94. Fuhrman, p. 108.
95. Fuhrman, pp. 113–116.
96. Fuhrman, pp. 123–131.
97. Fuhrman, pp. 133–134.
98. Fuhrman, pp. 138–139.
99. Fuhrman, pp. 247–248.
100. Fuhrman, pp. 155–156.
101. Fuhrman, pp. 150–151, 153.
102. Timothy Dumas, *A Wealth of Evil: The True Story of the Murder of Martha Moxley in America's Richest Community* (New York: Warner Books, 1998), p. 60.
103. Dumas, pp. 60–61.
104. Fuhrman, p. 244.
105. Dumas, p. 62.
106. Fuhrman, pp. 215–220; Dumas, pp. 150–152.
107. Dumas, pp. 64–65.
108. Fuhrman, pp. 209–213.

109. Dumas, pp. 153–154.
110. Fuhrman, pp. 244–245, 248–249, 245.
111. Dumas, p. 159.
112. Fuhrman, p. 150.
113. Dumas, pp. 179–180.
114. Fuhrman, p. 231.
115. Dumas, p. 171.
116. Dumas, pp. 173–175.
117. Dumas, p. 195.
118. Dumas, pp. 187, 195–196.
119. Dumas, p. 196.
120. Fuhrman, p. 253.
121. Dunne, p. 401.
122. Dunne, pp. 402–403.
123. Dumas, pp. 240–241.
124. Dumas, pp. 241–242.
125. Fuhrman, pp. 251–252.
126. Dumas, pp. 248–249.
127. Dumas, p. 249.
128. Fuhrman, p. 254.
129. Dunne, pp. 404–406.
130. Dunne, pp. 408–409.
131. Dunne, p. 409.
132. Fuhrman, p. 65.
133. Fuhrman, pp. 71–75.
134. Dumas, p. 4.
135. Fuhrman, pp. 264–265.
136. Fuhrman, pp. 272, 285–286.
137. Fuhrman, pp. 285–286.
138. Fuhrman, p. 289.
139. Fuhrman, pp. 290–293.
140. Fuhrman, pp. 295–296.
141. Fuhrman, pp. 275, 277–278.
142. Fuhrman, pp. 277–278.
143. Fuhrman, pp. 298–307.
144. Jack Batten, "Murder Among the Super–Rich," www.marthamoxley.com/
reviews/jbatten.htm, June 6, 1998.
145. Fuhrman, pp. 389–392.
146. Joseph Geringer, "Superior Court Weighs Trial Agenda,"

in *The Martha Moxley Murder*, Court TV's Crime Library, www.crimelibrary.com/notorious_murders/famous/moxley/index_1.html, p. 2.

147. Geringer, "Grand Jury," in *The Martha Moxley Murder*, p. 1.

148. Geringer, "Michael Skakel Arrest," in *The Martha Moxley Murder*, p. 1.

149. Geringer, "Superior Court Weighs Trial Agenda," p. 1.

150. Geringer, "Superior Court Weighs Trial Agenda," p. 2; Dunne, pp. 420–422.

151. Dunne, p. 412.

152. Dunne, pp. 416–419.

153. Patrick Bellamy, "The Latest Update April 22, 2002 to June 7, 2002: Skakel Trial Update," Court TV's Crime Library, www.crimelibrary.com/notorious_murders/famous/moxley/updates_1.html, pp. 7–9.

154. Bellamy, p. 8.

155. Bellamy, pp. 11–12.

156. Bellamy, pp. 14–15.

157. Bellamy, p. 24.

Chapter 7

1. Alan Dershowitz, *Reversal of Fortune* (New York: Pocket Books, 1986), p. 297.

2. Dershowitz, pp. 304, 303.

3. H.R.F. Keating, *Great Crimes* (Stamford, CT: Longmeadow Press, 1982), p. 77; Robert Sullivan, *Goodbye Lizzie Bordon* (New York: Penguin Books, 1974), p. 2; Martin Fido, "Lizzie Borden," in *Murders After Midnight: Gripping Cases from the Annals of True Crime* (London: Weidenfeld and Nicholson, 1990), p. 26.

4. Sullivan, p. 2.

5. Keating, p. 77.

6. Rick Geary, *The Borden Tragedy: A Memoir of the Infamous Double Murder at Fall River, Massachusetts, 1892* (New York: NBM Publishing, 2003), reader page.

7. Sullivan, pp. 6–9.

8. Sullivan, pp. 13–17.

9. Fido, "Lizzie Borden," p. 26.

10. Sullivan, pp. 20–21.
11. Martin Fido, *The Chronicle of Crime* (New York: Carroll and Graf, 1993), p. 90.
12. Sullivan, p. 25.
13. Sullivan, pp. 24–26.
14. Fido, "Lizzie Borden," p. 27.
15. Sullivan, pp. 25–27.
16. Sullivan, pp. 27–28.
17. Sullivan, p. 28; Fido, "Lizzie Borden," p. 28.
18. Sullivan, p. 29.
19. Sullivan, pp. 29–30; Fido, "Lizzie Borden," p. 28.
20. Sullivan, pp. 30–31.
21. Keating, p. 77.
22. Fido, "Lizzie Borden," pp. 28–29.
23. Sullivan, pp. 31–32.
24. Sullivan, p. 32.
25. Fido, "Lizzie Borden," p. 29.
26. Sullivan, p. 35.
27. Fido, "Lizzie Borden," p. 29.
28. Sullivan, p. 35.
29. Fido, "Lizzie Borden," p. 29.
30. Sullivan, p. 36.
31. Sullivan, p. 36.
32. Keating, p. 77.
33. Sullivan, p. 37.
34. Keating, p. 77; Fido, "Lizzie Borden," p. 29.
35. Sullivan, p. 40.
36. Sullivan, p. 40.
37. Fido, "Lizzie Borden," p. 29.
38. Sullivan, pp. 41, 44–51, 55.
39. Fido, "Lizzie Borden," p. 30.
40. Fido, "Lizzie Borden," p. 29.
41. Sullivan, pp. 63–66.
42. Sullivan, p. 69.
43. Sullivan, p. 69.
44. Sullivan, pp. 74–75.
45. Sullivan, pp. 77–79, 81–85.
46. Sullivan, pp. 97–101.
47. Sullivan, pp. 121–123.
48. Sullivan, pp. 127–134.

49. Sullivan, pp. 135–138.
50. Sullivan, pp. 142–143.
51. Sullivan, pp. 144–145, 147.
52. Sullivan, p. 165.
53. Sullivan, p. 166.
54. Sullivan, p. 168.
55. Fido, "Lizzie Borden," p. 29.
56. Sullivan, p. 169.
57. Sullivan, p. 172.
58. Sullivan, p. 173.
59. Sullivan, pp. 173–174.
60. Sullivan, p. 175.
61. Sullivan, pp. 177–178.
62. Fido, "Lizzie Borden," p. 30.
63. Keating, p. 91.
64. Sullivan, p. 183.
65. Sullivan, p. 207.
66. Fido, "Lizzie Borden," p. 30.
67. Sullivan, pp. 208–209.
68. Jay Robert Nash, *Murder Among the Rich and Famous: Celebrity Slayings that Shocked America* (New York: Arlington House, 1983), p. 300; William Wright, *The Von Bulow Affair* (New York: Dell Publishing, 1983), pp. 61–62.
69. Alan M. Dershowitz, *Reversal of Fortune* (New York: Pocket Books, 1986), p. xix.
70. Dershowitz, pp. xviii–xix.
71. Dershowitz, p. xviii; Wright, p. 42.
72. Wright, p. 51.
73. Wright, pp. 54–55; Dunne, pp. 88–89.
74. Wright, pp. 63–64.
75. Wright, pp. 66, 70–71.
76. Nash, p. 301.
77. Nash, p. 300.
78. Nash, p. 301; Wright, p. 68.
79. Wright, pp. 72–73.
80. Dershowitz, p. xx.
81. Wright, pp. 81–85.
82. Dominic Dunne, "Fatal Charm: The Social Web of Claus von Bulow," in *Justice: Crimes, Trials, and Punishment* (New York: Three Rivers Press, 2001), p. 86.

83. Wright, p. 74.
84. Wright, p. 75.
85. Wright, p. 76.
86. Wright, pp. 96–97.
87. Wright, p. 98.
88. Wright, pp. 100–103.
89. Wright, pp. 108–111.
90. Wright, pp. 111–112.
91. Wright, pp. 112–114.
92. Wright, pp. 116–117.
93. Wright, pp. 117–118.
94. Wright, pp. 118–123.
95. Wright, p. 129.
96. Wright, pp. 129–130.
97. Wright, pp. 131–134.
98. Wright, pp. 135–136.
99. Wright, pp. 137–141.
100. Wright, pp. 143–144.
101. Wright, pp. 144, 148–153, 156–157.
102. Wright, pp. 158–160.
103. Wright, p. 160.
104. Dershowitz, pp. 3–6.
105. Dershowitz, pp. 25, 27–29.
106. Dershowitz, pp. 32–37.
107. Dershowitz, pp. 41–43, 45–46.
108. Dershowitz, pp. 48–49.
109. Dershowitz, p. 42.
110. Dershowitz, pp. 63, 70–72.
111. Dershowitz, pp. 76–77.
112. Dershowitz, pp. 75–82.
113. Dershowitz, pp. 83–87.
114. Dershowitz, pp. 92–95, 106–112.
115. Dershowitz, pp. 119–125.
116. Dershowitz, pp. 128–132.
117. Dershowitz, pp. 136–139, 142–152, 155.
118. Dershowitz, p. 157.
119. Dershowitz, pp. 180–183.
120. Dershowitz, pp. 195–198.
121. Dershowitz, p. 197.
122. Dershowitz, p. 200.

123. Dershowitz, pp. 193, 213–220, 225, 228.
124. Dershowitz, pp. 231, 235.
125. Dershowitz, p. 248.
126. Dershowitz, pp. 268–278.
127. Dunne, pp. 95–96.
128. Dunne, pp. 97, 101–102.
129. Dunne, pp. 101–102.
130. Dunne, p. 78.
131. Roger Ebert, "Reversal of Fortune," *Chicago Sun Times*, October 17, 1990, www.suntimes.com/ebert/ebert_reviews/1990/10/572715.htm (accessed February 2004).

Chapter 8

1. Gilbert Geis and Leigh B. Bienen, "Leopold and Loeb (1924) and the Cause of the Crime," in *Crimes of the Century* (Boston: Northeastern University Press, 1998), p. 34.
2. Geis and Bienen, p. 40.
3. Geis and Bienen, p. 16.
4. Geis and Beinen, p. 14.
5. Hal Higdon, *Leopold and Loeb: The Crime of the Century* (Chicago: University of Illinois Press, 1975, 1999), pp. 66–67.
6. Higdon, p. 66.
7. Higdon, pp. 16–17.
8. Higdon, pp. 16–18.
9. Higdon, p. 20.
10. Higdon, pp. 18–19.
11. Higdon, pp. 251–252.
12. John Brophy, "1924: Leopold and Loeb: Murder by Genius," in *The Mammoth Book of Murder* (New York: Carroll and Graf, 1990), p. 352.
13. Higdon, p. 210.
14. Higdon, p. 209.
15. Higdon, p. 209.
16. Higdon, p. 147.
17. Higdon, pp. 147–148.
18. Higdon, pp. 148–149.
19. Higdon, p. 149.
20. Higdon, pp. 149–151.
21. Brophy, p. 353; Geis and Beinen, p. 16.

22. Higdon, p. 16.
23. Higdon, pp. 151–152.
24. Higdon, pp. 16–17.
25. Higdon, pp. 20–21.
26. Miriam Allen De Ford, "Superman's Crime: Leopold and Loeb," in *Murderers Sane and Mad* (New York: Abelard-Schuman, 1965), p. 154.
27. De Ford, pp. 154–155.
28. Higdon, pp. 24–25.
29. Higdon, pp. 25–26.
30. Higdon, pp. 30–31.
31. Higdon, pp. 31–32; De Ford, p. 156.
32. Higdon, pp. 32–33.
33. De Ford, p. 157.
34. Brophy, p. 355.
35. Higdon, pp. 41–42; De Ford, p. 158.
36. Higdon, pp. 39–43.
37. Higdon, pp. 44–45.
38. Higdon, pp. 46–47.
39. Higdon, pp. 48–49.
40. Higdon, pp. 50, 52–53.
41. Higdon, p. 53.
42. Higdon, pp. 54–55.
43. Higdon, pp. 57–61.
44. Higdon, p. 63.
45. Higdon, p. 62.
46. Higdon, pp. 64–65.
47. Higdon, pp. 67–68.
48. Higdon, pp. 76–77.
49. Higdon, pp. 77–78.
50. Higdon, pp. 77–83.
51. Higdon, pp. 83–84.
52. Higdon, pp. 86–88.
53. Higdon, pp. 89–91.
54. Higdon, pp. 91–92.
55. Higdon, pp. 92–94; Geis and Bienen, p. 16.
56. Higdon, pp. 96–98; Geis and Bienen, pp. 14–15.
57. Higdon, p. 96; Geis and Bienen, p. 13.
58. Higdon, pp. 97–110, 121.
59. Higdon, pp. 115–116.

60. Geis and Bienen, p. 16.
61. Geis and Bienen, p. 17.
62. Geis and Bienen, p. 17; Higdon, pp. 131, 135, 145.
63. Higdon, p. 163.
64. Geis and Bienen, p. 17.
65. Higdon, p. 145.
66. Higdon, p. 164.
67. Higdon, p. 164.
68. Higdon, p. 165.
69. Geis and Bienen, p. 18; Kevin Tierney, "The Million Dollar Defense," in *Darrow: A Biography* (New York: Thomas Y. Crowell, 1979).
70. Tierney, p. 340.
71. Geis and Bienen, p. 27.
72. Geis and Bienen, p. 20.
73. Tierney, p. 244.
74. Geis and Bienen, p. 20.
75. Geis and Bienen, pp. 25–26, 35.
76. Geis and Bienen, p. 41.
77. Higdon, pp. 292–293.
78. Geis and Bienen, pp. 23–24.
79. Ron Soble and John Johnson, *Blood Brothers: The Inside Story of the Menendez Murders* (New York: Onyx/The Penguin Group, 1994), pp. 4–6.
80. Soble and Johnson, pp. 6–8.
81. Soble and Johnson, pp. 9–11.
82. Soble and Johnson, pp. 15–16.
83. Dominick Dunne, "Nightmare on Elm Drive," in *Justice* (New York: Three Rivers Press, 2001), p. 110.
84. Davis, p. 77.
85. Soble and Johnson, p. 18.
86. Soble and Johnson, p. 19.
87. Soble and Johnson, p. 19.
88. Soble and Johnson, pp. 23–25.
89. Soble and Johnson, p. 27.
90. Soble and Johnson, p. 26.
91. Don Davis, *Bad Blood* (New York: St. Martin's Paperbacks, 1994), p. 59.
92. Dunne, p. 111; Davis, p. 96.
93. Dunne, p. 121; Davis, p. 83.

94. Dunne, p. 121.
95. Davis, pp. 86–87.
96. Soble and Johnson, p. 80; Dunne, p. 122.
97. Dunne, pp. 121–122.
98. Davis, pp. 96–97.
99. Soble and Johnson, pp. 81, 83.
100. Davis, p. 97.
101. Davis, pp. 97–98; Dunne, p. 122; Soble and Johnson, p. 82.
102. Soble and Johnson, pp. 182–184.
103. Soble and Johnson, pp. 191–193.
104. Soble and Johnson, p. 194.
105. Soble and Johnson, pp. 194–195.
106. Davis, pp. 103–104.
107. Davis, pp. 104–105.
108. Soble and Johnson, p. 206.
109. Soble and Johnson, p. 206.
110. Soble and Johnson, p. 206.
111. Dunne, pp. 130–131.
112. Davis, p. 106.
113. Soble and Johnson, pp. 206–207; Davis, pp. 106–107; Dunne, pp. 130–131.
114. Davis, p. 111.
115. Davis, p. 112.
116. Dunne, p. 127.
117. Davis, p. 113.
118. Davis, pp. 113–114.
119. Davis, pp. 115–116.
120. Davis, pp. 120–121.
121. Davis, pp. 129–130; Soble and Johnson, p. 219.
122. Dunne, p. 139; Soble and Johnson, p. 223.
123. Davis, p. 131.
124. Soble and Johnson, p. 219.
125. Davis, p. 158.
126. Davis, pp. 141–143.
127. Soble and Johnson, p. 244.
128. Davis, p. 216.
129. Davis, pp. 216–217.
130. Soble and Johnson, p. 303.
131. Soble and Johnson, pp. 335–347.

132. Norma Novelli with Mike Walker, *The Private Diary of Lyle Menendez in His Own Words* (Beverly Hills, CA: Dove Books, 1995), p. 28.

133. Davis, p. 141.

134. Davis, pp. 158–160.

135. Soble and Johnson, pp. 247–248.

136. Soble and Johnson, p. 310.

137. Soble and Johnson, pp. 327–328.

138. Soble and Johnson, p. 335.

139. Soble and Johnson, p. 337.

140. Novelli, p. 245.

141. Novelli, p. 247.

142. Soble and Johnson, p. 274.

143. Hazel Thornton, *Hung Jury: The Diary of a Menendez Juror* (Philadelphia: Temple University Press, 1995), pp. xx–xxi.

144. Pierce O'Donnell, "Reflections on the Con Artist as a Young Man," in Novelli, p. 228.

145. O'Donnell, p. 258.

146. "The Menendez Brothers," Forensic Files, Court TV, www.courttv.com/trials/Menendez (accessed March 2004).

147. "A Chat with a Menendez Juror," American Online's Center Stage, April 22, 1996, www.courttv.com/archive/casefiles/menendez/documents/jurorchat.html (accessed March 2004), p. 1.

Chapter 9

1. Dominick Dunne, *Fatal Charms and the Mansions of Limbo* (New York: Ballantine Books, 1999), p. xiii.

2. Norman Zierold, *Three Sisters in Black* (Boston: Little, Brown and Company, 1968), pp. 4–5.

3. Zierold, p. 5.

4. Zierold, p. 11.

5. Zierold, p. 12.

6. Zierold, pp. 19–20.

7. Zierold, pp. 21–22.

8. Zierold, p. 23.

9. Zierold, pp. 31–32.

10. Zierold, pp. 34–35.

11. Zierold, pp. 38–39.

12. Zierold, pp. 40–42.
13. Zierold, p. 43.
14. Zierold, pp. 44–45.
15. Zierold, p. 46.
16. Zierold, pp. 48–49.
17. Zierold, p. 48.
18. Zierold, pp. 76–82.
19. Zierold, pp. 86–88.
20. Zierold, pp. 104–105.
21. Zierold, p. 120.
22. Zierold, p. 127.
23. Zierold, p. 163.
24. Zierold, pp. 205–206.
25. Zierold, pp. 119–222.
26. Bill Ondine and Ralph Vigoda, *Fatal Match: Inside the Mind of Killer Millionnaire John du Pont* (New York: Avon Books, 1998), pp. 5–6.
27. Carol A. Turkington, *No Holds Barred: The Strange Life of John E. du Pont* (Atlanta: Turner Publishing, 1996), p. 18.
28. Ordine and Vigoda, p. 7; Turkington, p. 19.
29. Ordine and Vigoda, p. 8.
30. Ordine and Vigoda, p. 12; Turkington, p. 19.
31. Turkington, pp. 21–23.
32. Ordine and Vigoda, p. 22.
33. Turkington, p. 23.
34. Ordine and Vigoda, pp. 23–24.
35. Ordine and Vigoda, p. 27.
36. Turkington, p. 23.
37. Ordine and Vigoda, pp. 59–61; Turkington, pp. 24–26.
38. Ordine and Vigoda, pp. 73–75.
39. Turkington, pp. 33–35; Ordine and Vigoda, pp. 99–101.
40. Turkington, p. 37.
41. Turkington, p. 38.
42. Ordine and Vigoda, p. 102; Turkington, pp. 38–39.
43. Ordine and Vigoda, p. 102.
44. Ordine and Vigoda, pp. 104–105; Turkington, pp. 48–49.
45. Ordine and Vigoda, pp. 106–107.
46. Ordine and Vigoda, pp. 106–111; Turkington, pp. 70–71.
47. Turkington, p. 78.
48. Turkington, p. 94.

49. Turkington, p. 95.
50. Ordine and Vigoda, pp. 112–113.
51. Turkington, p. 96.
52. Turkington, pp. 84–85.
53. Turkington, pp. 81–89.
54. Turkington, pp. 85–89.
55. Ordine and Vigoda, p. 114.
56. Ordine and Vigoda, p. 117; Turkington, pp. 102–103.
57. Turkington, p. 105.
58. Turkington, p. 106; Ordine and Vigoda, p. 119.
59. Ordine and Vigoda, p. 121; Turkington, pp. 109–110.
60. Ordine and Vigoda, pp. 123–126; Turkington, pp. 110–111.
61. Ordine and Vigoda, p. 131.
62. Ordine and Vigoda, pp. 131–134; Turkington, pp. 124–126.
63. Ordine and Vigoda, pp. 136–138; Turkington, pp. 126–127.
64. Ordine and Vigoda, p. 139.
65. Turkington, p. 131.
66. Turkington, p. 133.
67. Ordine and Vigoda, pp. 140–141.
68. Ordine and Vigoda, p. 142.
69. Turkington, p. 135.
70. Turkington, pp. 142–143.
71. Turkington, p. 136.
72. Turkington, p. 140.
73. Ordine and Vigoda, pp. 142–143.
74. Ordine and Vigoda, pp. 156–157.
75. Turkington, p. 142.
76. Ordine and Vigoda, pp. 159–160.
77. Turkington, pp. 144–145; Ordine and Vigoda, pp. 170–171.
78. Ordine and Vigoda, p. 174.
79. Ordine and Vigoda, p. 177.
80. Ordine and Vigoda, p. 175.
81. Turkington, pp. 152–155; Ordine and Vigoda, pp. 181–187.
82. Ordine and Vigoda, pp. 188–189; Turkington, p. 157.
83. Turkington, p. 158.
84. Ordine and Vigoda, pp. 189–190.
85. Ordine and Vigoda, pp. 189–191.
86. Ordine and Vigoda, p. 192.
87. Ordine and Vigoda, pp. 192–193.
88. Ordine and Vigoda, p. 193.

89. Ordine and Vigoda, pp. 195–196.

90. Ordine and Vigoda, p. 213.

91. Ginny Dover and John Dover, "John du Pont Convicted of Murder," The Schizophrenia Homepage, www.schizophrenia.com/newsletter/397/397dupont.htm (accessed April 2004).

92. Ordine and Vigoda, pp. 208, 219.

93. Ordine and Vigoda, pp. 223–241, 211.

94. Ordine and Vigoda, pp. 213–214.

95. Ordine and Vigoda, p. 246.

96. Ordine and Vigoda, pp. 223, 226–227.

97. Ordine and Vigoda, pp. 277–278, 281, 291.

98. Ordine and Vigoda, pp. 293–294.

99. Henry Campbell Black, *Black's Law Dictionary* (St. Paul, MN: West Publishing Company, 1979), pp. 904–905.

100. Mark Gado, "The Holy Child," in *The Insanity Defense*, Court TV's Crime Library, www.crimelibrary.com/criminal_mind/psychology/insanity/10.html, p. 1; Ordine and Vigoda, p. 312.

101. "Du Pont Jury Resumes Deliberations," U.S. News Story Page, CNN Interactive, www.cnn.com/US/9702/19/dupont.trial (accessed April 2004), p. 1.

102. Ordine and Vigoda, p. 296.

103. Ordine and Vigoda, pp. 305–306.

104. Ordine and Vigoda, p. 314.

105. Gado, p. 2.

106. Ordine and Vigoda, p. 342.

107. Dover and Dover, p. 1.

108. Ordine and Vigoda, pp. 345–347.

109. Ordine and Vigoda, p. 348.

110. Ordine and Vigoda, pp. 349–351.

111. Turkington, pp. 187–188.

Bibliography

CHAPTER 1

Roland Burnham Molineux Case

Borowitz, Albert. "Packaged Death." In Johnathan Goodman, ed., *The Christmas Murders: Classic Stories of True Crime*. New York: Sphere Books Ltd., 1988, 49–67.

Molineux, Roland Burnham. *The Room with the Little Door*. New York: G. W. Dillingham, 1903.

"Molineux Guilty in First Degree." *New York Times*, February 11, 1900, 1–5.

"Molineux Murder Indictment Fails." *New York Times*, April 13, 1899, 1–2.

Nash, Jay Robert. *Bloodletters and Badmen*. New York: M. Evans and Company, 1995.

Candace Mossler Case

Nash, Jay Robert. *Murder Among the Rich and Famous: Celebrity Slayings that Shocked America*. New York: Arlington House, 1983, 155–164.

Wilson, Theo. *Headline Justice: Inside the Courtroom: The Country's Most Controversial Trials*. New York: Thunder's Mouth Press, 1998, 121–141.

CHAPTER 2

Linda Burfield Hazzard Case

Olsen, Gregg. *Starvation Heights*. New York: Warner Books, 1997.

Phone interview with Gregg Olsen, by the author, September, 1997.

Dr. Carl Coppolino Case

Bigart, Homer. "Coppolino Guilty and Gets Life in Slaying of Wife." *New York Times*, April 29, 1967, 1:3.

Block, Eugene B. "Trials in Contrast." In *The Fabric of Guilt*. Garden City, NY: Doubleday and Company, 1968.

"Colonel's Death in Jersey in '63 Is Called Murder by Grand Jury." *New York Times*, July 23, 1966, 26:3.

Fido, Martin. *The Chronicle of Crimes*. New York: Carroll and Graf, 1993.

Holmes, Paul. *The Trials of Dr. Coppolino*. New York: New American Library, 1968.

Katz, Leonard, *The Coppolino Murder Trial*. New York: Bee-Line Books, 1967.

Knappman, Edward W., ed. "Carl Anthony Coppolino Trials: 1966 & 1967." In *Great American Trials*. Detroit: Gale Research, 1994.

MacDonald, John D. *No Deadly Drug*. Garden City, NY: Doubleday and Company, 1968.

Nash, Jay Robert. *Bloodletters and Badmen*. New York: M. Evans and Company, 1995.

CHAPTER 3

Allen Blackthorne Case

"Blackthorne Stands Trial." www.CBSNews.com (accessed September 18, 2000).

Levesque, William R. "Two Life Sentences, Daughter's Hatred." *St. Petersburg Times*, November 3, 2000.

Minai, Leanora. "Blackthorne Portrayed as Bitter, Vindictive." *St. Petersburg Times*, June 16, 2000.

Minai, Leonora. "Blackthorne's Conduct Erased Juror's Doubts." *St. Petersburg Times*, July 8, 2000.

Minai, Leonora. "Case Closed." *St. Petersburg Times*, July 7, 2000.

Minai, Leonora and Jounice L. Nealy. "Court Releases Prosecutors' Documents in Bellush Case." *St. Petersburg Times*, June 23, 1998.

Rule, Ann. *Every Breath You Take*. New York: Pocket Books, 2001.

Times Staff Writers. "Chronology of Events." *St. Petersburg Times*, July 7, 2000.

"Who Is Allen Blackthorne?" www.CBSNews.com (accessed September 18, 2000).

CHAPTER 4

Albert Louis Luetgert Case

"Another Luetgert Murder?" *New York Times*, May 19, 1897, 1.

Fido, Martin. *The Chronicle of Crime*. New York: Carroll and Graf, 1993.

"Luetgert Case in Chicago," *New York Times*, June 18, 1897, 2:2.

"Luetgert Is Convicted," *New York Times*, February 19, 1898, 2–3.

"Luetgert Jury Disagrees," *New York Times*, October 22, 1897, 5:1.

Nash, Jay Robert. *Bloodletters and Badmen*. New York: M. Evans and Company, 1995.

Thomas Capano Case

Allen, Mary. "Capano Contests Sentence." *The News Journal*. www.delawareonline.com/newsjournal/local/2003/09/10capanocontestss.htm (accessed April 4, 2004).

Allen, Mary. "Lawyers Call Capano a Difficult Client." *The News Journal*. www.delawareonline.com/newsjournal/ local/2004/01/17lawyerscallcapa.htm (accessed April 4, 2004).

Anastasia, George. *The Summer Wind: Thomas Capano and the Murder of Anne Marie Fahey*. New York: Regan Books, 1999.

Barrish, Chris and Peter Meyer. *Fatal Embrace: The Inside Story of the Thomas Capano/Anne Marie Fahey Murder Case*. New York: St. Martin's Press, 1999.

Ramsland, Katherine. *The Rise and Fall of Thomas Capano*. Court TV's Crime Library. www.crimelibrary.com/notorious_murders/classics/capano/1.html (accessed April 4, 2004).

Rule, Ann. *And Never Let Her Go: Thomas Capano: The Deadly Seducer*. New York: Pocket Books, 1999.

Spangler, Todd. "Wealthy Scion to Stand Trial Over Ex-Girlfriend: Their Affair Ended, She Can't Be Found—And He's Charged with Her Murder." *San Francisco Chronicle*, October 5, 1998, A5.

CHAPTER 5

Harry Thaw Case

Fido, Martin. "Society Sex Scandals Behind New York Killing." In *The Chronicle of Crime*. New York: Carroll and Graf, 1993, 120.

Flint, Terrence. "Murder at Madison Square Garden." In Art Crockett, ed., *Celebrity Murders*. New York: Pinnacle Books, 1990, 153–179.

Jones, Richard Glyn, ed. "1906: Harry Thaw: Murder at Madison Square Garden." In *The Mammoth Book of Murder*. New York: Carroll and Graf, 1990, 236–238.

Keating, H.R.F. "Shots and Sex." In *Great Crimes*. Stamford, CT: Longmeadow Press, 1991, 13–14.

Nash, Jay Robert. "1906: Harry K. Thaw: The Millionaire Murderer." In *Murder Among the Rich and Famous*. New York: Arlington House, 1983, 20–40.

"Pictures of a Tragedy." *Smithsonian Magazine*, February 1999. www.smithsonianmag.si.edu/smithsonian/issues99/Feb99/object_feb99.html (accessed February 2004).

Wolf, Marvin J. and Mader, Katherine. "1906: Mad Harry, Evelyn, and the Beast." In *Rotten Apples: True Stories of New York Crime and Mystery 1689 to the Present.* New York: Ballantine Books, 1991, 153–163.

Susan Cummings Case

Associated Press. "Heiress Testifies Shooting Came After Weekend of Threats." *The Shawnee News Star*, May 9, 1998. www.news-star.com/stories/050998/new_shooting.html (accessed February 2004).

"Heiress Gets 60 Days for Killing Boyfriend: Convicted of Manslaughter, Not Murder." *San Francisco Chronicle*, May 14, 1998, A6.

"Luxury Life for Prison Queen: Cell of Splendor for Rich Killer." Tabloid News Services, May 5, 1998. www.tabloid.net/1998/05/22 (accessed February 2004).

"Mike's Comment of the Week." Interscan Corporation, June 12, 2000. www.gasdetection.com/MDS/m061200.html (accessed February 2004).

O'Neill, Anne-Marie. "Jail Break." *People*, June 6, 1998, 115–116.

Ordonez, Jennifer. "In Jail, Heiress Has Privileged Existence." *Washington Post*, May 21, 1998, A01.

Pulitzer, Lisa. *A Woman Scorned*. New York: St. Martin's Press, 1999.

Salmon, Jacqueline L. "Polo Match Turns Sour." *Washington Post*, September 9, 1997, A01.

"A Scandal in Hunt Country." *Dominick Dunne's Power, Privilege, and Justice*. CourtTV.com. www.courttv.com/onair/shows/dunne/episodes/scandal.html (accessed February 2004).

Wright, Paul. "The Crime of Being Poor." *Washington Free Press*, no. 65, September/October 2003. www.washingtonfreepress.org/65/crimeBeingPoor.htm (accessed February 2004).

CHAPTER 6

Cullen Davis Case

Cartwright, Gary. *Texas Justice: The Murder Trials of T. Cullen Davis*. New York: Pocket Books, 1994.

Gribben, Mark. *T. Cullen Davis: The Best Justice Money Can Buy*. Court TV's Crime Library. www.crimelibrary.com/notorious_murders/not_guilty/t_cullen_davis (accessed February 2004).

Naifeh, Steven and Gregory White Smith. *Final Justice*. New York: Onyx/The Penguin Group, 1994.

Thompson, Thomas. *Blood and Money*. New York: Dell, 1976.

Michael Skakel Case

Batten, Jack. "Murder Among the Super-Rich." www. marthamoxley.com/reviews/jbatten.htm (accessed February 2004).

Bellamy, Patrick. "The Latest Update April 22, 2002 to June 7, 2002: Skakel Trial Update." Court TV's Crime Library. www.crimelibrary.com/notorious_murders/famous/moxley/updates_1.html (accessed February 2004), 1–24.

Dumas, Timothy. *A Wealth of Evil: The True Story of the Murder of Martha Moxley in America's Richest Community*. New York: Warner Books, 1998.

Dunne, Dominick. "Trail of Guilt." In *Justice*. New York: Three Rivers Press, 1991, 400–426.

Fuhrman, Mark. *Murder in Greenwich*. New York: Avon Books, 1999.

Geringer, Joseph. *The Martha Moxley Murder*. Court TV's Crime Library. www.crimelibrary.com/notorious_murders/famous/moxley/index_1.html (accessed February 2004).

CHAPTER 7

Lizzie Borden Case

Brown, Arnold. *Lizzie Borden: The Legend, the Truth, the Final Chapter*. Nashville: Rutledge Hill Press, 1991. Reprint, New York: Dell, 1992.

Fido, Martin. *The Chronicle of Crime*. New York: Carroll and Graf, 1993.

Fido, Martin. "Lizzie Borden." In *Murder After Midnight: Gripping Cases from the Annals of True Crime*. London: Weidenfeld and Nicholson, 1990, 25–30.

Geary, Rick. *The Borden Tragedy: A Memoir of the Infamous Double Murder at Fall River, Massachusetts, 1892*. New York: NBM Publishing, 2003.

Keating, H.R.F. *Great Crimes*. Stamford, CT: Longmeadow Press, 1982.

Kent, David. *Forty Whacks: New Evidence in the Life and Legend of Lizzie Borden*. Emmaus, PA: Yankee Books, 1992.

Kent, David, ed. *The Lizzie Borden Sourcebook*. Boston: Branden Publishing Company, 1992.

Lincoln, Victoria. *A Private Disgrace: Lizzie Borden by Daylight*. New York: Time Life, 1990.

Masterson, William L. *Lizzie Didn't Do It!* Boston: Branden Publishing Company, 2000.

Sullivan, Robert. *Goodbye Lizzie Borden: The Story of the Trial of America's Most Famous Murderess*. New York: Penguin Books, 1974.

Claus von Bulow Case

Claus von Bulow Portal: Phoos, Mailing Addresses, Poster, and in the Media. www.celebrity-photos-crazy-com/Claus_Von_Bulow (accessed February 2004).

Dershowitz, Alan M. *Reversal of Fortune*. New York: Pocket Books, 1986.

Dunne, Dominick. "Fatal Charm: The Social Web of Claus von Bulow." In *Justice: Crimes, Trials, and Punishments*. New York: Three Rivers Press, 2001.

Ebert, Roger. "Reversal of Fortune." *Chicago Sun Times*, October 17, 1990. www.suntimes.com/ebert/ebert_reviews/1990/10/572715.htm (accessed February 2004).

Nash, Jay Robert. *Murder Among the Rich and Famous: Celebrity Slayings that Shocked America*. New York: Arlington House, 296–311.

"Von Bulow Testifies that Blake was 'Loving and Devoted Husband.'" *New Yorkish*, March 3, 2003. http:

//archives.newyorkish.net/030303/030303.htm (accessed February 2004).

Wright, William. *The Von Bulow Affair*. New York: Dell Publishing, 1983.

CHAPTER 8

Nathan Leopold and Richard Loeb Case

Brophy, John. "1924: Leopold and Loeb: Murder by Genius." In Richard Glyn Jones, ed., *The Mammoth Book of Murder*. New York: Carroll and Graf, 1990, 350–357.

De Ford, Miriam Allen. "Superman's Crime: Loeb and Leopold." In *Murderers Sane and Mad*. New York: Abelard-Schuman, 1965, 149–168.

Geis, Gilbert and Leigh B. Bienen. "Leopold and Loeb (1924) and the Cause of the Crime." In *Crimes of the Century*. Boston: Northeastern University Press, 1998, 13–47.

Higdon, Hal. *Leopold and Loeb: The Crime of the Century*. Chicago: University of Illinois Press, 1975, 1999.

Logan, John. *Never the Sinner: The Leopold and Loeb Story*. New York: Overlook Press, 1988.

Tierney, Kevin. "The Million-Dollar Defense." In *Darrow: A Biography*. New York: Thomas Y. Crowell, 1979, 334–351.

Lyle and Erik Menendez Case

"A Chat with a Menendez Juror." American Online's Center Stage, April 22, 1996. www.courttv.com/archive/casefiles/menendez/documents/jurorchat.html (accessed February 2004), 1–5.

Davis, Don. *Bad Blood*. New York: St. Martin's Paperbacks, 1994.

Dunne, Dominick. "Nightmare on Elm Drive." In *Justice: Crimes Trials, and Punishments*. New York: Three Rivers Press, 2001, 104–142.

"The Menendez Brothers." Forensic Files, Court TV. www.courttv.com/trials/Menendez (accessed February 2004).

Novelli, Norma, with Mike Walker. *The Private Diary of Lyle Menendez in His Own Words*. Beverly Hills, CA: Dove Books, 1995.

O'Donnell, Pierce. "Reflections on the Con Artist as a Young Man." In Norma Novelli with Mike Walker, *The Private Diary of Lyle Menendez in His Own Words*. Beverly Hills, CA: Dove Books, 1995, 251–263.

Soble, Ron and John Johnson. *Blood Brothers: The Inside Story of the Menendez Murders*. New York: Onyx/The Penguin Group, 1994.

Thornton, Hazel. *Hung Jury: The Diary of a Menendez Juror*. Philadelphia: Temple University Press, 1995.

CHAPTER 9

Dunne, Dominick. *Fatal Charms and the Mansions of Limbo*. New York: Ballantine Books, 1999.

Wardlow Sisters Case

Fido, Martin. *The Chronicle of Crime*. New York: Carroll and Graf, 1993.

Nash, Jay Robert. *Bloodletters and Badmen*. New York: M. Evans and Company, 1995.

Zierold, Norman. *Three Sisters in Black*. Boston: Little, Brown and Company, 1968.

John du Pont Case

Black, Henry Campbell. *Black's Law Dictionary*. St. Paul, MN: West Publishing Company, 1979.

Dover, Ginny and John Dover. "John du Pont Convicted of Murder." The Schizophrenia Home Page. www.schizophrenia.com/newsletter/397/397dupont.html (accessed March 2004).

"Du Pont Jury Resumes Deliberations." U.S. News Story Page, CNN Interactive. www.cnn.com/US/9702/19/ dupont.trial/ (accessed March 2004).

Ordine, Bill and Ralph Vigoda. *Fatal Match: Inside the Mind of*

Killer Millionaire John du Pont. New York: Avon Books, 1998.

Gado, Mark. "The Holy Child." In *The Insanity Defense.* Court TV's Crime Library. www.crimelibrary.com/ criminal_mind/psychology/insanity/10.html (accessed March 2004).

Turkington, Carol A. *No Holds Barred: The Strange Life of John E. du Pont*. Atlanta: Turner Publishing, 1996.

INDEX

GINI GRAHAM SCOTT has long been involved with the criminal justice and legal system. Besides getting a Ph.D. in Sociology from the University of California at Berkeley, an M.A. in anthropology from Cal State, East Bay, and a J.D. from the University of San Francisco Law School, many of her books are on these topics, including *Homicide: 100 Years of Murder in America*; *You the Jury: A Recovered Memory Case*; *Mind Your Own Business: The Battle for Personal Privacy*; *Private Eyes*; *The Truth about Lying*; and *Making Ethical Choices, Resolving Ethical Dilemmas*. She has a Certificate in the Administration of Justice and an A.A. in Police Sciences from Merritt College in Oakland, California, and has worked on various projects with the Oakland Police as a volunteer. She did a series of studies about police investigative techniques, including *Investigating Homicide in Oakland: An Analysis of Homicide Patterns and Investigative Approaches* in 1997, published by the Oakland Police Department in 1998; *Cops, Canines, and Community*, a study of the Oakland Police Canine Unit; and *Winning the Prostitution Clean-Up Campaign*, a study of the vice-prostitution unit in Oakland. She has been a member of the Oakland Citizen Police Academy Alumni Association since 1998, and was their vice president and public relations/community liaison from 1999 to 2003.

The website for the book is at www.richandfamoushomicide.com. Dr. Scott can be contacted at Changemakers, 6114 La Salle Avenue, #358, Oakland, CA 94611 or at giniscott@richandfamoushomicide.com.